D0014353

The LOST TRIBE of CONEY ISLAND

The LOST TRIBE of CONEY ISLAND

Headhunters, Luna Park, and the Man Who Pulled Off the Spectacle of the Century

Claire Prentice

New Harvest
Houghton Mifflin Harcourt
BOSTON NEW YORK
2014

This edition published by special arrangement with Amazon Publishing

For information about permission to reproduce selections from this book,
go to www.apub.com.

www.hmhco.com

Library of Congress Cataloging-in-Publication Data
Prentice, Claire (Journalist), author.
The lost tribe of Coney Island : headhunters, Luna Park, and the man who pulled off the spectacle of the century / Claire Prentice.
pages cm
ISBN 978-0-544-26228-7 (hardcover)
1. Igorot (Philippine people)—United States. 2. Exploitation. 3. Louisiana Purchase Exposition (1904 : Saint Louis, Mo.) 4. Hunt, Truman Knight. I. Title.
DS666.I2P74 2014
305.899'21—dc23 2014011690

Book design by Brian Moore

Printed in the United States of America
DOC 10 9 8 7 6 5 4 3 2 1

For Mum, David, and Bram

In memory of Dad and Gran, who inspired my love of stories

And with respect for the lives of Julio, Maria, Feloa, Dengay, Tainan, Friday, Fomoaley, and all the other Igorrotes who traveled to America

The Igorrotes at Luna Park, 1905

Contents

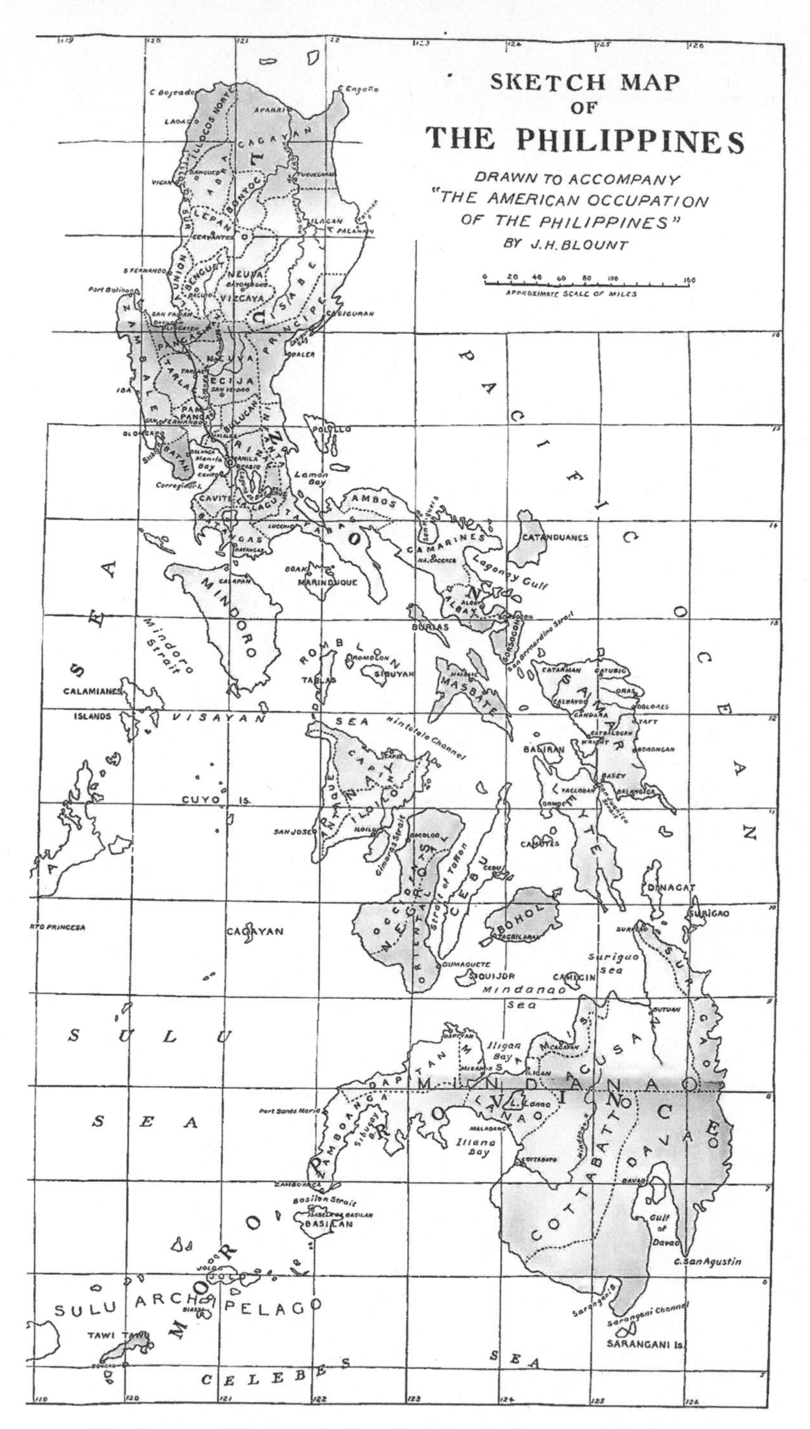

Sketch map of the Philippines showing Bontoc in the far north

NEPTUNE
MERMAID
AVE.
SURF
STILLWELL
AVE.
CANAL
GRAVESEND
CONEY IS
WAREHOUSE
W. 23RD
W. 21 ST.
W. 20TH
W. 19TH
W. 17TH
W. 16TH
W. 15TH
W. 12TH
HART PL.
PUBLIC SCHOOL No. 80
ICE PLANT
SEWERAGE DISPOSAL PLANT
BROOKLYN RAPID TRANSIT STATION
SCENIC RAILWAY B'LDG.
TRIP TO THE MOON
THE DELUGE
FRIEDE'S STEEL GLOBE TOWER
STEEPLECHASE PARK
(BURNT OUT)
RAVENHALL'S HOTEL
BROOKLYN CHILDREN'S AID SOCIETY
COTTAGE PL.
HIGHLAND VIEW AVE.
BOWERY
WALK
BOARDWALK
BATH HOUSE
HOTEL
BATHING
ROLLER COASTER
TOWER
STEEPLECHASE PIER
LAUREL HOUSE
ATLANTIC
ZIZ COASTER
FELTMAN'S
JONES

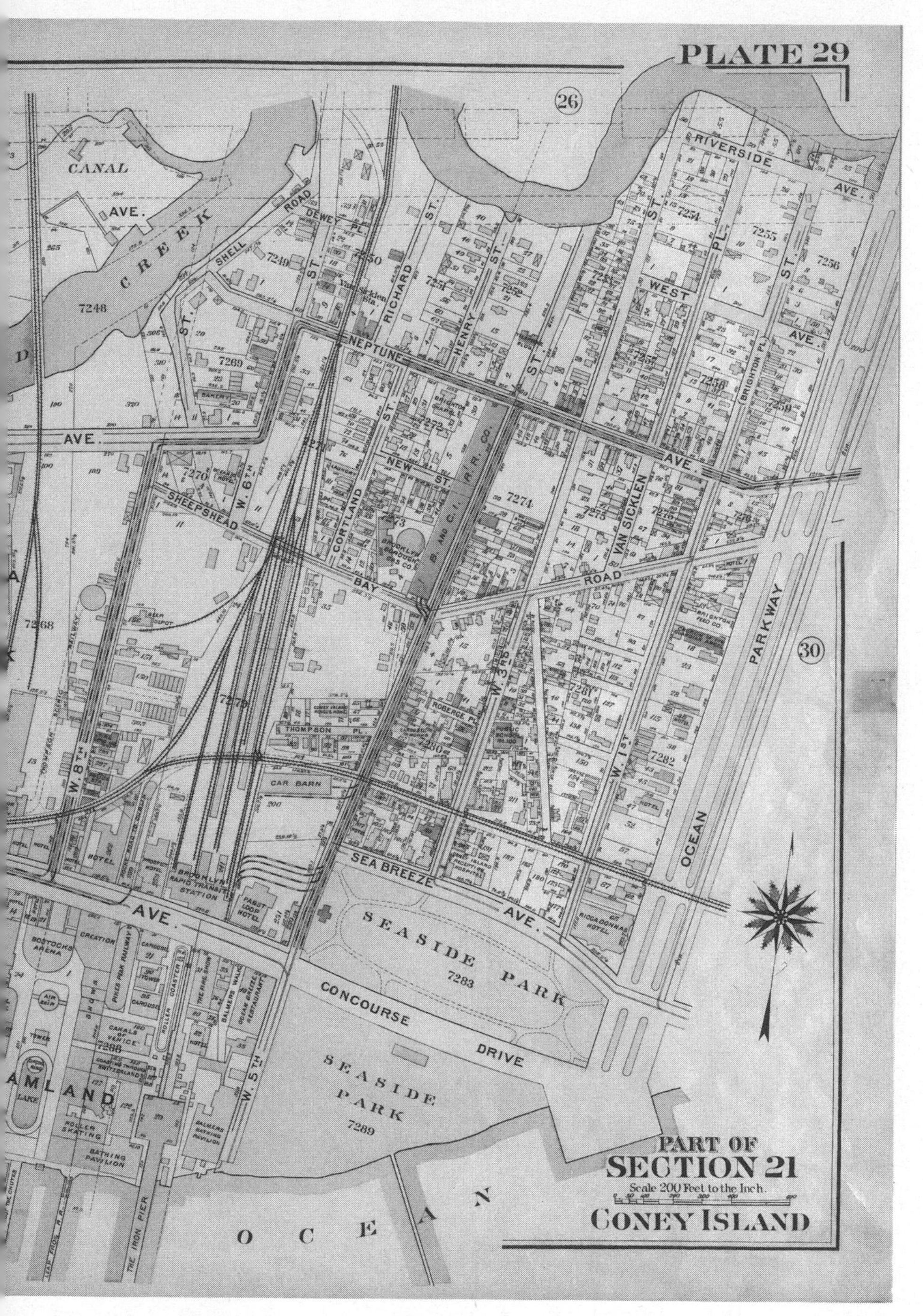

Map of Coney Island showing the three big parks—Luna Park, Dreamland, and Steeplechase Park, 1907–1908

Shall I tell you about life?... Well, it's like the big wheel at Luna Park.

—*Evelyn Waugh,* Decline and Fall, *1928*

I was healer of their bodies, father confessor of all their woes and troubles and the final arbiter in all disputed questions.

—*Dr. Truman Hunt describing his relationship with the Igorrotes when he lived among the tribe in Bontoc in the* San Antonio Sunday Light, *November 19, 1905*

[The Igorrotes] are so punctiliously truthful themselves that the smallest of white lies on our part would rob us of their confidence and friendship . . . If an Igorrote makes a promise to you, no matter how trivial it seems to you, he will fulfill it if it costs him his life. And he expects you to take the same pains to fulfill your promises to him.

—*George Fuller quoted in the* Brooklyn Daily Eagle, *June 4, 1905*

Cast of Characters

Truman Hunt: The Igorrotes' manager. A former medical doctor and lieutenant governor of Bontoc Province in the Philippines. He takes the Igorrotes from the mountains of the northern Philippines to exhibit them on America's fair and amusement park circuit.

Julio Balinag: Truman's twenty-one-year-old translator. He is half Igorrote and half Ilocano, a tribe regarded by Americans as superior to the Igorrotes. Julio is ambitious but principled, and takes great pride in his natty American wardrobe.

Maria: Julio's eighteen-year-old Igorrote wife is a mother hen who looks after the other members of the tribe.

Friday Strong: The baby of the group, seven-year-old orphan Friday belongs to a different tribe—the Negritos. He stands less than four feet tall, and always has a cigar clamped between his teeth.

Tainan: "The little boy with the big voice" becomes a favorite with the American public, not least for his performances of patriotic American songs, including "My Country, 'Tis of Thee." He is nine years old, and is friends with Friday.

Fomoaley Ponci: The tall, chubby tribal chief. He becomes the butt of the Igorrotes' jokes because of his self-importance and willingness to give lengthy interviews to the press.

Feloa: A natural leader and a popular, outspoken tribesman. He leaves his wife and three young children in the Philippines to travel to America to earn his fortune.

Dengay: A friend of Feloa's. Dengay has a wife and four young children in the Philippines.

Ed Callahan: The thirty-three-year-old former railroad clerk works in the Igorrote Village as Truman's security guard and right-hand man. He is intensely loyal to the showman.

Sallie Hunt: At the age of seventeen, the spirited Sallie left her large family behind in Kentucky to seek excitement at the 1904 St. Louis World's Fair. There Truman gave her a job as his stenographer and the two were married a few months later.

Adele von Groyss: A flamboyant and eccentric Austrian expatriate famed for her avant-garde parties. Truman's friend, she puts him and Sallie up in her Broadway home when they first arrive in New York in May 1905. Adele is fascinated by Igorrote culture.

Thompson and Dundy: Dubbed "the Kings of Coney," the founders of Luna Park think big and spend extravagantly. They are determined to book the Igorrotes for the 1905 season.

Samuel Gumpertz: The manager of Dreamland, Luna Park's main rival, which is situated just across Surf Avenue from Thompson and Dundy's park. He too wants the Igorrotes.

Frederick Barker: Truman's nemesis: the high-minded, dogged, and handsome government agent who is tasked with finding Truman and bringing him to justice.

Louis Blum: The Chicago attorney appointed by the government to prosecute Truman. Blum is an overweight bachelor with a ready wit. He's a born optimist with an encyclopedic knowledge of the law and current affairs.

Antoinette Funk: The tiny yet formidable attorney hired by Truman to defend him. She is of the surprising view that women don't belong in the professions.

Introduction

The Igorrotes on show at Coney Island, summer 1905

SITTING ON MY desk is a tattered black-and-white photograph of a group of tribesmen, women, and children, naked but for their G-strings. They are squatting on their haunches around a campfire. Several of them look directly into the camera. One points, another laughs and holds up a stone, as if pretending he is about to throw it at the photographer. Some of them are smiling, apparently sharing a private joke. In the background, a young boy and girl are making something out of bits of broken wood. Behind a low fence, a group of men in formal American clothes and derby hats stand watching the scene. If you look closely, you can see a few of them are laughing too. If it wasn't for the observers in Western clothes, it could be a scene taken from an ethnographic journal. But this is no documentary image of a distant people unaccustomed to contact with the rest of the world: this tribe is very aware we are watching, and they seem frankly amused by it.

When I first came across this photograph, I knew next to nothing about it, but the energy of the tribespeople drew me in. I immediately knew I had to find out who these people were. Where and when was the picture taken? What became of them?

My quest to unravel the story of the tribespeople in the picture has taken over several years of my life. It has been an addictive, fascinating, sometimes frustrating, but always fulfilling journey.

Now I know that the picture is one of a handful of photographic relics of an extraordinary episode in American history. It was taken more than a century ago at Coney Island, ten miles from downtown Manhattan.

The tribespeople are Bontoc Igorrotes, who became known in America simply as Igorrotes,[1] meaning "mountain people." Fifty of them were brought from their remote home in the northern Philippines to America and put on show at Luna Park in 1905. They were billed as "dog-eating, head-hunting savages" and "the most primitive people in the world." The tribespeople became the sensation of the summer season and were soon in demand all over the US.

Millions of Americans flocked to see the Igorrotes. The crowds were captivated by the tribe's vitality, and thrilled and scandalized in equal measure by their near nudity, their dog feasts, and their tattooed bodies, which, the public learned, indicated their prowess as hunters of human heads.

As I study the Igorrotes' faces in the picture on my desk, I have often wondered what it was that persuaded them to leave their homes to set up camp in America's most famous amusement park. What did they think of America and Americans? How did they find life under the gaze of an audience? How did the freedom-loving tribe cope with being locked up day and night at Luna Park? Did they regret their decision? What did they tell their families about their adventure when they returned home?

It is impossible to imagine what it was like for these premodern people to be thrust into the heart of the quintessential modern metropolis, New York.

This story is set at a time when disagreements about the political future of the Philippines had created a schism in American domestic politics. America had taken control of the Philippines from Spain following the 1898 Spanish-American War. But far from being welcomed with open arms, the American occupiers were met by a rebellion of Filipino nationalists led by Emilio Aguinaldo. The US deployed tens of thousands of soldiers to the islands. The three-year Philippine-American War that followed led to the deaths of over 4,200 American and 20,000 Filipino combatants. Hundreds of thousands of Filipino civilians were killed in the fighting, or died of disease and starvation in the famine that followed. America won the war but was widely criticized for using excessive force and brutality to overcome the opposition to her rule.

The assumption of American control over the overseas territory prompted deep soul-searching at home. Was it right for America to acquire an overseas empire? When, if ever, would the Filipinos be ready to take over the responsibility of governing themselves?

The Philippine issue was the determining foreign policy concern of the day, and the thread that connected the three presidencies of the early twentieth century. William McKinley reluctantly led the US into the war with Spain and won control of the islands. Theodore Roosevelt, who assumed the presidency in 1901 after McKinley's assassination, had unsuccessfully coveted the job of governor-general of the Philippines, and dreamed of guiding the people of the islands toward self-government, while William Howard Taft, Roosevelt's successor as president, had previously served as governor-general of the islands.

The Philippine Islands were not just a concern for the upper echelons of the American government. Service in the Philippines united Americans from all walks of life: time and time again in this story we encounter men and women who worked in the islands, as government servants, police officers, lawyers, doctors, nurses, teachers, engineers, preachers, soldiers, and politicians, and who viewed their time there as a unique bond.

As America was taking control of the islands, she was also sizing up her new subjects. Ethnologists were sent into far corners of the country to assess and report on the country's many indigenous tribes.

The islands' people were then categorized according to their level of "civilization," from barbaric to semibarbarous to those deemed cultured and educated.

The earliest American visitors to the Philippines were particularly taken with the "savage" Bontoc Igorrotes. In his major study, *The Bontoc Igorot*,[2] compiled in 1903, the American ethnologist Albert Ernest Jenks observed that, aside from cutting off the heads of neighboring villagers, the Bontoc Igorrotes were a peaceful, good-humored, honest, industrious, and likable people with low rates of crime. Jenks noted that they were true primitives who had no words for many items in modern culture, including shoes, pantaloons, umbrellas, chairs, or books.

In 1904, the American government spent $1.5 million taking thirteen hundred Filipinos from a dozen different tribes to the St. Louis Exposition. The Philippine Reservation became one of the most popular features of the fair, and the Igorrotes drew the largest crowds of all. By displaying the tribespeople in this manner, the US government hoped to gain popular support for its occupation of the Philippines by showing the American public that the Filipinos were innocents, a people far from ready for self-government, and in need of paternalistic American protection.

From the moment the Filipinos arrived on American soil, they were the subject of endless newspaper articles drawing comparisons between their culture and that of their American hosts. Many articles focused on the Igorrotes' disdain for Western clothes and what was portrayed as their insatiable appetite for that most domesticated of American pets, the dog. But the Igorrotes were also invoked in articles about premarital sexual relations, hard work, and the simple life versus the complexities of modern living, while their trusting and trustworthy nature often drew comment.

During this first visit to America by the Igorrotes, the *Macon Telegraph* provided its readers with an insight into the Filipinos: "The Igorrote is more honest and more honorable than the American. Knowing the value of money, he would not be tempted for one single instant to take that which did not belong to him, even if he were sure that his theft would never be found out. The property of another is absolutely safe in his possession."[3]

The Igorrotes were like a mirror held up to American society. America might be the more "advanced" culture, but while the host country took pleasure in patronizing the primitive tribe, it was not entirely immune to the idea that it might learn something from the Philippine visitors.

Displaying human beings for the entertainment and edification of the paying public seems shocking today, but "human zoos" were nothing new in the early 1900s. For more than four hundred years, exotic humans from faraway territories had been paraded in front of royal courts and wealthy patrons from Europe to Japan, and more recently at world's fairs and expositions as far afield as New York, Paris, and London. But what happened in Coney Island in 1905 was the result of two modern forces meshing: American imperialism and a popular taste for sensationalism. The Igorrotes who were brought from the Philippines became caught up in the debate about America's presence in Southeast Asia. They were used to push the case that America had a duty to protect, educate, and civilize such savage beings, and later, when the treatment they experienced became a national scandal, they were used to argue that America had no place in the Philippines at all.

The other force was equally irresistible. Early twentieth-century America was addicted to novelty and sensation. The human zoo that came from the Philippines and unpacked its bags at Coney Island in 1905 became the most talked-about show in town. The tribespeople were gawked at by everyone from ordinary members of the public willing to pay a quarter for the privilege of seeing human beings in the raw to anthropologists, politicians, celebrities, and even the daughter of the president.

But there was another ingredient in this potent mixture, a volatile one that propelled the Igorrotes onto the front pages.

Sitting next to the picture of the Igorrotes on my desk is another photograph, faded and torn in several places. In it, a man in a panama hat and an expensive-looking three-piece suit stands with a fat cigar in his hand, smiling for the camera. He is surrounded by a group of bare-chested Filipino tribesmen. He is Dr. Truman Knight Hunt, a former medical doctor who met the Igorrotes after he went to the Philippines following the outbreak of the 1898 Spanish-American War. It was Truman's idea to take the Igorrotes to Coney Island. There he transformed himself into one of the great publicists of his age, spinning a colorful web of stories about "his" tribe that the press and public lapped up.

No one could have predicted what would happen next.

In early American political, ethnological, and press accounts of the Philippines, Truman is a hero, revered by the Igorrotes for his strong leadership, his kindness, and his ability to heal their medical ills. Referring to Truman's decision to leave America in 1898 to go and live in the Philippines, one newspaper article described how he "forsook civilization because he was disgusted with the shams and the pretense of the social world, and went to live among the simple, honorable, natural Igorrotes . . . The Igorrotes have learned that he is their friend, as just and honorable as they are."[4] By 1906, when the Igorrotes wind up as witnesses in an American court of law, the Truman we discover is a much darker, more complex character, accused of exploiting the tribespeople, stealing their wages, and treating them like slaves.

What had happened to the former physician and civil servant–turned–showman in the intervening years? Were the allegations made against him true? Did the fame and fortune he earned as a showman warp him, transforming an upstanding American citizen into a greedy, heartless man?

These pages tell a story of adventure, ambition, betrayal, triumph, and tragedy. Much of it is shocking and sensational and all of it is true.

Throughout the process of writing *The Lost Tribe of Coney Island,* I have strived at all times to be faithful to the facts. There are frustrating gaps and inaccuracies in the archives and many of the accounts that do exist are open to question. When the Igorrotes first arrived in America, the press swallowed Truman's tall tales and printed them verbatim. The reporters were often as guilty of stretching the truth to entertain the public as Truman was. Later, as the story took a darker turn, Truman frequently deceived the police and the US government about where his groups were performing in order to throw them off his scent. He also lied to the authorities and to the press about details such as how many Igorrotes he had brought to America and about aspects of their culture. I have sifted through these lies and distortions to find the facts underneath. Ultimately, only Truman Hunt and the fifty-one Filipinos who traveled with him to America knew the precise details of everything that transpired between them.

From time to time, I describe the thoughts, feelings, and motivations of the lead characters. I have done so based on close consideration of my research. Anything that appears in quotation marks comes from a newspaper article, book, government report, official correspondence, court transcript, magazine, or journal article. Italicized dialogue that does not appear in quotation marks is imagined but is rooted in facts, real incidents, and a thorough examination of the character and circumstances of the people involved.

The Igorrotes were a national phenomenon in their day, yet they have been all but forgotten by history. Why? Perhaps this is because the Igorrote exhibition trade came to be regarded as a shameful episode in US history and in US-Filipino relations. Or maybe the popular culture of the day simply moved on to the next big thing, erasing the Igorrotes from the public consciousness. More than a century on, this extraordinary episode in history is a story that deserves to be told.

Researching this book I've often felt like a participant in a long and elaborate treasure hunt. It has lead from large institutions like the National Archives, the Library of Congress, and the New York Public Library to the cluttered, dusty archives of various county courts, member-run genealogical societies, nonprofit history and heritage centers, local newspapers, and small-town libraries, and on to The National Library of the Philippines and the National Archives of the Philippines in Manila, and Bontoc Municipal Library.

The search was complicated by the fact that the Igorrotes' names were often mangled by the journalists, ships' clerks, immigration officers, court officials, and police whom they encountered. Misspellings, phonetic approximations, and simple guesses mean that individual tribespeople were often called by several different names during their time in the US. Additionally, the Igorrotes didn't keep track of their own ages and they frequently changed their names throughout their lives. Typically they were given only one name at birth and did not adopt a family name as was customary in the West. When they arrived in America, most of the tribespeople in Truman's group were assigned a second name or simply plucked one from thin air.

If the Igorrotes' names have at times been perplexing, I've frequently been struck by the irony of Truman Hunt's name. Not only does Truman become the focus of an international manhunt, we are also in a sense hunting for the "true man," the real Truman Hunt behind the fanciful tales and headline-grabbing exploits.

Equally striking is the decency of the Igorrotes who conducted themselves with incredible dignity during their American sojourn despite the most extreme provocation. Ultimately, this is a story of a hero turned villain that makes us question who is civilized and who is savage.

The LOST TRIBE *of* CONEY ISLAND

1

From One Island to Another

BONTOC PUEBLO, NORTHERN PHILIPPINES, MARCH 1905

This is one of only two known surviving photographs of Truman Hunt and the Igorrotes. Taken at St. Louis, 1904.

IT WAS LATE in the evening when Dr. Truman Knight Hunt wrote the final name in the ledger. His body felt stiff as he eased himself out of his chair and stepped outside into the town—if a ramshackle collection of small, squat huts with dirt floors and thatched roofs could be called a town. There were no roads. In the distance he could make out the tribe's rice terraces, which clung precariously to the surrounding mountainsides. Truman breathed in the night air. He felt as if he had met every Igorrote tribesman, woman, and child in the Philippine Islands that day. A hopeful crowd was still waiting to be seen, little flickers of red glowing in the fading light as they sucked on their pipes, sending puffs of smoke into the still air. Children had dozed off in their parents' arms. A mangy-looking dog looked up and growled at the American stranger in a false show of strength. Truman picked up a stone and hurled it at the dog, which ran to take shelter behind a group of boys.

Truman gazed at the tribespeople who were gathered around campfires, cooking and chatting. They were barefoot and naked except for their breechcloths (known as *wa´-nĭs* in the local Bontoc dialect) and the little basket hats (*suk´-lâng*) that the men used to store their smoking pipes and tobacco. Aside from their bangs, which they chopped in a severe straight line, the men never cut their jet-black hair. Instead they greased it with fresh hog fat,[1] rolled it up, and tucked it under their basket hats. The women wore theirs in a loose knot. Some had blankets draped around their shoulders. Men and women alike wore huge ear ornaments made of copper wire, bamboo, or even teeth, and necklaces made of copper or beads.[2]

By the light of the campfire, Truman could see the tribe's intricate tattoos. They were made up of a series of fine India-ink lines, zigzags, and barbed-wire patterns that arced up over the men's chests and down their arms. Every time they took another human head from an enemy village, the community celebrated with a month of feasting and by inking their bodies with new tattoos. Dogs were slaughtered and eaten as a centerpiece of the feast.

A group of naked children ran past the spot where Truman stood, playing the native version of tag.

Truman shouted to get the Igorrotes' attention. Expectant faces looked up at him. The tribe's language sounded strange in his American mouth as he told them he wouldn't be interviewing anyone else. Anyone who hadn't already been seen should go home. They needn't bother coming back tomorrow. He had more than enough people and would be notifying the successful candidates shortly. A chorus of groans broke out. The tribespeople had been waiting all day and those who hadn't met the white man who promised the opportunity of a lifetime were anxious to do so. He ignored them, turned, and walked back into his hut, closing the door firmly behind him.

He was tired after a long day, but was filled with a growing sense of confidence about his new business venture. One by one he had appraised each man, woman, and child who had stood before him. Truman's criteria were simple. His tribespeople needed to be physically fit, sociable, and appealing—or at least not repulsive—to the eye. When they reached America, they would be put on show as live exhibits at fairs and amusement parks, so they couldn't be frightened by those who would pay good money to see them. They must be strong enough to survive the crossing. His group had to be able to take instructions. He couldn't stand willfulness and had sent anyone who had shown the slightest hint of it packing. In making his selection, Truman had relied on his gut. His instincts had served him well in his life so far.

As he eased his five-foot-eight-inch frame back into his chair, he sighed contentedly and congratulated himself on a good day's work. He crossed his hands over his stomach and stretched his legs out under the desk. His mind wandered through some of the tribespeople who had auditioned for him that day. There was beautiful Daipan, known locally as the belle of the village, with her flashing black eyes and her exquisite singing voice, and Tainan, the high-spirited nine-year-old nicknamed "the little boy with the big voice" by his countrymen and women. After waiting awhile for the crowd outside his hut to disperse, Truman got up and opened the door just wide enough to shout through the crack for his assistant, Julio, to come. A young Filipino man beautifully dressed in a light brown American suit and highly polished leather shoes stepped forward.

When Truman had offered Julio twenty-five dollars a month to act as his assistant and translator, the twenty-one-year-old had jumped at the chance. He spoke Bontoc along with several other Filipino dialects, Spanish, and English, and was hungry for adventure. With the money he could earn in America, he would be set up for life.

Under the light of a smoky oil lantern, Truman and Julio ran through the names of the candidates who had caught Truman's eye. Julio knew a number of those who had volunteered and his opinion on their character mattered to his boss. As Truman read out each name, Julio nodded his approval or indicated his doubts with a frown or a shake of the head. Truman went down his list, scoring out names and circling others. After conferring awhile with his young assistant, Truman selected forty-nine Igorrotes to journey with him and Julio to the Land of Opportunity. He added the name Friday Strong. The seven-year-old boy was an orphan and a member of a different tribe, the Negritos, the Philippine aboriginals. With his mop of wiry black hair, his huge grin, and his natural exuberance, Friday was too cute to be left behind.

The tribespeople Truman selected were young; all but ten of his new recruits were aged thirty-five or under. They came from a number of villages and towns throughout the region and included married couples, close friends, and relatives along with others who had never met before. Friday was the youngest. The tribal elder Falino Ygnichen, who looked youthful and strong for his sixty-something years, was the oldest. With the exception of Julio, who was half Igorrote and half Ilocano, and Friday, they were all from the same tribe, the Bontoc Igorrotes, believed by anthropologists to be descended from the Malayans. They would later be referred to by Truman and his fellow Americans simply as "Igorrotes."

Truman's own relationship with the Igorrotes had begun after he enlisted with the First Regiment, Washington Infantry, following the 1898 outbreak of the Spanish-American War. A trained physician, he had transferred to the hospital corps and, after being honorably discharged in 1899, he stayed on in the Philippines. He and a group of fellow former soldiers traveled north of Bontoc to prospect for gold in an Igorrote region famed for its extensive gold and copper deposits.

Truman's yearned-for fortune didn't materialize and in 1900 he settled among the Igorrotes in Bontoc pueblo in northern Luzon, taking with him "his medicines and forceps."[3] Before long he was famed throughout the region as the "Apo Medico" and Igorrotes traveled miles on foot to beg him to treat their sick relatives in neighboring communities. In 1901, when the Board of Health for the Philippine Islands created the role of "superintendent of public vaccination and inspection of infectious diseases for the provinces of Bontoc and Lepanto," Truman was the obvious man for the job.[4]

A cholera epidemic broke out the following year, and Truman volunteered to run the emergency hospital set up to house the diseased and the dying. He cut a heroic figure, laboring long hours in harrowing conditions and risking his own life to save his Filipino brothers and sisters.[5]

By the time he was made lieutenant governor of Lepanto-Bontoc in June 1902, he was viewed by the Igorrotes as a trusted friend and a "demi-God," thanks to his history of saving lives and his ability to pull teeth, dress wounds, and set broken bones.[6] In turn Truman viewed the Igorrotes as "the most virtuous and the happiest people . . . the most truthful, the most honest, the most industrious, the frankest, simplest, bravest, and best natured people . . . on earth."[7] This was despite the fact Truman had witnessed a head hunt at close quarters. In Bontoc each *a´-to* (village) had "a basket of soot-blackened skulls hidden away in a public building—they are all that remains of captured heads."[8] Some of the Igorrotes' ways baffled Truman but mostly he found the tribespeople entertaining, good-humored, and easy to get along with. As their lieutenant governor, he was firm but fair, and spoke enough of the tribe's complex dialect to make himself understood.

Truman had gotten the idea to exhibit his own group of Igorrotes at the St. Louis Exposition in 1904. Held to mark America's progress, the exposition was attended by twenty million Americans and featured exhibits from sixty-two countries. Thirteen hundred Filipinos from a dozen different tribes made up the Philippine Reservation, which covered forty acres and cost $1.5 million.[9] The Filipino tribes were exhibited in an anthropological diorama, surrounded by their native spears, drums, textiles, and pottery, and were presented as ranging from the Visayans, a "high and more intelligent class of natives" to the Moros, who were "fierce followers of Mohammed," the "monkey-like" Negritos, and the "picturesque" Igorrotes.[10]

Truman, who by this point had lived among the Igorrotes for several years and was one of the few Americans who could claim to know them well, had been made manager of the Igorrote Village in St. Louis. There he had watched with interest as Americans of all walks of life had flocked to see the scantily dressed, head-hunting, dog-eating Igorrotes in numbers far outstripping the organizers' most ambitious projections. The spirited Igorrotes were naturally outgoing and proved so popular they had become one of the biggest moneymakers at the fair, bringing in two hundred thousand dollars, three times more than any of the other Filipino tribes on exhibit.

At St. Louis a great debate had raged over whether the Igorrotes offended public decency by wearing only their G-strings. Fair organizers ordered Truman to cover the tribespeople in breeches made of "brilliant green and yellow and red silk."[11] A newspaper reporter summed up the view of many disappointed visitors when he wrote, "the Igorrote is endowed with a skin so beautiful it would be a crime to hide it."[12] When news of the controversy reached the White House, President Roosevelt declared that "if we were to have Igorrotes at the World's Fair, we should have real Igorrotes."[13] The trousers came off and news of the row made headlines from coast to coast, driving visitor numbers yet higher. In the words of one newspaperman, "the peculiarities of this one group of Philippine natives have done more than any other agency or feature toward advertising the greatest of all International Expositions."[14]

Despite the Filipinos' popularity with the public, America's presence in the Philippines had bitterly divided US public opinion. Among those who denounced the idea of an American empire were the industrialist Andrew Carnegie and the writer Mark Twain, who wrote of America's "assassination of the liberties of the people of the Archipelago."[15] William McKinley, who was president when America colonized the Philippines, had always insisted that America's motives were honorable, stating, "The Philippines are ours, not to exploit, but to develop, to civilize, to educate, to train in the science of self-government. This is the path of duty which we must follow, or be recreant to a mighty trust committed to us."[16] When it became clear that Theodore Roosevelt, who assumed office after McKinley was assassinated, had no plans for the prompt return of the islands to the Filipino people, the Anti-Imperialist League grew increasingly vocal. It campaigned in the press, on the streets, and in the corridors of power, pressing its case that America should withdraw from the Philippine archipelago on racial, moral, and economic grounds.

Against this political backdrop, the display of the Filipinos at St. Louis had an imperialist objective: to show that the civilizing American presence in the Philippines could only improve the lives of the savages. Though the display of the Filipinos was intended to be a one-off, Truman knew an opportunity when he saw one. He wanted to exhibit the Igorrotes in America again, this time in a more commercial setting.

Julio had been part of the group that traveled to St. Louis, along with his wife, Maria, and Friday Strong. The experience had given Julio a taste of the world beyond his doorstep and had whetted his appetite for more. When Julio had returned to Bontoc to begin recruiting for Truman's new exhibition group, he had not known what to expect. The Igorrotes were homebodies who typically ventured no more than the distance from their huts to the family rice fields. Some of the men went farther afield to trade or on their head-hunting expeditions, but it was rare for them to travel more than a day's journey from home. Julio was not certain whether many of them would be prepared to leave their families behind to journey to the other side of the world. But Truman was promising wages of fifteen dollars a month for each Igorrote who joined his venture, an incredibly large sum for the mountain people.

At first the tribespeople had come slowly, led by the brave younger ones, then in family groups and clusters of friends, picking their way through densely wooded forests and along winding dirt paths in search of the white man. Truman's proposal was audacious. Leave home. Leave family and friends behind. Board a ship and journey thousands of miles to a place where untold riches and adventures awaited. For the Igorrotes, who had no word for *ship* and who bartered with beeswax and tobacco, the opportunity to see the world beyond the mountains of Bontoc was an unimaginable prospect. Yet as soon as word got out, they came in numbers Truman could only have dreamed of. More than three hundred of them turned out that day.[17]

Truman's appeal for volunteers had been helped by the fact that returning veterans of the St. Louis World's Fair had become the closest thing their region had to celebrities, parading their American clothes, radios, flashlights, candies, and toys in front of their astonished neighbors. They included Antero, Truman's former houseboy, who posed for a photographer from the *Seattle Daily Times* in a G-string and silk top hat, carrying opera glasses and a cane.[18] A new term was coined to describe those who journeyed to America, *nikimalika*—"Malika" meaning America[19]—and they were treated with a mix of awe and envy.

Satisfied with his selections, Truman handed the final list of names to Julio and told him to inform the successful candidates.[20]

Every trace of light had vanished from the sky by the time Julio walked out of Truman's hut. Clearing his throat loudly to get the Igorrotes' attention, he explained that he was going to read out the names of those who had been selected to go to America. This group should wait behind for further instructions. Anyone who did not hear his or her name should go home. As Julio read out the names, there were gasps of joy, surprise, and disappointment. Several tribespeople who had not been selected begged Julio to persuade his new boss to let them go. Julio was sympathetic but firm, explaining that the decision was final.

The party would leave first thing in the morning in two days' time. Anyone not waiting outside Truman's hut shortly after sunrise would find his or her place had been given to someone else. They were to take only what they needed. They had a long journey ahead, including several hundred miles on foot, and they couldn't be weighed down by unnecessary baggage. The rejected candidates were each given two pesos and a bag of rice to last them on the walk home. But many of them were not willing to give up that easily. That night they bedded down outside Truman's hut, in the hope of persuading him to reconsider, or slipping unnoticed into his selected group before the time came to leave.

With the recruiting complete, Truman insisted that his favorite Filipino join him in his hut to smoke a cigar. Maybe he'd even tempt the good-natured Julio to drink a little *bá-si.* The natives typically only drank the potent local sugarcane spirit at weddings. Truman took a seat at his desk and invited Julio to do the same. He congratulated his assistant on his good work and handed him a cigar. The American struck a match and held it out across the desk. Julio leaned in for a light. He sucked the end of the cigar before exhaling the rich smoke. It tasted sweet and strange in his mouth. In this corner of the Philippines only the Americans smoked cigars; the tribespeople packed locally grown tobacco into clay, wood, and metal pipes, which they typically began to smoke around the age of six, boys and girls alike.

Without asking, Truman poured out two cups of *bá-si* and handed one to Julio. *To the Igorrote Exhibit Company,* said Truman, holding up his cup. Julio lifted his drink and joined Truman in the toast. The interpreter wasn't accustomed to drinking liquor and the cane spirit burned the back of his throat.

2

First Steps

BONTOC PUEBLO, MARCH 1905

Approach to the Bridge of Spain in the New Town, Manila, 1899

THE SUN WAS just beginning to rise and the air was cool as Julio got up and dressed. Outside his hut the atmosphere was festive and filled with expectation as the tribespeople packed up their belongings and gathered together to breakfast on rice and camotes, a local sweet potato. Julio picked up the gold watch he had bought in St. Louis and carried proudly every day since. The Igorrotes used the position of the sun to tell the time, but the interpreter preferred to be more precise. It was a quarter after six. He slipped the watch into his pocket and went to join the others, leaving his wife, Maria, sleeping in their hut.

Some of the Igorrotes had returned to their homes the previous day to say their farewells and gather a few things. Others lived too far away or had chosen not to go home for fear their families would try to persuade them not to go to America. As they breakfasted, they chatted animatedly about the adventure ahead of them. Their conversation woke Maria, who lay for a while listening. She hated the idea of leaving her family behind, but before she had time to wallow, she heard Julio shouting to get everyone's attention.

Maria draped a blanket around her shoulders. As she stepped outside, Julio looked over and smiled. She smiled back at him affectionately. Julio was holding Truman's list and had begun to call out each name in turn, just as the teachers had done in his Augustinian mission school. He ticked off the names of those who were there, then sent Friday and Tainan off to round up the others. Ed Callahan, Truman's American right-hand man, emerged from a tent nearby and stood for a few moments watching as the interpreter handed out pieces of paper, which he explained were contracts. By signing them the Igorrotes were agreeing to go to America with Truman and to be part of a Filipino exhibit there for a period of one year. They would dance, sing, weave, perform mock battles, and give other tribal displays. They would earn fifteen dollars a month each plus tips and whatever they earned selling their handmade jewelry, pipes, and other souvenirs. When the year was up, Truman would arrange and pay for their return transport to the Philippines. Given that the tribespeople couldn't read the English words on the contracts, let alone write their own names, Julio realized asking them to sign the documents was a pointless exercise, but he did as Truman had instructed him to do. Most of the Igorrotes scratched a cross; others made a scribble.

Julio looked around at their piles of possessions, which were spread out on the ground. There were gongs, shields, spears, baskets, handwoven clothing, and blankets. A few had brought head-hunting axes. They knew they wouldn't be able to use them in their new home, but Truman had told them to bring them along to show the American people.

Inside his hut Truman washed down his breakfast of eggs with a cup of hot, sweet coffee. Then he picked up his hat and walked outside to join his new employees. The first challenge was to get the Igorrotes 250 miles south to Manila, where he expected to find a telegram and a sum of money from his backer and business partner, Edmund Felder. There was no railroad in the region. They could walk to the west coast and take a boat, but Truman decided they would make the journey on foot. He called Julio and Callahan over and told them he was counting on them to make sure all the Igorrotes stayed together and on the right path. Julio nodded and, noticing Tainan and Friday appearing through a clearing with the final few members of the group, he informed Truman that they were ready to leave. Truman handed Julio a crudely drawn map showing him the route he should take, avoiding the major towns. It would take them longer that way, but Julio knew better than to argue. Truman told them to set off immediately. He would bring up the rear.

Insects buzzed around the group as they walked, the sun beating down on the Igorrotes' naked skin. A ragtag trail of volunteers who had been rejected by Truman followed behind, begging to be allowed to go too. Julio told them they were wasting their time, but his advice fell on deaf ears. Truman laughed at first. But as their pleas became more incessant and the sun got hotter, he grew annoyed. He turned around and shouted at them to go home. Many did. The more persistent ones walked on at a safe distance, hoping to replace any Igorrote who fell by the wayside or had a change of heart.

All day, the group trudged through the harsh yet beautiful landscape of jagged pine-covered peaks, described by the earlier Spanish rulers as La Montañosa. High in the mountains the temperature was cool and pleasant, but in the valleys the heat was punishing. One of the men at the back of the group suddenly came to a stop and began to sway. Truman rushed over and, as the man stumbled to the ground, he noticed it was Falino, the tribal elder. A crowd gathered round. Truman shouted to them to stand back and give Falino some air. *He is suffering from heat exhaustion. He will be fine.* When Falino came around, Truman lifted a cup of water to his lips and told him to drink. He shouted to two of the young men standing nearby to help him move the sick man under the trees so that he could rest in the shade until he felt strong again. They could all take a break. The tribespeople were glad of the opportunity to rest. The trek was hard going even for their muscular limbs.

Truman sat with Falino while the others smoked. He took the old man's pulse and asked how he was feeling. Only when he was certain

Falino was fine did Truman signal to Julio that it was time to get going again. They walked on and on for days. There were no roads, just thin paths leading through the forests, which were crisscrossed by thorn-covered creepers.[1] The strongest men carried sacks on their backs filled with rice, beans, and other provisions. When they had to ford a river, the Igorrotes held hands to keep each other upright. Julio and an imposing man named Fomoaley Ponci walked at the head of the group. Before they set out, Truman had instructed the tribe to elect a leader. They didn't understand why. Their communities were non-hierarchical, with no chiefs,[2] but they did as Truman said and chose Fomoaley. He was popular, outgoing, looked to be in his thirties (he didn't know how many years he'd been alive), and he had many heads to his credit. At around five foot six, Fomoaley was tall by Igorrote standards, most of the men being little more than five foot and the women a few inches shorter still. While the Igorrotes were typically lean from laboring hard in the rice fields, Fomoaley was plump. He was taken with the idea of being the leader and began imperiously ordering his countrymen and women around.

Julio and Fomoaley were soon joined at the front of the group by Feloa, a self-assured and outspoken young tribesman. The Igorrote men were accustomed to picking their way through the mountains when they went on head-hunting expeditions, and they clambered barefoot down steep, rocky slopes with the agility of mountain goats, sending stones and dirt flying in all directions. Callahan walked a short distance behind them. The Filipinos didn't care much for Truman's American right-hand man. He was surly, sullen, and rarely spoke to them except to bark out instructions. Julio regarded Callahan as ignorant and ill educated, though he did his best not to show it.

Truman walked at the back of the group feeling every one of his thirty-nine years. He and Callahan frequently "tangled themselves up in the creepers," which "held them back as if they were big snakes" as they gingerly picked their way along the paths.[3] The sight of them struggling amused the Filipinos. Once the light of the sun began to fade, Truman sent Friday and Tainan ahead to tell Julio to set up camp when they came to a suitable spot. Delighted to have an important job to do, the boys set off at full speed. Friday had brought his skinny pet dog and it followed in hot pursuit. The Negrito clutched a small pocket mirror in his hand as he ran. He'd been given it by a woman in St. Louis and it had become his most prized possession, after his dog.

When Truman and the other stragglers arrived, Julio, Callahan, Feloa, and Fomoaley had already rigged up blankets between the trees to create a makeshift camp and had built fires. Everyone was weary and, after a supper of rice and beans, they bedded down early.

This was the first time many of the Igorrotes had been apart from their families. Several lay awake under the night sky and wept for their loved ones. Others dreamed of the opportunities that lay ahead, the chance to earn real American money, of the things they would buy with it and the ways they would use it to build a better life for their families when they returned. Julio pictured himself as a successful businessman, living permanently in America with Maria and their growing family. It was a scenario he had played out in his head many times before.

Encouraged by Truman, Friday and Tainan imagined going to school for the first time. They knew a little bit about education from Julio and the local boys who had attended the missionary schools. Friday curled up beside his dog and nuzzled his face into its matted fur as he drifted into sleep. Maria, who was lying nearby, glanced over at the boy. She loved him dearly. He had been orphaned and then sold by his own relatives to an American newspaperman named George Fuller who had established the *Manila Freeman*, one of the earliest American newspapers in Manila. Despite the hardship and sorrow Friday had known in his short life, the boy was sunny and irrepressible. He was also "straightforward and truthful and absolutely fearless" and seemed "to know instinctively when he is right, and when he is no one can drive him."[4] Friday had told Maria that Mr. Fuller was going to visit them in America over the summer.

A short distance away, Truman lay under a canopy of netting. The tribespeople didn't seem to be bothered by mosquitoes, but the blasted creatures were hungry day and night for his American blood. Soon his skin stung all over from their bites. Truman was not athletic and his limbs ached from the trek. He looked up at the sky and thought of his wife.[5] She had been just seventeen, less than half his age, when they met in St. Louis the previous year. She was a girl just out of school, and she was named Sara.

Like thousands of young women and men, Sara had traveled to St. Louis to find work and excitement at the fair. She had left her widowed father, her brother, and her five sisters behind in her childhood home in Louisville, Kentucky, in the hope of making a new life for herself. She would get her dream, though she could hardly have imagined how her life would turn out. Truman had given her a job as his stenographer in the Igorrote Village. They married a few short months later, just days before Truman left America for the Philippines. On her wedding day she took new Christian and middle names to go with her new surname. From now on Sara A. Gallagher was Sallie G. Hunt.

Truman was an educated, intelligent man and his choice of bride surprised those who knew him. Sallie was a common little thing, though pretty and lively. Truman's airs and graces disguised the fact that he too was self-made, and friends and associates had imagined him settling down with a woman of learning and refinement. Despite their obvious differences, they were a happy couple. Sallie was in awe of her clever, worldly husband. Truman was madly in love with his beautiful wife, fiercely protective and quick to fly in to a jealous rage at the slightest (usually imagined) provocation. He had not been her only suitor at the fair, and with good reason. Sallie had a thick mane of chestnut hair, plump, kissable lips, and the most incredible emerald-green eyes he had ever seen. Truman found her looks and her youthful exuberance utterly bewitching. He had met many beautiful women in his travels, but none quite like Sallie. As he lay in the mosquito-thick mountains, he closed his eyes and imagined her warm embrace.

Truman had been raised in a modest farming family in Iowa, but he had always had big dreams of becoming a doctor and making a name for himself by saving many lives. He went to the University of Iowa to study medicine, graduating in 1887. Three years later, his father died. That same year, on December 3, Truman married his childhood sweetheart, Myrtle Potter, who was a Sunday school teacher at the local Methodist church. In 1892, she gave birth to their first child, a beautiful baby girl, Calista. It wasn't long after that Myrtle contracted the measles. She rallied but her body was left weakened and she died the following year. Truman was bereft. He sent Calista to live with his mother while he tried to pick up the pieces of his life. The handsome widower, who was still in his twenties, became a drifter, traveling across the continent in an attempt to heal his broken heart. It was that same wanderlust that led him to the Philippines.

At the turn of the twentieth century, the Philippines was the last frontier, a place not just for missionaries and colonial administrators, but for adventurers, explorers, and opportunists. Truman Hunt was all of those things.

In the distance, Truman heard Julio shouting at Tainan to quiet down and go to sleep. Truman was fond of Julio. He was ambitious and reminded Truman of himself. Admiring his sharp Western attire, Truman observed that Julio was the closest thing the northern Philippines had to a dandy. He'd always thought the young Filipino seemed different from the Igorrotes and recently he had learned that Julio was the son of an Igorrote mother and an Ilocano father, a tribe regarded by Americans as intellectually and culturally superior to the Igorrotes. In fact, Ilocanos were known as "the Yankees of the Philippines,"[6] on account of their energy, industry, and ways of doing business. Julio's father was a soldier turned trader and clerical worker who had once fought the Igorrotes. Despite this, the Igorrotes had accepted Julio as if he was one of their own. This was important to Truman—after all, his assistant had to be liked and respected by the group.

Truman, Callahan, and the tribespeople journeyed from dawn till dusk for more than two weeks. On their last day, Truman called Callahan and Julio to one side before they set out. They would reach Manila that day. The area surrounding the city was full of *ladrones*, robbers and insurgents who were fiercely opposed to American rule. These armed men would probably leave the headhunters alone, not least because there were so many of them, but Truman told them to be vigilant. The tribespeople walked without incident until the early afternoon, when Julio looked up and caught sight of a distant spot on the horizon. Built for the most part on a mud flat at the mouth of the Pasig River, Manila was so low it was almost level with the surrounding water. Julio recognized it immediately.

Truman was out of breath by the time he caught up with Julio and the others. Over the last seven years, Truman had come to know Manila well. The first time he visited, he had been struck by how ugly, gray, and dilapidated it looked. Despite its moniker of the Pearl of the Orient, Manila had none of the grandeur or beauty of other cities he had visited in the region, like Hong Kong or Kobe. Truman tripped over a crack in the sidewalk. The roads were a mess, badly paved and full of potholes.

The Igorrotes huddled close together as they walked. The streets teemed with people. Victorias, as the horse-drawn carts were known locally, clattered past, throwing up dust and dirt. They were laden with people and led by small, sturdy, thick-necked ponies, a crossbreed descended from Chinese and Spanish horses. Maria looked at one of the animals pulling a hired carriage. The beast looked fit to drop, but with one word from its driver, it took off at great speed. Carabao with huge horns snorted as they hauled carts laden with sacks of rice and tobacco. The city looked as if it had been thrown up in a hurry. To American eyes, there might not be much that was grand about the Philippine capital, but to the Igorrotes the scale and speed of life in the city was awe inspiring.

Feloa looked up at the towering electricity pylons and the tangle of cables strung between the buildings overhead. The air was thick with the smell of horse and carabao dung. White-skinned men in khaki army uniforms and broad-brimmed hats strode purposefully down the sidewalk. Friday caught sight of something up ahead and ran off down the street, with Julio in hot pursuit. The boy came to an abrupt stop outside the window of Clarkes, an ice cream parlor opened by an American entrepreneur named Met Clarke. Friday pressed his face up against the glass. Inside, women in white blouses and long skirts and men in linen suits sat at tables topped with fresh flowers, enjoying sundaes, sodas, and floats. One of the women looked up and, noticing Friday, nudged her friends. Friday pulled funny faces in the window to make them laugh. Julio grabbed the boy by the arm and hauled him back to join the others.

The tribespeople walked up the street, past Manila's first department store—the American Bazaar—and Botica Boie, which dispensed everything from potent medicines to club sandwiches. They peered in the windows of Estrella del Norte, an upmarket store owned by a Jewish family that sold perfumes from Paris, watches from Switzerland, and the first automobiles ever to land on Philippine soil.

Farther on, a jam of people pressed together, waiting to cross a bridge over the Pasig River. Tracks were being laid across the bridge to accommodate the new electric tram system that the colonial authority was building. American soldiers wearing white gloves directed the throng of pedestrians, carriages, and carts. All human life was there—priests and shopkeepers, beggars and gentlemen. An elegantly dressed lady sat in her carriage and looked over her fan as Truman and his band of natives passed.

In a nearby square, a group of local women dressed in apron skirts and brightly colored shawls stood chatting and shading themselves under a coconut palm. Truman flashed them a smile. There were some beauties among the native women. A barefoot man in dark trousers and a sleeveless shirt hurried past, carrying a pole across his shoulders with a large basket dangling from each end. Tainan stepped closer to peer inside and was almost knocked off his feet when the man stopped and turned around.

Though it wasn't unheard of for one or two members of a mountain tribe to venture into the capital to trade, the presence in the downtown area of four dozen tribespeople dressed in loincloths was enough to turn heads. While the Igorrotes gawked and were gawked at in return, the group leaders, Julio, Fomoaley, Feloa, and Callahan shepherded the tribespeople to a sheltered spot in the shadow of a church to rest. Truman handed Julio some money and told him to get them something to eat and drink. The interpreter should also buy them some proper clothes; they couldn't board the ship looking like that. He would return for them later.

Truman hurried down the street to the telegraph office. He was expecting to find a telegram and three thousand dollars from Edmund Felder. Felder had acted as executive officer of the Philippine Exposition Board at the St. Louis World's Fair and at the close of the fair he had agreed to go into business with Truman and set up an Igorrote exhibition company. The deal was that if Truman did the legwork and recruited a group, Felder would cover the expense of getting the tribe to America.

The clerk in the telegraph office informed him that he had nothing for anyone named Truman Hunt. Truman ordered the man to look again. But still there was nothing for him. Truman slammed his hand down on the counter in anger. Without the money, his scheme would founder before it had even begun. He needed the money to buy the tickets to get the fifty-one Filipinos to the US and to pay for the food they would consume on the voyage. Helpless, he fired off an angry cable to Felder.

Their ship, the SS *Minnesota*, was due to depart for Seattle the next day. Truman paced up and down the dusty, cracked sidewalk outside the telegraph office, cursing Felder and trying to think of alternative ways to get his hands on three thousand dollars. He wasn't prepared to let his plan falter. He fired off a flurry of telegrams. He informed friends and associates that he was sitting on the business opportunity of a lifetime and invited them to invest. For good measure, he sent a furious message Felder's way. While he waited for replies, Truman visited his old cronies in Manila in a desperate attempt to raise enough money to get the Igorrotes aboard.

But it was too late. On the morning of March 26, 1905, the funnels of the *Minnesota* blasted a farewell to Manila and she sailed out of port without any of the Igorrotes on board. Truman's mind raced. He would not be defeated. But how the heck could he scrounge up enough money to get the Igorrotes on a ship to the US? He must hold his nerve. He sent off a final round of telegrams, informing his friends and associates that he was giving them one last chance to buy into his Igorrote exhibition business and make their fortunes.

Truman then called in at the office of Dean Worcester, secretary of the interior of the Philippine Islands and a passionate imperialist. The two men were friendly and Worcester had given Truman's scheme his full backing, believing that the exhibition in America of primitive "non-Christian tribes" like the Igorrotes was a powerful way to demonstrate that the Philippine people were far from ready for self-government. Worcester had informed Truman he would need to provide a bond before taking the tribespeople out of their own country. But when Truman called at Worcester's office, he found his friend was traveling on business around the islands. Worcester's deputy, who knew little of the matter, had given Truman a document to sign. The bond was set at ten thousand pesos. Truman hastily scribbled his signature, then departed.

Unbeknownst to Worcester's deputy, lying underneath a pile of documents on Worcester's desk was a note from the provincial governor of Lepanto-Bontoc objecting to Truman's scheme and questioning whether he was a fit person to act as guardian of the tribe.

Truman was sweating when he arrived back at the telegraph office. The man behind the desk handed him a note. It was from one of his Manila contacts, Charles S. Moody, a former member of the American colonial administration. To Truman's great relief, Moody was offering to put up the money needed to get the tribespeople to America, on condition that he traveled with them and got a percentage of the profits.

With the finances in place, Truman rushed to the ticket office. There the clerk informed him that he couldn't get them on a ship to North America for another week. His best bet if he was in a hurry would be to secure the tribe's passage on the *Rubi*, the *Zafiro*, or one of the other mail steamers that plied the waters between Manila and Hong Kong. There, if they were lucky, they might catch up with the *Empress of China*, which was sailing to Vancouver. Truman rushed down to the dock. Luckily, he had grown accustomed to flying by the seat of his pants.

3

The Journey from the Tropics

HONG KONG HARBOR, MARCH 29, 1905

The RMS Empress of China

THE TRIBESPEOPLE BENT their heads back as far as they could, but still they couldn't see the tops of her funnels. Tainan felt a fluttering sensation in his stomach. With wide eyes, he jumped up, as if hoping the few extra inches would help him take in the ship's full splendor. Standing on the dock in Hong Kong, Daipan wished her father were there to witness the incredible sight before them. The RMS *Empress of China* was a huge, hulking beauty, 455 feet long and weighing 5,900 tons. Julio reached out and took Maria's hand. For the first time since they set out, Maria felt nervous. She had wanted to go to America again, but only now did the enormity of the journey ahead seem real. Fighting back tears, she smiled up at her husband and gave his hand a gentle squeeze.

Built in England at a cost of $1.2 million, the *Empress of China* had two funnels and three masts, and could accommodate more than a thousand passengers and crew. The sea lapped against the steamship's elegant bulk, creating a watery melody. Truman left the Igorrotes with Julio and Callahan and went to find a porter. Julio admired the way Truman did business. In Manila he had pulled out all the stops—and a fistful of dollar bills—to get them on a boat bound for Hong Kong. The sea had been choppy on the 360-mile voyage and Truman's prize cargo had traveled wedged between mailbags and cattle.

The dock in Hong Kong pulsed with life. Rickshaws and horse-drawn carriages offloaded passengers who were whisked up gang-planks where clerks in crisp white cotton shirts and neatly pressed beige trousers inspected tickets and checked names. Men in dark blue overalls carrying packing cases darted onto the ship before reemerging empty-handed and ready for the next load. Other steamers in the harbor belched out clouds of black smoke. Engineers carried out last-minute checks and repairs. The sound of their hammers on the ship's hull rang through the warm air.

Through the din of the dock, Fomoaley shouted to get their attention. With no Igorrote word for *ship*, he pointed up at the vessel and told the tribespeople that they would soon be boarding this "big canoe."[1] This would be their home for the next three weeks. Julio began tapping them on the shoulders and organizing them into small groups with Fomoaley, Feloa, Dengay,[2] Callahan, and himself as group leaders. Only a handful of the twenty-eight Filipino males and twenty-three females now walking toward the ship had ever left the mountains before. Julio was sensitive enough to realize that many would be feeling apprehensive. As well as being Truman's right-hand man, he felt it was his job to look after the others, especially Tainan and little Friday who had no family to guide them. Friday had been upset to leave his dog behind in Manila, but Julio had consoled him. There would be plenty of dogs in America.

Truman was traveling on a tight budget. The *Empress of China* could accommodate one hundred and twenty first-class, fifty second-class, and six hundred steerage passengers. As Truman and Moody took their places in their second-class cabins, the group leaders led the Igorrotes down to their accommodations in steerage. Truman had instructed Callahan to stay with the tribe. He could return to his own cabin in time for dinner. Belowdecks, the tribespeople would be living in close quarters with passengers from Europe, Japan, and China.

A double deck of bunks made from rough wooden boards ran along both sides of the ship, fore to aft. Another row ran along the middle of the ship with a narrow corridor on either side. It was dark and damp, with open hatches in the deck providing limited natural light and ventilation. The more experienced travelers in steerage claimed the best bunks, amidships, where the pitching and rolling of the vessel was at its least pronounced. If the ship was full, as many as six passengers would cram into one bunk. The Igorrotes and their fellow passengers discovered they were in luck—the *Empress* wasn't sailing at capacity that day. Though there was room to spread out, most of the Filipinos still chose to huddle three or four to a bunk. Before they departed, Truman had provided them with military blankets to sleep under and Western clothes to keep their bodies warm and their flesh concealed. But the *Empress* had barely set sail before they'd removed the long trousers and skirts. Already they loathed how the foreign clothes rubbed against their skin and hindered their movement.

Over the next twenty days and nights, they would travel eight thousand, five hundred miles across the Pacific under the command of Captain Rupert Archibald, a Canadian-born master mariner of Irish descent. On previous voyages, the vessel's distinguished passengers had included the Austrian archduke Franz Ferdinand, who traveled from Yokohama to Vancouver in a luxurious stateroom. This time around passengers included the English cricketing legend Lord Hawke, Lord and Lady Castlereagh, finely dressed but rather colorless members of the British aristocracy, and grizzled survivors of the SS *Tacoma*, a blockade runner that had been captured by the Japanese after it became caught in ice in the Soya Strait between Russia and Hokkaido. The Filipino tribe was not famous, at least not yet, and there would be no luxuries for them belowdecks.

Up above in the grand dining room, the wealthy passengers celebrated their departure with fine wines and the choice of five cuts of meat. Down in steerage the Igorrotes gathered at long unadorned tables in front of their bunks and poked through a watery stew full of lumps of gristle. Julio looked around the table and caught Feloa's eye. The two men smiled. Little had they known a few short years ago that their lives would bring them here.

Their enthusiasm for the trip was shared by the youngest members of the group. Not so long ago, Friday was an orphan being raised by a poor distant relative. When that relative had sold him to an American for less than one US dollar in order to buy food, Friday had cried himself to sleep. Now here he was, on his way back to America. He wanted to live there forever. His friend Tainan didn't know what he was looking forward to most—the incredible American inventions the *nikimalika* had described seeing, like telephones and automobiles, or the candies they had let him sample.

Some of the Igorrote women sat in their bunks chatting. They were too nervous to eat. Daipan was happy-go-lucky and not normally prone to introspection. But tonight anxiety had gotten ahold of her and, try as she might, she couldn't shake it. What if she hated America? What if the people they encountered were not kind to them? What if someone in her family back home got sick when she wasn't around to help? Maria's mind was also awhirl. Just as she laid one worry to rest, a dozen more flooded in to take its place. As the wife of Truman's assistant, Maria felt a responsibility to look after the other women and the children. She was only eighteen years old herself but she had her husband with her for support. A number of the tribespeople were traveling without any relatives. Maria forced her own worries from her mind and turned her attention to the girls beside her.

Daipan imagined herself at home, surrounded by her family. A hot tear formed in the corner of her eye. Maria looked over just as the tear began its slow descent. Taking a seat on the edge of Daipan's bunk, she put a hand on the young woman's arm. Daipan tried hard not to cry but the effort was too much. Soon her whole body was racked with aching sobs. The more she cried, the more her body shook and the better she felt. Maria put her arm around her. When finally her tears were spent, Daipan looked into Maria's dark brown eyes and managed a weak smile. Before long some of the other women and children came over and crowded into the bunk. Maria pulled the blankets up to cover them all. And that was how they slept that first night at sea, snuggled up together, a dozen or so, packed like sardines into one narrow bunk.

Boredom was not a feeling that the Igorrotes gave in to readily. At home their days were divided between tending their crops, animals, and children; hunting; cooking; eating; and sleeping. Time dragged on board the ship. With nothing else to do, they unpacked their native musical instruments, and began to play. Their impromptu concert was watched with interest and, in some quarters, with annoyance by their fellow passengers, who stayed within their own ethnic groups. Callahan, who had been sent by Truman to check up on the tribe, couldn't stand the high-pitched screeching of their instruments and stomped back to his own cabin for some peace and quiet. Maria lay awake for a long time at night, listening to the roar of the engine and the creaking and groaning of the cables that steered the rudder. It took her awhile to get used to the sensation of the ship moving beneath her body. Tainan had befriended one of the ship's cats, a skinny creature with straggly black fur. After every meal he rushed to deliver scraps of food he had saved to his new friend, distracting the cat from its job as chief rat catcher.

Rodents, fleas, and germs thrived on board. The Igorrotes' custom of keeping their hair long, both men and women, made them susceptible to catching lice. Their tribal clothes did little to keep out the cold. Several of them caught chills. Many got seasick. From time to time, the matron would come down to check on the health of the steerage passengers. The seasick Igorrotes were provided with beef tea, chicken broth, and arrowroot from the ship's store. Some were suspicious of the potions and left them untouched; others were grateful for whatever relief they could provide. There were primitive lavatories on each side of the ship. When the sea was rough, the hatches leading up onto the deck had to be closed, and the air below deck grew foul.

After catching a glimpse inside the boiler room one day, Fomoaley became fascinated by the flames, which burned in the heart of the ship. He rushed to describe the sight to the others: "A great fire burned all the time . . . I was afraid that it would burn us all up, but the white men knew how to shut it up."[3] The chief took to lurking in the doorway near the boiler room, hoping that the men would let him peer into the flames again.

Truman felt cramped in his second-class cabin, but he was a good deal more comfortable than his new employees. Each morning he took the time to dress in his finest clothes. He was a self-made man who believed in dressing to impress. After all, you never knew whom you might meet around the next corner. Truman broke up the monotony of the long days at sea with regular visits to the salon and the smoking room, and strolls round the deck. Usually he ate with Moody and Callahan, and sometimes with men and women they had met on the journey, but as the ship sailed north to Japan he chose to dine alone. He was in a melancholy frame of mind. The enforced inactivity of sea travel didn't suit him, and he didn't feel like making small talk. Truman wondered what Sallie was doing. Good old Sallie. Once upon a time he would never have imagined himself with someone like her. She was so different from his first wife, the kind, gentle, self-sacrificing Myrtle. Sallie was feisty, high-spirited, and spoiled. She could be stubborn and infuriating but he adored everything about her. Sallie's father said she'd inherited her hot blood from her Irish mother, who'd passed away when Sallie was an infant.

The announcement that the ship would soon be docking at Kobe interrupted Truman's thoughts. In the Japanese port, Truman took the opportunity to stretch his legs. He visited the telegraph office, where he sent a note to Sallie, telling her all was well and that he was due to arrive in Vancouver on April 18. He would be in touch again when they landed to make arrangements to meet up with her. He wired the organizers of the Lewis and Clark Exposition in Portland, Oregon; and sent another telegram to Frederic Thompson and Elmer "Skip" Dundy, the owners of Luna Park, the newest and best of the Coney Island amusement parks. With interest in the Igorrotes on the East and West coasts, Truman saw no reason why he couldn't do business with both parties, for the right price. He suggested to the Lewis and Clark organizers that he meet them to discuss an Igorrote exhibit, and then he invited Thompson and Dundy to make him an offer, stressing that they weren't the only party bidding.

The showman also sent messages to newspaper editors. He knew that if he sent a steady stream of tidbits ahead to excite the American public, he would have a ready-made audience waiting for them when they landed. He informed the editors that the Igorrotes hunted the heads of their neighbors for sport, then celebrated the kill with a month of feasting and by having new tattoos inked on their chests. He described how the Igorrotes, with their brown bodies covered only in flimsy loincloths, writhed and gyrated to the sound of tom-tom drums at their tribal feasts. To seal their reputation as uncivilized and exotic, he added that they ate dog and that the men, women, and children alike were all ferocious cigar smokers. The American public was in for a treat.

Though many of the Igorrotes in Truman's group had known each other before, others had never met. Now, forced together by circumstance, they formed new bonds. Minor quibbles were quickly quashed and Julio and the tribal elder, Falino,[4] worked hard to ensure disagreements were speedily resolved. The group would be living in close quarters for the next year and, as Julio pointed out, they could ill afford to make enemies among themselves.

As they sailed across the ocean, the men delighted the boys with vivid tales of their head-hunting expeditions from long ago. They were led by Falino, who, as the oldest, had more heads to his credit than all of the others. Falino had thought it strange when Truman asked him his age. Igorrotes didn't regard ages or dates as important. Their calendar revolved around the crop cycle and was divided into ten, not twelve, months. They used numbers in an impressionistic, rather than precise, fashion. If something was large or took a long time, then a big number was used to describe it. Their crossing of the Pacific, a journey of less than a month, was described among the Igorrotes as a voyage of "a thousand nights."[5]

Some of the Igorrotes were afraid of the vast ocean and didn't dare venture outside. Others went up on deck to survey the horizon. "I would never have believed there was so much water. For many days we saw no land, yet we kept on night and day. Even in dark nights when there was no moon or star we went on just as fast," marveled Fomoaley.[6] Friday was mesmerized by the seemingly infinite ocean and would willingly have stayed up on deck for the entire journey if he had been permitted. He spent many a happy hour with the menfolk, listening to the waves crashing against the hull, throwing bits of whatever he could find overboard and watching as they were quickly gobbled up by the sea. His favorite time was when he would sneak up alone after nightfall and stare up at the sky. He imagined he could see his mother between the stars, watching over him and his new life. Sometimes he took out his mirror and held the reflective side up toward the night sky, as if trying to catch the glow.

Life had settled into familiar rhythms belowdecks. The industrious Igorrotes took pleasure in the jobs they could find, like mending their musical instruments and darning holes in their blankets. When Julio called the tribe together one evening to announce that they would arrive in Vancouver the next day, the Igorrotes found the news unsettling. They had just grown used to life at sea and now another, much bigger challenge awaited them.

On Tuesday, April 18, 1905, the *Empress* reached port. It had been a largely uneventful crossing, which Captain Archibald put down to favorable weather conditions. In the early 1900s, Vancouver was one of the busiest ports on the northwest Pacific coast, receiving a massive daily traffic of goods, mail, and passengers. Without delay the *Empress of China* began to disgorge its nineteen hundred tons of cargo. Bales of Oriental silk bound for New York, burlap bags of rice, crates of tea, and packing cases were passed hand to hand by longshoremen onto the quayside as the first-class passengers began to descend the gangplank. The passenger lists were always scrutinized by the local press: when film stars or royalty were known to be on board, the crowds on the port could be dozens deep. That day Lord Hawke was the most famous man aboard and the cricketer happily signed autographs on the quayside. The Viscount and Viscountess Castlereagh disembarked without occasioning much excitement.

In steerage, the Filipinos were getting a pep talk from Julio. Callahan stood watching. He'd be glad to get off this stinking ship. It was claustrophobic and had made him yearn for life on land again. Julio knew that Truman was eager to get them across the city quickly and with a minimum of fuss; the interpreter instructed the Igorrotes to put on their American clothes. When a few of the tribespeople grumbled, Julio reminded them that they were working for Truman now and he was paying them to obey his orders. They were to stay together as a group. Anyone caught wandering off would be severely reprimanded. They would be fined, their first American wage withheld.

Truman pulled on his coat and left his cabin. He closed the door behind him and instructed the cabin boy to have his trunk delivered onto the quayside, where he would arrange for it, along with the steamer trunks filled with spears, shields, and strips of bamboo, to be taken to Vancouver's main train station. Then Truman and Moody descended the narrow companionway leading to steerage. Truman tried not to gag as the stale smell emanating from below deck pricked his nostrils. He surveyed the ragtag tribal group, who were still pulling on their new clothes. Behind them, Truman noticed Falino was leaning heavily against a bunk with his eyes closed. He approached Julio, who informed him that the old man was feeling unwell. It was just a cold, nothing to worry about. Truman told Julio not to leave the sick man's side in port. Then he instructed the interpreter and Callahan to begin herding the tribe up onto the deck. Feloa lent Falino a steadying arm.

On deck, quarantine officers inspected the new arrivals. Julio stood next to Falino and whispered to the old man to stand up straight. All immigrants were subject to a medical check, and could be refused entry or their guardian could be required to pay a three-hundred-dollar bond if they were discovered to be infirm, lunatic, idiotic, deaf, dumb, or blind, to ensure they did not become dependent on the Canadian state. Truman could not afford to throw three hundred dollars away like that. When it was Falino's turn to be examined, the medical inspector peered at him for what felt to Julio like a long time, asking him to show his gums and cough. A fine sweat broke out on Falino's brow. Finally the inspector nodded brusquely and moved on to the next man. When the medical inspectors were satisfied that the

Filipinos were not carrying any infectious diseases, they signaled to Truman that he could take them off the ship.

After three weeks spent living in an enclosed space with minimal fresh air and little natural light, the Igorrotes emerged blinking into the chill of an early-spring day in Vancouver. The tips of their fingers tingled, and the cool air caught in their throats. The port pulsated with life. The tribespeople stood for a moment, silently taking in the sights and sounds of the unfamiliar new land. Truman shouted at them to keep walking. The Igorrotes obeyed, their eyes darting all around as they followed Julio, and took their first tentative steps toward their new lives in the Land of Opportunity.

4

The Money Men

MIDTOWN MANHATTAN, APRIL 12, 1905

Frederic Thompson and Elmer "Skip" Dundy opened the Hippodrome in April 1905.

LONG BEFORE THE doors opened at seven o'clock, a crowd began to gather on the sidewalk. Women in furs and men in tuxedos spilled out of motorcars. A seemingly endless line of carriages ran as far as the eye could see along Sixth Avenue and round the corner, choking Forty-Third and Forty-Fourth Streets. Roundsman Fogarty, the police officer in charge of the patrol and a veteran of the theater squad, declared that he had never seen a longer line of carriages drawn up before any New York amusement enterprise in his entire career.[1]

Six thousand people turned out for the opening night of the Hippodrome Theater, affectionately dubbed "the Hippo" on account of its vast girth. Five thousand more came in the hope of buying tickets, but were turned away empty-handed.[2] Every seat in the house was taken. The expectant crowd milled around on the sidewalk waiting for the doors to open. They were illuminated by twenty-five thousand tiny white lights, which studded the towers at either end of the Hippodrome, shining out over neighboring Broadway. New Yorkers knew how to dress up for an occasion, but this was something special. They'd pulled out all the stops. The ladies wore evening dresses in pastel blues, greens, pinks, and peaches, made of the finest silks, velvet, and delicate chiffon layered over lace, embroidered with pearls, diamanté, and beads. They carried fans and evening bags in their gloved hands. The men wore top hats and tails. Their shoes were highly polished and their sideburns neatly trimmed.

The doors were unlocked and the audience surged inside. People chatted animatedly to strangers standing next to them in the line as they waited to have their tickets torn by men dressed in long red coats and black trousers with gold stripes down the sides. Nobody knew quite what to expect but with the Luna Park creators Frederic Thompson and Elmer "Skip" Dundy running the show, one thing was certain: they were in for a stunning night's entertainment. In the bar, the hum of conversation mingled with the sounds of corks popping and glasses clinking. There were rumors of swimming horses, lions in glass cases, and an epic battle scene. Just then the Vanderbilts entered the room. A hush descended as heads turned and necks craned. Other VIPs in attendance included the Guggenheims, the socialite Harry Payne Whitney, and Chauncey Depew, the New York senator and former president of the New York Central Railroad System. The millionaire showman James A. Bailey of Barnum and Bailey fame was overheard telling his party that it was the first time in thirty years he had visited a playhouse.[3] This was a night not to be missed; it was history in the making.

Standing in the plush lobby of the Hippodrome surrounded by bejeweled ladies, and gents in white bow ties and stiff collars, was a clean-shaven man in a striped brown suit with a black derby hat and a pair of muddy shoes. He stood out only for his ordinariness, dare anyone say it, even his scruffiness. "How are you, Fred?" shouted the millionaire John W. Gates, breaking away from his friends, and going over to shake the man's hand.[4] The young man he addressed was none other than Frederic Thompson, the creative genius behind Luna Park and the Hippodrome and a man, despite appearances, famed for his extravagant tastes. The two men stood chatting for a moment before someone else recognized Thompson and stopped to wish him luck.

At just thirty-three years of age, Thompson had a lot riding on that night. Not only had he put together the program, he and Dundy had spent $1.5 million[5] ($40 million in today's money) of their own and backers' money building the Hippodrome, swallowing up their savings and all their profits from Luna Park. Thompson himself designed the Hippodrome, along with the architect Jay H. Morgan, and together the two men had created a lavish theater that boasted a stage twelve times the size of the average Broadway stage. In short, the venture was the biggest gamble of Thompson and Dundy's professional lives. Thompson would be glad when the curtain went up and the show got underway. He was relieved to see Dundy striding toward him with a drink in each hand. Thompson excused himself from the group of well-wishers who had gathered around and walked over to greet his business partner.

Thompson and Dundy had a genius for the entertainment business. Their partnership was magical, with each egging the other on to greater triumphs of inventiveness.

Dundy had a broad frame, pleasant features, and was a gifted political operator. He was born in Omaha, Nebraska, in 1862, the son of a federal judge, and grew up in a large, comfortable house where the famous showman Buffalo Bill Cody was a regular guest of his parents. Under pressure from his father to enter the legal profession, Dundy started his career as a clerk of the court. But the law was not for him; Buffalo Bill's stories of life in the show ring had awakened in the young Dundy a fascination with the world of midways and fairs.

Though he was born into privilege, Dundy's early life was not without personal challenges. He had a stutter that he had to work hard to overcome, developing a system of "running" at his words that gave his speech a sense of urgency. This came in handy when he got his first job as a pitchman at a fair, ensuring that Dundy's pitches stood out from all the rest. Dundy had also gone prematurely bald and was very sensitive about his hair loss. But he turned this imperfection into a business advantage: whenever he was losing an argument, without saying a word, he would remove his center-parted toupee and put it in his pocket, in a bid to distract his opponents. It was a tactic he used on Thompson whenever his business partner's imagination and spending were getting out of hand.

Thompson was of slender build and had a long face and heavy-lidded eyes. High-strung, prodigiously energetic, and outgoing, he was one of the most popular men in the New York entertainment business. He had an unrivaled passion for his work and "tried to do four times as much work as most men would be satisfied to pass to their credit."[6] Thompson was born in Irontown, Ohio, and was a decade younger than Dundy, though he didn't look it. But what Thompson lacked in looks he more than made up for with charm. Thompson had begun his career as an office clerk and planned to start his own brokerage company, but a trip to the 1893 Chicago World's Fair changed that. At the fair he took a job as a janitor and, after impressing his bosses, was put in charge of an exhibit. From that moment on, he was hooked. He saw the enormous possibilities that the amusement business offered, both for generating profits and as an outlet for his pent-up creativity.

He wound up in Nashville, Tennessee, where he took a job as a draftsman. A competition to design buildings and pavilions for a local fair gave Thompson the break he needed. He won twenty-five hundred dollars for his entry, no small sum in 1896 (worth around sixty-seven thousand, five hundred dollars today). When the Nashville fair opened, Thompson's uncle turned a failing attraction over to him to see if he could make a go of it. It was called the Blue Grotto and Thompson didn't have to look hard to see why the damp and leaky papier-mâché exhibit was failing. While he didn't have money to dramatically alter the structure of the attraction, he could tinker at the edges and spend what little he had on causing a stir. He replaced the barker outside the grotto with an Edison cylinder phonograph, which, he reasoned, was so novel it was sure to attract the attention of passersby whom he could talk into buying a ticket. He wound it up and stood back. Within minutes a huge crowd had gathered around to discover where the crackling disembodied voice was coming from. The novelty paid off, the attraction turned a profit, and Thompson's career as a showman was launched.

Thompson and Dundy's first meeting, in 1898, was hardly auspicious. It took place at the Trans-Centennial Exposition in Omaha, where the two men were running rival—and coincidentally, remarkably similar—attractions. Thompson was there with a cyclorama called Darkness and Dawn, while Dundy was running The Mystic Garden. Both gave viewers a glimpse into what heaven and hell might look like. But, to Dundy's great annoyance, his attraction was inferior to and much less popular than Thompson's.

Their paths crossed again at the Pan-American Exposition in Buffalo, New York, three years later and they immediately recognized each other. Thompson had created a groundbreaking new attraction for Buffalo, called A Trip to the Moon (it predated the 1902 Georges Méliès film of the same name), which captivated the imagination of an audience eager for new experiences. At ten-minute intervals, would-be astronauts were invited, for a dime, to journey beyond the bounds of Earth, via a "combination of electrical mechanism and scenic and lighting effects . . . [which] produce the sensation of leaving Earth and flying through space amid stars, comets and planets to the Moon."[7] Unlike previous attractions that moved around the audience, this one took them on a journey using innovative electrical devices to lift them off the ground.

Dundy asked Thompson for a demonstration. Smiling, Thompson invited Dundy and his fellow passengers to board a cigar-shaped spacecraft. A gong sounded. The spacecraft's huge wings began to beat, slowly at first, then gathering speed, and the craft lurched forward with a whooshing sound. The "airship" was operated by a complicated system of gimbal bearings under the deck, which imparted a rocking motion, while the wings and large propellers were operated by powerful dynamos. Through the windows, images of the fairground receded into the distance to be replaced by clouds and the tiny lights of the earth below. Moments later the spacecraft touched down on the lunar surface. There the fairgoers were greeted by miniature moon men, singing "My Sweetheart's the Man in the Moon," and handing out chunks of green cheese. The moon dwellers led the visitors through a cavernous papier-mâché lunar landscape pocked with craters painted red, yellow, and green, and across a drawbridge that led into a castle. There the moon king and queen reclined on huge velvet thrones, dressed in robes and crowns, flanked by bronze griffins.

Astounding, was Dundy's verdict. He immediately asked his rival to go into business with him. Thompson said yes: if Dundy could learn from Thompson's creativity, then he could surely benefit from Dundy's focus and financial expertise.

A Trip to the Moon was the standout success of the Pan-American Exposition. After it closed, Thompson and Dundy were inundated with offers from amusement park owners across America who were eager to get their hands on the moneymaking attraction. They struck a deal with George Tilyou, the owner of Steeplechase Park at Coney Island, on the condition that they would continue to manage the attraction at Steeplechase and the three of them would split the profits. Tilyou agreed. Thompson and Dundy quickly made an impression at Coney. They staged a number of headline-grabbing publicity stunts, most famously the public electrocution of Topsy, a six-ton Indian elephant, who had killed her trainer (it later transpired that the trainer treated her cruelly and had put a lit cigar to the end of Topsy's trunk). Edison power company workers hooked up electrodes to her feet, then turned on the current. Smoke rose from the great beast's hide. She convulsed, then seconds later she toppled over, dead. Thompson preserved Topsy's feet and part of her hide for an office chair.

When Tilyou offered Thompson and Dundy a reduced share of the profits the following season, Thompson and Dundy ditched their business partner, taking A Trip to the Moon with them. The enterprising duo bought up the neighboring Sea Lion Park, where they set about creating a theme park to beat them all. They would name it after Dundy's sister, Luna.

While Dundy took care of the finances, wining and dining potential investors from Wall Street and the Coney Island racing crowd,

Thompson lived on-site at Luna Park, sacrificing sleep and surviving on little but adrenaline and creative inspiration as he drew up plans for thrilling and outlandish attractions. Luna Park opened on May 16, 1903, and was an immediate success. Top attractions included a replica of Venice, complete with gondolas paddling along the Grand Canal; the War of the Worlds, a spectacle in which miniature versions of the navies of the allied European powers attacked New York Harbor; and Twenty Thousand Leagues Under the Sea, a submarine ride to the polar regions.

Thompson and Dundy made a great team but they couldn't have been more different, in their backgrounds or temperament. Thompson was a spendthrift with a weakness for drink. Dundy was focused and had a steely core. He helped keep his business partner on track and was the one person who could persuade Thompson to leave the bar when alcohol got too strong a grip on him. But Dundy had his own vices, namely women and gambling. Just as Dundy helped him, Thompson would return the favor on occasion, turning up at the gaming tables when he got word that Dundy was on a losing streak. The two men worked hard and didn't believe in keeping books.[8] Despite their differences, they rarely argued, perhaps because of their shared worldview that in order to make a fortune they would first have to spend one.

It was this shared worldview that had led them to where they now stood on the evening of April 12, 1905, in an office high above the Hippodrome stage, where they took a few moments away from the crowds to drink a toast to each other and their latest venture. If they could pull this off, the Hippodrome's opening-night spectacular, then the sky really was the limit. Two upstarts from Coney Island dragging the theater spotlight away from Broadway and over to Sixth Avenue. Who'd ever heard the like? They looked each other in the eye as they threw back their drinks. A knock at the door of Thompson's office signaled it was time to go.

Thompson slapped Dundy firmly on the back. The two men put down their glasses and stepped outside the door. They would meet again when the curtain fell. By then their fate would be known.

Thompson made his way downstairs. He wanted to make a final check backstage. Dundy was far more superstitious than he cared to admit, and, during his time at Coney, he had come to regard elephants as his lucky charm. At his insistence, the auditorium of the Hippodrome had been festooned with ornamental bronze Indian and African elephant heads, cast especially for him at great expense. Their tusks held electric lightbulbs. Before seating himself in his box, Dundy reached up to give the trunk of one of his beloved elephant lamps a rub for good luck. Thompson had taken two boxes next to Dundy's for himself and his friends but Thompson's own seat would remain empty for most of the evening as the popular frontman dashed around backstage, ensuring the show went off without a hitch.

Dundy surveyed the crowded auditorium. Along with the rich and famous in their fine evening wear were hundreds of ordinary hardworking Americans dressed in their Sunday best. It was exactly the mix Thompson and Dundy strove to bring to all of their attractions. Tickets for that night's opening gala ranged from $575 for a seat in a private box down to 25 cents for a seat in the family circle—the same price Thompson and Dundy charged for their top attractions at Luna Park. To their delight, the pair would learn later that the Hippodrome's box office raked in twenty thousand dollars that night (more than half a million dollars in today's money).[9]

The audience was treated to the show of a lifetime. Beautiful young women in pink leotards spun in midair using nothing but their teeth to grip the thinnest of ropes. Dundy's beloved elephants danced. Cavalry troops on horseback dodged gunfire and explosions in a mock battle that raged across an eight-thousand-gallon clear glass water tank that was raised from below the stage by hydraulic pistons. A thousand dancers, actors, and circus performers filled the stage with color and action. "Magnificent, astounding and almost paralysing in its brilliance," was the verdict of one critic.[10] New York had never seen anything like it. When the curtain came down, the audience leaped to their feet, clapping, cheering, and shouting, "Hip, hip for The Hippodrome."[11]

The triumphant opening would have satisfied the ambitions of lesser men but it only served to drive Thompson and Dundy on, as they turned their attention to their next scheme.

The Igorrotes were coming. Thompson was determined to get them for Luna Park—at any price. By now they must have landed on American soil. When Truman had cabled from Kobe, Thompson had made him an offer and urged Truman to give him first refusal on the Igorrotes. He was expecting to hear from the showman again any day now.

5

Welcome to America

EN ROUTE TO SEATTLE, APRIL 18, 1905

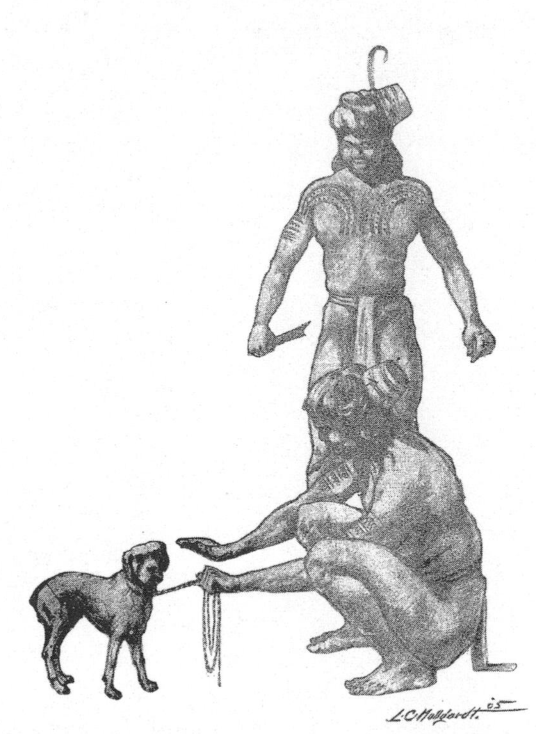

Sketch from the Seattle Sunday Times *of two Igorrote men and a dog they are about to slaughter for a canine feast, by the artist L. C. Mullgardt*

TRUMAN WOKE UP to the acrid smell of burning. Smoke was pouring from the hat in his lap. Throwing it onto the floor, he stamped the fire out. The Igorrotes looked over, intrigued. A cinder must have drifted across from the stove; it had burned a hole the size of a silver dollar in the crown. Darn it, that hat had cost him five dollars. Julio stifled a smile. Callahan and Moody laughed. Truman shot them a furious glance.

Truman and his charges were traveling in a private car attached to the Canadian Pacific regular passenger train. Most of the Igorrotes had never set eyes on a train before and it took them awhile to get used to its endless rocking and jolting. All of a sudden, Truman heard a loud retching sound. He looked around and saw Tainan bent double, with his head between his legs, vomit running down his bare calves. Truman gagged. He got up and moved to the other end of the carriage.

The showman rubbed his eyes. The air was heavy with the Igorrotes' pipe smoke and fumes from the stoves and kerosene lamps. The conductor's many duties included removing cinders from passengers' eyes. The Filipinos were not permitted to eat in the dining car. For one thing Truman didn't have the money; for another, the American passengers would have complained. Instead the tribespeople cooked rice and beans for themselves over a coal stove. They had just a bucket of sand to protect them and their wooden train car if the fire got out of control.

Truman cast his mind back to a more pleasant journey—the luxurious Pullman car that had carried him and Sallie from St. Louis to Oregon the previous year. They'd been on their way to be married and had been full of excitement, not to mention the numerous flutes of champagne they drank on the journey.

He was jolted out of his happy memory as the train screeched to a stop. Sedro-Woolley was a glorified railroad junction, where four lines converged just south of the Canadian border. It was an undistinguished place for the Igorrotes to make their American premiere, but Truman had banked on the fact that nothing ever happened here. He leaped from his seat and peered through the window. As he had planned, the platform was lined with pressmen and eager townsfolk. In this nowhere place, the arrival of the Igorrotes was big news.

The showman led the tribespeople on to the platform and turned to the waiting group of reporters. In a booming voice, he told them that his Igorrotes were "tired from their long sea voyage and complaining of being so long denied their customary diet of dog meat."[1] A burly man standing on the platform with a hunting dog recognized his cue and discreetly took the dog's leash off.

At a signal from Fomoaley, the tribespeople charged along the platform. The crowd watched as the Filipinos closed in on the dog. When Tainan made a grab for its tail, the animal squealed and snarled.

Truman shouted a few harsh words in Bontoc and the Igorrotes came to a sudden stop. Feigning fury, Truman ushered them back onto the train. Tomorrow the newspapers from Seattle to Portland would be full of tales of the Igorrote savages who had burst from their carriage to attack an innocent American dog. Truman saved a final wave for the dog's owner (who had been primed several days earlier by Truman's advance man) as the train puffed on, taking the tribe closer to their fame.

The sky was already growing dark when they arrived in Seattle on the evening of April 19, 1905. Truman had rented a small cottage on Blanchard Street, an area given over to manufacturing and workers' houses. They could stay there for a night or two until his local fixer found them somewhere cheaper. Truman told the Igorrotes to rest, though he could hear them talking long into the night. The showman sat up smoking. He felt excited about what lay ahead. A great adventure was about to begin.

The next morning Truman took a streetcar to the offices of the *Seattle Daily Times*, where a reporter was waiting to conduct the first big interview with the Filipinos' manager. Truman needed little prodding to sell the tribe. "It's a fine lot we have . . . The natives are excellent dancers," he enthused, though he confessed in a conspiratorial tone that "There was not much keen enjoyment in gathering the party [in their Philippine mountain home] . . . I walked more than 250 miles. It was impossible to ride or get through the country in any other way than on foot."[2]

The showman said he had been inundated with volunteers, far more than he needed, due largely to the positive experience of the Igorrotes who had exhibited at the St. Louis Exposition the previous year. "The natives were greatly impressed by the stories told of the American visit [by] the party that attended the St. Louis Exposition," said Truman.[3] "All of those natives took home trinkets and money that created a great deal of comment and envy, but the stories of their travels and the unending versions of America's wonderful development were the matters which aroused the deepest interest among the Igorrotes. They all wanted to see and to hear, and we could have brought almost any number had it been possible to do so,"[4] he added.

Truman was ready to talk next about head-hunting rituals and dog feasts and was taken aback to find that the reporter wanted instead to discuss a new system of taxation that the Philippine Commission was considering rolling out to the remote areas of the islands. Puzzled, but never stuck for words, Truman said the group traveling with him was "strongly opposed to the collection of taxes."[5]

The reporter called a photographer over, and Truman began dusting imaginary pieces of lint off his jacket and straightening his tie. Thankfully, he had worn his smartest suit. He must buy several copies of the paper, enough for his mother and sister back in Iowa, and Sallie, too. She would get a kick out of her husband's newfound fame.

After his interview, Truman called in at the telegraph office. There was a message waiting for him from Henry W. Goode, the president of the Lewis and Clark Exposition, inviting him to Portland that week to discuss terms for setting up an Igorrote Village there. Truman telegraphed his reply: he would be delighted to take up the invitation. Thompson and Dundy would be waiting to hear from him, but Truman decided to hold off making contact until he heard what Goode had to say. There was another note from his local fixer, informing Truman that he'd found lodgings for the showman and his charges, over on Pike Street, near the wharf. Truman put the piece of paper with the address in his jacket pocket.

Truman was in good spirits when he returned to the little house on Blanchard Street. He opened the front door to discover the Igorrotes' clothes hanging all over the place. The tribe had spent the day doing their laundry. The showman smiled and shouted to Julio to tell them all to pack up. They were moving to new accommodations.

Pike Street was a low, wide thoroughfare by the port and the railroad tracks. The smell from the San Juan fish-packing company mingled with the aroma of burning fat and animal flesh from the tannery across the street. Truman led the Igorrotes up to number twenty-two and opened the door. This would be their home until he decided where they were going next. The accommodations were basic, two big empty rooms, but they would do fine. Best of all, there was space for them to give performances, which would bring in some much-needed money. The showman instructed the Filipinos to make themselves at home. He was going out to spread the word that an exotic tribe had arrived in town, and they were giving daily performances in their Pike Street lodgings.

When Truman and his business partner Edmund Felder first came up with their plan to exhibit the tribe in America, they had written to the War Department seeking permission. In their letter, they declared their intention "to arrange for [the Igorrotes'] stay in this country for about two years, exhibiting them at the Portland Exhibition, at Coney Island, or other amusement centers, and at the larger State Fairs."[6]

Clarence Edwards, head of the War Department's Bureau of Insular Affairs, approved the plan to put the Igorrotes on display at the Lewis and Clark Exposition in Portland, timed to mark the centennial of Lewis and Clark passing through Oregon on their epic trek westward. The Exposition was planned as a piece of economic boosterism that would celebrate local, national, and international culture. But if exhibiting the Igorrotes in the educational, anthropological setting of an exposition was acceptable, Edwards had major doubts about showing the tribe in an amusement park.

Edwards wrote to the civil governor of the Philippines about Truman and Felder's request, stating, "I rather deprecate the idea of taking these people to Coney Island and giving the people of the United States the idea that the majority of the people of the Philippines are similar to the Igorrots [*sic*] and Negritos, in the same way as I would rather deprecate the idea of having Apachee [*sic*] Indians travelling around to represent Americans."[7]

By exhibiting the tribe in Portland, Truman would be abiding by the terms of his agreement with the government. But could the showman resist the lure of Coney's big bucks?

• • •

Truman arrived in Portland on the morning of April 23, 1905, to find the Exposition grounds a hive of activity. He had brought Moody, Julio, and Fomoaley with him. Henry Goode welcomed his visitors and invited them to take a tour with him. The sound of hammers, shovels, and picks rang out as builders, carpenters, and plumbers put the finishing touches on the Exposition buildings. Once marshland forested with dogwoods, blackberry vines, and flowering currants, the grounds had been transformed into a wonderland of Spanish Renaissance-style buildings and ornamental gardens. The man charged with taming the wilderness was John Olmstead, the nephew of Frederick Law Olmstead, the celebrated creator of New York's Central Park.

Goode showed them the large patch of ground he had earmarked for the Igorrotes and began enthusing about what a beautiful setting it was. The spot was overlooked by a hill. Truman pointed to it. This wouldn't do at all. Goode was confused. Why was that a problem? Truman spoke slowly, as if to a child. If the Igorrote village could be seen from a hill, then any fairgoer would be able to climb up the slope and peer down into his village without paying a cent. The village needed to be moved. As they argued a third man walked over to join them. Truman, already in a foul mood at Goode's stupidity, turned and noticed the man standing beside him was Edmund Felder. Without stopping to think, he swung for his erstwhile business partner but Goode grabbed his arm and held him back. Fomoaley and Julio stood silently watching the scene. Truman demanded to know what Felder was doing there. Without waiting for an answer, he screamed at him that he didn't want to hear an apology, he would never forgive Felder for leaving him stranded in Manila without any money to get the tribespeople to America. But Felder ignored him. He was there to claim his share in the enterprise that he had been instrumental in setting up. Truman was livid.

Goode turned to the showman and tried to persuade him to cut Felder in on the deal as per their original plan. Outraged, Truman accused Goode of double-dealing and stormed off, threatening to sue Felder and vowing to take his Igorrotes elsewhere. The Portland deal was off. Moody, Julio, and Fomoaley hurried after him.

The Exposition's director of concessions, John Wakefield, had been standing nearby and had witnessed the whole scene. He'd heard rumors that Truman had been speaking to Thompson and Dundy and sensed the showman was up to no good. When a group of reporters called later that day, Wakefield told them that Truman had stormed out of Portland in order "to raise a big hullabaloo and have the fact that [the Igorrotes] are here advertised over the country . . . as a result of the advertising they will receive they will be sought by all the amusement managers of the country."[8] Asked whether they would miss the Igorrotes in Portland, Wakefield, who as director of concessions had had a vested financial interest in the Igorrote deal, couldn't contain his rage: "The majority of the board does not think [the Igorrotes] would be a great benefit to the Exposition any way, as they consider them a band of dirty little cannibals."[9]

On the train to Seattle, Truman's mind whirled with possibilities. Exhibiting the Igorrotes in Portland would have been easy money and would have satisfied the authorities who were anxious that the tribespeople should be exhibited in an "authentic" setting. But Truman felt sure he could make much more money at Coney Island or elsewhere on the American fair and amusement circuit. Getting the tribe to New York would be a logistical and financial headache, but once they were there the returns could be astronomical. Truman needed to come up with a plan fast.

The showman sent a telegram to Thompson as soon as he got back to Seattle. He lied that he had had a better offer for the Igorrotes and invited the Coney showman to increase his own bid. Then he made his way to Pike Street. When he opened the door to the Igorrotes' room, he found them gathered around Falino, who lay on a pile of blankets on the floor. Maria was wiping the old man's forehead with a damp cloth while Daipan tried to get him to drink sips of water. Truman went over and placed his hand on the patient's brow. He had a raging fever and seemed to be slipping in and out of consciousness. There was no alternative but to get him to a hospital.

Truman spent much of the night at Providence Hospital with Falino, until a nurse sent him home. He was worried about the old man but decided to focus his attention on work. The next morning he contacted every newspaper in the area to tell them that the Igorrote tribespeople had landed safely on American soil and were celebrating with a huge outdoor show. Their tribal spectacular would be held an hour from downtown Seattle, in the forests of Blake Island. Here, on the former ancestral camping ground of the Suquamish tribe, the Filipinos would perform tribal dances, sing their native songs, throw spears, and cook up an authentic dogmeat feast.

The location was chosen, Truman bluffed, to ensure the Igorrotes' privacy. To safeguard that privacy, Truman invited the reporters to come along and witness the event. In reality, the location suited Truman because it lay outside the city limits, precluding interference by municipal authorities.

The only way to reach Blake Island was by boat. The steamer that left Seattle at 9:45 on the morning of April 23 was named the *Dix*, and she carried Truman, Moody, Callahan, the Igorrotes, a dozen newspapermen, a variety of Igorrote musical instruments, cooking pots, a bag of rice, and three mutts brought from the city pound, along with its usual mixture of nature lovers and trekkers. Truman called the reporters to gather around. That morning they would witness one of the most remarkable sights of their life; a *canao*, which was the name the tribespeople gave their native feast and dance.[10] In the Philippines these could last for weeks without pause, but here, owing to the restrictions of the steamer schedule, the grand spectacle would last six hours.

On the island Truman selected a stretch of beach a short walk from the dock. Watched by the waiting reporters, the tribespeople threw off their "street dress"[11] and the men got straight down to the serious business of preparing for the feast. The women collected water and began cleaning the pots. The men built fires and washed the rice for cooking. Then they "seized [their] native cymbals" and "plunged into a thanksgiving dance . . . they swayed to and fro with a rhythmic motion that indicated a lighthearted and care-free condition of mind. As the preparations for the slaughter of the dogs proceeded the dance changed, and, as the old braves seized a luckless pup and dragged him away to the block, the dance became animated."[12]

Assisted by two of his countrymen, Fomoaley tied the snarling mutt's feet to a wooden post. When they were satisfied that the dog could not escape, the men lifted the animal above their heads. The dog's snaps and snarls turned to helpless yelps as it dangled upside down. Fomoaley took a knife from his belt and, with one deft stroke, slit the dog's throat. The mutt let out an ear-piercing sound that was "brutal and revolting."[13] As it gasped its final breath, Fomoaley sliced the dog's tail off.

W. P. Romans, the photographer sent by the *Seattle Daily Times*, stood close by, furiously releasing the shutter button on his camera. He knew the paper would never print his picture of the dog's throat being slit but it was too good a shot to miss. He moved around the scene, capturing it from various angles.

"The dancers suddenly squatted, and, with eyes turned toward the cooks, broke into a song. Then the women and young boys leaped to their feet again."[14] The chief threw the lifeless dog's body into a pot of water that was boiling over a huge bonfire.

Truman called to the women to follow him to a spot farther along the island.

When the showman returned, Romans asked where the women had gone. Truman replied that during the dog feast they were banished to another patch of ground, for their own less exotic feast of boiled rice and clams. Truman explained that dogmeat was a delicacy that the Igorrotes believed made them fierce, giving them strength to carry out their head-hunting expeditions. As such, women were forbidden from eating it, for fear it would make them aggressive. The only time women were allowed to taste the canine flesh, Truman said, was as a treat on their wedding day, when they needed fire in their bellies to carry out their conjugal duties. The reporters smirked.

The Igorrote men and boys gave thanks with a wailing song for the feast they were about to eat. When they were satisfied that the meat had boiled for long enough to fall off the bone in chunks, they gathered around, ready to gorge themselves. The Igorrote elders were the first to taste the lean dogmeat, picking it up with their bare hands and shoveling it into their mouths. Only when they had finished were the younger men allowed to partake in the canine feast.[15]

Friday never ate dogmeat. But that day he gnawed fiercely on a dog bone, then, barking wildly, he threw himself around on the grass in a spontaneous show of savagery for the benefit of the reporters.

The Igorrotes slaughtered the two remaining dogs, then threw them into the pot to cook. They feasted, sang, and danced with wild abandon. Friday and Tainan waved axes above their heads as they danced a jig. The boys were not beautiful according to American tastes, but their ever-smiling faces and tireless energy charmed the watching reporters.

Next the women reappeared. The tribal chief began to chant and the whole group formed a circle around him, beating tom-toms, singing, and writhing to the music. This, Truman explained, was a wedding dance. To American eyes, the Igorrotes looked possessed, as if by some strange spirit.

While the others danced and sang, Friday peered out from behind a clump of bushes, firing an imaginary bow and arrow at them and "hunting" them by creeping slowly forward until he was close enough to pounce. The Igorrotes were too busy to notice him, but the reporters weren't. They laughed as he jumped out with a shout. Then Friday withdrew to a safe distance to begin the performance again.

Before concluding the festivities, the tribe ran races, threw spears and stones, and wrestled each other to the ground. An odd, American touch saw the winners of a singing competition rewarded with a box of cigars, which they sucked on contentedly. At five thirty in the afternoon, Truman signaled to the tribespeople to pack up, ready to catch the steamer *Manette* back to Seattle.

The event was the talk of the town the next morning when families across the city sat down to read their newspapers over breakfast. Unable to leave a good story alone, Truman had thrown in a homey promise: he was taking the entire tribal group to his family's farm in Iowa for a vacation before the start of the summer season. Whatever would the good farming folk of Iowa make of the G-string–clad Filipinos?

Buoyed by his triumph, Truman announced that the Igorrotes were holding another huge dog feast and this time everyone was invited. It would take place in Madison Park in downtown Seattle the following Sunday. But the police had other ideas. They told the showman they would arrest him if he took a dog anywhere near the place. "Igorrotes Can Have No More Dog Say Authorities—Gentle Calves and Lambs Killed Daily but Fido Is Protected . . . the Igorrotes are pressing emaciated hands to depressed stomachs and wondering if this is after all the land of the free,"[16] read the front-page story in the *Seattle Daily Times.* The reporter got creative, summing up the position of the Seattle Police and the Humane Society with a verse:

Backward, turn backward,
O child of Luzon!
Lower thy bolo and put thy shoes on.
Poor little Fido, just stand back of me,
And I will protect thee from this crueltee.[17]

Truman didn't get his dog feast, but that didn't matter: he got the publicity he craved.

Word spread about Seattle's exotic new residents, and crowds began to descend on Pike Street, handing over their nickels and dimes at the door. The visitors included L. C. Mullgardt, a Harvard-educated artist and architect. As he left the Washington Hotel, where he was staying, and turned the corner, "a brazen tumult assailed his ears as he passed the temporary Igorrote camp on Pike Street. Entering, [he] saw the broad-shouldered, swarthy Igorrote men swaying in the mazes of their native dances to the ear-splitting accompaniment of brass cymbals. It was a weird but interesting scene."[18] When the show was over, Mullgardt stayed for a while and, with Julio interpreting, he engaged the tribespeople in conversation.

So taken was the artist with the Filipinos that he postponed pressing business engagements in Portland and San Francisco so that he could return to Pike Street the following day with his sketchbook. For the next five nights, he sat in the dimly lit front room gazing intently at the tribe, who danced and sang native songs. He worked quickly, sketching the tribespeople in charcoal.

A reporter from the *Seattle Daily Times*, there at Truman's invitation, noticed Mullgardt's drawings of the "strong and virile"[19] warriors, and went over to talk to him. Explaining his fascination, the artist said, "Frankly, I confess that the more I saw of the Igorrotes after a most casual visit to them last Tuesday, the more I became interested in them and the more fixed became my desire to picture them and to study their ways."[20] The reporter persuaded Mullgardt to let him print his sketches of the nearly naked Filipinos alongside his article in the paper.

Invigorated by the attention the tribe was garnering and delighted to have some money in his pocket again, Truman sent a telegram to Thompson and Dundy, accepting their latest offer and promising he and the Igorrotes would arrive at Coney Island within a fortnight. Finally, things were looking up for Truman Hunt and his Igorrote exhibition business.

But not everything ran to Truman's carefully orchestrated plan. On May 10, just as he was preparing to set out with the tribe on their journey, he received word from the hospital that Falino had died of pneumonia.

Truman must tell the tribe, but how? He knew the Igorrotes well enough to know that the old man's death, alone, in a Western hospital and on foreign soil, would hit them hard, not least because they couldn't give the tribal elder a traditional burial.

The showman recalled the funeral of an Igorrote elder he had known named Som-kad'. The tribe had washed the deceased, then dressed the body in a burial robe and placed it upright in a chair which they positioned at the open door of the deceased man's house with the corpse facing out. They lit a small fire underneath the body to overpower the odors that would naturally emanate from it. For several days and nights, the dead man remained there, in full view of those who passed. Family, friends, and neighbors sat with the body, singing soothing songs and going about their daily lives. The women swatted the flies away from the corpse and spun threads, nursed their babies, chatted and laughed, while the children played at the dead man's feet. After a day or two, the men gathered to drink *bá-si*, the local alcohol, and to peacefully divide up the property of the deceased. They hunted animals—carabao, pigs, chickens, and a dog—to be eaten at the burial feast.[21]

On the day Som-kad′ was to be buried, the villagers gathered at the dead man's home. One of the tribesmen lifted the corpse—by now "a black, bloated, inhuman-looking thing" with an odor "most sickening to an American"[22]— and carried it over to a coffin. "Streams of rusty-brown liquid"[23] poured from the body. The coffin was lowered into the ground, then the men threw themselves onto the piles of loose dirt at the graveside. Using their bare hands, they scooped up the soil and buried the coffin in the shortest time possible—Igorrote custom dictated that if a crow flew over the grave, or a dog barked or a snake slithered past before the body was fully covered, a dire evil would affect the community. Next the men hurried to the river to wash. Depending on the wealth and status of the deceased, Igorrote burials were followed by feasting and funeral rites lasting from two to eight days.[24]

Short of furtively engaging in an authentic burial ritual, which would surely bring the police after them, Truman was at a loss as to what the tribe could do to honor the dead man. Maybe, he thought to himself, they could do something to mark the occasion when they reached Coney. He had no idea what, but he would come up with something.

The showman entered the front room of the Pike Street house. The Igorrotes had just finished eating and were smoking their pipes. Julio looked up. He could see from Truman's face that something was wrong. Truman beckoned to his assistant to come over. Without preamble he told him the tribal elder was dead. The interpreter had known the old man was seriously ill, but the news of his death came as a shock. Weren't American hospitals the best there were? Maria glanced over. Julio's eyes filled with tears. As the oldest Igorrote traveling with them, Falino had had special status within the group. He was admired, and respected as Igorrotes believed a wise elder should be. The showman placed a fatherly hand on Julio's shoulder. *Do you want me to tell to the others?* Julio shook his head, he would do it. What would they do with the body? Truman would have it embalmed and stored until he could make arrangements to return it to the Philippines for a proper Igorrote burial. Julio nodded.

The interpreter turned to face his countrymen and women and

called to them to listen. Truman stood silently at his side. *Falino is dead,* Julio said abruptly. There was silence for a moment, then one of the women started to sob. Soon the room was filled with the unmistakable sound of grief. Truman closed his eyes, as if trying to shut out their pain. The showman left the house and went outside for a walk. He gagged as the smell of fish caught in the back of his throat. The tribe's reaction to Falino's death had stoked up old memories of dear Myrtle's passing. He would find somewhere else to sleep that night.

When Truman finally returned to Pike Street, he told Julio to get his coat. Moody was taking him and Fomoaley on a special trip downtown. They would all leave for New York the following day. Julio didn't feel like going out, but when Truman mentioned that he had arranged a sightseeing tour of the offices of the *Seattle Daily Times,* Julio could not resist. Since his arrival in Seattle, he had become a regular reader of the press and had taken an ill-concealed pride in the many stories the paper had carried about the tribe. Now he was intrigued to see how the publication was put together.

If Julio was fascinated by the workings of the paper, the journalists at the *Seattle Daily Times* were no less intrigued by the Igorrotes who had provided them with pages of colorful copy. The editor took them on a tour of the entire plant, from the copy rooms by way of the composing room, stereotyping room, the mailing and delivery rooms. At the culmination of their visit, Julio stood in open-mouthed wonder before the big presses of the *Times* as they thundered, printing that day's paper. He was unable to make any comment except to exclaim, wonderingly, occasionally: "Quick."[25]

The Dexter Horton and Company bank was next on the Filipinos' itinerary. The telephone rang just as the special guests arrived, trailed by a reporter from the *Seattle Daily Times.* The bank manager, N. H. Latimer, rushed to answer it. He listened for a moment, then handed the receiver to Fomoaley. The chief, upon hearing a voice emanating from "the stick," took fright and dropped it. Laughing, the manager invited Julio and Fomoaley to follow him into the vaults. The men's eyes widened as Latimer informed them they were looking at two million dollars' worth of gold, silver, and currency. *What would you do with the money if you owned it?* asked Latimer. "If I had that money I would buy the Philippine Islands," replied the Igorrote chief. "What would you do with the Philippines?" inquired the bank manager. "If I owned Philippines I'd be big chief," said Fomoaley, his eyes glistening at the prospect.[26] "The mere proprietorship of the Philippines and the homage that would be paid him was all the Igorrote chief coveted," observed the reporter.[27]

In a nearby fur store, Fomoaley stroked the animal skins, exclaiming "All [is] big here in America. Big men, big women, big houses, big city, these big. Not like our deer," he added, pointing toward an elk skin.[28]

Their last stop was a baseball game. Julio watched with interest and did his best to memorize the rules. "Maybe [the] Igorrotes will learn baseball. I think Igorrotes can understand how to play."[29] Turning to Moody, he asked, "You say Japanese play baseball? If Japanese play baseball then Igorrotes can."[30]

That night Julio and Fomoaley described their day to their countrymen and women. Friday, who had learned to play baseball when he was living with the Fuller family and had "a good batting eye,"[31] joined in as Julio explained the game. The tribespeople took comfort in having something to think about besides Falino's death.

Truman woke them early the following morning. What lay ahead for the Filipinos was a vast transcontinental journey, in its way just as enormous as the one they had already taken across the Pacific. Two and a half thousand miles of railroad track led from Seattle to Coney Island. Their final destination was not an ethnological exhibit, or government-sponsored display. They were headed into the heart of America's show land, into a place of sensation, shocks, and raucous laughter.

By the early 1900s, the circus, amusement park, and midway business was booming as blue-collar Americans sought ever more vivid distractions from the daily grind. Ringling Brothers, and Barnum and Bailey were household names. Visiting fairs and temporary expositions held in towns and cities across America attracted people from all walks of life, and demand for new eye-catching exhibits was insatiable. As interest in these forms of entertainment soared, the trade had begun to attract characters ranging from the merely colorful to the blatantly corrupt. Many of the entrepreneurs of this world walked a fine line between legitimate business and hucksterism. Truman had an unusual pedigree for a sideshow man, with his background in medicine and government service, but over the next few months he would show himself to be just as talented at wheeling and dealing as those who had been born into the business.

Truman was gripped by a familiar sense of anticipation as they boarded the train in Seattle. He had negotiated with the railroad company to provide a private carriage for the Igorrotes at a discounted price. It would allow them to travel together and would afford them some protection from prying eyes and racist taunts. Anti-Asian sentiment ran high in the American Northwest, largely directed at Chinese immigrants but loosely applied to anyone who looked Asian, and Truman thought it was in everybody's best interests to seclude the tribe from the other passengers. But that hadn't prevented a constant stream of curious travelers from coming to the end of the car to peer in at the tattooed foreigners with their huge earlobe stretchers and odd-looking hats.

The Igorrotes gazed out of the window as the train trundled through one-horse towns and sprawling cities. Describing their train journey, Fomoaley later enthused, "We were carried for many days in houses that went on wheels and flew along like birds. And now it seemed as if the land would never end. We must have come nearly a hundred days' journey in a week."[32]

While the tribe sat smoking and speaking in low voices at one end of the carriage, Truman sat dreaming up publicity stunts at the other.

At every station stop, Truman's advance man had tipped off a new set of newspapermen that the Igorrotes, the latest sensation coming to Coney Island, were passing through town. The showman was never disappointed: a pack of newspapermen was always waiting. If there was time, Truman would arrange interviews and stunts with local reporters, joyfully spinning them lines. He sent word ahead to New York's newspapers. A train was coming, and it carried the story of the century.

Truman had a keen eye for what would excite Americans about the Igorrotes. He described the customs of the head-hunting Filipinos in vivid detail. At a time when America was expanding her global reach, her citizens were developing a fascination for savages and foreign cultures. Against this backdrop the Igorrotes were portrayed in the media as an exceptionally primitive people, living virtually naked in mud huts, hunting their neighbors' heads and eating their own pets. In interviews, Truman portrayed himself as a paternalistic patron. The newspapers could not get enough of them: FROM LUZON TO LUNA: IGOROTS COMING, 51 STRONG, TO BUILD VILLAGE AT CONEY, read the headline in the *New York Tribune* on May 9, 1905.

In Chicago the group, now well drilled in Truman's choreographed antics, threw on their American shirts, skirts and pants, ready to change stations. Outside on the street, the Igorrotes stood in silent wonder. If Manila had seemed overwhelming, then this was on a whole new scale. Chicago was an assault on the senses. The air reeked, of what the Igorrotes did not know, crowds surged along the sidewalk, and the buildings seemed to disappear into the sky. At the turn of the century, Chicago was a bustling metropolis, home to two million people and some of the tallest, most handsome buildings in the world and proud of its hard-fought status as America's second city. But it was also caked in grime and ridden with crime. The Igorrotes huddled together as the elevated train thundered along the tracks overhead, carrying thousands of commuters into the city. For the mountain-dwelling tribe, walking the city streets was like landing on the moon.

A sense of relief washed over the Igorrotes when they reached the station and stepped in off the sidewalk. Truman asked a railroad worker where they would catch the train to New York City. The man pointed to a platform in the distance. Their new home was within striking distance. What would happen next would make the Igorrotes a household name.

6

Making an Entrance

NEW YORK CITY, MAY 15, 1905

Park Row station at the Manhattan end of the Brooklyn Bridge, 1905

The Filipinos' private car rolled into the train yards just north of New York's Grand Central Station. It was wet, windy, and not yet daybreak. The train slowed and Julio gazed through the rain-streaked window at the dark, foreboding sky, the cold glass numbing his cheek. Great plumes of smoke billowed out as the train squealed and hissed to a halt. Julio could just make out a group of figures moving around in the murk outside. He strained to get a better look. Suddenly out of the gloom a pale face streaked in oil and grime pressed up against the glass, almost a mirror image of his own. Julio instinctively pulled his head back as the face opposite his opened its mouth and began to shout.

The trainman couldn't believe what he was seeing. He shouted to the other men working in the yard to come over. Within a few moments, a group had gathered around. They gawked through the window in slack-jawed amazement. Dark-skinned men and women wearing hardly any clothes peered back at them. One, a child with skin as black as coal, waved. Where, one of the trainmen wondered aloud, were they going? Madison Square Garden? To the port to catch a ship back to wherever they had come from? No, it must be Coney Island, insisted another, that was where the freaks of the world ended up. The trainmen would certainly have a story to tell their families that night. The foreman shouted at them to get back to work.

The engineer let off the brakes, and the train trundled down the track toward Grand Central. It was just before 5:15 a.m. on Monday, May 15, 1905,[1] when the Igorrotes' car pulled up to the platform, giving a jolt, which woke the handful of tribespeople who were sleeping under a pile of rough military blankets. Grand Central was accustomed to welcoming eight hundred trains and seventy-five thousand passengers daily, but it had never seen a cargo like this.[2] The Igorrotes experienced a now familiar blend of excited bewilderment. They had journeyed halfway across the world, and had rattled across eleven US states, through wide-open plains and busy railroad junctions. They had grown accustomed to new sights and sounds but nothing could have prepared them for their arrival in America's greatest city.

Outside, newspaper reporters and photographers jostled to get a view of the savages through the windows. They turned to each other as if to confirm what they were seeing. "The men looked the part of head-hunters with a vengeance," observed one. "Both the men and women were tattooed from head to foot, the marks on the chest of some of the men indicating . . . that they were fully-fledged harvesters of heads. The women sat in the window smoking big, black cigars with great contentment, and one of them had two spools attached to large pieces of wire in her ears. Both sexes wore large brass earrings which were remarkably suggestive of the dog tags used in this city."[3]

Truman Hunt was usually cool under pressure. But today was different. After more than six months of planning, it was almost time for the show to begin. He could hardly wait. The Igorrotes were going to be the talk of Coney Island. No, of the nation. Before they left the train, he gave them a pep talk. Truman was an enthusiastic, if sometimes inexact, speaker of the Bontoc language. None of the tribe could mistake the energy of what he was saying but Julio had to step in from time to time to help when Truman couldn't find the right words. The tribespeople were to be on their best behavior. Those who knew some English were permitted to speak to the reporters, provided they didn't stray from the script they'd rehearsed with Truman and Julio on the journey.

Egged on by Truman, Tainan and Friday began to cavort for the crowd. Fomoaley pushed to the front and puffed out his chest as he posed for the cameras. Around his neck the chief wore strings of beads decorated with what looked like human hair. Truman pointed out the tattoos on his body, which indicated his prowess as a headhunter. This was not the first time several of the photographers had stood this close to a murderer but, they thought, this one seemed remarkably good-humored. *Hold up your spear and look angry so we can get a picture of you in a ferocious pose,* shouted one of the photographers. Smiling graciously, the headhunter obliged.

Reporters crowded around the Igorrotes and began shouting out questions. *What do you think of America? Is it true that you eat dogs? Will you be hunting human heads here in America?* Truman had a well-rehearsed answer at the ready. "The only heads they will take in this country will be those of the goddess of Liberty, inscribed on the good American dollar, at gay Coney Island this summer," he said.[4]

The newspapermen were struck by how friendly Truman and the tribespeople were with each other, laughing and joking in the Igorrotes' native tongue. Truman had the air of an indulgent parent as he relayed the tale of how the superstitious tribespeople had spent the last part of the journey attempting to fight off the ghost of one of their countrymen who had died of pneumonia in Seattle and who they were convinced was haunting their train. Tunnels were particularly problematic. A couple of nights before their arrival in New York, the Igorrotes' fears had reached a climax. It was late at night when one of them let out a bloodcurdling scream. Assuming that an intruder had burst into their train car, the tribesmen grabbed their battle-axes and yelled at the enemy to prepare to be massacred. The commotion had woken Truman, who, bleary-eyed, told them there was no one there. It was some time, the American added, before he could persuade the Filipinos to put down their arms.[5] The reporters laughed.

Behind the handful of Igorrotes who were reveling in the attention, many more stood rooted to the spot, struck dumb by the extraordinary scene of one of America's biggest, busiest cities jolting to life. Newsboys yelled out the day's top headlines, shoeshine boys were setting up shop, and the first wave of commuters streamed through the station. Men carrying briefcases took a moment out of their busy lives to stop and stare, and children tugged at their mothers' coats and pointed at the new arrivals. The Igorrotes peered back in awe at what they saw. The smell of hot coffee filled their nostrils.

As the newspapermen asked their final questions, Truman bought a copy of the *New York Times* from a passing newsboy and scanned the front-page headlines. His eyes alighted on a report about a two-week battle on the southern Philippine island of Jolo between American troops and the followers of the outlaw chief of the Moro tribe, which had resulted in the deaths of three hundred Filipinos and seven Americans. The outlaw and his surviving army were reported to be in a swamp surrounded by American troops.[6]

The Americans had made great progress in the Philippines, thought Truman, introducing a new system of law and order and building schools, roads, and hospitals, but there was still a lot of work to be done. And while President Theodore Roosevelt's government liked to give the impression that American rule had been embraced as a force for good by the Philippine population, those who had been to the islands knew the reality was a good deal more complicated. Truman tucked the newspaper under his arm, and shouted to Julio and Callahan to herd the Igorrotes down a ramp leading to the subway platform. There they would board a train for the thirteen-minute ride downtown.

A short distance from where the Igorrotes stood, the new season at Coney Island was already underway. Among the Shoot the Chutes waterslides and the dancing horses, wedged between the fat lady and the scenic railway, a large, empty lot awaited the arrival of the Filipino tribe. The park lost money every minute the lot sat unoccupied and money was Coney's lifeblood.

The new season had gotten off to a promising start, despite the missing Igorrotes. Spirits were high on opening day, Saturday, May 13, 1905. The sweet smell of cotton candy mingled with the salty sea air. Ballyhoo men yelled, music blared, and men, women, and children swarmed off steamboats, trains, and open trams, dressed in their finery for the occasion and intent on having fun. They had come from all over New York, New Jersey, Connecticut, Pennsylvania, and beyond. For most of them, a trip to Coney was a once-a-year escape from the daily grind.

Coney Island was made of tall tales. The birthplace of the hot dog and the roller coaster, it was the poor man's paradise, offering sensation for a nickel. Coney bent the rules of time and space. Its currency was the huge and the tiny, the ten-ton woman and the ten-inch man. Freaks and curiosities lived alongside detailed recreations of kingdoms from beyond the seas. Part Victorian cabinet of curiosities, part compendium of global delights, at Coney the extraordinary was commonplace and the humdrum of everyday life could be forgotten.

By the early twentieth century, it was America's most popular seaside resort. On summer Sundays a quarter of a million people could be found in its three big amusement parks—Luna Park, Steeplechase Park, and Dreamland. "If Paris is France, then Coney Island, between June and September, is the world," declared Steeplechase's owner, George Tilyou.[7] For most visitors the train or steamboat ride to Coney was as close as they were likely to get to foreign travel.

For the ten-cent park entrance fee, even the most hard-up visitor could stand on the picturesque banks of the Grand Canal at Luna Park's very own replica of Venice. Those with an additional quarter to spare could treat their beloved to a gondola ride in authentic narrow boats propelled by men in striped jerseys and straw boater hats, or take them to the Japanese tea garden to be waited on by geisha girls in stunning floor-length gowns of the finest silk.

If Coney was a fantastical land, it was a land with two kings. Just two years previously, Thompson and Dundy had plowed everything they owned, along with three quarters of a million borrowed dollars

($18.4 million in today's money), into creating Luna Park. Money was so tight that when Thompson went to Dundy shortly before the grand opening requesting a couple of dollars to buy a new pair of trousers, Dundy, who controlled their finances, refused. In a bid to save money, the pair had been rooming together in an apartment with so many leaks in the roof that whenever it rained, they had to sleep under a canopy of umbrellas.

But just seven weeks after the park opened in 1903, Thompson and Dundy had paid off all their debts. Before long, they were so rich that Thompson could afford to take up residence in a suite of rooms at the Algonquin Hotel, where he had a dumbwaiter installed so the chefs in the kitchens below could send their dishes upstairs to be served by his Japanese butler, Sato.

Famously nicknamed "Sodom by the sea," due to the criminals, prostitutes, and rowdy beer halls that had been a feature of the area since the resort's early days in the 1880s, Coney Island had done a lot in recent years to clean up its act. This was due in no small part to the genius of the new breed of showmen like Thompson and Dundy, whose great innovation had been to enclose their amusement parks, giving them an excuse to charge an admission fee as well as keeping the riffraff out. True, a large criminal element still hung around the Bowery, but there they were somebody else's problem.

Grand hotels sprung up along the seafront, offering guests every luxury they could imagine, many imported directly from Europe, from Parisian soap in the bathrooms to luxurious Italian bed linens. The hotels had deep wraparound verandas and wide green lawns running down to the sea. The ornate dining rooms served menus of roast lamb, littleneck clams, and baked bluefish, followed by ice cream on a bed of meringue. Guests were treated to live music and fireworks while Pinkerton detectives patrolled the grounds to make sure undesirables stayed out.

While Coney was changing the face of leisure, it was also making its mark on popular culture. Luna Park was immortalized by the popular vaudeville singer Billy Murray in the song "Meet Me Down At Luna, Lena." In the song, a young man by the name of Herman invites the object of his desires, a German girl, Lena, to join him for a day out at Luna Park, "a real place for lovers," where they would ride on Thompson's famous attraction, A Trip to the Moon:

Meet me down at Luna, Lena
Meet me at the gate.
Do not disappoint me, Lena
I'll be there at eight.
We'll make the trip up to the moon,
For that is the place for a lark.
So meet me down at Luna, Lena
Down at Luna Park.[8]

By 1905 Thompson and Dundy knew their business inside out, and they knew that the Igorrotes were destined to be the standout hit of the new season. The Kings of Coney had taken out advertisements in all the major New York newspapers to boast of their newest attraction. Reporters came to interview Thompson and Dundy, who informed them that the Igorrotes were bringing bamboo, straw, and other building materials with them from the Philippines. "They will build their own peculiar houses, and will live exactly as if they were in their own mountain home," said Thompson.[9] For a quarter—the highest fee charged at any of Luna's attractions—visitors would gain access to a scene straight from the wilds of the Philippines: Igorrotes weaving baskets, making copper pipes, cooking, and carving shields and spears. If they were lucky—and they would be lucky "every hour, on the hour"—they might witness the Igorrotes performing tribal dances, head-hunting chants, and spear-throwing demonstrations.

Thompson and Dundy didn't like to be kept waiting. They'd received a telegram from Truman informing them that he would be arriving with the Igorrotes that same day. There was nothing for it but to wait.

Goose bumps pricked Friday's arms as he stood on the platform at the Park Row elevated train station in lower Manhattan. He gazed down at the tracks just in time to see a rat scurry along the rails below. He held up the small mirror from which he was never parted and attempted to throw the light of the morning sun into the rodent's eyes. He edged closer for a better look as the creature's long tail disappeared through a crack. Maria reached forward and grabbed the boy by the arm. Reluctantly, Friday stepped back, clutching the mirror tightly in his hand. As the Igorrotes waited on the platform for a train to take them over the Brooklyn Bridge, the city streets were waking up below them. Commuters hurried along the sidewalk accompanied by the roar of streetcars delivering New York's newspapermen, attorneys, and government officials to their offices.

Along the platform, Julio reflected that he knew almost nothing about New York beyond the scraps he had gleaned from his conversations with Truman. It had been two months since they had left the Philippines. And here they were, just a short train ride from the place they would soon call home. Julio was excited about the challenge ahead. When he came to America the last time, he was just another member of the group. This time was different. He was their leader, of sorts, and he felt the weight of responsibility on his young shoulders.

Feloa had been one of the first to volunteer to take part in Truman's scheme. If he stayed in the Philippines, he knew that life would bring few surprises. He had already married his sweetheart, and together they had had four children. It had been hard to leave them behind, but Feloa wanted to provide his family with a better future. If he had not taken this opportunity, he would forever have wondered what might have been. Feloa looked at the American men and women waiting for the train, then gazed down at his own clothes.

Before they left Seattle, Truman had spent $1.41 on new clothes for the entire group, intended to keep out the cold and minimize unwanted attention when they made their way through towns and cities.[10] But even with the addition of long skirts and pants, the tattooed, bead-wearing tribespeople looked incongruous among the early-morning collection of businessmen, salesclerks, and secretaries. A few feet from where Feloa stood, a young woman stole a polite sideways glance. When the tribesman looked up, she turned her head away hurriedly.

The Igorrotes were late, Truman could no longer remember by how many days. Ever since his posting to the wilds of Bontoc, his timekeeping had become atrocious. While stationed there he had planned to spend one Christmas with the soldiers at the nearest American army base 150 miles away, but he'd lost track of time and turned up ten days late. Truman was used to doing things his own way. Besides, the Igorrotes were the biggest attraction of the year—the owners of Luna Park could afford to wait. Anticipation would only make the reward sweeter.

Speaking of which, Truman couldn't wait to take Sallie in his arms that evening. Not that they would have much privacy. They would be staying in the spacious and rather grand Broadway home of their friends Adele and George Wilkins, until Truman found them somewhere of their own. A bungalow would be provided on-site at Coney for the Igorrotes' manager, but he wasn't sure it would be a suitable place for Sallie to live.

Truman had first met Adele von Groyss—to use her rather grand maiden name, which she preferred to be known by—in the Philippines, where she was volunteering with the medical corps. She was born in Austria and claimed to be a baroness. He had no idea if it was true but he cared little. The baroness was small and plump with extravagantly coiffured blonde hair and a taste for elaborate hats. Of more interest to Truman, his friend was extraordinarily well connected, and had thrown some of the best parties he had ever attended. Her New York home was decorated boldly with tribal masks and abstract art. The showman was glad that Sallie would have some female company during her first weeks in a new city when he would be working day and night. As he looked down the tracks for the train, Truman made a mental note to ask Thompson for a restaurant recommendation when they got to Luna Park. If any man could point him in the direction of a good dinner, it would be Thompson, who, like Truman, only ever ate in the finest restaurants. He would take Sallie, Adele, and George out to dinner to celebrate the tribe's safe arrival in New York.

A train drew up and Truman yelled to Callahan and Julio to get the tribespeople on board. The few passengers who shared the Igorrotes' train car were unable to hide their astonishment; some looked on with open mouths, others hurriedly moved on to another car.

These reactions no longer surprised the Igorrotes. But Julio felt a mixture of hurt and annoyance at their negative reactions. Did they feel frightened of them, he wondered. Or was it revulsion? Did they regard him in the same way, despite his fine clothes? His thoughts were interrupted as the doors closed and they pulled out of the station.

The train jerked and clanked as its wheels gripped the tracks, pulling its cargo onto the Brooklyn Bridge. Julio instinctively looked back toward Manhattan as they journeyed across the water. Without uttering a word, he threw up his arm and pointed to the rest of the tribe to look up. Their eyes darted from the soaring St. Paul Building, up to the Park Row Building, the world's tallest building when it was completed in 1899, to the trio of towers making up "newspaper row"—the New York Times Building, the Tribune Building with its thin clock tower, and the Pulitzer Building with its distinctive dome. Tainan ran from his seat to the window and pressed his face against the glass. Friday followed. Maria clutched Daipan's arm. The panorama of the Manhattan skyline grew wider and more spectacular as they drew farther away. Julio's usually sophisticated veneer dissolved as he gazed up in amazement. He caught Maria's eye and grinned. Julio knew the sight would stay in his memory forever. Truman looked up from his newspaper. He wasn't given to sentimentality, but his heart stirred at the sight of the tribespeople. The Filipinos sat in silent wonder as the train continued across the bridge and down into Brooklyn. They hadn't seen anything yet.

7

Meeting Uncle Sam

LUNA PARK, MAY 15, 1905

The Igorrotes meet Uncle Sam, June 1905.

THOMPSON KEPT A showman's hours and was rarely up before noon. But he rose early that day, eager to welcome his new stars. It was ten thirty in the morning and the park was not yet open when he got word that the Igorrotes had arrived. He left his bungalow and hurried over to meet them near the park entrance. As he turned the corner and caught his first glimpse of the Filipinos, he smiled broadly, stopping for a moment to admire them. The Igorrotes had already pulled off their American clothes and stood in their G-strings, rummaging in their basket hats for their pipes, unaware they were being watched. Thompson's eyes wandered over the head-hunting tattoos that covered the men's chests. He noticed the huge bamboo plugs in some of the women's ears. The tribespeople were magnificent. They were going to make him a fortune. He strode over to meet them.

Shaking Truman's hand, he glanced from Fomoaley, whom Truman introduced as the tribal chief, to Tainan and Daipan. Thompson could hardly contain his delight as he looked around his new exhibit. Julio stepped forward and extended his own hand. The park boss took it gladly and told the interpreter he was thrilled to welcome the tribe to Luna Park. He had reserved a prime spot for them and invited them to come and inspect it for themselves. Thompson led the way to a far corner, which he'd deliberately chosen so that the tribe's many visitors would have to walk past all the other enticing rides and attractions before they reached the Igorrotes.

The tribespeople walked past the gates leading to a dozen other attractions, unable to read the signs announcing the thrilling rides and spectacles waiting inside. *Your spot is over*—began Thompson, but he was interrupted by a loud trumpeting noise that made Tainan shriek with fright. Truman and Thompson laughed. The elephant stables lay just behind the plot where the Igorrotes would live.

There was a fence around the Igorrote Village, intended to make sure no one but those who paid to enter could enjoy the show. A sign had already been hung over the entrance, announcing that this was the home of the Filipino tribe. Truman eyed the wording. There was no mention of dog eating. He would get that added. The site looked ideal. There was plenty of room for the tribespeople to build their homes, along with a large arena for their tribal performances. Truman indicated his approval to Thompson and told him they would set to work building the village immediately; they would do without rest. Thompson told him not to hurry. He planned to stage a second grand opening to announce the arrival of the tribespeople on Saturday. In the meantime, they would offer those who came to Luna Park a sneak preview of the tribe building their village. Truman smiled. He liked his new business associate's style.

Luna Park occupied thirty-eight acres and operated like a self-contained town, employing more than a thousand people and housing its own telegraph office and long-distance telephone service. Dubbed an "electric Eden," it was a dream world lit by one million tiny electric lightbulbs (the electric bill was four thousand dollars a week[1]) and filled with domes, spires, minarets, lagoons, colonnades, and castles. In the park grounds, Thompson and Dundy staged dramatic dioramas of real and imagined events like The War of the Worlds, The Kansas Cyclone, and The Fall of Port Arthur. They were designed to take advantage of the public's fascination with wars, disasters, and distant lands and people at a time when newspapers carried few photographs. Thompson and Dundy believed that novelty was the key to success. Each year they scrapped any attractions that weren't creating a buzz and replaced them with new, more spectacular creations.

Brand-new for the 1905 season was The Dragon's Gorge, created by Ohio-born inventor LaMarcus Adna Thompson, known as L. A. Thompson.[2] For ten cents it took passengers on a six-minute scenic railroad ride to the North Pole, past icebergs and "a real polar bear hungrily eyeing a real Esquimo paddling about in a real canoe on real water"[3] specially imported from the Arctic, then on to the Orient and the dizzying heights of the Rocky Mountains. En route, it visited Havana Harbor the morning after the February 1898 destruction of the USS *Maine*, a crucial milestone on the road to the Spanish-American War, which led to America taking control of the Philippine Islands. Without this important event in US history, Truman Hunt would likely never have ended up in the Philippines and America might never have laid eyes on the Igorrotes.

Over at Fire and Flames, a fire chief yelled into his trumpet that a real-life fire was about to break out. Crowds handed over their money and hurried inside. To their surprise, behind the entrance the atmosphere was festive, with a marching band leading a parade up the street. Just as the onlookers were starting to get restless, a man came running out of a hotel screaming, "Fire," setting in motion an exquisitely choreographed presentation featuring one thousand performers. Alarm bells clanged and horse-drawn fire wagons rushed to the scene of a blazing six-story building. On the opposite side of the specially built fake street, firefighters battled to overcome the (real) flames while men, women, and children (all actors paid to take part in the staged event) jumped from the windows of the building into nets below. In Dr. Martin Couney's Infant Incubators, mewling rows of premature babies were kept alive using costly state-of-the-art equipment, more advanced than anything in New York's hospitals. One of the oddest attractions in a resort filled with the bizarre was The Fatal Wedding, a five-cent show in which a lovely young woman in a bridal gown and veil with orange blossoms in her hair walked behind a screen, only for herself and her beloved to be transformed into skeletons who were then served a sumptuous wedding feast.[4]

If Thompson was the brains behind Luna Park's most imaginative spectaculars, then Dundy deserved the credit for filling it with exotic animals. His love of elephants bordered on an obsession and he imported the largest show herd in the world to Luna Park. For a dime apiece, a stenographer from Hoboken and her mailman beau could enjoy a five-minute ride of a lifetime perched atop one of Dundy's prized beasts.

Despite Thompson's insistence on novelty, one attraction was too popular to be torn down. A Trip to the Moon, the ride that had brought Thompson and Dundy into business together four years earlier, was still delighting crowds. Could the Igorrote Village succeed in surpassing the profits of Thompson and Dundy's most popular ride? Ever the betting man, Dundy felt confident that they would.

Finally, on Saturday, May 20, 1905, a week behind schedule, the Igorrote Village opened to the public. Crowds thronged Stillwell and Surf Avenues. Sixty thousand people surged through the gates of Luna Park. Many made straight for the Igorrote Village. Feloa had been given the job of barker to draw in the crowds, and stood at the entrance shouting in his native tongue. The men, women, and children who passed him gazed at his tattooed, nearly naked dark skin. Hypnotized by the sight of this fierce headhunter from another world, they handed over their quarters. As they entered the Philippine attraction, the visitors stopped and stood in wonder. Even by Coney's standards, the Igorrote Village was an astonishing sight. Against the backdrop of the Electric Tower, the Helter Skelter slide, and the outdoor circus, the Filipinos were living in small huts with thatched roofs and walls constructed using a mix of straw, mud, and bricks. Their village was surrounded by a bamboo fence and was decorated with spears, shields, and skulls. In a confidential tone, Truman told the visitors that these skulls were the mortal remains of the Igorrotes' enemies. In fact they were the skulls of animals, but, Truman reasoned, nobody need know this but him.

The architecture of the village was very loosely based on the Igorrote settlements of northern Luzon. Igorrote homes in the Philippines were typically squat structures, too small for a full-grown adult to stand up in. They were dirty, dark, and damp with low thatched roofs and mud floors. Rice and corn hung from the roof beams to dry. Each hut had a sleeping room at one end into which the entire family retired at night, carefully shutting the door behind them. When it was cold, a fire would burn all night in the center of this room so that by morning the tribespeople were covered in soot, their eyes burning red from the smoke. An adjoining room was used as a storeroom. The family hens and pigs lived inside, or in a small pen underneath the hut.

At Luna Park, Truman Americanized the design, making the huts taller and more spacious to accommodate visitors to the park and adding a front door flanked on either side by white wooden shutters to make them look more appealing to American eyes. These would help keep out Coney's bright lights but did little to keep the resort's noise at bay. Over the following weeks the Igorrotes would build and rebuild these structures, so that visitors could see them involved in constant activity.

Under orders from Truman, the tribespeople were still building their homes on opening day. To the amazement of the onlookers, the agile Igorrotes climbed up the bamboo frames of their huts using their bare hands and feet, carrying bales of straw balanced on their backs. Fomoaley watched over the construction, shouting out instructions in the Igorrotes' clipped tongue. Truman, who was standing at the edge of the village, offered a commentary for the crowd. *Look,* he said, *at the Igorrote men's unusually long big toes, which splay out to the side.* He explained that these had evolved over time to work like thumbs, helping the men climb the tall trees in their native habitat.

Truman pointed to a tower standing at the entrance to the Igorrotes' enclosure. *This,* he explained, *is an authentic headhunters' watchtower. These can be found at the entrance to Igorrote towns and villages in the Philippines. From these towers the tribespeople keep a constant lookout for advancing enemy headhunters hoping to take them by surprise.* The crowd looked at the imposing structure. It towered over the Igorrotes' homes. At its top stood a platform ringed by a bamboo fence and topped with an umbrella-shaped thatched roof. A door at its base led inside to some steps, which they could climb to the top. The Igorrotes had been puzzled as to why in a country without headhunters they needed to build a tower, but they had done as Truman asked. Though he had said nothing, Julio understood that it was part of the show, there to shock and awe. Less authentic were the telegraph poles behind the village, which could be seen over the tops of the Igorrotes' huts.

In the center of their community, the Igorrotes were busy building a hut raised on stilts four feet above the ground. It was entered by a small ladder that could be drawn up into the single living and sleeping room inside. *This hut,* Truman told visitors, *is the home of Manidol, the medicine man* (this was another new tribal post created by Truman). *The medicine man,* he continued, *is second in importance only to the tribal chiefs, and he is treated with a great deal of respect by his countrymen and women.* His job was "to exorcise troublesome spirits and allay bodily pains," making him, in the words of the *Brooklyn Daily Eagle,* "a cross between a voodoo doctor and a Christian Scientist."[5] At one side of the village was a small hut where Callahan spent his nights, allowing him to keep a watchful eye over the tribe. Aside from Julio, the Igorrotes were not permitted to leave the village at any time, not even to venture out into Luna Park's grounds.

The Igorrotes were miners and agricultural workers at home, renowned for their highly skilled irrigation and cultivation techniques, which enabled them transform even the steepest mountainside into thriving rice terraces. There was no room for rice terraces or mines at Luna Park, so Truman had them erect a copper-smelting plant across from the medicine man's hut, which the Igorrotes would use to make their smoking pipes, along with jewelry and other trinkets to sell to their visitors. Under their agreement with Truman, along with their monthly wages of fifteen dollars each, they could keep all the money they raised from selling souvenirs—rings, bracelets, necklaces, earrings, textiles, spears, and shields. As the visitors milled around, Julio invited a group of American men to throw coins to a distance of about five yards from where several Igorrote boys stood. The men obliged. The boys took aim and fired their arrows at the coins. When one of them made a bad miss, laughter rang through the village as the others teased him.

Do the boys hunt heads? someone in the crowd wanted to know. But before Truman could answer, Fomoaley let out a yell. The Igorrotes laid down their tools. One by one they walked forward and began to form a circle around Fomoaley, who stood erect. Truman informed the crowd that this man was the tribal chief. Quietly at first, Fomoaley began to utter a stream of guttural sounds. Gradually his voice grew louder and more rhythmic as the rest of the tribe joined in his chant. Their chant turned to song and the Igorrotes began to sway in time to the beat of the tom-tom drums. Truman decided that he would let the strange scene speak for itself. He watched with a satisfied smile as the crowd of onlookers grew until there wasn't an inch of standing room to be found.

Women pushed to the front of the crowd; children were lifted onto their fathers' shoulders. A young Igorrote man struck a gong and the chief picked up a thin strip of bamboo. Another tribesman appeared carrying a live hen. Fomoaley lifted his hand and closed his eyes as if in silent prayer. What happened next led several people, men among them, to faint. With a flash, the tribal chief lowered his hand and began to beat the bird with the bamboo strip, first its wings, then its neck and finally its head, his strokes growing faster and faster.

Women threw their hands up to cover their eyes. Young boys looked on with morbid delight. The crowd gasped as the bird fell dead.

Fomoaley picked the hen up by its rubbery orange feet and held it over the fire, burning its feathers to a crisp and rubbing them off with sticks. Then, with one deft stroke, he sliced open its stomach and, with a flick of his wrist, ripped out the blue-green tangle of its guts. A young Igorrote man held out a small ceramic beaker to catch the blood. When enough of the dark red liquid had dripped inside, Fomoaley lifted the cup and, chanting quietly under his breath, walked over to his hut. There, watched over by the medicine man, he sprinkled a few drops of blood over the roof. One by one the men of the village came forward and took the beaker, each sprinkling the hen's blood over a hut. It was exactly as they had rehearsed it. Truman spoke again, informing the crowd that this was a tribal custom intended to ward off evil. The onlookers stood in stunned silence.

The sacrifice of the hen brought the American Humane Association knocking on Truman's door. They had received a number of complaints about the bloody incident and arrived at Luna Park to investigate. Truman put up a rigorous defense of the practice, explaining that it was an important Igorrote custom. As well as blessing their homes, Truman said that the bird's slaughter was part of a sacred funeral rite, held to mark the sad passing of their tribal elder in Seattle, which the group had been unable to commemorate while they were traveling. After a few words in the right ears from Thompson, the authorities accepted Truman's explanation.

But the controversy surrounding the incident with the hen was nothing compared to that which would soon be provoked by another tribal ritual. Less than a week after the opening of the Igorrote Village, a woman turned up in a state of agitation, claiming her beloved dog, Prince, had been devoured by the Filipinos. According to Mrs. Mary Jackman, she had been visiting Luna Park with Prince and, after she was distracted by a circus performer, she turned around to find her pet dog had gone. At first Mrs. Jackman assumed the dog had found its own way home, but when she returned and discovered her house empty, she pointed the finger of blame at the Filipinos.

The Coney police were called in to question the Igorrotes, with Julio and Truman translating. When that failed to yield results, Truman promised to undertake his own investigation under the watchful gaze of the Coney crowd. With Julio in tow, he mounted a theatrical search of the Igorrote enclosure. The public looked on eagerly as the two men searched the Igorrotes' homes, rifling through their possessions before emerging every now and again to show that their hands were empty. Then Truman went over to a native kettle, sitting beside the fire. When he peered inside it, he discovered a number of bones. Holding them up, he declared that they "may belong to Prince."[6]

This show served its purpose. Cartoons appeared in the newspapers depicting the Igorrotes stealing dogs from American homes. CHAIN UP YOUR DOG, screamed the headlines. No one seemed to notice (or care) that Mrs. Jackman was the wife of the proprietor of Coney's musical railways and a neighbor of Truman's. In every sense the disappearance of Prince was an inside job. The American Humane Association came calling again. Truman was ready for them and insisted the dog feasts were a vital part of tribal life and could not be stopped.

With combined glee and revulsion, the New York press reported that dog was the only meat the Igorrotes ever ate. In reality, the Igorrotes only ate dogmeat on special occasions like weddings, funerals, and after a successful head-hunting foray, but Truman had a showman's impulse not to let the facts interfere with a good story. He informed the public that young, short-haired dogs of around four years of age were regarded by the Igorrotes to be the tastiest and were typically served boiled with sweet potatoes.

The sacrifice of a dog was an important Igorrote custom and, though they were reluctant to say anything at first, some of the tribe felt the daily dog feasts at Coney were undermining their cultural significance. Not only that, but their bodies couldn't digest all of the meat that they were being given. On behalf of them all, the tribal chief approached Julio with a request that they be allowed to return to a more varied and authentic diet of chicken, pork, fish, rice, beans, and vegetables, with occasional servings of dog.

Julio was a gifted negotiator, trusted and well liked by the Igorrotes. They didn't seem to mind that he was treated differently by their American bosses and that he was excused from the dancing and other tribal displays. The dogmeat problem was the first serious test of Julio's loyalty, and he felt it deeply. But though he was eager to help his countrymen, he knew this was one battle he couldn't win. Visitors came to Coney wanting to see the tribe eat dog, so eat dog they must. He decided that on this one occasion he would keep quiet. Truman wasn't paying him twenty-five dollars a month to make trouble. In the Philippines he'd be lucky to be earning five dollars a month, even in a good government job or teaching post. If the rest of the group had stayed at home, with little or no education, they might never have had the chance to earn wages. Instead they would have faced a lifetime of tending their land and raising a few animals. Truman was paying them generously. For that they must learn to adapt and tolerate the occasional hardship. In time, Julio thought, the tribespeople would grow accustomed to the change in their diet. If they didn't, well, then he would see what he could do.

Life under Coney's bright lights forced the Igorrotes to adapt in other ways too. The industrious mountain dwellers were accustomed to getting up before sunrise and going to bed when the sun set. In their new home, they continued to wake early but they had to stay up until midnight, putting on a show for their visitors. It was hard for some of them to stay awake and it wasn't unheard of in the weeks following their arrival for one or two of the weary tribespeople to doze off.

Friday was so awed by his surroundings that he found it difficult to sleep at all. Day and night he could hear music, shouting, and the sounds of people having fun. In northern Luzon, there was little noise to speak of, save for the birds and wild cats. Friday didn't mind Coney's noise but he yearned to see the source of it for himself. He would be content to stay within Luna Park's gates if he could only catch a glimpse of the rest of the park and the amusements the visitors enjoyed.

When Julio returned to the village after a trip to the store one afternoon, Friday begged the interpreter to take him with him the next time. Julio didn't want to upset the boy, so he said he would ask Truman. Friday's belly rumbled as he imagined the American candies he would buy at the store.

Still smiling at the thought of his sugary feast, Friday walked over to where a group of the women and girls were busy weaving, and sat down at their feet. An immense cigar dangled permanently from the corner of the boy's mouth. To the American visitors it looked odd, but the boy had been smoking for as long as he could remember. Just as Julio had promised back in Manila, Friday had a new playmate, a filthy mutt, which had so far been spared the fate of the other dogs brought to the tribe from the New York pound. It had become the young boy's constant companion.

The women chatted and laughed while Friday threw stones for the dog to chase. Tiring of this game, the Negrito waited until none of the women were looking, then he reached up and hurriedly tied one of their dangling threads to the dog's tail. He then picked up a stick and threw it. The mutt ran after the stick, pulling the women's threads with him. The women leaped up and began to shout. Running after the dog, they attempted to untangle him and recover their handiwork. Friday stood watching the chaos with satisfaction until Fomoaley strode over and slapped him across the shoulders. The young boy sloped off to find some other source of entertainment.

The mud had barely set on the walls of the tribe's huts before they were enveloped in yet another outcry, this time over their lack of clothing. Coney Island society, never known for its high morals, was shocked by the Filipinos' scanty attire and, according to a report in the *New York Morning Telegraph*, "for the first time in its life, protested."[7] Never one to shy away from publicity, Truman waded into the debate, insisting that it was "imperative" that the tribespeople be allowed to wear their own minimal clothing. "They would die of colds were they to wear our heavy clothing,"[8] said the doctor inexplicably. The truth, of course, was that if he covered them up, he knew no one would come and see them.

In early June, Willis Brooks, a reporter from the *Brooklyn Daily Eagle*, stopped by and said he wanted to write a big article on the Filipino tribe for the front page of that weekend's paper. Truman was away and had left George Fuller, Friday's guardian who had recently joined them in New York, in charge.

Like Truman, Fuller had served with the US Army in the Philippines and had gotten to know the tribespeople there. Fuller was happy to show the journalist around, but he stressed that his esteemed colleague, Dr. Hunt, was the number-one authority on the tribe, and "probably knows more about the Igorrotes than any other white man on earth."[9]

During their long association with the tribe, Fuller and Truman had both formed the opinion that the Igorrotes were the most honest people they had ever encountered. "We have to handle these little people as carefully as you would dynamite. They are so punctiliously truthful themselves that the smallest of white lies on our part would rob us of their confidence and friendship,"[10] said Fuller. "There is nothing halfway about them. They give you either their full confidence or none; and when they withdraw their confidence all friendship is at an end . . . They are frankly, openly, courageously your enemy until you can convince them that you did not mean to deceive them . . . If an Igorrote makes a promise to you, no matter how trivial it seems to you, he will fulfill it if it costs him his life."

Brooks was accompanied by a cartoonist who'd come along to sketch the tribe. He wandered through the village with Julio, observing the Igorrotes as they went about their daily activities. He drew Manidol the medicine man, who was delighted to learn that his face would be in the newspaper and asked Julio to buy him a copy so he could show it to his friends back home. Julio agreed, secretly amused at the tribesman's vanity.

The cartoonist walked around the village and noticed a pretty young woman whom Julio informed him was Daipan. The artist asked her if she would be willing to pose for a sketch. Blushing, Daipan agreed. He sat down and rested his sketchbook on his lap. He drew quickly and began asking her questions as he worked. *How old are you?* She told him she was around sixteen, and that she was the daughter of a distinguished headhunter who had been killed during the Spanish-American War. The girl's eyes filled with tears. He looked at her sympathetically, then wrote her name underneath the sketch alongside the words "the belle of the village." It was an opinion shared by the reporter, who noted that she was "a plump little thing, shapely and far from ugly to look upon."[11]

The most entertaining subject, though, was Friday. The boy danced around and tried out the handful of English phrases and words he'd picked up. Though the Negrito boy didn't like dogmeat, he was happy to oblige when the cartoonist asked him to demonstrate how he looked and felt before and after a dog feast. For the "before" sketch, Friday looked pained, as if he would die if he didn't taste the dog's succulent flesh in the next instant. For the "after" drawing, the young boy puffed out his belly and clutched his sides as if he might burst. When he was finished, the artist thanked the boy and slipped him a nickel.

Fuller took Brooks inside one of the Igorrotes' huts. He explained that they were homebodies by nature who rarely traveled more than three miles from their villages, making this appearance at Luna Park a unique opportunity for the public to witness the tribe up close.

Noticing the axes that every Igorrote man possessed, Brooks asked Fuller to tell him about the tribe's head-hunting custom. Fuller explained that every Igorrote town was at war with its neighbors. A head hunt began with a tribesman throwing a rock at an approaching enemy. Then one of the other men in his group would throw a spear at the enemy's abdomen. If it struck him, a young Igorrote who had not taken a head before would be given the honor of slicing the still breathing victim's head off with his virgin ax. "The Igorrotes go out hunting enemies just as we hunt bears,"[12] explained Fuller, picking up an ax. "When a hunter has killed an enemy of his people, he cuts his head off with a hatchet such as you see here and brings it home in this sort of basket." He held up a basket that one of the men had finished weaving (all basket work was traditionally done by the men). After the kill the other men often joined in, hacking off the slain enemy's hands, feet, arms, and legs so that soon only his torso was left. The reporter sat wide-eyed. Fuller continued, "Then they tattoo one of those fancy lines upon his breast. Every line means a head."[13]

After a successful head hunt, the village would erupt into a celebration, with singing, dancing, and feasting. The following morning the head was taken to the river to be washed. The lower jaw was cut from the head, boiled to remove the flesh, and turned into a handle for the victor's *gang´-sa*, a gong-like instrument. There followed a month of feasting and holidays. Carabao, hogs, dogs, and chickens were killed and eaten. No work except that which was absolutely necessary was performed. *Why do they do it?* asked Brooks. *What would the man have done? Nothing*, said Fuller with a smile, *they do it because they are bored and want some excitement.*[14]

Brooks shook hands with Fuller and Fomoaley and prepared to leave. Gathering up his belongings, the reporter felt a shiver run down his spine as he eyed the many lines inked on the tribal chief's chest.

Over the coming weeks, the Igorrotes cemented their reputation as Coney's biggest attraction. The public couldn't get enough of them. Those who could afford to returned again and again. Some visitors had favorite Igorrotes, typically children, for whom they brought gifts and money. There were offers of adoption, education, and patronage. They received parcels of clothes, candies, and cigars from all over the country.

Before long news of the Igorrotes' arrival at Coney reached the White House. Among the dignitaries who came to see them in 1905 was President Theodore Roosevelt's eldest daughter, Alice, then aged twenty-one. Miss Roosevelt arrived at Coney in a touring car with a group of friends, as guests of the philanthropist, investor, and racehorse breeder Payne Whitney. They toured the park grounds, trailed by a gaggle of press agents.

In the Igorrote enclosure, Alice and her friends were greeted by Julio, wearing his signature American suit and leather shoes. Behind him, the rest of the "savages," wearing their most festive G-strings, blankets, and beads, got down on their knees to welcome her. Miss Roosevelt told Julio that she planned to follow in her father's footsteps and visit the Philippines herself as part of an American diplomatic and trade mission to Japan, and the Far East later that year. The visiting VIP and her friends then watched with evident pleasure as the tribe sang and danced.[15]

Soon the Igorrotes' fame spread across the country. Souvenir postcards had been popular since the 1893 Chicago World's Fair. By the time the Igorrotes arrived at Coney, stalls up and down the beachfront were selling hundreds of thousands of postcards each week, featuring photographs of the Eskimos, the Lilliputian village, and the big wheel. Vacationers scrawled messages on them boasting of the fun they were having and sent them to friends and family back home. One of the most popular postcards in the summer of 1905 featured a tall man dressed as Uncle Sam in red and white striped trousers, a blue jacket, and a top hat. There was nothing special about Uncle Sam, an out-of-work actor who strode the boardwalk all day, drumming up interest in Coney's attractions. But surrounding him and looking up at Uncle Sam was a family of diminutive Igorrotes. The image symbolized an encounter between two worlds. Just ten miles from downtown Manhattan, metropolis of the modern age, Stone Age men and women were living in a village by the sea.

8

Divided Loyalties

LUNA PARK, JULY 1905

The Igorrotes at Luna Park, with Julio on the far right, sitting next to Maria, and Friday on the far left

IN THE TWO months they had been living among the eight-thousand-strong Coney community, Julio had made a few friends outside the village. He often went to visit Judy the elephant, and took her fruit whenever he had some. Her trainer, Barlow, showed Julio the leathery spot behind Judy's huge flapping ears where she loved to be patted. He also met Alexander, "the Hindu Magician," who lived in a hut behind the Igorrote Village, and whose act involved firing lead balls from his mouth. Alexander had been a big hit at the Hippodrome and had been invited by Thompson to transfer his act over to Luna Park. Julio enjoyed watching his tricks and hearing his stories of the many places he had been, but the truth was the Filipino interpreter frequently felt out of place among the "freaks" and human curiosities at Coney. He didn't feel as if he was one of them, but neither was he one of the bosses or managers. He had plenty of friends in the Igorrote Village but his job as Truman's assistant created a distance between him and his countrymen and women. The animals were easy company.

That day as he walked out through the park gates and onto Surf Avenue to buy provisions, the interpreter thought back to the first time he had ventured outside alone into the crowded New York streets. Though he would never have admitted it to anyone, he had felt overwhelmed by the great throngs of people and more than a little afraid. Of what, he wasn't sure. But he had forced himself to keep going. In time the fear had turned to wonder. Now he loved these expeditions. He wandered alone among the day-trippers and vacationers, looking at the ladies' long dresses and picture hats and at the men's elegant suits, and imagined that one day he and Maria would dress like that. He was already planning to buy a straw boater as soon as he had enough money. But that day he hardly noticed the other people on the street.

He pulled open the door of the store and two young men, not far from his own age, emerged from inside. They were laughing at some tale one of them had told. Julio stood back to let them pass and watched them for a moment. Sighing, he went inside. It dawned on Julio that, for the first time since leaving home, he felt lonely. He couldn't mention it to Maria. It had been his idea to come, and besides he knew that Maria had been feeling homesick lately. He had to be strong for her.

Julio scooped up an armful of candies and cookies. He asked the man behind the counter for some of their cheapest tobacco. Truman gave him an allowance each week to buy supplies for the tribe, but the money didn't last long. Standing in the store, Julio was suddenly overcome with an unfamiliar sadness. In that moment he would have given anything to talk to his older brother, Nicasio. The two of them shared a similar temperament, and they were both hardworking, intellectually curious, and ambitious. Julio wondered what Nicasio would say if he could see him now. He would probably tell Julio to stop feeling so sorry for himself. The thought made the interpreter smile. He took his groceries off the counter. Truman had given him an incredible opportunity and he must make the most of it.

Julio walked over to the door but a headline in one of the newspapers stopped him in his tracks: IGORROTES AND WHITES IN BATTLE.[1] He stepped forward to take a closer look. The article described how Thompson and Dundy had been summoned to the Igorrote Village early that morning after a huge fight broke out between the Filipinos and the white residents of Coney Island. The cause, it claimed, was the tribe's love of dogmeat. So greedy were they for the succulent canine flesh, they had broken into the stables housing Albert Carre's circus under cover of darkness and stolen several fox terriers and a Russian wolfhound. When the circus man awoke, he immediately noticed the missing animals and rushed to find the culprits. The smoldering embers of a fire had led him to the Igorrote Village, where he found singed dog hairs scattered all over the place. According to the article, forty men rushed to punish the Igorrotes, carrying pitchforks, whips, and shovels. The Igorrotes reportedly grabbed their spears and let out shrill war cries. Only when the elephant trainer intervened by turning the hose on the Igorrotes did the battle subside. Fearing that the Igorrotes would try to stage a similar theft again, Thompson said he had erected a twenty-foot-tall fence around the Filipinos and had sent all the Luna Park special policemen to watch over the tribe. Julio was even mentioned in the article as innocently denying the thefts.[2]

The interpreter frowned. Far from being greedy for dog, the tribe were sick of the sight of it. There was indeed a new, higher fence around the village, but Truman had had it put up because he felt the previous one was too low to prevent passersby from seeing inside the village without first buying a ticket. The events described in the story had never happened. Julio knew this was part of the business they had signed up for, but some of Truman's farfetched stories made him feel uncomfortable, especially the portrayal of his countrymen as violent savages.

Back at Luna Park, Feloa and Dengay sat sharpening their spears and talking in hushed tones. The men were sick of being locked up in the village all the time; they had to do something about it.

Before they left the Philippines, Julio had warned them that they would have to make sacrifices. But they hadn't anticipated the extent to which their lives would change. The tribe prided themselves on the fact they were largely self-sufficient in their native environment. They were strong headhunters, free to roam as they pleased and physically fit and active. At Coney, they spent their days cooped up in a pen, their every move watched by thousands of strangers. Overnight they had become entirely dependent on Truman for everything.

The tribal ceremonies which accompanied the Igorrotes' agricultural labors in their homeland were a high point of the calendar. Now, with no land or crops to tend, their tribal dances and songs felt meaningless. They had a crude smelting plant to produce the copper they needed to make their pipes and jewelry, but it was little more than a tourist attraction. They had no choice but to eat the dog their new bosses gave them, and their only work was creating a show for their visitors. Without physical work to do in the fields, they felt idle and got little exercise. A roll of flesh hung over the bands of their loincloths. Their Coney diet was making them fat. More than anything, the tribespeople longed to leave their village and see something of the world outside.

Julio had promised the previous night that he would talk to Truman about it but Feloa and Dengay weren't sure if they could trust him. Both men knew that the interpreter and their boss were friendly. The tribesmen had complained many times to Julio about all the dogmeat they were given to eat and nothing had changed.

Callahan wandered through the village and spotted the two Igorrote men huddled together. He walked around the back of the huts and hid behind one, close to where they were sitting. Truman's security guard and right-hand man was no great linguist. He'd picked up a few Bontoc words and phrases but not enough to understand their conversation. He did, however, sense rumblings of discontent. He moved closer and accidentally trod on the tail of one of the mutts tied to the fence for that night's dog feast. The dogs began to bark. Feloa looked up and, noticing Callahan, abruptly stopped speaking.

The security guard knew that he should speak to Julio first, but

Truman's two assistants didn't have much time for each other. Callahan preferred to deal with things himself or go straight to Truman. He walked over to one of the other security men working in the village and told him to watch over things while he went to see the boss.

Callahan was still in Truman's office when Julio happened to call in on his way back from the store. The interpreter often visited his boss and that day he had something he wanted to talk to him about. He wouldn't mention the newspaper article, for he knew it wouldn't achieve anything other than getting Truman's back up. The showman would simply say he was doing his job.

Truman invited Julio to take a seat and asked him if there were any problems in the village. The interpreter paused for a moment and looked from Truman to Callahan. He would have preferred to speak to Truman about the tribe's complaints in private, but now that he had asked him directly, Julio could hardly lie. *Some of the tribespeople have been asking if they could be permitted to leave the village to go for a walk. Might it be possible?* Julio asked hopefully. He suggested letting them go out in small groups with him, or with Truman or Callahan.

Truman looked serious for a moment. *No,* he said firmly, *it's out of the question.* Noticing Julio's crestfallen expression, the showman said he was keeping them locked up with good reason, because he wanted to protect them from racists and scoundrels. Americans had not yet embraced people whose skin was not white like their own. Truman told Julio of a terrible incident he had heard about recently: a gang of two hundred white men had gone, armed with clubs and stones, to the shacks where a group of black laborers were living just across the water in Weehawken, New Jersey, "bent upon wiping out the negro gang."[3]

If the Igorrotes ventured out into the New York streets with little clothing and even less common sense, Truman continued, he dreaded to think what might happen to them. Though he didn't say so to his assistant, he also knew that if ordinary Americans could see his Igorrotes on the city streets for free, they would stop paying to see them at Coney. It was safe, Truman said, for Julio to go out because he wasn't naive like the others, and besides, his lighter skin and smart Western clothes meant he didn't stand out like his countrymen. Flattered but reluctant to give up, Julio pressed on: *Could they just have a walk around Luna Park? They could wear their American clothes.* Truman shook his head.

Sensing that he had pushed it as far as he could, Julio got up to leave. He noticed the smug expression on Callahan's face. It was important to Julio that Feloa, Dengay, Fomoaley, and the others knew that he had put their case to Truman, that he was doing what he could to make their lives better, but he didn't know how to tell them what the showman had said. It seemed so final. Did Truman intend to keep them locked up like prisoners for a full year, until their contracts expired?

9

Tribal Life in the City

LUNA PARK, JULY 1905

A section of the Igorrote Village at Luna Park, showing two of the tribal huts and the headhunters' watchtower

TRUMAN ENTERED THE hut to find the women gathered around Laguima. The atmosphere was festive as family and friends fussed over her, fixing her ceremonial apron and headdress in place. It was a big day in the Igorrote Village. Laguima was getting married, to the "full-fledged warrior" Bocosso.[1] The impending nuptials had been widely advertised in all the New York newspapers. Those who came would have a chance to watch history being made.

One of the older women stepped forward and presented Laguima with the bridal trousseau. The women had spent many hours weaving the beautiful patterned cloth using red, yellow, orange, blue, pink, and purple threads. The bride-to-be clutched it to her chest.

This was not quite how Laguima had imagined her wedding day, but she knew what was expected of her. She picked up her pipe and sucked deeply on it, filling the hut with smoke. All the Igorrotes loved their pipes, but perhaps none more so than Laguima, who had smoked constantly during the wedding rehearsal.

Truman looked on admiringly as the young woman gave her audience a twirl. He tried not to look at her large ornamental ear stretchers. All the women, and many of the men, wore them and considered them to look most attractive, but they turned their manager's stomach. Truman watched Laguima chattering excitedly with her friends, and couldn't help but think of Calista, his daughter back in Iowa. She would be thirteen now, not that much younger than Laguima. It was a long time since he'd seen her and he wondered what she looked like now. Did she have her mother's fine features?

Doctor? Truman's thoughts were interrupted by Laguima. Proudly, she stepped forward to show him her bridal outfit. *You look exquisite*, said Truman. He told her he was providing a special wedding banquet for her and Bocosso, and he wanted them to savor every moment of the day. Laguima smiled up at her boss and thanked him. The wedding might be a staged event,[2] designed not to unite two young lives forever as one but simply as a show for the unsuspecting crowds. But it was still a feast. They might as well enjoy themselves, thought Laguima, tucking a flower in her hair.

Outside, the crowds had been arriving since the park opened. A section had been roped off for the press. Photographers were busy getting into position. Truman began briefing reporters on what to expect. Everyone jostled for the best view. Bocosso, the groom-to-be, appeared from the men's quarters, flanked by his fellow tribesmen. After a respectable delay, Laguima emerged from her hut. She looked over at Bocosso and smiled before taking a few tentative steps toward him. Standing at the front of the enclosure, Truman informed the public that, unlike in a typical American wedding ceremony, no promise and no advice were given at an Igorrote wedding. The showman had placed the tribe's copper gongs around the fence of the enclosure so that the crowds could show their appreciation for the wedding spectacle by throwing coins into them.

A tribal elder, Byungasiu, stepped forward and assumed a position in front of Bocosso and Laguima. The couple stood silently while Byungasiu placed a hen's egg, some rice, and a dash of *tapui,* the fermented rice drink consumed on special occasions, in a bowl. Then the elder began to speak. Truman explained that he was addressing the Igorrote god, Lumawig, and began to translate: "Thou, Lumawig, now these children desire to unite in marriage. They wish to be blessed with many children. When they possess pigs, may they grow large. When they cultivate their palay, may it have large fruit heads. May their chickens also grow large. When they plant their beans, may they spread over the ground. May they dwell quietly together in harmony. May the man's vitality quicken the seed of the woman."[3]

The women of the tribe began walking toward the center of the village, where they started to sway with their heads held aloft. A few of the men held tom-tom drums, which they began to beat with increasing urgency. Another tribesman stepped forward holding a *gang´-sa,* which he struck with a short stick. The leader sang an improvised song, with his last few words being taken up in refrain by the rest of the men. Their voices gradually grew quieter and the women took up the song.

Clutching their spears and shields, the tribesmen bent over at the waist and began to lurch forward with strange jerky movements, joining the women in a constantly moving circle. The dance grew faster and faster until their nearly naked bodies dripped with sweat. The crowd looked on, not quite sure what to make of the scene unfolding in front of them. Two of the tribesmen appeared carrying a dog, "a species of Coney Island cur," which, Truman explained, had been specially fattened for a week. (At home the Igorrotes usually starved their dogs for several weeks before the slaughter, preferring their dogmeat lean.) On seeing the dog, the centerpiece of any Igorrote wedding feast, the Igorrotes howled with joy and danced with wild abandon.[4]

Two of the groom's closest friends were selected by the bride to hold the dog aloft, taking two paws each. The dog twisted and squealed. Feloa slit the beast's throat, and, as its warm blood spilled out onto the dust, he walked around and cut off its tail. Dengay came forward and placed an iron pot under the dog's throat to catch the gushing blood. The execution was deft and, Truman insisted, it had less horror and pain than was witnessed in American abattoirs. The canine's body was taken to the center of the village, where it was held over an open fire. When all of its hair had been singed off, the bald, tailless body was thrown into a large pot. There it simmered into a pulpy mass. Truman invited the reporters, and any members of the public with a stomach strong enough, to step forward to peer into the pot.[5]

The tribespeople gathered around as the dogmeat was ladled into bowls. The bride and groom were given their serving first. Scooping it up with their hands, the couple greedily tore off chunks with their teeth. The tribesmen and boys were fed next. Contradicting his statement in Seattle that women were only permitted to eat dog on their wedding day, Truman told the crowd that now that the newly married couple and all the male members of the tribe had sated their hunger, all the women and girls were allowed to eat whatever canine scraps were left over.[6] The showman then signaled to the groom that it was time to adopt an American custom and kiss his bride. Bocosso embraced Laguima tightly, making the young woman blush. The audience whooped and threw coins into the copper gongs.

Truman decided he would take the opportunity to educate the American public about Igorrote mating rituals. It was a fact, he told the newspapermen, that among the Igorrotes marriage almost never took place prior to sexual intimacy, and rarely prior to pregnancy. The reason was that no man wanted to risk marrying a woman who could not bear him a child. Furthermore, he explained, it was customary for a young man to be sexually intimate with two, three, or even more girls before he reached a decision as to who he wished to take as his bride.

Though Igorrote women were not given quite as much sexual freedom as the men, they nonetheless had a lot more of it than their American counterparts. An Igorrote woman was almost invariably faithful to her temporary lover, though she too was free to experiment with different lovers (though not simultaneously) until she decided which man was for her. Truman continued: contrary to the social mores in their new host country, when an unmarried Igorrote woman became pregnant, it was viewed as a virtue, not a stigma, for she had proven her fertility.

In Igorrote courtship rituals, it was typically the woman who made the first move. She would declare her interest in a new lover by using a flirtatious trick, such as stealing a man's pipe, his pocket hat, or even the breechcloth he was wearing. The man would then be forced to chase after her into the *o´-lâg* (the sleeping place of all unmarried girls and young women, which their lovers were permitted to visit). Truman left the rest up to the newspapermen's, and in turn the public's, imaginations.

Americans declared themselves shocked and, in some cases, quietly envious.

That night, Truman paid a visit to the Brooklyn Lodge of the Benevolent and Protective Order of Elks on his way home from Coney. The five-story clubhouse was an imposing brownstone building on Schermerhorn Street, with a large bay window and, lest any member should miss it, a statue of an elk standing outside the door. Truman was a member of the society and whenever he traveled he found that visiting the local lodge was an excellent way to get established in the city.

The showman sat in the parlor with a tumbler of whiskey in hand. A huge pair of elk antlers hung on the wall above his head. Surrounding him were some of the most powerful men in the city—judges, senior police officials, politicians, businessmen, wealthy merchants, doctors, architects, and the like. Such acquaintances could come in very handy. Noticing a newspaper editor he knew, Truman got up and walked over to greet him. Just then a bell started to toll. The Elks gathered round and raised their glasses as a lodge official intoned, "It is the hour of recollection." The Exalted Ruler, the most important man in the room, stepped forward to give the eleven o'clock toast:

> You have heard the tolling of eleven strokes.
>
> This is to remind us that with Elks, the hour of eleven has a tender significance.
>
> Wherever Elks may roam, whatever their lot in life may be, when this hour falls upon the dial of night, the great heart of Elkdom swells and throbs.
>
> It is the golden hour of recollection, the homecoming of those who wander, the mystic roll call of those who will come no more.
>
> Living or dead, Elks are never forgotten, never forsaken.
>
> Morning and noon may pass them by, the light of day sink heedlessly in the West, but 'ere the shadows of midnight shall fall, the chimes of memory will be pealing forth the friendly message,
>
> 'To our absent members'.[7]

These words, or a variation on them, were a nightly ritual at every Elks Lodge in America. The toast was a highlight of the evening, for it signaled that the time had come to drink heartily and make merry. Throwing back his whiskey, Truman approached the Exalted Ruler. It was time they became friends.

Truman was on a roll. The wedding might have been a sham, but the public hadn't realized that and they had loved it. At last Truman was making good money, and he had to admit he was enjoying the attention. Work could not be going better. He'd been so busy he had rather neglected poor Sallie. He and Sallie were still staying with Adele and George Wilkins. They had been most generous hosts, but Sallie was beginning to tire of living in someone else's house.

Adele was charming, but Sallie longed for the company of someone of her own age and background. She also wished her husband were home more. It was seven months since they had married and in that time she'd hardly seen him. He kept telling her that things would settle down soon, but there was little sign of it. He often came home in the early hours reeking of alcohol and sometimes he didn't come home at all, complaining that he had been detained by work and had stayed over in his Coney bungalow. She had written to Catherine, her favorite of her four sisters, seeking advice. Catherine wrote back telling Sallie to insist Truman pay her more attention. How Sallie loved receiving her sister's letters. They arrived once a week without fail. Catherine wrote of life back home, and of their father, sisters, and brother, in such a chatty, newsy way that Sallie almost felt as if she were there talking to her.

One morning toward the end of July, Sallie cornered her husband over breakfast. George Wilkins was out at work and Adele was at a charity meeting, leaving Sallie and Truman alone. Pouring Truman's coffee, Sallie begged her husband to take her out. She looked so sad that Truman found it impossible to say no. He would pick her up at eight. She should wear the new evening gown he had bought her. He was taking her somewhere special.

Truman arrived home early. He found Sallie sitting at the dressing table in her pale pink gown, with her hair up, just a few wisps curling around her face. She looked ravishing. Truman strode over to her and, bending down, kissed her passionately. She tilted her head back and pressed her lips firmly against his. After they parted, Truman told her to close her eyes. Then he put his hand inside his jacket pocket, produced a long, slim box tied with red ribbon, and placed it in her hands. Opening the box, she gasped. Diamonds sparkled in the glow of the lamp. She threw her arms around Truman, smothering him in kisses.

Truman took the necklace and fastened it around Sallie's neck. Standing back to admire her, he told his wife he had never seen her look more beautiful. Her face flushed as she scolded her husband for spoiling her. He was always buying her gifts. Truman promised Sallie that he was going to make up for neglecting her that night. He was taking her to New York's smartest restaurant. After that they would go on to the opening night of a new club. It was by invitation only. An associate from the Elks had gotten him on the guest list. Sallie clapped her hands with joy. She had some news to tell Truman, and she wanted to pick a special moment to do it.

The next morning Truman woke up with a pounding headache. He'd drunk a lot of champagne and had very little sleep. His brain began slowly processing the events of the previous night. Had Sallie really told him what he thought she did? Or had he dreamed it? Sallie yawned and rolled over to face him. She gazed at him lovingly. Then, propping herself up on her elbow she leaned over and trilled, *Good morning, Daddy,* before kissing him deeply. Sallie was too happy to notice that her husband wasn't smiling. She leaned back against a pile of pillows and, resting her hands on her belly, begged Truman to stay in bed awhile. He could go to work late—surely they could manage without him for a few hours. Truman sat up with his back to her. He thought of the last time someone had called him "Daddy."

The showman stood up suddenly. He had a publicity stunt to get working on. He would tell Sallie all about it that night. He left without taking breakfast.

Over at Luna Park, Truman called in to see Thompson. Every summer Thompson traveled to Europe to comb the fairs, exhibitions, and amusement parks for innovative new acts and exhibits. He'd recently returned from such a trip, and had brought several acts back with him to give Luna Park a midseason boost. They included an acrobatic dog act (he was already imagining the headlines about the encounters they might have with the Igorrotes) and the celebrated father, mother, and daughter contortionist act the Pantzer Trio.

The pickings had been slim this time around, Thompson said. Truman should get a group of Igorrotes together to take over there. They would love them in London and Paris. It was an off-the-cuff remark, but Truman took note. Coney Island was just the beginning for the Igorrotes. Maybe he could get Thompson to put up the money for a European tour.

Speaking of the Igorrotes, Thompson had heard from Dundy that there was some trouble in the village while he was away. Truman laughed and explained that there had been something of a power struggle between the tribe and Fomoaley, whom they'd elected to be their leader. Fomoaley had been throwing his weight around and the rest of the tribe, growing tired of his iron rule, had begun to rebel. Fomoaley had been accused of letting his newfound power and fame go to his head. While some of the tribe had stood by their leader, a majority had demanded the selection of a new chief. Fearing the disagreement could turn violent, Truman had intervened, insisting the tribe adopt an American custom and settle their dispute at the ballot box. Reluctantly the tribesmen had been persuaded to put down their arms and cast their votes. With fifty tribespeople living in the village, Feloa had received thirty-two of their votes and was duly elected the new tribal chief.[8]

At the same time, the tribespeople had voted for a "mother" of the tribe. As the wife of Truman's assistant, Maria was not eligible for the role, though she performed it unofficially. In her place, the tribe selected a popular young woman named Langasa to the position with thirty-five votes, making her a clear winner over her nearest rival, Gumay.[9] Thompson wished all his concession managers took so much trouble to keep their attractions fresh. He could do with a few more men of Truman's caliber. He told him to keep up the good work.

Truman had an idea for a new stunt that he wanted to run by Thompson, involving Judy, Dundy's favorite elephant. Thompson smiled as the Igorrote manager described his plan. Thompson loved it and told Truman to go and speak to Barlow, the elephant handler. He should tell him he had Thompson's approval.

Over at the elephant stables, the showman outlined his scheme to Barlow. Judy had a canine companion, a plump little terrier by the name of Howard, who followed her everywhere and slept with her in her straw bed at night. What if the Igorrotes tried to steal Howard for one of their dog feasts and Judy went on the rampage through the Igorrote Village? Barlow smiled. What did he need to do?

Truman sent Feloa and Dengay to the elephant stables. There they were instructed to grab Howard. The park wasn't open yet, so Truman took care of the rest. It wasn't necessary to have Judy destroy the Igorrote Village, but there was no harm in Truman and Callahan tearing it up a bit to give the impression that Judy had wreaked havoc. Once they were finished, Truman invited the press to come and inspect the damage for themselves.

He showed the reporters around the village, and described how, spying Howard about to be thrown into the Igorrote cooking pot, Judy had wrenched herself free of the iron shackles that secured her hind feet and "let out a trumpet note of rage and grief"[10] as she rushed into the Igorrote village like a "terrifying avenger,"[11] sending the tribe running for cover. But Feloa was too slow. Judy had tossed him in the air and the Filipino landed on the porch of Truman's bungalow, narrowly escaping death. Sensing that Judy wasn't done with him yet, Feloa had jumped down the back of Truman's quarters and hidden in the horse stables. Judy then "started on a career of destruction."[12] She'd bulldozed Feloa's house to the ground, torn pieces from three other huts and ripped through Truman's bungalow, pulling down the porch and kitchen. All the while Howard was standing at her side, barking encouragement.

By the time Judy was finished, "the camp of the brown savages from Luzon looked as if it had gone through fire and wreck and battle and murder and sudden death. Judy had gone about the rescue of her friend from the stewing pot in a manner prompt and cataclysmic."[13] None of this was true, of course, but the press loved it. So too did the public, who came in their thousands to watch the tribespeople put their homes back together again.

It had been some time since an exhibit at Luna Park had generated so much excitement. The Igorrotes had been everything Thompson and Dundy had wished for and more. Thompson recognized in Truman a kindred spirit. Truman was a born salesman—there were some things you couldn't teach.

In Washington, DC, 230 miles away, a clerk in the government's Bureau of Insular Affairs was reading about the escapades of Judy the elephant and the Igorrotes as he ate breakfast. Unlike most readers, he was not amused. He had encountered the tribespeople while working as a law clerk in Manila and he found it vexing and distasteful that an indigenous tribe should be exhibited in such a way. What was worse, he knew that the American authorities in the Philippines had given permission for the tribe to be put on show. The clerk pointed the article out to his wife, then kissed her good-bye and left for the office.

Interest in the Igorrotes was not confined to the popular press. The *Independent*, a learned journal "Devoted to the Consideration of Politics, Social and Economic Tendencies, History, Literature, and the Arts," also sent a writer along to meet the tribe. Clarence W. Bowen, the paper's editor, didn't go in for the kind of sensationalist stories found in many of the city's newspapers, but he had a long-standing interest in the Philippines and felt certain the journal's educated, politically aware readers would enjoy reading an informative piece about the tribespeople who were living in their midst. Maybe they could interview the tribal chief about his impressions of America.

Truman was delighted when the *Independent*'s man came calling.[14] It wasn't every day he and his Filipino charges received a visit from a representative of such a distinguished publication, he gushed to the reporter.

Truman introduced the man to Julio and Fomoaley. Though Feloa was now their chief, Truman didn't entirely trust the young man and felt he could rely on Fomoaley to give a better interview. Truman told Fomoaley the man wanted to know all about life in Bontoc and what he and the others thought about America. The showman and Julio would translate. Never one to shy away from the limelight, Fomoaley nodded his approval. The journalist eyed him. In his notebook, he scribbled his first impressions of the leader, who was "a large, plump Filipino whose age was probably forty-eight. He was clad in two necklaces, two bracelets, some tattoo marks and a loin cloth."[15]

The journalist looked up from his notebook and asked his first question: *Why did you come to Coney Island?* "I have come here with my people in order to show the white people our civilization. [Truman] the white man that lives in our town asked me to come, and said that Americans were anxious to see us. Since we have been here great crowds of white people have come and watched us, and they seem pleased."[16]

Why, the reporter asked, *did so many Igorrotes want to come to America?* Fomoaley replied that it was because of the stories the tribespeople who had been exhibited at St. Louis told. "When they came back they had so many wonders to tell us that it took six of them three days and three nights, standing up before our people talking all the time," he said.

The reporter turned next to the question on every American's lips. *Why do you hunt heads?* "Among our people a young man must have taken a head before he is made a warrior. Our young women will not marry a man unless he has taken a head. We take the heads of our enemies. Sometimes these are the people of some other Igorrote town, sometimes they are the little black people [members of other tribes] who shoot with poisoned arrows, sometimes it may be some family that lives close by and has taken a head from your family . . . The Americans don't like us to take heads, but what can we do? Other people take heads from us. We have always done it. The women won't marry our men if they do not take heads."

Fingering the beads of his necklaces, Fomoaley described the first head he ever took. He had been walking beside a spring when he noticed a man in the distance walking toward him, as if coming over to get a drink of water. Fomoaley shouted at the man, who then shot an arrow at him. The Igorrote chief raised his shield and ran toward him, "then I speared him and cut off his head with my bolo. When I returned to my town I went straight to the house where the girl [who I wanted to marry] lived, but she would not look at me till I showed her [the] head. That pleased her very much, because it showed that I was a warrior and could kill enemies. So we were married."

Truman interjected, explaining to the reporter that the Igorrotes regarded head-hunting in much the same way as Americans viewed sports, as an enjoyable leisure activity and a good way to expend excess energy. Head-hunting, the showman added, allowed the tribespeople to relieve the boredom of their routine rural existence, for every head hunt was celebrated with an elaborate feast, a high point in the Igorrote social diary.

The man from the *Independent* asked Fomoaley how the tribe felt about the Americans coming to live in their country. Truman indicated to Julio that he would translate the answer. "The American people are our friends and want to learn our civilization . . . Our civilization is so much older than theirs that it is no wonder if they do not know some things."

What do you mean? asked the reporter.

Fomoaley grew suddenly animated and began to wax lyrical, with a little help from Truman. "We are the oldest people in the world. All others come from us. The first man and women—there were two women—lived on our mountains and their children lived there after them, till they grew bad and God sent a great flood that drowned them, all except seven, who escaped in a canoes and landed, after the flood went down, on a high mountain . . . The white men have some stories, too, like that. Perhaps they have heard them from one of us.

"Our God is the great God who lives in the sky and shines through the sun. He makes our rice and sugar cane grow and looks out for us—he gives us the heads of our enemies. We have heard of the white man's God, but ours is better." Fomoaley told the reporter about a priest who had come to Bontoc, years earlier when the Philippine Islands were under Spanish rule, to try and convert the Igorrotes. "That man told us that God had a son who died for us, and that we ought to leave our God and go to him. But our Chief said: 'We did not want him to die for us. We can die for ourselves.' No, we will be true to our own God, who has always been good to us. We never give him anything. How could a man give anything to God? [The priest] told us that if we were very good and did what he said, we would go to the white man's heaven, up in the sky. He said that people there could fly like birds, but that they spent all their time singing praises of the white man's God. We did not think we'd care to go there. Our own heaven, where the fruit is always ripe and the game is plenty, suits us far better."[17]

Why, the reporter asked, *does the tribe eat dog?* "We eat dogs when we are going to war because they make us fierce and help us to hear, see and smell well."

The chief was enjoying himself. He began to describe the many incredible inventions he had seen since his arrival. "The most wonderful thing that I have seen here is the stick that you talk in and another man hears your voice a day's journey away [a telephone]. I have walked all around and looked at the back, but I can't see how it does it. But we don't need that [in Bontoc]; we can call as far as we want to by pounding on a hollow tree with a club."

The reporter wanted to know what Fomoaley thought of the American people. Truman translated, putting his own imaginative spin on the chief's answer. "They are good people, but they do not look well. They all wear clothes, even the children. It is bad that any one should wear clothes, but much worse for the children. We pity them. They cannot be well, unless they leave their clothes off and let the wind and the sun get to their skins. Perhaps they are ashamed because they don't look well with their clothes off. They are thin and stooping and pale. That is because they work so much. It is very foolish to work. Men who work hard do not live long. Everything we want grows in the forest; we make our houses out of cane, rattan and leaves, our women weave our loin cloths, and we get our food from the trees and from the fields of rice and sweet potatoes and sugar cane. Why cannot the Americans live like that? I would tell them about our ways if I could because I feel sorry for them."

The man from the *Independent* raised his eyebrows. He had come expecting to hear the tribe marvel at the wonders of American life, not to talk of the ways the colonizers could learn from them. This would make for a most interesting and controversial article, the sort that readers had come to enjoy and expect from the *Independent.*

The interview was published under the headline VIEWS OF AN IGORROTE CHIEF and ran to six pages with three photographs of the tribespeople posing in "American" and "savage costume," holding spears and native musical instruments and poised as if about to start dancing. The same issue of the journal included articles on subjects ranging from Cuba's political quarrels to the separation of Norway and Sweden, and the need of leadership in America's labor unions.

That week's *Independent* also featured a page-long article describing a speech given by Secretary Taft on his return to America following a visit to the Philippines. It read: "Conditions there, he said, were not entirely satisfactory, but evidence of progress was to be seen in a more efficient Government, the elimination of inefficient men, economy, and the substitution of Filipinos for Americans in the public service . . . Some young men of education had been advocating immediate independence. Therefore, it was necessary to declare the policy of the Administration and to point out that independence was not possible for a generation. The Secretary heartily commended the self-restraint and moderation of the Democratic members of the party [traveling with him], who patriotically agreed to refrain from political argument and to leave all statements of policy to himself, as the representative of the Administration. Senator Patterson, one of the Democrats, says the gulf between Americans and Filipinos is widening. He fears the Philippines are a smoldering volcano."[18]

A few short months earlier, most Americans had had no idea what Igorrotes were. Since then the word *Igorrote* had entered the American language as shorthand for a naive, savage human being. The Filipino tribespeople had become a regular feature in newspaper cartoons and editorials. They appeared everywhere from fashion magazines to advertising campaigns. Everyone had an opinion on the tribe.

Americans couldn't decide if they pitied or envied them. The *New York Morning Telegraph* printed a poem reflecting that the simple life of an Igorrote was preferable to that of a magnate:

I fain would be an Igorrote,
Without a stitch of clothes,
And dwell upon the sandy beach
Where the cooling sea-breeze blows.
Iron-jointed, supple-sinewed,
I would walk—would almost fly,
Catch the stray dog by the hair,
And work him over into pie.

There I'd live the life idyllic,
Caring naught for Summer suns,
Caring naught for scorching cities,
Where the perspiration runs.
Dressed alone in my complexion,
With a palm-leaf fan, perchance,
I would rather be a savage
Than a magnate, wearing "pants."[19]

The *Buffalo Courier* considered a statement made by Fomoaley in the *Independent* that Igorrote women wouldn't marry their men until they had taken a head. "Those Igorrote girls seem to be mighty particular," read the article. "An American girl will be pleased with fine clothes and plenty of ice cream, but the Igorrote belle must be attracted by the exhibition of a head lopped off some neighbor. Tastes differ the world over."[20]

Sometimes the tribespeople found unlikely allies. Following an outcry from humane societies, *Vogue* sprang to the Filipinos' defense. Of their taste for dog, the writer reflected, "Shocking, very, but after all is there any real difference between killing a calf and eating its flesh and performing a like operation on a dog?"[21]

The tribespeople even had a puzzle named after them, the Igorrote Double Cross puzzle, "made of Philippine mahogany," and described as "difficult and fascinating."[22]

But the real sign that the Igorrotes had been taken to America's heart came in an advertising campaign. The Los Angeles–based company Bowles Bros. began using the Filipino tribe to sell their Short-O cooking oil with the words:

> *We poked fun at the Igorrote*
> *Because he dined on dog*
> *And he, within, indulged a grin*
> *Because we fried potatoes in*
> *The fuming fat of hog.*
> *But that was many moons ago;*
> *We now are better bred.*
> *No more our distant, savage ward*
> *Can laugh because we fry in lard—*
> *It's SHORT-O oil instead.*
> *SHORT-O Fries Everything*[23]

They were famous. America had fallen in love with them. But not everyone was in favor of the way the Filipino tribe was being exhibited. Cultural commentators and newspaper editorials called for them to be displayed in a more dignified, appropriate setting such as a museum or university. Others called for them to be returned to their homes in the Philippines. The *Post Standard* of Syracuse took a stand, demanding: "The less we have of exhibits of dog-eating Igorrotes and other backward people the better we shall be able to look the lower animals in the face."[24]

Savage or innocent, noble or childlike. The Igorrotes were like one of the distorting mirrors at the Coney funfair. How they were portrayed reflected the views of those looking at them more often than it gave a true picture of the Igorrotes themselves. And though the tribespeople never expressed a word about politics, they were constantly drawn into the debate about America's place in the Philippines.

The Filipinos who had been portrayed in a stereographic image popular at the 1904 World's Fair as "Members of Uncle Sam's Infant Class" were constantly signed up for one side in the argument or the other. The Democratic-leaning newspapers called for America to pull out of the Philippines, while those on the right pointed to the "savage" Igorrotes as evidence that the Filipinos were incapable of running their own country. This view was in stark contrast to that expressed in the *New York Tribune*, which described the Igorrotes as "stalwart specimens of mankind, so high in morality and industry that it has been said of them that they will eventually become dominant among the [Philippine] island people."[25]

Such lofty arguments couldn't have been further from the minds of the crowds who came to see the tribe. On busy Saturdays and Sundays, they threw so many coins into the village that Truman instructed Callahan to go around with cloth bags every half hour to collect the money. When he took the coins to Truman in his office, the showman stuck his hand inside one of the bags and gave Callahan a handful. He wasn't paying him much but he knew it was in his best interests to keep his security man happy.

After Callahan had gone, Truman took the cloth bags one by one and tipped them upside down. Nickels, dimes, quarters, and silver dollars spilled out onto his desk. The showman began counting them. The tips totaled almost as much as the gate receipts. The tribe's ability to make money had vastly outstripped even Truman's expectations.

10

Head-hunting the Star Attraction

LUNA PARK, JULY 1905

The entrance to Luna Park, 1905

IN THE SUMMER of 1905, a leading vaudeville promoter named Colonel John D. Hopkins came to Coney Island to see Truman. Colonel Hopkins's military rank was honorary and self-awarded. He was a plump, white-haired, bespectacled man whose vigor made him seem a good deal younger than his seventy-five years. He was exceptionally vain and routinely deducted a decade and a half from his age. Hopkins was tenacious, quick-witted, and irascible. A former prizefighter in his native Australia, he had never lost his desire to win. No price was too high when it came to getting a star he wanted.[1] The impresario's gambles were frequently disastrous, though he hit gold regularly enough to stay comfortably afloat. One of the productions that almost sank him was the operetta *HMS Pinafore*, which he staged on a ship docked in a river. The extravagant production wiped out his savings but with typical resilience he quickly bounced back.[2] He had many friends—and enemies—in the theatrical world. His friends included the actor John Wilkes Booth, who conversed with Hopkins just an hour before he assassinated President Lincoln in 1865, a fact Hopkins never tired of mentioning.[3]

The day before his meeting with Truman, Hopkins caught a train from his home in St. Louis to New York City. He was determined not to return home without a contract in his pocket bearing the signature of Truman and giving him the right to exhibit the Igorrotes in America.

He arrived at Luna Park to find Truman in a cheerful frame of mind. The two men shared a no-nonsense style and after exchanging a few pleasantries, they got straight down to business. Hopkins proposed using his many contacts to organize an Igorrote tour that would take the tribespeople to theaters, amusement parks, and town and county fairs across America. The impresario would put up the money to cover the initial costs of taking the tribe on the road. He could deliver confirmed bookings in Kentucky, Tennessee, Missouri, and Kansas, with many more to follow. In return he wanted 50 percent of the profits.

The prospect of a nationwide tour thrilled Truman. There was a lot of money to be made from stacking up short engagements. He had hoped to arrange a similar tour himself through the Elks. There was a lodge in most large American towns and cities and they often arranged charity events and carnivals. But so far Truman's plan had failed. The lodges were run at the local level and trying to coordinate anything centrally was proving complicated.

By October, Hopkins reasoned, Coney Island's gates would be closed for the season. As temperatures dropped in the Northeast, bookings would become increasingly thin on the ground. Taking the fifty tribespeople farther afield would be costly. All this was true, but Truman was reluctant to give up half of his business without a fight. For three hours Truman and Hopkins wrangled and blustered with each other. By turns Hopkins was jovial and profane. A bottle of whiskey was sent for. Truman's cigar box grew empty. The Igorrotes were going nowhere without Truman. But Hopkins had contacts, expertise, and exceedingly deep pockets, which could take them far. Finally the two men reached an agreement.

Truman would allow fifteen of the tribespeople to go on the road with Hopkins. Hopkins would arrange the bookings for this group and he would take 60 percent of the profits they generated, with the rest going to Truman. Truman would keep the other thirty-five Filipinos. But, added the showman, he would retain overall control of all the tribespeople, including Hopkins's group. Hopkins agreed. He had no intention of complying with such a ludicrous condition, but they would deal with that later. Contracts were drawn up and signed. That night the two men celebrated with a first-rate meal. During dinner, Hopkins mentioned that he wanted to leave with his Igorrotes as soon as possible. He planned to show them first in Kansas City and then in Louisville and St. Louis. Truman understood Hopkins' impatience, but he explained that the tribespeople had to be handled carefully. He would have to choose the right moment to tell them of the arrangement.

Truman arrived home that night to find Sallie already asleep. Lying in bed next to her, the showman stared up at the ceiling and pondered the best way to tell the Igorrotes that the group was to be split up. He could ask Julio to do it. No, that wasn't fair. He was their boss. And their friend. He should tell them himself. They would be upset. He wondered whether he could soften the blow by telling them it was just for a short time. He didn't want to upset them any more than necessary.

There was something about the colonel that Truman didn't like or entirely trust, but he wasn't in this game to make friends. Hopkins was a successful businessman and his grand tour would earn them a handsome profit. The showman would welcome the extra money.

At the end of the week, Truman called the Filipinos together to tell them of his plan. He did his best to present the split as temporary. He read out the names of the fifteen Igorrotes who were going with Hopkins. The tribespeople sat in silence, digesting the news. Feloa, who was not part of the colonel's group, was the first to speak up: When were they going? And for how long? Truman said that Hopkins would be taking them on the train the following morning. The other details were still to be finalized, but he hoped they wouldn't be apart long. This wasn't true, but Truman told himself it was a white lie. The tribespeople barely slept that night. The thought had never occurred to them that they might be split up.

The following morning when the time came to say their goodbyes, Maria hugged Tainan tightly. Hopkins had wanted to take Julio and Maria, but Truman had refused. He'd offered him Tainan instead. The boy spoke some English and could help translate. Tears coursed down Maria's cheeks as Hopkins and his fifteen Igorrotes exited the village. Daipan, who was standing close by, put her arms around Maria and reminded her the others would be back soon. Truman gazed over at them. He caught Daipan's eye and hurriedly looked away. He felt for them. Being alone in a strange place together had made the bonds between the tribespeople closer than ever.

Coney Island had been good to Truman, but he didn't want to get stuck there. His ambitions were bigger than Luna Park. He wanted to be the talk of America. And though he didn't have Hopkins's personal connections, Truman had already received offers for the Igorrotes from fair and amusement park operators in several US states. On top of that, Truman had just been made a handsome offer closer to home. He knew the gentlemanly thing to do would be to discuss it with Thompson first, but he was feeling impetuous.

The rivalry between the three big Coney parks—Dreamland, Luna Park, and Steeplechase—was intense. No trick was too dirty, no stunt too cheap when it came to getting one over on the competition. Despite the bitterness that existed between George Tilyou, the owner of Steeplechase; Thompson and Dundy at Luna Park; and Dreamland's William Reynolds, together the men had been hailed as the saviors of Coney, rescuing the seaside resort from its corrupt, criminal past of debauchery.

The lion's share of the praise belonged to Frederic Thompson, most observers agreed, the young man with the panatela, the slouch hat, the winning smile, and the unrivaled reserves of energy. "Do you remember Coney Island in the old days—a place where frothy beer, bold eyed females, strong-armed thugs and the foul-mouthed offspring of every gutter in the land ran things with an utter disregard of law and the rights of decent folk?"[4] asked an article in the *Spotlight*, the weekly political and current affairs newspaper. "Fred Thompson is the man who delivered the solar plexus [punch] to this picaresque social cesspool and he did it by opening Luna Park as a place where a man could bring his wife, his mother, his sister or his sweetheart without running the risk of having her confounded with the ladies of the-less-than-half-world."[5]

Dreamland was the newest of the three big parks, having opened the previous summer, and so far its owner William Reynolds, a former New York senator turned real estate developer, had failed in his bid to overtake Luna Park as the most popular, most profitable park in Coney Island. Reynolds was a businessman first and he didn't have the same feeling for amusement parks that his competitors over at Steeplechase and Luna Park had. If Luna Park was colorful and chaotic, Reynolds wanted Dreamland to be refined and elegant. Inspired by the Court of Honor at the heart of the Chicago World's Fair, Reynolds insisted that all the buildings in Dreamland be painted white. The former politician thought this would make his park seem classy, but visitors to Dreamland complained that it lacked the exoticism of Thompson's wonder world.

Where Thompson and Dundy were always pushing forward with new and exciting innovations, Reynolds simply ripped them off, creating replicas of his rivals' most popular attractions within his own gates. Where Reynolds did succeed was in portraying his park as a family-friendly place with an emphasis on wholesome fun and exhibits with a strong moral message, like The End of the World and Creation, which depicted the creation of the Earth in realistic scenes, from chaos to man. His most popular attraction was the Lilliputian Village, a miniature town populated by midgets, in which everything, from the vehicles and the houses to the furniture, was built to scale. It was Samuel Gumpertz who brought the vision for Lilliputia to life after he scoured America and beyond looking for little people to fill the town. Though business was brisk at Dreamland, Reynolds was not raking in the huge sums he had anticipated. He promoted Gumpertz to the position of general manager and charged him with turning things around.

Gumpertz had been pestering Truman for weeks to break his contract with Thompson and Dundy and bring the tribe over to his rival park. At first Truman had resisted, but Gumpertz had kept upping his offer until Truman could no longer refuse. Behind Thompson and Dundy's backs, Truman had agreed to deliver the Igorrotes to Dreamland on Sunday, August 6, 1905.

Truman summoned Julio to his office the day before the move and told him they were relocating across Coney Island to another park. The tribespeople would be better off at Dreamland. Thompson and Dundy had put a lot of pressure on him to make the dog feasts a daily feature of the village, said Truman. Samuel Gumpertz, the manager of Dreamland, would be more respectful of their customs. Julio was surprised. They had finally settled in at Luna Park and had assumed that they would be there till the end of the season. But if what Truman was saying was true, that at Dreamland they could present a more accurate version of their customs, then of course that was good news.

Before Julio could say anything, Truman told him that he had to go away on business that afternoon. Julio should have everyone ready to leave Luna Park early the following day, Sunday. They would go before the park opened. They should take their belongings with them along with whatever bits of the Igorrote Village they could carry. They would need to move quickly. Thompson lived on-site at Luna Park and he might try to stop them. They must not leave through Luna's main gates; rather, Callahan and Julio were to smuggle them out through a side exit. *Won't all the gates be locked?* asked the interpreter. *Callahan will take care of that*, said the showman. Once they arrived at Dreamland, Gumpertz would look after them. He had some publicity stunts lined up to announce their arrival and the Igorrotes should go along with them. Truman would be back within a few days. If there were any problems with the new arrangement, he would sort them out on his return.

When Julio woke the tribe early the next day and told them they were moving, all the tribespeople had one question: Why? Weren't they the stars of Luna Park? Julio relayed what Truman had said. Excited chatter broke out. But not all the tribespeople believed what they were hearing. Feloa and Dengay exchanged a suspicious glance. Fomoaley walked over to join them. Just then Callahan appeared and told everyone to get a move on. They had not a minute to lose. The tribespeople did as they were told and began packing up their possessions. The women scooped up armfuls of rings, bracelets, and fabrics.

A park worker noticed the commotion and rushed to fetch Thompson. The owner of Luna Park was fast asleep when the man called. He threw on his clothes and dashed over to the Igorrote Village just in time to see the tribespeople bundling up the last of their belongings.

It took a lot to anger Thompson. But he despised disloyalty and double-dealing. *Where are you going?* he demanded to know. Julio avoided his gaze. The tribe stood in silence. Someone must have offered Truman more money than he could say no to, thought the owner of Luna Park. Why hadn't Truman come to him first instead of going behind his back?

Thompson could hardly force the Igorrotes to stay against their will. They were wards of the United States government, and the government had given permission to Truman, and Truman alone, to exhibit them. Thompson had no choice but to watch as his biggest moneymaker walked out of Luna Park's gates. Where was that scoundrel Truman? It had been bad enough that the showman had leased some of the Igorrotes out to Hopkins, but now, to have the rest of the tribe simply leave like this and for Truman not even to have the decency to show up and give an account of himself, was unforgivable. Thompson had met many rogues in his career but Truman beat them all. Thompson vowed that he would make the showman pay for this.

Led by Callahan and trailed by Thompson, the Igorrotes emerged from the self-contained wonder world of Luna Park and out onto Surf Avenue. With the exception of Julio, it was the first time any of the Filipinos had stepped outside the park grounds in the three months since they had arrived in New York. An automobile glided past, its engine thrumming. Friday ran over to the edge of the sidewalk to get a better look. As the vehicle disappeared into the distance, the street fell eerily quiet. It would be several hours before the crowds arrived and the shooting gallery, the Boer War attraction, and the shops and sideshows opened up for another day. But this was not a sightseeing trip for the Filipinos. Callahan shouted at them to hurry up and cross the street. He could see Dreamland in the distance.

Thompson stood in the road cursing Truman, the Igorrotes, Gumpertz, and the whole double-dealing profession of hucksters and sideshow men that had deprived him of his tribe. Impotently he watched as the Filipino headhunters walked toward the gates of his biggest rival.

To the surprise of the American men and women who came to Luna Park later that day, they were greeted by a large sign in front of the Filipinos' deserted enclosure, which read, "The Igorrote Village has been closed by Messrs Thompson & Dundy because they would not permit the Igorrotes exhibiting some objectionable features."[6] It was a gesture designed to save face. The owners of Luna Park didn't want anyone to know that their biggest attraction had pulled up stakes and would soon be on display at Dreamland. But there was an irony in their choice of words; after all, it was the tribe's "objectionable features"—the near nudity, the dog slaughtering, and relative sexual freedom—that had made the Igorrotes such a hit.

Truman delivered a parting gift for Thompson and Dundy. After the tribe's departure, he sent a note to a reporter friend of his at the *New York Times* in which he quoted the tribal leader saying the dispute with the owners of Luna Park began as a labor strike in protest against the Americanization of their diet. According to the note, the Igorrotes had pleaded with Thompson and Dundy to allow them to return to a more authentic diet and a simpler life like the one they enjoyed back in the north Luzon wilds, and had "refused to dance a single step or utter one note of Igorrote music until their demands were recognized."[7] When Thompson and Dundy had refused, the Igorrotes had upped and left.

Though the Igorrotes were nervous about uprooting their lives again so soon, many of them were relieved to have left Luna Park. They had been complaining for weeks about their food and about some aspects of the show that they felt demeaned their customs. Truman had seemed sympathetic, but he was a busy man and in recent weeks he had been increasingly absent from Coney Island. Julio had heard good things said about Gumpertz, and with all this talk about a return to a more "authentic" way of life, the Igorrotes were hopeful that finally their complaints were going to be addressed.

Gumpertz was a balding, kind-looking man whose tiny spectacles gave him a scholarly air. The son of a lawyer, at the age of nine he'd run off to join the circus, working as an acrobat until a crash landing on his head from the top of the human pyramid abruptly ended his circus career. Undeterred, he went on to work with Buffalo Bill as one of his Congress of Rough Riders and later managed Harry Houdini. By 1905 he was regarded as one of the best men in the business and he knew his well-earned reputation was riding on this summer season. Eager to generate some publicity for his Igorrote Village, Gumpertz planned to transport his new arrivals back across the Brooklyn Bridge to Manhattan. Then they would return to Coney Island, where they would be presented to the press and the public as if they had just arrived direct from the Philippine Islands. Dreamland's press agent, a former journalist by the name of George Wotherspoon, had come up with the scheme and had invited a bunch of his newspaper friends to come along and meet the tribe. If anyone saw through the stunt, Gumpertz would simply say some of the Luna Park Igorrotes had joined his own group fresh off the boat from Manila.

Aware that the tribal chief and the translator might be recognized, Gumpertz told them to wait behind at Dreamland. Reporters, not remembering the faces of the Igorrotes they had already met, greeted the "new arrivals," who described the excitement they felt on seeing the New York skyline up close. The *Brooklyn Daily Eagle* recounted the moment when one of the tribesmen first clapped eyes on the Brooklyn Bridge and exclaimed, "The American man, he is god; he can do anything."[8] Gumpertz congratulated himself on pulling off his trick. Only the *New York Times* appeared to notice that the "new" Igorrotes at Dreamland had been living at Coney all summer, but no one else seemed to care.

Gumpertz had once managed a chain of seventeen theaters for Col. Hopkins and the two remained friendly. Hopkins happened to be in New York on business when Gumpertz took delivery of the Igorrotes and the colonel had suggested another stunt to intrigue the press: what if they invited a dentist along to inspect the teeth of Dreamland's newest residents?[9]

The Igorrotes had never seen a dentist in their lives and the public who turned out to witness the spectacle wondered whether their teeth would pass muster. The dentist arrived promptly, dressed in black trousers and a white cotton dental jacket, and proceeded to rig up a chair in the Igorrotes' enclosure, with a rope on each side. He selected two Igorrote helpers, whom he instructed to pull gently on the ropes whenever he raised his hand, thereby tipping the chair back so he could see inside his patients' mouths. The tribespeople were instructed to line up, roughly in order of age. Few of the Filipinos knew their real ages, though it mattered little—it was all just part of the show. The dentist then called each of the tribespeople forward individually and invited them to lie back while he peered into their mouths. Every now and again, he would reach for one of his instruments and poke around inside as if investigating some potentially troublesome discovery. When the last of the Igorrotes had been summoned to the chair and the inspection was complete, the dentist declared, to everyone's surprise, that the tribe's teeth were by and large in excellent condition.

After the show, Gumpertz encouraged the visitors to mill around inside the Igorrote Village and talk to the tribespeople. He wanted his exhibit to be more interactive than the village had been over at Luna. The Filipinos invited their visitors to come inside their half-built homes for a tour. The younger Igorrotes typically spoke better English than the older members of their tribe, having picked a bit up since they arrived in the country. They felt relaxed about Gumpertz's request that they mix with the Americans. They tried on their hats and gave them spears and shields in return.

By now the Igorrotes were utterly unselfconscious in front of their visitors. They invited them to dance and make music with them and praised those who joined in with the English words they'd picked up.

"Good boys," they cried as besuited American men danced around their campfire. The Igorrotes performed with renewed energy and vigor. For the first time in a while, they felt optimistic about what the future held. Their happiness would be short-lived.

Standing on a platform at the entrance to the village, Gumpertz announced that the Filipino tribespeople were about to celebrate their arrival at Dreamland with a dog feast, "the first they have had in several days as it was impossible to allow them the privilege while crossing the continent."[10] Feloa looked at Dengay. What was the meaning of this? Julio looked over at them. It must be a one-off, he thought. Truman had given them his word.

Crowds swarmed into the tribe's enclosure, eager to see the bizarre Igorrote custom. Gumpertz nodded to Callahan to bring in the dogs. The Igorrotes could see they had no choice: the show must go on.

The week after their move to Dreamland, Truman took twelve Igorrotes for a short trip to Atlantic City. There he led them on to the beach and instructed them to throw off their American clothes and run into the sea. The vacationers relaxing on the golden sand couldn't believe their eyes. Many got up from where they'd been sitting and rushed toward the ocean for a closer look. Women shielded their eyes. A murmur of unease passed through the crowd. A few teenage boys began to scoop up fistfuls of sand and throw it in the direction of the nearly naked tribespeople, who were gaily splashing in the surf. Soon the Filipinos were being pelted with stinging wet sand and the younger tribesmen started to square up for a fight. Lifeguards came running. Someone was sent to fetch the police and the mayor.[11]

The spectacle was the talk of the town. "Their attire was shocking," read the report on page one of the next day's *Atlantic City Daily Press*. "These Filipinos, in their native garb, would not be permitted to attend any function where scrutinizing eyes would glance them over. Their sole wearing apparel would not fill a trunk larger than a snuff box. At home, the laws of the wilds and woods, in which they live, do not call for full dress suits or overcoats. They simply roam around with the least possible amount of clothing. When they came to Atlantic City this week they did not take the trouble to go to the tailor and order new suits but held to their native dress. So when they appeared on the beach front yesterday, in their rather shocking garbs, the life crew found it necessary to order them off, or to don full-fledged American bathing suits. The crowd in that vicinity was hilarious for a time."[12] On the boat back to Coney, Truman praised the tribe for what he viewed as yet another publicity coup.

Coincidentally, and more soberly, that same week Secretary Taft gave a major speech in Manila about the future of the Philippines. "His frank declaration that while the United States want to give the people of the islands self-government this could not be done until they become capable of it will perhaps increase the dissatisfaction in a certain restless contingent. Among the American residents, as well as among the more substantial and intelligent Filipinos, however, this frank declaration that existing conditions are not to be disturbed will inspire a feeling of confidence that will stimulate material progress," concluded the *New York Herald*.[13]

In late August Truman appeared at the Dreamland Igorrote Village and announced he had some exciting news. That day they would be receiving two very special visitors. Ever since the Igorrotes had first arrived on American soil, Truman had seized on every opportunity to play up their anthropological and educational appeal. Now two well-known amateur anthropologists and photographers, Elizabeth and Sarah Metcalf, were coming to spend a week in the Igorrote Village. The spinster sisters, both in their late forties, had a long-held fascination with the Filipino tribes and would soon leave America to travel to the Philippines. There they planned to live among the tribespeople, photographing them at work and at play. At Coney they decided they would make a record of a different kind.[14]

"I have read and heard so much about the Igorrotes that I fully made up my mind to visit Dreamland and endeavor to have an interview with this peculiar race, and study their ways and language, the latter I am most anxious to learn," explained Sarah Metcalf, a graduate from the school of languages in Boston.[15]

The sisters brought a phonograph with them from their Massachusetts home. A crowd began to gather in the Igorrotes' enclosure as the sisters set up the machine. Truman looked on eagerly. He was delighted to see a large audience had turned out to witness the encounter for themselves. First, the Metcalfs played Filipino tribal folk tunes. To the Americans they sounded baleful and wailing, but the Igorrotes looked on with evident pleasure. When the recording reached an end, one of the sisters carefully removed the cylinder and replaced it with another, featuring popular American tunes. The crowd sang along, while one or two Igorrote children entertained them by dancing a jig. When the music finished, the sisters carefully placed a blank cylinder in the machine.[16]

Before they had set out for Coney, they had thought how marvelous it would be if they could make a recording of the Igorrotes' voices. It would be, they believed, the first time anyone had made an audio recording of Igorrote speech. Truman had given his permission. At the sisters' request, Gatonan,[17] one of the tribal elders, took up a position beside the phonograph and began to recite the Igorrote "headhunter's challenge," not realizing that he was being recorded. Truman explained to the crowd that this was a semisacred oath that preceded the decapitation of their enemies. At the showman's insistence, it had been worked into their daily displays at Coney. Gatonan finished speaking, and Elizabeth Metcalf wound up the phonograph so it would play the recording back. No one, not even Truman, could have anticipated what happened next.

The Igorrotes, upon hearing the headhunter's challenge emanate from a wooden box and not recognizing the voice, reacted with alarm, kicking the machine over into the Coney dirt. The public gasped. Several took fright and ran for the exit. Truman explained that the tribe had been afraid, assuming that the phonograph had been possessed by an evil spirit. The showman helped the sisters to pick up their machine, and reflected that he couldn't have dreamed up a better stunt himself. He was delighted to have an incident of such ethnological significance to report in case the authorities wrote requesting an update on the tribe's progress.

The appeal of the Igorrotes was anything but short-lived. Their famous fans included the popular Irish film actor Cyril Scott and the

Broadway and vaudeville star Blanche Deyo, who gave Truman a generous cash donation that she told him to use toward sending the Filipino children to school.[18] Scott brought a string of frankfurters, which he distributed to the tribe, quipping that he had considered bringing a dog but thought such a gift might get him into trouble.[19] He visited the Igorrotes so often that rumors began to circulate that he was set to play the role of a dusky Igorrote in his new play, *The Prince Chap*, at the Madison Square Theater the following month. For once, Truman wasn't behind the story.

By the height of the 1905 summer season, the Igorrotes were bringing in twenty thousand dollars a week (around five hundred and twenty-five thousand dollars in today's money), unimaginable riches at a time when an apartment could be rented on 42nd Street for four dollars a week and a mink coat sold on Fifth Avenue for around sixty dollars. If he had been careful, Truman could have lived off his earnings for years. But it wasn't in the showman's nature to save. He'd grown accustomed to the high life, living it up with Sallie in New York's finest restaurants and most exclusive clubs. And he had no intention of giving it up any time soon.

The showman's celebrations were rudely interrupted, however, when he got word that a rival promoter, Richard Schneidewind, had arrived in America with his own group of Igorrotes. Schneidewind had gotten his first booking at the Lewis and Clark Exposition in Portland, filling the gap left after Truman pulled out. Truman knew Schneidewind from the Philippines and St. Louis. From what he heard, he was working with Edmund Felder, the man who had left Truman stranded in Manila without any money to transport the tribe to America.

Truman had no desire to share his lucrative trade with anyone else. He would do whatever it took to put a stop to Schneidewind's business venture before it got off the ground. If Coney was anything to go by, Truman could soon have an Igorrote group in fairs and sideshows in every state in the union. He resolved to make this happen. Grabbing his hat, he made his way to the telegraph office. He had some pressing business to attend to.

11

Unexpected Arrivals

DREAMLAND, LATE AUGUST 1905

The Coney Island emergency hospital ambulance, c. 1905

SQUATTING ON THE dirt floor of her bamboo hut, Castro Mordez grimaced. As another stabbing pain shot through her pelvis, the young Filipina let out a shuddering moan. Reaching up with one hand, she clutched her swollen belly and inhaled deeply. The child wasn't due for weeks yet, but her body told her it was on its way. Luckily, the Igorrote women were accustomed to delivering babies. One tribeswoman stood rubbing Castro's back, two more positioned themselves on either side of her, and the eldest, most experienced woman in the tribe knelt on the ground between the woman's legs. Fairgoers milled around outside enjoying the sweltering summer's day, oblivious to the fact that a few feet away Coney's first-ever Igorrote baby was about to be born.

Arriving breathless at the door of Truman's bungalow, Julio banged loudly and shouted to his boss to come quickly. Castro was having a baby. The showman ran after Julio. They arrived at the hut where Castro lay just in time to hear an unmistakable squalling sound. *It's a boy,* shouted one of the women.

The minute Truman laid eyes on the boy, cradled in his mother's arms, he knew he would need help if he was going to thrive. The baby had a thick mop of black hair but was as tiny and fragile as a rabbit taken out of a trap. At the turn of the twentieth century, a baby born prematurely faced dismal chances of survival. "Weaklings," as babies born before thirty-seven weeks' gestation were known, were in most cases expected to die.

Ironically, the Igorrote baby had been born in the one place that offered the best chance of its survival—not a hospital, but Coney Island itself. Alongside the freak shows and the exotic people and animals, Coney was home to Dr. Couney's Infant Incubators attraction.

Truman begged the new mother to put her baby in one of the incubators. Born in Alsace, France, and trained in Berlin, Dr. Couney was a heavyset man with a pronounced stoop and a graying mustache who had "the firm but gentle grasp that a man might have after a life of handling canary birds."[1] He wore spats and a suit of dark broadcloth and never went out without his derby and crook-handled cane.

The doctor began his work at a time when incubators were catching on in European hospitals, but America had been slow to embrace the new technology. He took in premature babies from New York hospitals that lacked the facilities to care for them. Others were brought to him directly by their desperate parents. All were placed in tiny incubators where a thermostat-controlled system blew filtered air over hot-water pipes to maintain the proper incubator temperature. The doctor employed fifteen trained nurses and medical technicians to look after the babies along with five wet nurses who fed the babies with breast milk. For twenty-five cents, the public could peer through the glass at the incubator babies, boys tied with blue ribbons and girls with pink. In 1905, each baby cost around fifteen dollars a day to care for. The parents weren't charged a penny by the doctor, who recouped all the costs from the entrance fees.

Dr. Couney's groundbreaking exhibit was credited with saving six and a half thousand tiny lives before he finally retired in 1943.[2]

His patients included his own daughter, Hildegarde, who was born weighing less than three pounds, but who, on graduating from the incubators, went on to become one of his nurses.

Truman crouched down beside Castro and asked if he could hold the baby. She nodded and Truman scooped him from her hands. He could feel the boy's heart fluttering in his tiny rib cage. They would go to see Dr. Couney now. The sooner the child was put in an incubator, the greater his chance of survival. Castro shook her head; the best place for him was with her, not in a glass box. She would trust his fate to Lumawig, the Igorrotes' god. The other tribespeople standing around her agreed.

Truman frowned. He might not be able to persuade her to use the infant incubators, but he would insist that mother and child go to the hospital. Coney's first Igorrote baby was too precious to take any chances with. Truman hurried over to the telephone exchange. There he placed a call to the Coney Emergency Hospital, asking for an ambulance to be sent over immediately. They didn't have incubators, but they had nurses and doctors who he would pay handsomely to save the child.

A small, wooden building, one block from the beach, the Coney hospital had twenty beds and was only open in the summer. Its staff was more accustomed to taking care of revelers who had imbibed too much alcohol in Coney's beer halls or cut their feet while paddling in the sea than looking after the newborn babies of exotic tribespeople.

Staff immediately whisked the mother and baby off in different directions to be cared for in separate parts of the hospital, as was customary at the time. The nurses looking after the baby placed him on the scales. He weighed just three and a half pounds, roughly the same as a newborn piglet. Castro spoke no English and had been hysterical when her baby was taken away, but Truman assured her that the child would receive the best care possible. He sat with her awhile and told her she would see her baby later. On his way out, Truman approached the nurses' station. Addressing the youngest, most attractive one in the group, he told her to call for him at Dreamland if there was any change in mother or baby's condition.

When the nurse went to check on her new patient, she found the pretty, dark-skinned Filipina had fallen into a deep sleep. Her black hair cascaded over the starched, white hospital sheets. She looked tiny in her huge sterile bed. The nurse wrapped her fingers around Castro's wrist and felt for her pulse. The new mother was breathing deeply. She seemed well, considering all she had been through. The nurse walked around to the foot of the bed and picked up her notes—her records said she was in her twenties but she didn't look a day over sixteen. Castro stirred and nuzzled her face back into her pillow as the nurse turned to leave.

She wondered how this young woman, who had turned up at the hospital wearing nothing but a blanket, had gotten to Brooklyn. How does someone from the Philippines end up on show at Coney Island? And where had she gotten such an unusual name? If only the two women had spoken the same language, Castro Mordez could have explained that she had plucked the name from the air when she came to America.

The nurse left her patient to rest. Outside a reporter was hanging around. He begged the nurse to let him see the new mother, just for a minute. She shook her head. The young woman had been through a lot and she needed rest, she said, pointing him toward the exit. Reluctantly, the newspaperman put his notebook in his pocket. He had learned enough earlier from his contact on the ward to write a story about Mrs. Castro Mordez. Though, according to his source, there might be reason to doubt the "Mrs." part. He would come back early the next day.

Truman was sitting in his office the morning after the baby's birth, plotting his next move. He was busier than ever. Not only were the Igorrotes attracting record crowds at Dreamland, but Truman had more bookings piling up. He was tired after all the excitement of the new arrival and had drunk more coffee than he probably should in a bid to stay awake. The Igorrote baby would be a major boost for business. The tribe was already bringing in a handsome profit, but it was always good to have something novel to sell. And now he did, something very special indeed. The first-ever Igorrote child born at Coney Island. Now that was something.

He took out his pen and began composing a press announcement. Strictly speaking it was the Dreamland press agent's job, but Truman preferred to take care of these things himself. He would send it out to newspapers all over America and beyond. The *Manchester Guardian* in England had written about Truman and his Igorrotes before. He must send news of the birth to the paper's editor.

But first he would take a quick look at the newspapers. It paid to stay abreast of what was happening in the world. Truman picked up the *New York Times.* The birth of baby Mordez on Wednesday, August 30, had coincided with a partial solar eclipse, which had been watched by astronomers and citizens in countries all over the world. Truman thought this auspicious for the next chapter of his Igorrote venture. He continued reading and began to laugh; according to the article, New Yorkers who had scrambled out of bed before five o'clock in the hope of witnessing something extraordinary hadn't been able to see a thing, so heavy were the rain clouds that had obscured their view entirely.[3]

Truman tossed the paper aside and picked up the *Tribune.* A headline on page three caught his eye: FILIPINOS NOT FIT TO RULE—CONGRESSMEN REPORTED OPPOSED TO GRANTING SPEEDY INDEPENDENCE.[4] It was a special report from the Philippines on the ongoing visit of Secretary Taft. The article summed up the consensus of opinion among Taft and the congressmen present at a conference in Manila that "the Filipinos are altogether unfit for immediate independence. Apart from the problems presented in the civilization of the Igorrotes, the Moros, Macabebes and other tribes, it would be cruel, it is believed to the people of the islands at large to turn them over to the mercies of theorists and demagogues."[5]

There was a loud knock at the door. Truman walked over and opened it. Standing outside his bungalow were two men he didn't recognize. The first announced himself as Thomas McGuire and said he was a state detective. He produced his shield, number 133. Behind him was an officer who said he had been sent by Captain Dooley of Coney Island's West Eighth Street Police Station.[6] They asked if he was Dr. Truman Knight Hunt. Truman glanced around outside the door and invited the two men to step into his office.

Confirming his identity, Truman offered the men coffee. Or if they fancied something stronger, he had a fine bottle of whiskey. Both men declined. This was not a social call. They were here on official business, namely a charge of bigamy, which had been lodged by a Mrs. Else Hunt. McGuire searched Truman's face for signs of guilt. The showman was impassive as he declared the accusation against him most odd. He had indeed been married before, to a girl named Myrtle. But his first wife had died tragically young, twelve years previously. McGuire asked Truman if he would be so good as to accompany them to the police station to answer a few questions. Truman picked up his hat and coat, and followed the men out the door.

12

Another Unwelcome Visitor

NEW YORK CITY, AUGUST 31, 1905

DR. HUNT ARRESTED AT CONEY.

Bigamy Charge, Say Police—Non-Support, Says Wife's Lawyer.

Headline from the New York Sun, *September 1, 1905*

THE STEAK DINNER sat cold and untouched on the dining room table. Sallie tried not to worry. Business often took Truman away on short notice and he had made a point of impressing this on Sallie early on in their courtship. It had only made him seem more mysterious and appealing. Besides, truth be told, he could be a little forgetful when it came to his appointments. Sallie sat at the table, staring at all the food. What a waste. She didn't enjoy cooking and wasn't particularly good at it, but she had made a special effort that night. There seemed little point sulking, though. What good would it do? Truman would be in later, full of stories about his day. He always had interesting tales to tell of people he'd met and things that had happened. For these, and the excitement he brought with him, she could forgive him just about anything.

Sallie smiled. What interesting lives they had compared to their relatives back home. She missed her daddy, her sisters, her brother, and her aunt back in Kentucky. She had lived with them her whole life until she moved to St. Louis and met Truman. But she wouldn't trade the life she had now—the fine restaurants, the jewels, the thrills—for anything. Just that week, Truman had bought her another beautiful evening gown. It was made of silk and was the prettiest shade of peach. It wasn't even her birthday. During the day she often opened the doors of her closet and gazed at it, sometimes taking it out and holding it against her body. The baby wasn't showing yet, but she felt certain it would soon. Truman was sending her to White's, the photographers on Broadway, to have a portrait photograph done. She'd joked that she'd better go soon before she got too fat.

Sallie pushed her chair back from the table and got up. She liked to be up to welcome Truman when he came home, but it was late and she could barely keep her eyes open. She scribbled him a note, apologizing for going to bed before he got in, and left it on the table. Before taking off her clothes and putting on her nightgown, she opened her closet and peeked at her new dress. She hoped she would get a chance to wear it that weekend. Maybe Truman would take her to the new French restaurant he'd been talking about.

Truman's mother always said her boy could talk himself out of anything. Her theory was being put to the test at the West Eighth Street Police Station, just a stone's throw from Dreamland. Truman told McGuire and the police captain, Robert Dooley, that he had not and would not treat any lady badly, let alone engage in a bigamous marriage. He searched for possible explanations. Maybe his accuser was a madwoman. Or an opportunist who had read about the enormous success of the Igorrotes. Or maybe it was someone who'd known Myrtle, his first wife, and didn't know she'd passed away. Captain Dooley had been stationed in Coney Island for two years and in that time he had heard every excuse going. He bid Truman a good night and turned the key in the cell door. Instead of enjoying the warm embrace of his wife, the showman would be spending the night with the Coney thieves and drunks.

Though the thought didn't occur to Truman, his cell was roughly equivalent in both size and comfort to the Igorrotes' huts at Coney. He was lucky—though he didn't feel lucky that night—that his arrest was not on a weekend. On Saturdays and Sundays, every thug, troublemaker, and opportunist operating along the eastern coast of America seemed to descend on the rougher parts of Coney Island, packing the cells to bursting point. He was also lucky that the recent hot weather had finally broken. When the mercury climbed, the cells became unbearable with the heat and the stench of urine and sweat.

It didn't take long for word to get out among New York's newspapermen that Truman was in a bit of trouble. His success, not to mention his frequent visits with Sallie to New York's most expensive restaurants and clubs, had made him a well-known figure in the city. Bigamy was unusual in early-twentieth-century America. It was regarded as a serious and shameful crime, punishable with up to five years in prison and a fine of five hundred dollars. If Truman was found guilty, disgrace beckoned.

A pack of reporters sat waiting as Truman was led into the Harlem courtroom of Magistrate Voorhees the following morning. Truman eyed the empty prosecution table. Voorhees called for the complainant to make herself known, but there was no sign of Else Hunt, her attorney, or the arresting officer. Raising his eyebrows, the magistrate looked at Truman. Under the circumstances, he told him, he had no option but to discharge him. Truman stood up and put on his hat, inwardly sighing in relief as he made for the exit. Outside the courtroom he was pounced on by the group of waiting reporters. The showman greeted them with a friendly smile but refused to make any comment. He had no desire for his personal life to make headlines.

Sallie was delighted when her husband showed up later that morning. What on earth had happened to him, she wanted to know, as she gazed at his disheveled appearance. Truman explained that some unexpected business had kept him away. He'd missed her and had impulsively decided to pay her a visit before returning to work. Sallie fussed over him and fixed him something to eat. Then she disappeared into the bedroom to find him clean clothes to wear.

She was so loving and devoted to him that Truman found it difficult to tear himself away, but he couldn't stay long. Yesterday's unexpected events had put him behind schedule. He must visit the hospital and find out how the Igorrote mother and baby were doing.

Truman stirred sugar into his coffee. He had received a request from the Kentucky State Fair to take the Igorrotes there. He couldn't wait to tell Sallie, but he would hold off on sharing the news until the deal was signed. He planned to invite her whole family to visit the fair at his expense. Their families hadn't been at their wedding because it had been arranged in too much of a hurry. Truman wanted to make up for that. The showman got on well with Sallie's favorite sister, Catherine, whom he'd met when she visited St. Louis, but he sensed he had not gotten off to the best start with her father, who he knew meant the world to her.

Truman thought of his own father, who had died fifteen years earlier. Myrtle had passed away three years later, and Truman had believed he would never be able to love another woman again. When he went to the Philippines, he didn't want for attention from women. He had met Else there, the woman now accusing him of bigamy. How he wished he had never set eyes on her. Their first meeting felt like a lifetime ago.

Sallie's sweet singsong voice calling from the bedroom interrupted his reverie. This nasty business had stoked up a lot of memories that were best left in the past. He must get to work.

The weather was pleasant, sunny but not too hot, the day after Truman's arrest. The showman stepped onto the train to Coney and immediately felt his mood improve as he caught the eye of a pretty stranger sitting near the door. He tipped his hat in her direction and flashed her a broad smile. He couldn't resist. It was Friday and he felt his equilibrium restoring. The takings always went through the roof on the weekends. He would take Sallie out to dinner on Saturday night. Somewhere fancy. They would go to a show afterward. Truman made a mental list of tasks for the day ahead. After checking on the village, he'd go to the hospital. He needed a new baby story to sell. Maybe they could run a competition to name the baby, get visitors to come up with suggestions and offer a prize for the winner. He was distracted momentarily as the pretty woman got up to leave the train. Truman smiled, his blue eyes following her as she walked over to the door. She smiled back and was gone. He wondered where she was headed.

The showman had bought an armful of newspapers on his way to the train and now, free of distractions, he began leafing through them. The papers would have received his press statement about the baby the previous day and he wanted to see what they had written. He opened the *New York Tribune* and began scanning the headlines. His eyes alighted on a story under the headline MRS. T. K. HUNT, WIFE OF IGORROTE MANAGER, CHARGES HUSBAND WITH BIGAMY.[1] The article described his arrest at Dreamland and said he'd spent a night in the cells. Truman hurriedly stuffed the paper under his arm. Then he opened the *New York Times*. His arrest had made page three.[2] What was a quality paper like the *Times* doing reporting this nonstory? There was no charge to answer—the alleged complainant had not come to court. Truman had assumed that when he left court that would be the end of the matter, but how wrong he had been. His face was growing red. He couldn't stop himself from opening the *Brooklyn Daily Eagle*. There it was, at the bottom of the left-hand column on page three, DR. TRUMAN HUNT ARRESTED ON BIGAMY CHARGE.[3]

His arrest had made all the papers. Apparently he was as newsworthy as the Igorrotes themselves. And for once he wasn't the one controlling the stories. He didn't like it one bit.

Truman didn't want to read any more. But before he could stop himself, his eyes alighted on a headline on the front page of the *New York Sun:* DR. HUNT ARRESTED AT CONEY.[4] The *Sun* was alone in having spoken to the complainant's attorney, Fred C. McLaughlin, who said Truman had met the complainant four years previously in the Philippines, where she was working as a nurse. Shaking his head, Truman read on. McLaughlin accused Truman of abandoning his wife and a three-year-old child and leaving them destitute.

Truman was so angry he almost missed his stop. He rushed from his seat and got off the train. He would go and see the editor of the *Sun* that day to demand an apology. The showman was well connected in the newspaper industry. He would contact the editors of all of these rags to complain. You didn't rubbish the reputation of Dr. Truman Hunt and get away with it. He was thankful that he didn't get any newspapers delivered at home.

If anyone asked him about it, he'd tell them it was a vicious lie made up by a rival who was envious of his success. This was true—all the other showmen were jealous of his Igorrote group and the fortune they were making him. Coney would soon close for the season. For four months, the Igorrotes had been the star attraction, vastly outearning everything else. This fact alone had earned him many enemies, who, he knew, would be delighted to see his enterprise founder.

Truman walked up Surf Avenue and tried to put the matter from his mind. He always felt comforted by the sights and sounds of Coney Island. Walking through the gates of Dreamland, he felt in a strange way as if he was coming home. As a boy growing up in Iowa, he'd loved fairs and circuses and thought how marvelous it must be to be a Barnum or a Bailey. He had looked forward with great excitement to the annual state fair, and would never forget the legendary trick rider C. L. DeWolf, who rode twenty miles in one hour and five minutes at the 1878 fair, changing horses every half mile. He rode the last half mile with no saddle or bridle and lassoed a buffalo.

Now here Truman was, living his own dream. He loved his work and the freedom it gave him to pull up stakes and move around at a moment's notice. At first Sallie had not understood his lifestyle and had begged him to buy them a home. But when he had explained that his business required him to spend much of the year traveling, it hadn't taken much to persuade her of the romanticism of such a nomadic existence. Until the previous year, she had never been outside of Kentucky. With Truman she would get to see the whole country, something most Americans could only dream of.

No one could feel down at Coney for long. The bright lights, the smiling faces, and all the fun of the fair had a cheering effect. So too did counting the day's profits. He and Sallie deserved a treat. She had been tired and was suffering badly with pregnancy sickness. They would go away for a short break. A change of scene would do them good. Julio and Callahan could look after the Igorrotes. He would tell them that he'd be gone for a few days.

Just as soon as he'd collected the takings and paid a quick visit to the hospital, he would go home and tell Sallie to pack a bag. As he walked toward his office, Truman was startled to hear a voice in his ear. Beside him was a man in the distinctive black peaked cap and bronze badge of the New York Police Department. The man announced himself as Officer John J. Allen. There was another man with him but Truman didn't catch his name. They handed Truman some official looking papers. Looking down, Truman saw the typewritten words *wife abandonment* and *bigamy*. He felt his stomach lurch.

Trying to hand the papers back to the officer, Truman said there must have been a mistake, the matter had been cleared up the previous day. When Officer Allen persisted, Truman grew exasperated. The officer held up the warrant, signed by Magistrate Sewell Barker of the Fifth District Court in Manhattan. The complainant was Mrs. Else W. Hunt. Truman didn't want to cause a scene, not here in his own workplace. He agreed to go with the officer, but first he said he must have a brief word with one of his business associates.

Gumpertz was in his office when Truman called. Problems with the law were not unheard of at Coney. When Truman explained the trouble, the Dreamland manager offered to go with him. He could post bail on the spot if necessary. They must secure an attorney. Gumpertz knew of a first-rate chap, named Ridgway. He would telephone his office immediately. The last thing Gumpertz needed was to lose the manager of his most popular attraction.

Across Surf Avenue in Luna Park, Fred Thompson roared with delight as he read of Truman's night in the cells in that day's newspapers. Thompson picked up the receiver. He was going to telephone his newspaper friends to give them a few more juicy tidbits about his former business partner. That would teach Truman to double-cross him.

Truman's day was going from bad to worse. He found himself back in the Harlem courtroom of Magistrate Voorhees on Friday, September 1, and this time Else Hunt, the complainant, was there too. Truman listened as the charges of bigamy and wife abandonment were read out. Voorhees asked Else for her address, which she gave as 109 West 135th Street, Manhattan. Then Voorhees invited her to state her case.

The magistrate detected a lilt to her accent. Truman looked at the woman standing across the courtroom with barely concealed loathing. Purposely avoiding Truman's gaze, Else said that she was born in Germany and had come to America in 1888, aged eighteen. Her home since that time had mostly been in New York. She was a trained nurse and in late 1899, her work had taken her to the Philippines.

There she met Truman Hunt and they had a whirlwind romance, marrying on June 9, 1902. Two days before the couple celebrated their first wedding anniversary, Else gave birth to a son, whom they named Philip after the Philippine Islands where he was born. In 1904, she and Philip had journeyed back to America with Truman, who had a job at the St. Louis World's Fair. Truman worked long hours at the fair and Else felt isolated, spending her days at home with a young baby. Truman suggested Else and Philip go to live for a time in New York, where she had many friends. Else had agreed to the plan. But after she moved to New York, she had hardly heard from her husband. Since the spring of 1904, she had seen him only once, when he had come to her apartment and had stayed just an hour.

Else wept as she explained she had been trying to find her husband since December 1904, when he had abruptly, and without warning, stopped paying her a monthly sum of one hundred dollars to cover the living costs of herself and Philip. She knew Truman wasn't hard up. He had earned at least ten thousand dollars from the St. Louis Igorrote Village and she believed he had earned many times that at Coney this summer. Someone in the press gallery whistled. That was a lot of money. The magistrate called for silence and invited Else to continue. She explained that she had finally been alerted to the whereabouts of her missing husband when a friend of hers had read about the Igorrote Village at Coney Island.

Else paused for a moment. Swallowing hard, she continued: mutual friends had informed her that Truman had married another woman, Sallie Gallagher, despite still being married to her, Else. Sallie and Truman had been cohabiting in New York all summer. Looking down, Else spoke softly, as if she couldn't bear to hear what she had to say next. Truman had cheated on her—not just with Sallie, there had been other women too. The magistrate asked her to speak up.

Else repeated what she had just said. *Do you mean to allege that your husband committed adultery with more than one woman?* asked Voorhees. *Yes, sir*, replied Else, her face a picture of misery.

When it was his turn to speak, Truman's attorney, James W. Ridgway, insisted that his client was an innocent man and dismissed Else's claims as an outrage. "My client, Dr. Hunt, is under $10,000 bonds to the United States [government] to guarantee the Igorrote people, and such an action in taking a man of his education and refinement and throwing him into a cell is simply outrageous," he continued, referring to the showman's recent incarceration.[5] The judge set bail at five hundred dollars and adjourned proceedings until the following Wednesday. Gumpertz paid the bail money and Truman was released. How Truman wished Else would crawl back into whichever gutter she'd emerged from. He sincerely hoped he could keep Else and this unpleasantness a secret from Sallie.

Two days after Truman's second arrest, on Sunday, September 3, 1905, a reporter from the *Nashville American* walked up Seventh Street in Louisville, Kentucky, looking for the home of Mr. Patrick Gallagher, a railroad clerk. When he found number 1139, he knocked firmly on the door. He heard footsteps from inside and a few seconds later the door opened. The reporter looked up at the man standing in the doorway. He was in his fifties with graying hair and tired-looking eyes. The newspaperman asked him if he was Patrick Gallagher, father of Sallie. Patrick Gallagher frowned and confirmed that he was. The reporter asked if Sallie was married to a man by the name of Truman Hunt. Gallagher nodded and looked suddenly concerned. Had something happened to her?

Did you know, Mr. Gallagher, the reporter continued, *that your daughter's husband was recently arrested at Coney Island on a charge of bigamy?* Gallagher's face crumpled in confusion. There must be some mistake. Truman was a doctor and a successful businessman. The reporter asked Sallie's father if he had any comment to make. Patrick Gallagher stood silently for a moment. Then, slowly closing the door in the man's face, he muttered that, no, he had nothing to say.[6] Inside, Sallie's father sat down at the kitchen table. It couldn't be true. They must have confused Truman with someone else. He would speak to Sallie. But how could he bring the subject up? No, he must put the matter from his mind.

That same day, an article appeared in the *St. Louis Globe Democrat* under the headline, DID HUNT MARRY FILIPINO WOMAN?[7] The article was short, with little in the way of concrete facts, but it was enough to spark rumors among Truman's acquaintances and those who knew of the recent Igorrote birth at Coney. There had been no mention of the baby's father. Truman had earned a reputation as a ladies' man when he was in St. Louis. In the Philippines he had flirted freely with the local women. Could he have gone further and sired an Igorrote's child? There was more to come. According to the article, when Truman married Sallie Gallagher it was understood by those who knew the showman in the Philippines that she would become the second Mrs. Hunt, the first having gotten divorced while visiting friends in Germany. There was no mention of Myrtle. Sitting at his desk in St. Louis reading the article, Col. Hopkins guffawed. He had been asked to comment but, in the interests of remaining on good terms with his business partner, he had declined to say anything beyond stating that he didn't know of any Filipino bride.

On Wednesday, September 6, *Hunt v. Hunt* was called in the Fifth District Court in Manhattan. Truman could hardly bring himself to look at Else again. Just when his life had been going so well, she had come along to destroy everything—his work, his reputation, his personal life—and had made the last seven days among the most unpleasant of his existence. A pack of reporters looked on, hopeful that they were about to get a juicy story for the next edition.

The clerk read the charges out before Magistrate Sewell Barker. Truman forced himself to look at Else. She met his gaze and held it for a moment before looking away. The showman found it hard to believe that he had once loved this woman. More than a year had passed since he had last visited her. Else had been beautiful in her prime, her Germanic roots giving her an exotic air. Now, standing there in court, she was unrecognizable. Truman was no longer listening as she described the misery he had inflicted on her. She might as well have been describing someone else. Her vitality had once bewitched him, but it had gone, leaving behind a haggard, middle-aged woman. He looked at her eyes. He had always loved her eyes. But now they were sad and jaded. Truman wondered what Philip, his first and only son, looked like now. He would be two. Whom did he take after? He was bound to be bright. The showman's second wife might have grown old and lined, but she wasn't lacking in intelligence.

In St. Louis he and Else had tried to play at being a happy family, but their fights had grown more frequent and increasingly bitter. Truman was hardly ever at home. He had grown tired of Else and of having a screaming infant around. He had also met Sallie during this time. He said he was working day and night, but Else had accused him of going out drinking and taking up with other women. Truman couldn't stand it anymore and, after a month of arguments, he had suggested that Else and Philip go and get an apartment in New York, where she had lived before their marriage and still had many friends. He told her he would send them money and would visit as often as he could. But he went just once to the Manhattan boardinghouse where she took a room. They spent only a short time together that day in the summer of 1904 and all they did was argue. Truman had left in a rage, hoping never to set eyes on her again. But he hadn't reconciled himself to losing all contact with his son. He liked to think that he and Philip would be reunited one day. That was, if Else hadn't poisoned the boy's mind against him. A son, especially a first son, was a special person in a man's life.

Three months after that last meeting with Else, the showman had proposed to Sallie. They held their wedding ceremony in the Igorrote Village in St. Louis. Truman had suggested it and, seeing how much it meant to him, Sallie had gone along with it, but afterward she had begged him to marry her again, this time in a Catholic church. Her Irish Catholic family's approval meant everything to her, even if they couldn't be at the service. The couple's second wedding, in December 1904, was a short service before two witnesses in a church in Portland, Oregon.

Deep down, Truman knew that he was not at liberty to marry Sallie. But divorce did not come cheap and the laws in New York, where Else was living, were among the toughest in the nation. Besides, his marriage to Else had taken place in the Philippines; it was hardly the same as a bona fide marriage in America. He told himself that what he and Else had in the Philippines was more like a common-law arrangement. Truman could persuade himself of anything if it made his own life easier. The day he married Sallie, Truman stopped sending the checks to Else.

Truman had a faraway gaze as Else recounted how she had no means of supporting herself and their son after Truman stopped sending her money. She couldn't return to her job as a nurse with an infant to care for and she didn't want to write to her family in Germany asking for funds. She still had her pride and she couldn't bring herself to tell her parents what a rogue her husband had turned out to be. She knew there were charities in New York for women in her position, but she didn't want to live off handouts. Why should she, when her husband and the father of her child was a wealthy man?

Else had waited awhile after Truman lost touch, assuming she would hear from him again in time. He had always had a habit of disappearing and then resurfacing again when it suited him, with little in the way of an explanation. But when the weeks turned into months and still she didn't hear anything, she had grown concerned. She had contacted friends, former colleagues in the Philippines, and people she'd met in St. Louis, inquiring about her husband's whereabouts. She and Truman had had their troubles like any couple, but she couldn't believe he would just disappear like that without so much as a word.

Recently a trusted friend had come to visit and had shown her an article in the *New York Times* about the Igorrotes who were at Coney Island with their former lieutenant governor, Truman Hunt. Else knew her husband was far from perfect, but how could he have been in New York and not even called to see how they were? Did he really believe he could just cast her and Philip aside as if he had never known them? Had he already erased them from his mind?

Magistrate Barker looked pityingly at the complainant. He had a good deal of sympathy for abandoned women and children. He was a firm believer in the sanctity of marriage and felt strongly that bigamists should be punished in the most severe terms. But try as he might to find a way to move forward and examine the charges against Truman Hunt, there were legal technicalities. Crucially, it had come to his attention that neither party had a permanent address in New York. This, Barker judged, meant the court had no jurisdiction in the matter. Despite Dr. Hunt's evident wealth, he had no legal residence anywhere. And Else Hunt was living in temporary accommodation. Under these circumstances, Barker had no option but to discharge the prisoner. The magistrate announced his verdict and declared that any case against Dr. Hunt would have to be brought in the Philippines, where the two had allegedly married and had their child. Truman Hunt was a free man. Else broke down and sobbed.

The showman breathed a sigh of relief. He never wanted to hear about the filthy business again. Leaving the courtroom, he refused to give any comment to the waiting newspapermen beyond stating that the allegations against him were lies. Those who knew Truman were faced with one of two explanations. Either he was the subject of a bizarre allegation made by a deranged woman or he was a man capable of denying the existence of his own wife and infant child.

13

The End of the American Dream

DREAMLAND, EARLY SEPTEMBER 1905

Dreamland, 1905

TRUMAN CALLED JULIO into his office just after one o'clock in the morning and instructed him to tell the tribe to pack up. The interpreter looked puzzled. Truman told him they were going on a trip and handed Julio a list of names. Those whose names were on the list were traveling with him by train that night. The rest were to stay behind at Dreamland until the close of the season. Julio looked at the list and noticed his own name and Maria's. He read on and opened his mouth to protest. *You have split up some of the married couples*, he said, begging Truman to allow him to amend the list. Truman looked momentarily confused, then told him to make the changes quickly. Julio's hand glided over the paper, scoring out names and adding others. When he was satisfied that he had made the best selection he could, he showed the paper to his boss. Truman glanced at it and nodded his approval. Then he shooed the interpreter out of his bungalow with the instruction to make sure those who were leaving were packed up and ready to go within the hour.

The park gates were locked and all the attractions had been shut up for the night. Julio called to the tribespeople to gather around. He was going to read out a list of names and those people were to start packing immediately. They would be leaving Dreamland before daybreak. Maria looked up at him, unable to believe what she was hearing. Julio began calling out names, aware that many of them would be leaving behind relatives and close friends. The Filipinos looked at one another. Where were they going? Julio shrugged and, with a sorrowful expression, confessed he didn't know.

Friday rushed up to the interpreter. Could he take his dog? Julio was about to answer that he couldn't when he was interrupted by Feloa. How long would they be apart? Would they be joining the others who had left with Col. Hopkins weeks earlier? Julio told them to keep their voices down. He wondered whether Samuel Gumpertz knew he was about to lose half of his Igorrotes. The interpreter sensed that the uncertainty over the arrangements was making everyone nervous. Julio looked over at Maria, who had started helping some of the younger ones to pack. Maria liked Dreamland. Gumpertz had taken a paternalistic interest in the tribe and, despite their initial fears, he had not pressured them to eat dog every day. Julio knew she would be sorry to leave.

While the Igorrotes packed, Truman was gathering his own things. He took out his watch; it was just after one-thirty. He sat down and lit a cigar. He had made this decision on impulse. The reappearance of Else had unsettled him in a way that he did not fully understand. He was used to writing his own story; he hated surprises. Who knew what that woman might do next? Even Sallie, who could usually see no wrong in her husband, had noticed that Truman had been irritable and moody lately. How he hated Else for what she had done. Just as his life was going so well, up she'd popped to make trouble and to try and grab his money. He would do everything in his power to make sure she didn't get any of it. He had a new wife now, and soon there would be a new baby. If Sallie got her wish, there would be many more children to follow.

There was another factor, of course, in his decision to tour the tribe: money. Truman had earned a fortune at Coney, but he had also spent one. He and Sallie had been enjoying the high life for months, and in New York a fortune could be lost with remarkable ease. Truman didn't want to trouble his wife but he was worried about money. Even though he'd gotten off the bigamy charge, it had cost him dearly. Ridgway was a gifted attorney and his prices were scaled to match his reputation.

The Coney season would soon be drawing to a close. Farther south there were state fairs crying out for headline acts, not to mention amusement parks that ran right through the winter months. As the Igorrotes' fame had spread out from New York, Truman had been inundated with offers from as far afield as Memphis, St. Louis, Detroit, Dallas, Atlanta, and New Orleans. He had confirmed bookings in Memphis, Macon, and Dallas. He had enough money in his wallet to get half of the thirty-five tribespeople at Dreamland to Memphis, their first stop. They would be living hand-to-mouth for a while, but in Memphis they would soon make enough in ticket sales to pay for their train travel to their next stop. When the season closed at Dreamland, he would send someone to collect the others.

Truman often daydreamed about the grand tour of America he would take his Igorrotes on. But why stop at America? They could soon be performing in front of the King of England in London and at the Presidential Palace in Paris. He felt certain that the tribe's success at Coney could be replicated anywhere he chose to take them.

The showman was excited about getting on the road again. He was eager to put some distance between himself and his second wife. He hadn't told Sallie about Else. He knew he should—he didn't want her hearing from anyone else. But he had to find the right moment. Sallie had a jealous streak and a mean Irish temper. She had been able to accept the existence of his daughter, Calista. The fact that her mother was no longer alive helped, but if she knew Truman had had another child, especially a son and heir, with yet another woman, she would be crushed. Once they were out of New York, Truman would tell her about Else. Not the truth, of course—he would say they had worked together and she had been infatuated with him. When he had turned down her advances, she had gone mad with rage and had come to New York to seek her revenge. He would claim to have no knowledge of Philip.

Adele was the only friend of Truman's in New York who had known Else. He knew he could trust his old friend not to speak to his second wife, or gossip about the past to anyone else. The showman had introduced Adele to Else in the Philippines. The two women had bonded over their European roots but Adele's loyalties lay with Truman. The pair shared a talent for self-invention and a deep bond based on mutual respect and admiration. When the trouble with Else had first blown up, Truman had toyed with the idea of asking Adele to pay his second wife a visit. Maybe she could gently persuade Else to drop the matter. In the end he had decided against it. Adele was a wealthy, well-connected society lady. It didn't seem appropriate to involve her.

The showman awoke from his reverie and noticed his cigar had gone out. He relit it and swept the papers on his desk into a briefcase. Outside he could hear Julio shouting orders. They would be out of Coney by the time it got light. A car in the early morning train to Memphis was reserved and waiting. They would soon leave New York far, far behind them.

14

Tall Tales

MEMPHIS, EARLY SEPTEMBER 1905

The Elks Lodge at 69–71 Jefferson in Memphis

TRUMAN ENJOYED MEMPHIS. The city was corrupt and no one tried very hard to hide it. Downtown, dice parlors, gin mills, pool halls, and bawdy houses jostled for attention. The showman had been in Memphis the previous year and he was looking forward to getting reacquainted with the city. Truman's wit and his ability to spin a yarn won him friends wherever he went, and nowhere more so than in Memphis. He had met a lot of them through the local Elks Lodge, which was famous among members for being a hard-drinking establishment, full of powerful members cutting deals and leveraging their connections.

But before he started enjoying himself, he needed to get the Igorrotes settled at East End Park. Truman walked through the park grounds, past a red-roofed pavilion nestled in a clump of sycamore trees. Two boys in school caps and blazers chased a liver-spotted hound round and round the pavilion. The park occupied a picturesque spot, popular with picnickers on account of the rolling lawns and pretty views. Truman stopped in front of a handsome structure with a conical dome at each end of the roof. Behind it, a Ferris wheel turned in the distance. He felt as if he were a million miles from New York City. Sallie would love it.

She had traveled some of the way with Truman and the Igorrotes by train but he had sent her on to Louisville to stay with her family for a while. She missed them all, especially her father and Catherine. Being on the road, changing cities every other week, was no life for a woman in her condition. She needed rest. Her family would look after her. The couple had not parted well, however. On the train from New York, Truman had told Sallie about Else. He'd neglected to mention Philip. Though he was certain Sallie believed his story about Else, the thought of another woman claiming Truman as her own gravely vexed Sallie. She had become sullen and argumentative. When they said good-bye, she was quiet and distant, far from her usual cheerful self.

He would send her a letter that night, something sentimental. He would beg her to forget about Else. Else was a poisonous woman who had never had any claim on him. Truman rarely wrote letters and he knew the gesture would mean a lot to Sallie.

The showman entered the Igorrote village and was delighted to discover the tribespeople had almost finished building their homes. Their village was smaller than at Coney Island, but Truman was happy with how it was shaping up. There was no room for a watchtower, a community building, or the medicine man's hut, but it would do just fine. They wouldn't be staying more than a few weeks, though they didn't know it yet.

Eager to drive huge crowds to his new village, Truman placed advertisements in the Memphis newspapers, declaring, "Attraction Extraordinary—Dr. T. K. Hunt, late governor province of Bontoc,

Island of Luzon, presents the premier attraction of the St. Louis Exposition, the famous head-hunting tribe of Igorrotes. 2,000,000 people have witnessed this remarkable exhibition, and have proclaimed it to be the greatest attraction of the World's Fair. Don't fail to witness their weird native dances—See the women Weaving 'Dress Suits' for their husbands."[1] In another advertisement Truman upped the ante, declaring that the Igorrotes had been "Pronounced by the press and public to be the greatest attraction ever presented in this country."[2]

When the park gates opened on the Igorrotes' first day, great crowds descended on their village. By the evening Truman had to stop letting them in, for the enclosure was crammed to capacity. The showman was so overwhelmed with visitors he had to institute a new policy, limiting each of them to just thirty minutes in the village. The ticket seller couldn't keep up, so Truman began taking the money himself. With each new wave of visitors that arrived, his pockets grew heavy.

Late one night, after the Igorrotes had finished their last tribal show for the day, Truman took a walk through the park grounds. He was in bright spirits. The change of scene had been good for him. As he turned the corner, his mood improved further as he looked up and noticed a sign advertising the pretty vaudeville singer Flo Adler, who was also appearing at East End Park. The two had met before, at Coney, and had instantly hit it off. Flo had a good sense of humor and a childish love of practical jokes. Truman entered the hall where the singer was performing and got there just in time to catch the second half of her show. She must be nearing thirty, but she looked stunning, with her thick dark hair, her big, brown eyes, and her perfect hourglass figure. As she sang a comic song about love, Truman had an idea.

He slipped backstage after the show and found her in her dressing room, sitting with her back to the open door. Her long brunette curls were piled loosely on her head. Truman glanced at her bare shoulders. *Miss Adler,* he said softly, *it's a pleasure to see you again.* Flo spun round in her seat and smiled broadly. Taking her hand in his, Truman continued: *I have a proposal which might interest you.*

In a saloon near the entrance to East End Park the following afternoon, Truman sat with a reporter from the *Memphis Commercial Appeal* who had been lured there with the promise of an exclusive. Leaning in close so that no one would overhear, Truman asked the reporter if he'd heard of the popular singer Flo Adler. *Of course, she's one of the best in the business.* Truman smiled, adding, *Well, she has become besotted by one of the Igorrote headhunters.* The reporter urged him to continue. Beckoning to the barman to bring them drinks, Truman went on: she had confessed to lusting after the Igorrote's "powerful physique, his manliness and great strength."[3] She'd even given him a pet name, "Hooligan," as a jokey reference to his spirited tribal performances.

The reporter took a swig from his glass. Truman explained that when he'd first learned of the singer's infatuation, he had advised her to put the Filipino from her mind. The tribesman was no match for her. But try as she might, she couldn't get over him. Just the night before, overcome with passion, she had stolen a ladder from the groundsman's hut and broken into the Igorrote Village under cover of darkness. She carried with her a smart American suit for her lover, which he was to don to disguise his tribal identity. When Flo entered the hut, however, she discovered to her dismay that the object of her affection was fast asleep and, accidentally stepping on the tail of "Igorrote Jack," the hound whose job it was to guard the tribe at night, she screamed as Jack began snarling at her, alerting the entire village to her presence. Truman had come to see what the commotion was, and Flo had confessed, with tears streaming down her cheeks, that she and "Hooligan" had planned to elope.[4]

What's a beauty like her doing getting involved with a brown-skinned savage? asked the reporter, going along with Truman's yarn. *She's in love, and we both know what that can do to a woman,* said Truman with a wink. The only thing she didn't like about the Filipino was his taste for canine flesh, added the showman, but her Filipino lover had offered to give it up when she became his bride. *What happened to them?* asked the reporter. *Flo is heartbroken,* said Truman. *And her lover is being punished. He has been placed in shackles to prevent him from making any future attempts at escape and placed on a diet of bread and water.*[5]

The story appeared in the next edition of the paper, exactly as

Truman had told it. The showman would celebrate that night. He had been meaning to pay a visit to the Elks Lodge since he arrived in Memphis. What better occasion than this?

Truman walked up the steps of the imposing redbrick building and identified himself to the man on the door. The home of the Memphis Elks was one of the most comfortable Truman had ever set foot inside, with chandeliers, palms, and deep red walls. The showman spotted a group of men he knew and went over to say hello. They included several prominent newspapermen, a judge, and a sheriff. Bidding them good evening and shaking hands with each of them in turn, the showman gladly accepted when they invited him to join them, settling himself into a comfortable club chair.

Truman had enjoyed the company of the lodge men in Brooklyn, but he felt altogether more at home here. He eyed the opulent decor, taking in the ornamental dark wooden pillars and the huge gold leaf vase that dominated the room. The aesthetic appealed to Truman, with his love of the extravagant and the exotic. The showman reached inside his jacket pocket and took out his cigar case. He always kept it stocked with the finest imported brands, which he now began offering around. The men asked how his exhibit was going. They'd read about Flo Adler and her tribal lover. The newspapermen wanted to know if he had any more juicy stories for them. Truman and his fellow Elks enjoyed a long and good-humored night. The showman was reminded of his old bachelor days. He would be sorry to leave Memphis. It was his kind of town.

One afternoon in late September 1905, Truman walked up Seventh Street in Limerick, so-named, Sallie had told him, because nearly all the residents who had come there to work in the Louisville and Nashville Railroad freight yard had emigrated from the Irish county of the same name. A gritty, working-class neighborhood, it was one mile south of downtown Louisville, Kentucky. As Truman neared Sallie's childhood home, he hoped that she had managed to forget about Else. The last thing he wanted was for Else to drive a wedge between them. That was why he had made the trip to Louisville that day, in order to put the matter behind them once and for all.

He hadn't told Sallie he was coming. The showman knocked on the door, hoping she would be at home. After a moment or two, Sallie appeared in the doorway and threw her arms around her husband's neck. Standing in the hallway, Truman kissed her tenderly, then held her back so he could get a good look at her. She was blooming. Last time he saw her she was pinched and pale. Now she was round faced with rosy cheeks.

Sallie took Truman's hands in hers and led him through to the kitchen. No one else was home. Pointing to a chair, she told him to sit while she made him something to eat. He must be hungry after his journey. Sallie noticed her husband had grown paunchy without her around to keep an eye on his diet, and began teasing him about it. Truman had recently turned forty and though mentally he felt young and vibrant, all his good living was starting to take its toll on his body. He had always been prone to weight gain and he had to admit his suits had been feeling tighter recently.

How long was he staying, asked Sallie. Truman said he had to go back to Memphis that night. He had come because he missed her and desperately wanted to see her. Sallie was disappointed he couldn't stay, but she thought it very romantic that he had taken an eight-hundred-mile round trip just to surprise her. She couldn't wait to tell her sisters.

Truman told his wife to come and sit at the table beside him. He had some exciting news. She did as he said and looked at him expectantly. *I'm bringing the Igorrotes to the Kentucky State Fair.* Sallie threw her arms up and squealed with joy. The fair was the biggest event of the season in her home state. She would tell everyone. She couldn't be prouder of her husband. Sallie didn't mention Else once during his visit. Truman felt hopeful that they had finally put the matter behind them.

The season had drawn to a close at Coney Island. At the request of his sister, Dora, Truman had agreed to employ his brother-in-law Edwin Fox in his Igorrote enterprise. Fox had left his home in Iowa and traveled to New York to collect the tribe. At Dreamland he met up with Callahan and Moody. Under Truman's orders, the three men split the Dreamland Igorrotes into two groups. Callahan and Fox took one, and Moody took the other. Truman sent them a list of the towns and cities each group was scheduled to visit, with a note of the dates they were expected. Moody had mentioned earlier to Truman that he wanted to add a couple of bookings but the showman had told him to hold off. They could discuss it when they next met. Truman planned to make regular, unannounced visits to check up on both groups and to collect his share of the takings. One group left for Michigan and the second was going to Georgia.

After Memphis, Truman took his own group to Lexington to the Kentucky State Fair, and then on another eight hundred miles to the Texas State Fair. Though the travel was expensive, Truman was glad to be making good money again. Having three groups touring simultaneously promised to be very lucrative indeed.

The weather was splendid, with clear blue skies and bright sunshine, on the morning of Friday, October 27, when Truman and the Igorrotes arrived in Dallas. To the tribe's disappointment, there hadn't been a great deal of building work to be done in their new village. At Coney the tribe had had space to move around. But now, with only eighteen of them in the group and with most bookings lasting only a week or two, their villages were becoming smaller and less picturesque.

The Igorrotes were sharing the bill with "Romeo, the talking pony," "the Prince—the smallest midget in the world," "Willie Stout, the Texas fat boy," and *Beautiful Baghdad*, a glittering show combining opera, musical comedy, and ballet.[6]

Truman had hired a local man, R. J. Marsh, to assist him in the village and had given him a crash course in Igorrote culture. Marsh had immediately impressed Truman with his flair for publicity. When a reporter from the *Dallas Morning News* came calling, Marsh invited the man to tour the village with him and began describing his charges as though he had known them for years: "[The Igorrotes] are remarkable for health, physical development, strength and longevity . . . They are the only people whose hair does not turn white when they are old."[7] He pointed out three men to the reporter who, he said, were ninety-two, ninety-five, and ninety-seven years, respectively, not one of whom had a gray hair or showed any signs of physical decay beyond the fact that their faces were lined. In fact, not one of the Igorrotes in Dallas was a day over sixty. But the reporter was more concerned with getting a good story than checking the accuracy of what he was told.

Next, Marsh pointed out a tribesman in his thirties named Domonick. His real name was Domoniog Paicao, but Marsh believed in keeping things simple. According to Marsh, the thirty-two-year-old tribesman had been declared by sculptors all over the country to be the finest specimen of a man they had ever set eyes on. These sculptors were so taken with his handsome features that they had made life-sized models of him, which now stood in museums all over the United States. "The strength of the Igorrotes is something wonderful," continued Marsh, warming to his theme. "Any of these men can pick up 500 pounds and carry it with ease."[8]

The reporter asked if they could set up a stunt to demonstrate their strength. Maybe they could get one of the men to pull the park manager's automobile or lift the Texas fat boy. Marsh agreed it was a splendid idea but said he'd have to run it by Truman first, and unfortunately the showman was away on business.

Marsh pressed on. "They are almost entirely free from disease. They are patient and industrious and no other women in the world have an easier time. The men do all the work, even the cooking. The women, however, make the clothes. They make the thread and do the weaving by hand. The clothes they have on are their own handiwork. They are absolutely truthful and strictly honest. They have never needed words for lying, stealing or drunkenness, for there is no practice corresponding to those words in their intercourse. Immorality is unknown among them, and whatever they have is a community property. If one of them gets hold of even a bottle of soda water all of them will drink of it. I have to provide three dogs every day for them. Boiled dog flesh is not distinguishable by taste from boiled beef."[9]

Marsh concluded the interview by turning to politics, explaining that the prospects for the Igorrotes in the Philippines were great under American rule: "The Igorrotes are intelligent and very imitative, and with half a chance they will fall in with the procession of civilization and go right along with it."[10]

Truman returned to Dallas after an absence of several days to find the Igorrote Village doing brisk business. He congratulated Marsh, and went to find Julio. The interpreter gave his boss a warm welcome. Though the tribe had had increasingly mixed feelings about Truman since he'd split them into different groups, Julio found his own job was easier when the showman was around. The Igorrotes still respected Truman and did what he said, even though they didn't like some of his rules. During his absences, they grumbled more about being locked up and being made to eat dog and about aspects of their performance they didn't like. Truman asked Julio whether there had been any problems while he was away. The expression on the interpreter's face told him there had. He invited Julio to come and have a drink with him.

They took their seats in a nearby saloon. Truman ordered two large whiskeys and asked Julio what was the matter. The showman seemed on edge. He usually made small talk and asked after Maria, and some of his favorite Igorrotes, but today there were no pleasantries. The barman brought the drinks. Truman knocked his back and ordered another. The interpreter knew his boss would not be pleased to hear what he had to say but the others had been nagging him to bring up the subject of their wages. Julio had been keeping a tally of their earnings. Truman had promised to pay each of the tribespeople fifteen dollars a month, and twenty-five dollars to Julio. They had been in America for six months and so far they hadn't seen a penny of their earnings. By Julio's reckoning, they were due around five thousand dollars, plus another thousand, maybe even two, from the sale of their souvenirs, money that Truman had been collecting. Taking a deep breath, Julio began: *Feloa has a large family back home and he is worried about them. He wants to send some of his money to them.* Truman said he would see to it that Feloa's family were given what they needed right away. He would send a telegram to the lieutenant governor in Bontoc.

What about the rest of us? Julio asked, his voice sounding braver than he felt. *Could we be paid some of our wages now?* Truman frowned. He wished he could pay them but the government had asked him to keep the money safe until they returned to the Philippines. If they got hold of it now, the government feared the tribespeople would gamble and drink the money away, like some of them did in St. Louis. Julio's face fell. It was true that a few of the men had been caught gambling, throwing dice, and betting on the numbers for money, but it was only a small group of men. The interpreter felt compelled to stand up for his Filipino brothers and sisters. *The Igorrotes are not gamblers and drinkers,* said Julio, eyeing his own full glass sitting beside Truman's empty one.

Truman was sorry but his hands were tied. He had given his word to the authorities. However, if they needed money for something, they just needed to ask him for it, as Julio did. He was a man of his word. They could trust him.

Is there anything else? asked the showman. *Yes,* said Julio. *Where does the money the visitors throw into the village go?* Julio was sticking his neck out now. Truman slammed his fist down on the bar. His eyes flashed with anger. Julio recoiled. He'd never seen his boss like this. *Who wants to know?* demanded Truman. *Feloa? That other troublemaker Dengay? Or is it you?* The showman didn't wait for an answer. He stormed out of the bar, leaving Julio rummaging in his pockets for coins to pay the barman.

Julio was shaken up. As he walked back toward the park, he thought of something Maria had mentioned recently. At the close of the St. Louis Fair, the Igorrotes were told by the organizers of the Philippine Reservation that they would receive the balance of their wages when they reached home, amounting to just under four thousand dollars. It was Truman who had accompanied them on the journey, but back in Manila, he claimed he had not been given the money. Julio, who had been paid before they left St. Louis, had no reason to doubt what his boss said. He'd assumed it was a mix-up. Truman might be a ruthless businessman, but he was not a liar. But now, with Truman withholding all of their wages, including his own, Julio couldn't help but wonder whether the showman might have pocketed the tribe's money himself. Could he have already spent their Coney Island wages?

Julio decided not to mention the incident in the saloon to any of the others. Truman had had a lot to drink. Maybe he'd caught him at a bad moment.

Truman rarely turned a booking down. Sometimes that meant double booking the tribespeople if one fair or amusement park wanted them before their previous engagement was over. As a result they were frequently late in arriving for a new engagement. Truman reasoned that by the time they got there, the fair organizers would be so relieved to see them and the crowds would be so big that all would be forgotten. Besides, he always had the excuse that shepherding a group of savages around America brought inevitable delays.

The group led by Edwin Fox turned up late at the Georgia State Fair in Macon, hot on the heels of Governor Terrell and his staff, whose train from Atlanta pulled into the train depot an hour ahead of the Filipinos' special car.[11] The excitement surrounding the arrival of the guest of honor was nothing compared to that generated by the first appearance on Georgian soil of the special guests from the Philippines.

Among the tribe's visitors at the Fair was Judge James H. Blount, who had lived in the Philippines for six years, where he'd been a judge in one of the Philippines' highest courts and had helped codify a new legal system for the islands. Like many Americans who had worked there, Judge Blount had returned home with the conviction that America should not hold on to the islands indefinitely, but should give the Filipinos independence. He had become an outspoken member of the Anti-Imperialist League, regularly expounding his views at political gatherings across the country.[12]

Describing his travels among the headhunters in northern Luzon, the judge said he never went anywhere without an armed guard. "The Igorrotes are not at heart a malicious people, and regret as much as anybody the necessity of cutting off people's heads, but they regard it as a part of their duty, for neglect of which they will suffer," said the judge, adding that he tried to avoid being anywhere near the Igorrotes when a particular native plant with red flowers was in bloom, as this was a time when the tribe believed that by sacrificing a human head and putting it on a pole, they would be rewarded with a good crop.[13] Edwin Fox chuckled over this novel piece of native trivia. The tribespeople seemed to inspire people to great heights of storytelling wherever they went.

Ever since Else had resurfaced in New York, Truman had become increasingly wary of being in the spotlight and frequently made himself scarce when reporters came to the village. The last thing he wanted was for Else to find out where he was and start making trouble again. But one October day a reporter from the *Dallas Morning News* happened to catch him in ebullient spirits. Truman told the reporter to call on him later in his rooms at the Oriental Hotel. He would give him an exclusive interview.

Dr. Hunt must be a wealthy man, thought the reporter as he walked up Akard Street toward the handsome redbrick hotel with its distinctive onion-domed turret. The Oriental was the priciest hotel in the city. It was where politicians and other dignitaries stayed when they came to town. That very year, the president himself had spent the night there. Stepping in off the street, the reporter stood silently for a moment as he took in the full splendor of the lobby: the marble floors, the huge exotic plants, the sweeping staircase. The desk informed him that Dr. Hunt was waiting for him in his rooms.

The showman invited the reporter to make himself at home. Then, handing him a generous tumbler of whiskey, Truman launched into a medley of his favorite stories, without any questions or prodding. The newspaperman sat back in his seat, his notebook resting on his lap. Anyone who knew the showman well was accustomed to the exaggerations and embellishments that made a good Truman Hunt story a great one, but the reporter was a novice who took everything the Igorrote manager said over the next couple of hours at face value, and wrote it down verbatim.

Truman went back to the beginning, describing his decision, in April 1898, to volunteer with the medical corps at the outbreak of the Spanish-American War. The showman described sailing to the

Philippines with the First Washington Volunteers in the capacity of captain assistant surgeon (in reality he was a far more junior private, then a hospital steward). When the regiment returned to the US in 1899, "Surgeon" Hunt said that he remained in Manila, where he was commissioned "Major Surgeon of the volunteer medical staff" (in reality, he received an honorable discharge from his position as a hospital steward with the army in August 1899 and went off prospecting for gold in the mountains of the northern Philippines).[14]

Refilling their glasses, the showman moved on to his arrival in the remote wilds of the Bontoc region, emphasizing his bravery and the dangers he encountered in the home of the ferocious headhunters. Without so much as a guide or translator, he lived in a simple army tent while a frame house was built for him. The Igorrotes were suspicious of him at first, but Truman described how he won them over with his medical skills. "I had a cinch on all the local medical men because I could not only cure various bodily ills, but I could also set a bone and pull a tooth. Neither of the latter feats could be performed by native medicine men and I was, therefore, looked upon as the greatest of them all.

"I pulled teeth for several poor people of the tribe who were really suffering from toothache and after the first day I was much surprised to have the chief of the tribe and the majority of the head men call at my tent and insist that I should pull out one tooth for each of them, although they were perfectly sound and such as many an American would have given hundreds of dollars to have retained in his head. As a rule, they all preferred that a front tooth be taken out so as to give them what they considered greater distinction.

"I had occasion frequently to bandage wounded limbs for the natives and in every instance I found that the next day everyone who could contrive to get a strip of anything in the line of cloth or cotton or even of bark wore strips so as to be in fashion." The reporter laughed and sipped from his glass.

What do the natives eat, Governor? he asked eagerly.

"Their food consists principally of rice, sweet potatoes, chicken, and dogs. They raise the latter just as we do hogs, for food. The species of dog preferred by them is the Chinese 'Chow' dog, which grows to the size of about eight or ten pounds. They like full-grown dogs best, but at a pinch will eat a month-old pup or 'Igorrote broiler,' as it is known to Americans."

Asked whether he had ever eaten dogmeat, Truman replied, "Yes, I am not ashamed to own it, I have eaten dog—in fact, was obliged to or starve. It was not a question of the manner of eating it, or the nature of the thing eaten, it was to eat it at once to keep life in."

In the nineteen months he spent living alone among the "naked and savage Igorrotes," Truman said he "lost the reckoning of the days and months" and didn't see a single white man or woman, nor did he receive so much as "a letter or message from those of his own race or kin whom he had left behind." This was a barefaced lie—there were at least five other Americans staying in Bontoc while he was there, including his own wife, Else, along with an American teacher, the constabulary lieutenant, and the ethnologist Ernest Jenks and his wife, Maud. But when Truman got going his storytelling knew no bounds.

As the interview went on, Hunt exaggerated his qualifications and inflated his job titles, describing how Secretary Taft had personally invited him to take up the position of governor of the Lepanto-Bontoc province (in fact he never rose higher than lieutenant governor). He was given the job, Truman explained, on account of his knowledge of the Igorrote language and his skills as a doctor, which meant he was "feared and held in awe by the superstitious natives."

Truman was a busy man, but he enjoyed telling his own story and seemed to have all the time in the world. Bontoc province was "about 235 miles from north to south and from 90 to 190 [miles] wide" with a population of six hundred thousand. "I was judge as well as governor of the province and in four years had only two cases of murder among 600,000. This is truely [*sic*] a record for the best governed American communities," boasted Truman. In fact he was lieutenant governor for one year, not four. The showman was happy to take all the credit for his peaceful community, adding that he was so well respected by the tribe that he became their spiritual guide as well as their governor and judge. "The object of my going there was to establish civil government in a crude form—something that would not be contrary to the best that was in their primitive form of tribunal government," said Truman. "Kindness and not force was the underlying principle of my regime. I was healer of their bodies, father confessor of all their woes and troubles and the final arbiter in all disputed questions. They knew I was perfectly disinterested in every way, as I received nothing for my services, and were also fully convinced that I only sought their good. The result of it all was that I had a well satisfied, contented and orderly lot of subjects."

The Igorrotes' manager said he was under a ten-thousand-dollar bond[15] to the US government to care for the tribe; to feed, clothe, and house them; and to return them to their own country at the end of their contracts, even in the event of death. He mentioned the death of one of the Igorrote men from pneumonia in Seattle, and the reporter could've sworn he saw tears in his eyes. He regarded all the Igorrotes as his friends—*no, scratch that, they are like family*, he said. The reporter amended his notes. Truman smiled, lifting his glass to his lips.

The reporter had heard that the tribe were not Christians and asked the showman to tell him about their beliefs. "Their religion is Pagan. They believe in a great Spirit behind the sun whom they worship at all times. They also venerate their male ancestors. A woman is not allowed to participate in this worship; the men do it for her, either the head of the family or the oldest boy. In this respect they remind one of the primitive Japanese in their religious forms of worship."

If Truman's earlier tone was self-congratulatory, he also had plenty of praise left over for the tribe. He described the Igorrotes' defining characteristic as their inherent honesty: "Honesty is . . . held in high esteem by them. I have never known a case of theft. True, this may result, as you say, because they have little in their possession to steal; but they have property that they consider valuable, although we might not think so according to our notions of value. I have had native Igorrotes carry United States Government money to the amount of several thousand dollars for over 200 miles, and not a single cent was missing."

Next, Truman launched into a spirited but largely inaccurate account of Igorrote marriage customs. "The marriage tie is held strictly sacred. Boys and girls are all paired off by their fathers as soon as they are born, similar to the Chinese custom. When the girl reaches the age of 12 or 14, and the boy 14 or 16, they are married. The nuptial ceremony consists of feasting and dancing and prayers offered by the oldest man in the village or community, irrespective of his station. Chastity is rigorously enforced under penalty of death. The two murders that I referred to previously were the result of infidelity and both the man and the woman were speared to death."

Do you feel the Igorrotes can learn from their American rulers? asked the reporter. Truman was uncharacteristically outspoken in his answer, perhaps due to the speed with which he had been swigging from his glass. "If the present system of educating the natives and preparing them for our form of government is followed and persisted in, there is not the slightest doubt in my mind that in twenty years they will be among our most loyal citizens," he said. He generously praised the former governor-general of the Philippines: "Governor Taft grasped the situation in a masterly way at the outset in inaugurating a simple and primitive form of government that was immediately accepted by them. This form was outlined so as not to conflict with anything that was good in their pagan form of government, while it aimed at the extermination of all that was bad."

It was a bravura performance. The reporter had enough material to fill the entire newspaper. Intriguingly, Truman ended his interview by telling the reporter that in 1898 he was known as Dr. G. T. Hunt and was living in the Washington town of Spokane Falls, after graduating from Bellevue Hospital College, New York, in 1889. Truman offered no further explanation as to why he, whose parents named him Truman Knight Hunt, might once have gone by the initials G. T. Hunt. Truman had obtained his MD at the University of Iowa, not in New York, and Bellevue did not have any student named Truman K. Hunt or G. T. Hunt enrolled there in the late 1880s. Was it a simple mistake on the part of the reporter? It seemed a careless and unlikely mistake. Odder still, the same information was published twice, in October and November, in two separate stories in two different Texas newspapers.[16] If the inaccuracies in the first article were the fault of the reporter, then why had Truman, who loved to read his own publicity, not corrected them before the second article was published? Was Truman simply drunk and lying for the sake of it? Or had he begun deliberately reinventing himself, in an attempt to make it impossible for his past to catch up with him again?

Previously Truman's inventions had been joyous exaggerations designed to snare the interest of the public and the press. Now his own story was slipping through his fingers like quicksilver. Within a matter of days, he would be forced to explain exactly who he was and what he had promised the Igorrotes.

15

Fighting for Control

TAMPA, NOVEMBER 29, 1905

Form No. 1.

THE WESTERN UNION TELEGRAPH COMPANY.

INCORPORATED

23,000 OFFICES IN AMERICA. CABLE SERVICE TO ALL THE WORLD.

This Company TRANSMITS and DELIVERS messages only on conditions limiting its liability, which have been assented to by the sender of the following message. Errors can be guarded against only by repeating a message back to the sending station for comparison, and the Company will not hold itself liable for errors or delays in transmission or delivery of Unrepeated Messages beyond the amount of tolls paid thereon, nor in any case where the claim is not presented in writing within sixty days after the message is filed with the Company for transmission.

This is an UNREPEATED MESSAGE, and is delivered by request of the sender, under the conditions named above.

ROBERT C. CLOWRY, President and General Manager. 323

NUMBER 88a SENT BY J RECD BY Cr 11 Paid CHECK

RECEIVED at Wyatt Building, Cor. 14th and F Streets, Washington, D. C NOV 29 1905 190

TELEPHONES: M 4106, M 2144 AND M 1707.

Dated Tampa Flo 29

To War Department
WDC

Has Dr Hunt made arrangements to return Igorotes to their home

H E Deputy

CHIEF CLERK DEC 1 1905 WAR DEPT.

ALWAYS OPEN. MONEY TRANSFERRED BY TELEGRAPH. CABLE OFFICE.

Telegram from H. E. Deputy to the War Department

IT WAS A pleasant winter's day with temperatures in the low seventies when the case of *Hunt v. Moody* was called before Court Commissioner Larimore in Tampa, Florida. The showman looked polished in a three-piece suit he had had made in Dallas, along with a new pair of fine leather shoes. He stared across the room at Charles Moody, the man who had put up the money to get the Igorrotes to America. Moody glowered back at him. The two men were the only people present who knew the precise details of the arrangement between them.

Truman had been in San Antonio, relaxing in his hotel bar, when the telegram from another of his business associates had arrived, informing him that Moody had started taking bookings for the Igorrotes and had gone with a group of them to Tampa without Truman's permission. Furious, the showman had taken the next train to Tampa. He, and only he, arranged the bookings. Moody knew that.

Truman felt confident that he would be awarded custody of the Filipinos. In his pocket, he had a copy of the document he had signed in Worcester's office in Manila, stating that he had permission to take the tribespeople to America. Since arriving in Tampa the previous day, Truman had hired two local attorneys, Peter Knight and C. C. Whitaker, to help him regain control of the tribespeople.

The showman had briefed his legal representatives well, informing them of his business partner's weak points, yet neglecting to tell them that without Moody's money he would never have been able to exhibit the tribe in the first place.

Standing before the Court Commissioner, Truman explained that the Filipinos had come to the United States under a contract with him, which would expire the following year. He produced a copy of the contract, along with the document he had signed in Worcester's office. After giving Larimore a moment to study them, Truman said that he, and he alone, had the personal permission of the governor-general of the Philippines to exhibit the tribe, adding that he was under a ten-thousand-dollar bond to care for them and to return them to their homeland at the end of their contract. Moody had taken the tribe without his permission. Before Moody kidnapped them, some of the tribespeople had told Truman that they were homesick and wished to return to the Philippines without delay. Truman planned to honor their request and take them home, but, by keeping them against their will, Moody was preventing him from doing this.

Truman explained that the Igorrotes were simple, innocent people who spoke little or no English. They were of low intelligence and, as if to illustrate this point, he added that there was no written form of their language. The tribespeople had to be cared for as if they were children and watched over morning, noon, and night to keep them out of harm's reach.

Moody's representative, F. M. Simonton, interjected. His client was Truman's main financial backer. He had given Truman three thousand dollars to get the tribe to America and in return he had been made Truman's business manager. As such, he had the right to take bookings for them. Truman's attorneys objected: none of this was true. Court Commissioner Larimore asked Simonton if his client had brought with him a copy of their agreement, to which Moody replied that it had been a gentleman's agreement. He had trusted Truman and had not asked him for a receipt for the money he had given him. Larimore was unmoved by his story.

A small smile passed over Truman's lips. This case was as good as won. Catching Larimore's eye and anxious not to appear too confident, he adopted a serious expression and asked if he might be allowed to speak again. Larimore nodded. Truman had lived among the tribe for years and knew them well. He had come to court to protect them. Here in a foreign land, they were vulnerable and he would do everything in his power to make sure they were not exploited. Moody didn't even speak their language, so how could he possibly know what they wanted?

Moody's lawyer objected; his client spoke a little of their dialect, as well as some Spanish, which a number of them had learned when the Philippine Islands were under Spanish rule.

While Truman, Moody, and their attorneys argued it out, Julio, whom Truman had brought with him, and eighteen Igorrotes sat in an office along the corridor, waiting to be called. Under the watchful gaze of a court official, they sat smoking their pipes and puffing their cigars. The *Tampa Morning Tribune* would later report that they were "apparently unconscious of what was going on."[1]

If the newspapers portrayed them as savages who were unconcerned about their future at the mercy of their master, the reality was very different. The Igorrotes knew their fate was being decided and they couldn't understand why no one wanted to hear what they had to say. As the hours passed and still no one called for them, the tribespeople grew restless. The Igorrotes didn't like Moody much and they trusted him even less. But they were hardly spoiled for choice when it came to their American bosses. Fox had a mean streak. They had seen less and less of Truman since they left Coney Island. Though they had always liked the showman, their feelings had become increasingly ambivalent toward him.

Moody had briefed Simonton that Truman was prone to exaggerations, fabrications, and outright lies. Eager to catch Truman out, Simonton grilled him about Bontoc Province, which he claimed to have governed, when in reality he had served only as lieutenant governor. "How many square miles are there in the province of which you were the Governor?" asked Simonton. "I cannot tell you," answered Truman with a smirk, adding, "but I can say it was not square."[2] Unimpressed by the showman's attempt at humor, Simonton accused Truman of exploiting the tribespeople. Contrary to Truman's claims, Simonton argued, it was Moody who was trying to protect them from Truman Hunt. The man was a rogue who "was in arrears in paying the Filipinos."[3] Truman's contracts with the Igorrotes expired that month and they all wanted to go home immediately, but he was refusing to take them.

Larimore glanced over at Truman. He seemed a decent sort. He was educated, a medical doctor. He had worked for the United States government and clearly knew the tribe well. While Moody had failed to provide any evidence to substantiate his claims, Truman had produced a document that indicated clearly that the tribespeople had been entrusted to him by the authorities in Manila. Before he made up his mind, the Court Commissioner wanted to hear what the Igorrotes had to say. He instructed the clerk to fetch them.

There was a palpable air of anticipation in the courtroom. Several local newspapermen had come to report on the case, along with a reporter for the *Associated Press.* The Igorrotes were a big national story and the agency man knew his report of the courtroom drama would be picked up by newspapers the length and breadth of the country. After all, it wasn't every day that a dozen and a half dusky-skinned savages from northern Luzon set foot in an American court of law.

The clerk opened the door of the office where the Igorrotes and Julio waited and told them they were wanted in court. Delighted that at last they were being given the chance to speak, the tribespeople cheered. They got up from the floor, "threw aside Nature's costume,"[4] and picked up clothes from a pile the clerk had managed to find from somewhere for them. The men put on overalls and overcoats of an ancient vintage while the women threw blankets around their bare shoulders.

Larimore couldn't help but smile at the tribe's odd appearance. He welcomed them and the deputy sheriff began to read out the names of each of the tribespeople with an "eloquence" that has "seldom been heard in any civilized country. As though he had been a resident of the Philippines for years, he rattled the names off with a regularity and pertinacity that caused the attorneys and others present to marvel."[5] The group consisted of ten men and eight women.

The Court Commissioner instructed Julio to ask each of them who their boss was and what they wanted to do: continue exhibiting in the United States or return to the Philippines. Julio avoided Truman's eye. He knew that his boss would want him to distort the tribe's answers, but he would not do it. He turned to the Filipinos and posed the questions. Everyone listened intently, eager to hear what the Igorrotes sounded like. The first to speak was a man named Pucuan. He pointed to Truman, indicating that he was his boss, and then said he wanted to go home. Julio worked his way down the line of Igorrotes and got the same answers each time. Truman was their boss and they wanted to go home.

Larimore nodded. The Filipinos, taking this gesture as a sign they were going home, erupted into demonstrations of joy. Larimore told Truman that he was delivering the tribespeople in to his custody, adding that he expected him to take good care of them and to return them to the Philippines as soon as was practical. Truman thanked him and promised he would take them from the city on the next train.[6]

The showman ushered his charges out of the municipal building and into the winter sun. He had no intention of keeping his promise. The Igorrotes would be going back to the Philippines, but not yet. They were far too valuable to him. The next day was the last day of the Florida State Fair. They would leave immediately for New Orleans. He had been offered a lot of money to exhibit them there for the rest of the winter.

Truman was convinced he wasn't doing anything wrong. Some of the Igorrotes had recently begun insisting that they had signed a contract with him for ten months, which in the Igorrote calendar was a full year, as dictated by their crop cycles. This period would come to an end by the close of the year. But this was nonsense—they had agreed to work for him for twelve months from the day they arrived in America, which meant their contracts wouldn't be up for several months. As far as the showman was concerned, it was the Igorrotes' ignorance that was the cause of their discontent. These primitive people had clearly not understood what they had signed.

He had asked Julio to clear up the confusion, but even he hadn't been able to persuade them. Truman was sick of hearing about the matter. His venture was a success, the Igorrotes were famous and would soon be rich, and he had no intention of giving up his business just yet. In fact, he saw no reason why he couldn't keep exhibiting them indefinitely. What were they going back to, anyway? A life of hunting each other in the wilds?

Later that afternoon, Larimore found his thoughts returning to the Filipinos. When he handed down his verdict, he had felt sure it was the right course of action. Truman had come across well during his courtroom appearance, but there was something about the behavior of the showman, the way he herded the tribe out of the courtroom, that was troubling Larimore. He was probably imagining it, thought the Court Commissioner, trying to put the matter from his mind.

Across town, a business associate of Moody's named H. E. Deputy stood in the telegraph office. He was dictating a note to the War Department in Washington, DC. It read: "Has Dr. Hunt made arrangements to return Igorrotes to their home." Deputy's eyes narrowed. That should set the War Department on Truman's trail.[7]

16

A Break for Freedom

EN ROUTE TO NEW ORLEANS, DECEMBER 1905

New Orleans, c. 1909. The tall building on far left is the Central Police Station, with the infamous red-light district of Storyville behind and right of it.

THE TRAIN TRUNDLED through northern Florida and the tribe gave in to the lazy languor of long-distance travel. They knew from their first cross-country trip, seven months earlier, that it would take many days to get back to the port where their American adventure had begun. But the prospect of returning to Bontoc and being reunited with their loved ones kept their spirits up. If they had doubted Truman's word before, now they felt secure in the knowledge that the showman was acting under the orders of the court in Florida. At last, they were going home.

The Igorrotes paid little attention to their surroundings as they passed through one station after another. The restlessness some of them had felt earlier had gone. So had the grumblings of discontent. Their only concern was making sure they got all the money they were due. According to Julio's calculations, Truman owed the whole group around seven thousand dollars in wages, plus several thousand dollars more in souvenir money. That would make around two hundred dollars each when divided between fifty of them.[1]

Despite Truman's insistence that he was under orders to deposit their wages and souvenir money in the bank for them, the tribespeople were no longer certain they could believe what he said. They had started keeping some of what they earned selling their souvenirs. They hid the money in their basket hats, inside the linings of their traveling clothes, under the waistbands of their loincloths, and in their traveling trunks.

As they sat on the train, only Julio knew that they were not going directly home. The secret weighed heavily on him. He had overheard Truman and Callahan talking about it and had spent the whole day waiting for an opportunity to tell Maria. Sitting cooped up in the train car with Truman, however, he hadn't had chance. That night he waited until everyone was asleep, then he placed a hand on his wife's shoulder and whispered her name in her ear. Maria stirred from her slumber and looked up at him. Though she was still half-asleep, she immediately saw from her husband's face that something was wrong. Julio looked around the car. Just as he was about to speak, he saw Truman, sitting in the shadows at the end of the carriage, looking directly at him. Julio looked back at his wife and told her not to worry, it was nothing. Julio had grown wary of his boss since the incident in the Dallas bar. Truman had apologized to him afterward, but there was something about the expression on the showman's face that day that he found hard to forget.

The Igorrotes had expected to be on the train for many days, but the following afternoon Truman clapped his hands together and told them they were getting off. Most of them had been asleep and so felt disoriented as they stepped down onto the platform. Only Julio could read the sign telling them they were in New Orleans. Truman led them out of the station and onto a streetcar. The tribespeople sat in silence, looking through the windows as they journeyed farther and farther out of town. Were they going to another station? Or to the port?

On and on they rode. After several miles they found themselves in the middle of what felt like nowhere, surrounded by dairies and fields. Was this the way home? It wasn't until they reached Athletic Park, a baseball stadium on the outskirts of the city that was transformed into a temporary amusement park in the winter months, that Truman delivered the bombshell that they were not going directly home. He had good news for them. They would do one last booking in America and go out with a bang. They would stay for two or three months in New Orleans, though Truman didn't intend to share this information with the tribe.

The Filipinos looked around at each other as Truman continued talking: the booking was a top-notch one, far too good to turn down. They were going to make a fortune in tips and souvenir sales. Truman knew they were homesick, but they'd be home soon enough. *Besides*, he added, *just think of how far the extra money will go back in the Philippines.* The tribespeople sat in stunned silence. They felt angry, betrayed yet again by their so-called American friend. After a few moments, they found their voices.

What about what the judge said in Florida? asked Feloa. He had given his permission for one last booking, replied Truman, adding that they must have missed this because they didn't speak English. Julio looked at him. That wasn't true. Julio wanted to challenge his boss, but he couldn't—not there, like that, in front of everyone. He didn't want to provoke him. *How long are we staying?* asked Dengay. *A short time*, lied Truman. *But we want to go home*, said Maria quietly, looking down at her hands. Pretending he hadn't heard her, the showman excused himself and left. On his way out he instructed Callahan to keep a close eye on them.

Despite their unhappiness, the Filipinos knew they had little choice but to start building their village.

Late one night, Truman returned to the Igorrote Village after an absence of several days. To the delight of the tribe, Tainan was with him. The boy ran toward his countrymen and women, shouting at the top of his voice, a huge grin plastered over his face. Maria threw her arms around him. Friday ran over and poked his friend in the ribs. It was the first time they had seen him in months. When the rest of Truman's original group poured through the gates after him, the village erupted. They might be stranded thousands of miles from home, but this was a homecoming of sorts. For the first time in months, they had something to celebrate.

The tribe sat up late talking. Daipan wondered aloud whether the fact they were all together again was a sign the showman was taking them home soon. Feloa tutted. *Do you really believe anything Truman says anymore?* Dengay joined in: *Truman promised we were going home and now here we are in another new place with yet another show ahead of us.* The new arrivals listened as Feloa described the many promises Truman had broken recently, not least his promise to the court that he would take them home immediately.

The chief told them to be on their guard. They couldn't trust anything Truman said. He still hadn't paid them any of their wages. He had taken their souvenir money. How long they might stay in New Orleans was anybody's guess. Daipan's earlier optimism vanished and she began to cry. Maria didn't say anything to the others, not even Julio, but she had noticed that their new village was more picturesque and less bare than some of their previous homes. Their huts were surrounded by plants and trees. Why, she wondered, would Truman and the park people have gone to all this trouble if they were only going to be staying a short time?

Twelve hundred miles away in New York, the Coney Island postmaster took delivery of a most unusual letter. Sent by a man named McIntyre in the War Department's Bureau of Insular Affairs, it inquired as to the whereabouts of Dr. Truman Hunt.[2] McIntyre understood that Truman had been at Coney with his Igorrote troupe and wondered if the postmaster knew where they'd gone at the close of the season. Some of the showmen and performers left forwarding addresses, but many more chose not to. They all had their own reasons. The assistant postmaster wrote back, stating that Dr. Hunt had left no contact information.[3]

Dengay and Feloa sat up talking in their hut one night after the others had gone to bed. In the Philippines they were fearsome warriors who had no qualms about hacking off the heads of their enemies while they were still breathing. In America, at the mercy of one man, Dengay and Feloa experienced an unfamiliar sense of powerlessness. They had been forced to live by a different set of rules, rules they didn't understand. Though he would never have admitted it to the rest of the tribe, Dengay felt afraid. He spoke very little English and in this foreign universe he feared what might become of them. Feloa confessed to his friend that he fantasized about picking up his head-hunting ax and turning it on Truman, but he knew that wasn't the answer. Igorrote custom dictated that they hunted the heads of enemy villagers, not random rogues. Besides, they weren't at home now. If he took his ax to an American, he would be sent to prison and never see home again. What would his family do then?

As long as Truman was making money from them, he would keep them in America. They had to find a way to escape. But what would they do once they got outside the park? They had no idea where they were. They didn't have enough money to get home and, even if they did, how would they find the way? At that moment, Julio walked past the entrance to the hut. Dengay and Feloa fell silent. They looked at each other. Could Julio possibly have heard what they were saying? They had been talking quietly but they had carelessly left the door ajar. If he had heard them, would he say anything?

Julio had always been accepted by the tribe but since they'd come to America, some of the men felt that his position as Truman's assistant meant they couldn't entirely trust him. The interpreter was different from the rest of them. In addition to the freedom he had to leave their enclosure, he looked, thought, and acted more like an American than an Igorrote. Many of the young boys looked up to him. He seemed worldly and wise, but some of the tribespeople had grown resentful and suspicious of his motives. Julio sensed this. It bothered him, but he wasn't sure what he could do to change it.

Sundays were always busy in the Igorrote Village and January 28, 1906, was no exception. Crowds of men, women, and children stood watching as the tribespeople went about the carefully orchestrated amusement park version of their daily lives. The women wove cloth and made rattan rings. On the other side of their enclosure, the tribesmen were hollering and running at each other with spears in the first sham battle of the day.

Feloa looked up and noticed Pucuan charging toward him, his spear held aloft. Feloa stepped to the side and threw up his shield to protect himself. Instead of turning and swiping at his opponent again, Pucuan staggered forward as if he'd lost his balance. Feloa instinctively reached out to grab him. With an odd, faraway expression on his face, Pucuan toppled forward and crashed into the bamboo fence. Feloa and Dengay tossed their spears and shields to the ground and, taking hold of Pucuan under the arms, they led him over to a hut. Inside, Feloa tried to ask what was wrong but Pucuan was gasping for breath. Clutching his chest, he made a rasping sound. Pucuan's sister and several tribesmen came in to see what was the matter. They looked on in shock as Pucuan slumped forward, apparently unconscious.

Julio ran to fetch Truman. The showman entered the hut and knelt down beside Pucuan. He felt for a pulse and, finding none, checked him over. *Coronary*, he said under his breath. They clearly couldn't move the dead tribesman with crowds milling around outside. They would have to close off the hut where the body lay and put a couple of the tribespeople outside to stop any of the visitors wandering in. Truman told Julio to make the necessary arrangements. The showman felt sorry for the Igorrotes, especially the man's sister. The death of one tribesman had been bad enough; two seemed especially cruel.

The Filipinos drifted into the hut to see the scene for themselves. Truman knew it was their custom to visit with the dead, but there was a large crowd outside and they needed to be entertained. The showman raised his voice just enough to get their attention. He needed them to go outside and continue the show. They could all take turns to sit with the dead man later, after the park closed. In the meantime, Truman gave Pucuan's sister and Feloa permission to stay with the body. He wasn't completely heartless.

The Igorrotes were a fatalistic tribe. Their belief in animism extended to illness, which they viewed as the work of evil anitos, or spirits. The only cure, as far as they were concerned, was for a good anito to drive out the evil one. If this didn't happen, then they believed the sick person was not meant to survive. They carried out funeral rites but did not typically enter into a long period of mourning, as was customary in their host country.[4] Despite the degree of comfort their fatalism gave them, it was a fact that Igorrotes liked to die in their own homes. Pucuan's death on foreign soil added immeasurably to the tribe's grief. He was popular and had been stronger and fitter than Falino, the old Igorrote who had died in Seattle. His death had come as a shock.

The tribe's anguish was made worse still by the fact that they couldn't bury Pucuan in the customary Igorrote way. Here, living inside an American baseball park, they could hardly put the corpse on display for a week while they sat with the body singing, chanting, and burning fires under it, though from what they'd seen of this country, the people would probably pay extra to witness such a scene. As they did with Falino in Seattle, they would have to make do with an improvised funeral ceremony. They insisted on carrying it out in private, away from the hordes of visitors who had become onlookers at some of their most intimate moments.

Truman gave his permission for their plan, though he told Julio they would need to keep it short. He would arrange for an undertaker to come first thing in the morning to take the body away. Truman wished he could persuade them to hold their ceremony when the park was open, but he knew they would resist. He didn't want to push them. No, he could still turn the Igorrote death into a publicity coup.

It was after midnight when the tribe began their funeral rites. All night they stayed up chanting, singing baleful-sounding dirges, and beating their gongs and tom-tom drums. Truman stood watching for a while from a distance, then retreated into his office. Before he went to bed that night, he took out a pen and composed a brief description of the scene he had witnessed. He would send it to all the newspapers. For good measure, Truman posthumously promoted Pucuan to tribal chief, a title that, he explained, made the funeral all the more important.

The news of Pucuan's passing made headlines across the country, from Texas to Indiana. "Puc Aa-Un [*sic*], one of the biggest chiefs of the Igorrote tribes on the Island of Luzon, died here of heart disease yesterday at the winter quarters of the band of Igorrotes which were brought here by Dr. TK Hunt a year ago," reported the *Fort Wayne News*, adding, "The native burial ceremonies of the tribes were all carried out before the savages would allow the undertaker to take the body to embalm. The blood of freshly killed chickens was sprinkled over the body and the noise of the tom-toms is being kept up all night to drive away the evil spirits."[5]

When Mr. Lynch, the undertaker, came from his premises on Tulane Avenue, to collect the body, Truman instructed him to have it embalmed and to await further instructions. Under the terms of his agreement with the US government, Truman was obliged to inform the Bureau of Insular Affairs if a member of his group died. He still hadn't gotten around to telling them about Falino's death the previous May. He would make contact soon, but not yet.

The death of Pucuan came at the end of a particularly trying period that left Truman feeling tense and distracted. The baby was due in two months, and Sallie kept writing to ask him when they would be reunited. He and the tribe had been traveling for three months before they reached New Orleans. In that time Truman had lost count of the number of towns and cities they'd visited. Life on the road suited him. It reminded him of his old bachelor days and he enjoyed the freedom. But it had brought its own stresses: every other week he had to secure new bookings and find money for train tickets along with somewhere for the tribe to live when accommodations were not provided on-site. The unplanned trip to Tampa had been another expense he could have done without. Money was tight again. The Igorrotes were still making him a handsome profit, but Truman was blowing the money as fast as he earned it, on drink, fine clothes, lavish gifts, clubs, and expensive restaurants and hotels.

Julio had been pestering him again, wanting to know when they were going home and asking about their earnings. They should count themselves lucky, thought Truman. Plenty of their countrymen and women would give their right arms to trade places.

• • •

Truman called Callahan into his office the following night. The security guard had never seen Truman so agitated before. The showman had been drinking and was pacing up and down raging that the Igorrotes were cheating him. He felt certain they had been hiding money from him and he wanted Callahan to go to their village with him now to take it from them. Callahan had noticed Feloa had started carrying a little rattan bag on his shoulders. Maybe he kept his money in there.

The park was closed when Callahan and Truman entered the village and walked over to where the tribespeople sat together talking. Callahan approached Feloa and demanded he hand over his bag and all his money. *No,* Feloa said calmly, *it is mine.* Truman, furious at the tribal chief's insolence, suddenly lunged at Feloa. Julio looked up just in time to see Truman raise his fist before bringing it down in a flash, striking Feloa violently on the back. Truman then ripped the bag from the chief's back and tipped it upside down.[6]

Coins poured onto the ground at the tribe's feet. Julio gasped. Several of the women standing nearby cried out. Truman shouted at them to be quiet, and bent down to pick up the coins. The tribespeople looked on as Truman and Callahan scrabbled around on their hands and knees, counting up Feloa's money. There was fifty dollars in total. Truman piled the money into his pockets. How dare Feloa keep fifty dollars hidden from him when he had been instructed to hand over his earnings. Truman was keeping their money safe for them. The showman looked around at the tribe. From now on, they must give their money to him, did they understand? Otherwise they, and he, would be in big trouble with the government. He would return later with a receipt.[7]

Truman told Callahan to stay and watch over them. Then he retired to his quarters for a drink. As long as he deprived the Igorrotes of funds, Truman reasoned, they would remain entirely dependent on him. If they had money, they could plan their escape. Without it, they were going nowhere.

Feloa had other ideas, though. He might be penniless again, but he was determined they were not going to remain here as Truman's slaves any longer. They would escape. He, Dengay, and a few of the other men would climb over the fence and make a run for it. If they were caught, they would scatter so as to maximize the chances of one of them finding the police. They didn't know where they'd find them, but they would ask someone in the street. It wasn't a flawless plan, Feloa knew that, but the alternative—living locked up indefinitely under Truman—was much worse.

The following night, January 30, 1906, one of the young boys came running to tell Feloa that their guard had finally succumbed to sleep. The men sprang into action. The bamboo stockade surrounding their village was high but they had no trouble scaling it. In the Philippines they were accustomed to climbing thirty-foot-tall trees to look for their enemies. Now, as the last man dropped down on the other side of their enclosure, the Igorrotes stood for a moment, glancing all around to make sure they weren't being watched. Then, at Feloa's signal, they began to run through the darkness across the park.

At the perimeter fence, they scrambled one by one up and over the top. Once they were safely on the other side, they began to run as fast as their legs would carry them. They didn't know where they were headed, but they assumed that if they ran toward the lights of the city then sooner or later they would find someone who would tell them where to find the police. It was after two o'clock in the morning and the streets were deserted.

They ran on and on, turning now and again to make sure no one was giving chase. They ran for more than three miles, until they reached a busy road. Unbeknownst to them, they were right across the street from the Elks Lodge, which Truman had been frequenting since their arrival in New Orleans. On Tulane Avenue, they saw a man on the other side of the road, walking with his head down. Feloa rushed up to him. *Police,* said the tribal chief. The man looked up and stared at the tattooed tribal leader. His mouth fell open and he blinked his eyes in disbelief. *Police,* said Feloa again, a note of urgency creeping into his voice. The man wordlessly pointed down the street to a building in the distance with a tall spire, one of the few that was still illuminated despite the late hour. Without stopping a moment longer, the man hurried off. The Igorrotes ran toward the lights.

Bursting through the doors of the Central Police Station, the breathless, nearly naked tribespeople were a sight to behold. The officer on the desk thought he must be dreaming. He stood silently for a moment and looked them up and down. Without Julio, whom they'd chosen not to involve in their plan, there was no one among them who spoke English fluently. Feloa had picked up a few words and phrases and launched into a muddled account of what had brought them here. The others joined in, shouting and gesticulating wildly. The officer picked up something about Athletic Park and guessed they were on show there. Before he had time to hear more, Truman came rushing through the doors with two policemen.[8]

Truman wasn't fit or especially healthy, thanks to his diet of rich food and liquor, and all the excitement had stirred him up. He could feel his heart pounding. Thankfully, he'd learned long ago how to appear composed in high-pressure situations. Striding up to the desk, Truman dabbed the sweat from his forehead with his silk handkerchief and introduced himself to the officer in charge, who had been joined by several gaping colleagues.

Truman explained that he was employed by the US government, which had contracted him to exhibit the tribe here in the city. If the officers hadn't already visited Athletic Park to see them, they would be very welcome to do so as his guests. Then, in a conspiratorial tone, Truman told the officer in charge that the group had been shaken by the recent death of one of their tribe. They were simple mountain people and that night, he explained, they had become convinced that they were being visited by the ghost of their dead countryman. Terrified, they had fled Athletic Park and run through the streets of New Orleans, shouting and screaming until finally they reached the police station.

The officer had no reason to doubt the smart, well-spoken government employee. The Igorrotes, not understanding what their boss was saying, looked at the police officer, wordlessly imploring him to help them. But the officer was laughing now at something Truman said, and the Igorrotes sensed that their escape was doomed. Turning his attention to them, the showman started to speak, his voice not betraying a hint of the anger he felt. In Bontoc dialect, he smiled as he calmly told the group that they would be locked up in the cells if they didn't come with him immediately. Feloa and Dengay looked at the policeman. Feloa opened his mouth to speak, but before he could get his words out, Truman put an arm around him and guided him toward the door.

Back in Athletic Park, the showman handed Feloa his bag without uttering a word. The tribal chief opened it. Inside were his tobacco and his pipe. All his money had been taken. He looked up to protest, but Truman was gone.

Truman asked the park bosses for a couple of extra security guards to watch over the Igorrotes that night. With the tribe safely locked up in their enclosure, he and the press agent got down to work. They would have to sacrifice sleep. Truman composed one of his best notices for the press yet, complete with his own imaginative spin.

The *Dallas Morning News* was among the newspapers that reported the showman's story, under the headline IGORROTES TERRIFIED—IN TURN THEY TERRIFY EVERY ONE WHO SAW THEM STAMPEDE, SPOOKS AFTER THEM.[9] The article read, "New Orleans, La., Jan. 30—The colony of Igorrotes from the Philippine Islands, who are wintering at Athletic Park, created a great uproar in that section of the city today and it was necessary to turn in a riot call for the police before the Filipinos could be subdued. Puc Aa Un [*sic*], the chief of the colony, died Sunday, and the Igorrotes imagine that they are being haunted by his ghost. They became so panic-stricken with fear this morning that they broke out and started uptown yelling and screaming at every step, and beating tin pans and other noise-producing instruments to scare off the spooks. Dr. Hunter [*sic*], who has charge of the band, and who is under bond to return the crowd to the Philippines, was unable to control the mob and turned in a riot call for the police. A platoon of bluecoats were dispatched to the scene and compelled the frightened Filipinos to return to the park."

Truman congratulated himself on yet another publicity coup and a crisis averted. He had never imagined life would bring him here. But here he was, master of his domain. As he'd shown time and time again, he was untouchable.

17

Dear Dr. Hunt

WASHINGTON, DC, FEBRUARY 1906

The State, War, and Navy Building in Washington, DC, c. 1915

Captain Frank McIntyre

IN A CITY dominated by somber classical revival architecture, the flamboyant State, War, and Navy Building stood out for miles around. Occupying an area equivalent to eleven and a half football fields, right next door to the White House, it was a curiously extravagant building given its solemn function. The building boasted nearly two miles of black slate- and white marble-floored corridors, decorative mansards, and ironwork sculptures, peaks, porticoes, and pillars, nine hundred of them on the exterior alone.

Inside, sober-suited government officials were hard at work formulating and conducting American foreign policy, which was transforming the country into a global power.

On a cold winter's day in early 1906, Captain Frank McIntyre sat at his desk in one of the vast network of rooms occupied by the Bureau of Insular Affairs. A division of the War Department, the bureau had been established after the Spanish-American War to administer America's newly acquired territories, including the Philippines, Cuba, and Puerto Rico. McIntyre was assistant to the bureau chief, Colonel Clarence Edwards.

Both men had served in the Philippines and knew the politics of the islands inside out. When the Igorrotes visited the president during the St. Louis World's Fair, they also called on Edwards and presented him with a set of hand-carved wooden miniatures of Igorrote weapons.[1] The tiny spear, head-hunting ax, and bolo now had pride of place in a display case in Edwards's office, just along the corridor from where McIntyre sat.

McIntyre had the stiff manner common among military men but his face was pleasant, with smiling eyes and a neatly trimmed mustache. On this particular day his expression was grave as he dictated a letter to his secretary. In the letter addressed to E. S. Whitaker, the inspector of the New Orleans police, McIntyre expressed his desire to discover the whereabouts of Dr. Truman Hunt, a former government employee whom he believed was in New Orleans exhibiting a group of Filipino tribespeople.[2] Would Inspector Whitaker have one of his men find Truman and make discreet inquiries about his business? McIntyre would be grateful if the inspector could treat his request as confidential.

McIntyre instructed his secretary to type the letter up immediately. He wanted to get it mailed out that morning. He rested his elbows on the edge of his desk and rubbed his eyes. He wished this particular problem would go away.

Capt. McIntyre's career was on the up. The son of Irish immigrants, McIntyre had been raised in Montgomery, Alabama, and had entered the United States Military Academy at the age of seventeen. After serving in Puerto Rico and the Philippines, he returned to the United States in 1902 to begin his long service with the Bureau of Insular Affairs. His resourcefulness and sound judgment had won him the support of his superiors, not least Secretary of War William Howard Taft.

McIntyre had a sure touch for the complex issues that crossed his desk and an ability to identify and defuse potential problems. His department had been aware for some time that Truman had been exhibiting a group of Igorrotes around the country. From what McIntyre understood, Truman had been given permission from US officials in Manila to take the tribe out of the country, and the Filipinos had all volunteered to join Truman's enterprise in return for a monthly salary. Because Truman was operating a private enterprise—and not a government-organized exhibit, as had been the case in St. Louis—he had been left to his own devices.

But the arrival of a mysterious telegram addressed to the War Department from a man named H. E. Deputy inquiring whether Truman had taken the Igorrotes home, as he'd promised the court official in Tampa he would, raised the alarm.[3] Fearing a political scandal, the chief of the Bureau of Insular Affairs had ordered McIntyre to find Truman and ascertain what had happened to the Filipinos. It was one thing for an American showman to exhibit a willing group of tribespeople, but if he was coercing them, that was quite another matter. And how on earth had they ended up in Florida? McIntyre's secretary dug out all the files they had on Truman Hunt and the Igorrotes in the bureau's archives. Letters, reports, and official communications sat in several piles on the desk in front of him.

From McIntyre's initial scan through the files, Truman emerged as an upstanding citizen who had run a cholera hospital, served as a provincial lieutenant governor, and been a popular leader. Among the many documents was a report written by Dean Worcester, secretary of the interior for the US Insular Government and one of the most powerful colonial administrators in the Philippines. In it, Worcester praised Truman for conducting a "very successful"[4] Igorrote exhibit at the St. Louis Fair. He added, "Dr. Hunt thoroughly understands the handling of such people, and has, furthermore, demonstrated his ability and willingness to live up to his agreements relative to proper care and kind treatment of the peoples which he has been allowed to take and which he returned safely to their home."[5] On this basis, Worcester wrote that he had no objection to Truman exhibiting another group of Igorrotes as a private enterprise in the United States—as he was now doing—"provided suitable bonds were given for the humane treatment and safe return of such people as might be taken to the United States by him."[6]

It was only as McIntyre read on that cracks began to appear in Truman's record. McIntyre picked up a letter in which Col. Edwards, the bureau chief, had approved Truman and his former business partner Felder's plan to exhibit the tribe at the Lewis and Clark Exposition in Portland but had expressly warned against taking them to Coney Island or other amusement parks of its ilk.[7] Yet Truman had gone ahead and taken the tribe to Coney anyway.

Then there was the telegram sent by William Reed, the provincial governor of Lepanto-Bontoc, to Worcester, stamped at 8:22 on the morning of March 14, 1905, just as Truman and the Igorrotes were setting out from the region on the long journey to America.[8] In the telegram Reed, apparently having just learned of their impending voyage, protested against Truman taking the tribespeople out of the country, adding that "the troubles which have arisen as a result of the St. Louis Exposition and [claims] of Igorrotes that they have not received all their money indicate what might be expected from a private enterprise."[9]

The last sentence of the provincial governor's telegram referred to claims made by the St. Louis Igorrotes that Truman had not paid them the balance of their salaries when they returned to the Philippines, but had kept the money for himself. Their share of the profits was no small sum, amounting to $3,866.98.[10] An official in Manila had taken the matter up and written to his colleagues in Washington requesting clarification as to whether Truman had been given the money, but nothing had come of it and the claims had been all but forgotten. Until now.

Worcester had dismissed Governor Reed's concerns out of hand and had insisted that the showman would be made to provide a suitable bond.[11] But, as McIntyre read on, he learned to his dismay that Worcester's own office had failed in their duty to make Truman give a proper bond. Worcester was away on business when Truman arrived at his office in Manila. His deputy, acting in his absence, had given Truman a document to sign. The bond had been set at ten thousand pesos (around five thousand dollars). It had since transpired that the bond was worthless, as it only applied to employees of the insular government, which Truman was not. Furthermore, it failed to specify any conditions Truman was required to fulfill with regard to the care of the Igorrotes.

There was worse to come. Worcester himself had written to the bureau in late 1905, describing a conversation he had had with a former employee of Truman's, a Lepanto miner who had acted as Truman's assistant at the St. Louis Fair. What the man told Worcester had left him feeling "especially uneasy."[12] According to the miner, Truman had proposed to him that "they should get together an aggregation of Bontoc Igorrotes, take them to the US, run the exhibit as long as it paid, and then abandon the Igorrotes there."[13] From the way the miner spoke, it was clear that he did not hold his former boss in high regard, Worcester observed. Maybe the miner had an old score to settle. But when Worcester asked around the local community, he learned that the Filipino man had a reputation for being "responsible and truthful."[14]

Alone, each of these incidents could be dismissed or explained away. But cumulatively they made for uncomfortable reading. McIntyre had come across men like Truman Hunt before. He had been stationed in the Philippines long enough to see that in the climate of upheaval and lawlessness that prevailed in the new colony at the turn of the century, even honest men had been known to commit dishonest acts. Embezzlement, theft, drunkenness, gambling, exploitation of the tribespeople, and licentious association with native women were among the vices that thrived among the islands' new American populace.[15] An early *Report of the Philippine Commission* noted, "Many [men] leave the United States honest, but with the weakening of the restraints of home associations and with the anxious desire to make so long a trip result successfully in a pecuniary advantage, demoralization and dishonesty are much more likely to follow than at home."[16]

At forty-one, McIntyre was an ambitious man and still had much he wanted to achieve. The last thing he needed was to become embroiled in a messy scandal at a time when America's involvement in the Philippines was high on the political agenda. Erving Winslow, the abrasive and outspoken secretary of the Anti-Imperialist League, was hunting for grounds to make trouble over the exhibition of the Igorrotes. Winslow was a powerful man, capable of causing a lot of bother. McIntyre must do everything he could to ensure the Secretary of War and Henry Clay Ide, the acting governor-general of the Philippines, remained one step ahead of their opponents at all times.

The matter must be given the utmost priority. If word got out, this could be a huge political embarrassment. They had to find Truman and get him under bonds. If he refused, the Igorrotes would be taken from him and sent home on the next ship.

One thousand miles away in New Orleans, on February 11, 1906, Inspector Whitaker received an envelope bearing the US government seal. Ripping it open, he read Capt. McIntyre's letter with interest. It wasn't every day you got a request for help from the government. Whitaker would be happy to assist.

The inspector knew of Truman Hunt and the Igorrote Village. He made it his business to know who was in town and what they were doing. Truman and several of the Igorrotes had recently turned up at the Central Police Station, shouting about having seen a ghost. They were always in the local newspapers, chasing after dogs or getting up to some stunt. Truman was a regular in the Elks Lodge, just along the road from the police headquarters. Given how many policemen in the city were members too, it wouldn't be hard to find him. Whitaker told one of his officers to go and pay Truman a friendly visit and find out as much as he could about him and the group.

At Athletic Park the police officer was informed that the group had recently moved on. The park manager had heard they were in temporary accommodations on North Rampart Street, a lively area adjacent to Storyville, New Orleans's infamous red light district. The Filipinos were giving impromptu performances there during the carnival season. The police, and many of the city's most distinguished citizens, knew the area well. Alongside the dance halls and saloons were elegant mansions devoted to high-end prostitution, whose wealthy former residents had fled the area as vice took hold. Those looking for cheaper thrills frequented the boisterous cribs, single rooms in creaky, run-down buildings, furnished with little more than a mattress and a whore.

The police officer knocked on doors up and down North Rampart Street, which eventually led him to a saloon where he found the showman holding court, a cigar in one hand and a drink in the other. The officer approached and introduced himself. Truman shook his hand and ordered a round of whiskey. The officer said it was a friendly call. The inspector of the New Orleans police liked his officers to get out and meet with new members of the community. Smiling, Truman said he would be happy to tell the officer anything he wanted to know. The showman introduced the two men sitting beside him as his business associates, J. L. Miller and Edwin C. Fox.[17]

The four men struck up a cordial conversation. Truman described how he had first met the tribe in the Philippines. He talked about their taste for dogmeat and their head-hunting. Before long the conversation turned to the incident with the ghost at Athletic Park. The tribe had become so afraid, said Truman, that he had been forced to arrange alternative accommodations for them. The police officer was enjoying himself. It wasn't every day he met the manager of an exotic tribe, and Truman was an entertaining host.

The showman was forthcoming about all aspects of his business, falsely stating that he was under a ten-thousand-dollar bond to the US government for the care and safety of the tribe. According to Truman, they had journeyed for a month by sea and rail before reaching their first stop, in Seattle, on April 19, 1905. There were twenty-seven males and twenty-three females in the group, plus an interpreter. Truman fell silent for a moment, then added that two of the males had since passed away.[18]

Where, the police officer asked, *has the tribe been showing since they got to America?* Truman thought for a moment. They had been to so many places since they left Coney Island. Before New Orleans they had been in San Antonio, Texas, and before that they spent a couple of weeks in Dallas. They'd also been showing in Memphis; St. Louis; Louisville; Kansas City; Lincoln, Nebraska; and Springfield, Illinois.[19] There were other places too but he couldn't remember them all.

When the discussion turned to money, Truman was surprisingly open, even boastful. Admission was twenty-five cents and visitors came in the tens and sometimes hundreds of thousands each week. The Igorrotes were the biggest attraction on the fair and amusement park circuit this year. The officer asked Truman how long he planned to remain in town. The Igorrotes would be there for a while longer with one of his associates, but he was planning to travel to St. Louis in a few days, the showman lied. As the officer got up to leave, Truman told him they had a booking lined up in Nashville next (in reality they were going on to Jackson, Mississippi). That should throw them off his scent.

The officer left with a favorable impression of Truman and his associates. Yes, Truman bragged and liked the sound of his own voice. But he was up-front, likable, and humorous. He was a gentleman compared to some of the scoundrels working in the fairs and amusement parks. The police officer relayed to Whitaker what Truman had told him and speculated that the tribespeople must be making him a very wealthy man.

The news that Truman had been located offered McIntyre some relief, but he was eager to make contact with the showman himself. From what Inspector Whitaker said, there was no point in writing to Truman at his address in New Orleans, as he would be out of town by the time the letter arrived. McIntyre had recently discovered that Truman had been working with a St. Louis theatrical man named Col. John Hopkins. On February 14, 1906, Captain McIntyre wrote to Hopkins inquiring as to the well-being of Truman's Igorrote group.[20]

From where Hopkins stood on the grounds of Forest Park Highlands amusement park, he could just about see the site where the Igorrotes had first wowed America nearly two years earlier at the St. Louis World's Fair. He wondered how many millions of Americans had seen them since then—two, three, maybe even four million?

The theatrical impresario was still leasing some of Truman's Igorrotes from him, but the showman had turned up out of the blue recently and demanded that Hopkins give them back to him for a short time so that he could honor a booking. When Hopkins had refused, Truman had reacted with anger and threatened to bring habeas corpus proceedings to regain control of the group. His behavior was unseemly and unprofessional and Hopkins didn't like it one bit.

Hopkins was used to drama. He had earned his living from the theater for as long as he could remember. In that time he had become accustomed to doing business with all sorts of characters. He didn't know Truman well, and didn't wish to. He had learned enough about the showman's methods to know he would be wise to distance himself from his business associate.

Hopkins's reply to McIntyre was brief and stressed that his interest in the Igorrotes was "simply that of a booking agent."[21] His job was to "arrange dates for them and contract for their appearance at various places, under an agreement made with Dr. Hunt. I have booked them at various places throughout the country the coming summer. Wonderland Park, Boston, is one of the places at which they have been booked by me."[22] He added that Truman was currently in New Orleans with the Igorrotes and had been there since around December. To the best of his knowledge, Hopkins said, all of the tribespeople were in excellent health except one of the older men, who had died a few weeks ago.

McIntyre was glad to hear from Hopkins, though he was alarmed to discover that Truman planned to keep showing the tribespeople through the next summer season. Flawed bonds aside, this was a clear breach of the gentleman's agreement Truman had made with Worcester to take them out of the Philippines for no more than a year.

He decided to write to Truman, care of Col. Hopkins in St. Louis. In his letter, dated February 17, 1906, McIntyre told the showman that he wanted to keep in touch with him while he was touring the country and would appreciate a report from him each month as to the tribe's health and well-being. He added, "I understand that two of the party have died since their arrival in this country. Will you kindly advise us as to the cause of death, the disposition of their remains, and also of their effects."[23]

A fortnight passed without any reply from Truman. On March 9, 1906, McIntyre wrote to him again, this time at North Rampart Street, New Orleans, the address provided by the chief of police there.[24] Official interest in the Igorrotes was growing. Three months had elapsed since the telegram had arrived from H. E. Deputy in Florida, raising the alarm that all might not be well with Truman and the Igorrotes. They needed to find Truman fast.

McIntyre's second letter did indeed reach Truman. The showman was irritated. The last thing he needed was for some meddling government official to start checking up on his business. Truman never wrote a letter if he could avoid it, but he feared the government would only intensify their search if they didn't hear from him. He had a better idea.

On the morning that he and the Igorrotes were due to leave New Orleans, Truman finally got around to composing his reply. In the letter, dated March 15, 1906, he wrote, "the people [Igorrotes] are all well and perfectly contented. The party at the present time here [New Orleans] but will leave soon for the north with weather permitting. One member of the party died in Seattle upon our arrival there. Body is embalmed and will be returned to his home, he having no effects except salary which will be paid to proper officials in the Philippines. He died of Pneumonia. Pucuan, another male Igorrote, died here Jan 25th,[25] body embalmed and will be returned with us. His effects are all sealed and in possession of his sister. I will say I did not receive your first letter addressed to me at St. Louis. My permanent address this summer will be 1139 7th St., Louisville, Ky. Will be pleased to make you reports monthly or weekly, as you may desire. Your very truly T.K. Hunt."[26]

On his way to the station, Truman called in at the Elks Lodge, where he handed the letter to a friend of his and asked him to post it in two days' time. Why should he make it easy for the government to find him?

At long last McIntyre had made contact with Truman, but there was something about the tone of the showman's letter that he didn't like.

He had given only the briefest details about the tribespeople under his care and seemed to be operating under the arrogant assumption that the Igorrotes were his to do with as he pleased, for as long as he wished. Truman had failed to provide a new and proper bond for the Igorrotes, despite receiving a request from Manila to do so. His contract to exhibit the Filipinos expired that month, yet here he was flaunting the fact that he had no plans to take them home.

McIntyre had recently made contact with several people who had firsthand experience of Truman's business arrangements and they had been only too happy to talk. According to them, the showman had split his original group of fifty Igorrotes into three, four, maybe even five groups, and leased them out to other showmen, traveling carnival companies, would-be-entrepreneurs, and drinking buddies. The bureau hadn't been able to confirm yet whether this was true, but if it was, they faced an even bigger challenge than they had at first thought. Discovering the whereabouts of one group had been difficult enough. McIntyre didn't relish the prospect of repeating the exercise several times over and then sending agents out to gather them all up before transporting them home.

Rumors that Truman had begun importing additional groups of the tribespeople direct from the Philippines without first securing official permission had reached the War Department. There was a suggestion that the showman was mixing these new arrivals up with his original group so as to evade any attempts to track them down. McIntyre needed to know whether there was any truth to the rumors. He had to find out where the elusive Dr. Hunt was going next.

18

A Rival Enters the Fray

CHUTES PARK, LOS ANGELES, FEBRUARY 1906

Richard Schneidewind

WHILE IT HAD taken McIntyre months to locate Truman's Igorrote group, it couldn't have been easier to find the rival troupe being exhibited by Richard Schneidewind and Edmund Felder. Schneidewind himself had written to the Bureau of Insular Affairs inviting the government to send a man along to inspect the Igorrotes and their village at Chutes Park, Los Angeles. McIntyre decided that he would do just that. He would be glad to hear that at least some of the Igorrotes in America were faring well, not least because he would have a rare piece of good news about the tribe for the bureau chief. There was a large pool of retired army officers who had served in the Philippines that he could draw on for this job. The man McIntyre selected to carry out the inspection was Lieutenant Colonel William Hamner, who had served in the Spanish-American War.

The moment Hamner stepped inside the Chutes Park Igorrote Village, he felt as if he were in the Philippine Islands. The village occupied an attractive piece of ground, around an acre in size, and was filled with pretty straw-thatched huts, shaded from the Californian sun by palm, pepper, and eucalyptus trees.[1] A handsome, well-groomed man with a mustache approached and introduced himself as Richard Schneidewind. He looked to be around thirty years of age and was dressed in a linen suit. He invited Hamner to wander freely through the village, and to talk to anyone he wished. Antero, the interpreter, would be on hand to translate.

Antero was a helpful and likable guide. He spoke excellent English and was clearly popular with the tribe. The interpreter, who had once worked as Truman and Else Hunt's houseboy in the Philippines, showed Hamner around. He informed him that there were thirty-five Igorrotes living in the village—eighteen males and seventeen females. The tribe's living accommodations consisted of a large "rich man's house" for Domingo, the head chief, who was reported to have seventeen heads to his name, a *pa-ba-fu´-nan*, which was a dormitory for the unmarried men, an *o´-lâg*, the dormitory for the girls and unmarried women, and separate huts for the group's two young married couples. Next they visited the granary and the municipal building at the center of Igorrote community life. The village was clean and pleasant. Particularly appealing, thought the inspector, were the miniature rice fields showing the Igorrotes' advanced methods of cultivation. He watched with interest as a group of tribespeople sowed rice.

From its authentic village layout to the informative lectures that Schneidewind arranged, it was clear to Hamner that the Los Angeles Igorrote exhibit had a strong educational ethos. Flyers advertising the village contained passages taken from Albert Jenks's ethnological study of the tribe, *The Bontoc Igorot*.[2] The contrast with Truman's village could not have been starker.

Hamner approached the chief and, with Antero translating, he asked him how he was enjoying working for Schneidewind. The chief replied that he was comfortable, well fed, and well cared for. He was happy to stay on and travel to Chicago, where they were due to be exhibited next. The inspector spoke to most of the tribe and they all gave the impression of being contented. They appeared to speak freely and did not give the impression of talking from a prerehearsed script. Schneidewind paid them their salaries on the same day each month and, so far, they had never needed to remind him. The Igorrotes were allowed to retain all the money they earned from the sale of rings, spears, and other souvenirs they made. Some of them kept their earnings in their luggage in the village, while others had already remitted much or all of it to the Philippines. Owing to their popularity with the public, their pay had recently been increased from $7.50 per month to $12.50 each for the chiefs and "head women," and from $5 to $10 for all other tribespeople. Hamner scribbled the figures in his notebook.

Several of the boys, including Antero, were attending the 16th Street School, just beside the park. Antero asked Hamner if he knew anything about the other Igorrote group that was exhibiting in America. They had not seen their friends and family in Truman's group in a year and were eager for news of them. Hamner shook his head—no, he knew nothing about a second group.

The following day Hamner wrote up his report, in which he concluded that Schneidewind was operating a model Filipino village and that the tribespeople were "in excellent physical condition."[3] He enclosed a photograph of the Chutes Park tribe, which seemed to confirm his favorable impression.

McIntyre received a newsy eight-page report from Schneidewind several days later, which was also sent to Dean Worcester, secretary of the interior in Manila. In it, Schneidewind wrote about the good health and happiness of the tribe, adding, "It is the purpose of the management, in all ca[s]es, to take the people only to thoroughly reputable places, and the overtures of travelling [*sic*] carnival companies and others of that ilk have not been entertained, as a correct representation of their life, manners and customs cannot be properly portrayed under such circumstances. It is hoped that this attitude of the management will be pleasing to the Government of the Philippine Islands, for it is not believed that the Government would sanction their exhibition on a plane with dime museum freaks, or where the really interesting features of the home life of these remarkable people cannot be faithfully shown."[4] McIntyre raised his eyebrows. He assumed this was a dig at Truman Hunt.

Schneidewind concluded: "The management is endeavoring to show the best side of the Igorrote. The dog feasts, which were of daily occurrence in St. Louis at the World's Fair, have occurred very rarely, because it is believed that they have but a small part in the life of the Igorrote and that they give a degraded impression of these fine people to the American public."[5] Schneidewind enclosed photographs of the Igorrotes and an advertising flyer.

McIntyre frowned. What was the true purpose of this letter? Like Truman, Schneidewind and Felder were on good terms with a number of senior officials in Washington and Manila. Had they learned that the bureau was investigating Truman Hunt, and written the letter in an attempt to distance themselves from Truman and his style of doing business? Were they simply protecting their own interests? Or were they laying the groundwork before stirring up trouble for their rival? And, given his eye for good publicity, why was Truman not taking similar steps to appease the authorities?

McIntyre wasn't the only person taking a keen interest in Felder and Schneidewind's Igorrote Village. Truman had recently sent an associate of his to Chutes Park to take a look around and see if he could learn anything about where his rival's group was going next. He had an old score to settle.

19

Memphis Blues

MEMPHIS, APRIL 1906

IGORROTES SICK OF AMERICA.

Newspaper headline from a file the US government kept on Truman and the Igorrotes

THE SMALL FRAME house at number 446 North Front Street had seen better days. Outside the paint was cracked and peeling, exposing beams of rotten wood. The two front windows were filthy. The scrappy front yard was overgrown with weeds and the gate leading to it was hanging off its hinges.

Truman drew up outside in a horse-drawn carriage just as the last light was fading from the sky. The showman climbed out and looked up at the house. He would never think of staying in such a place, but then, he didn't have to. He handed the driver some money and turned around as a convoy of wagons approached. One by one the Igorrotes emerged from inside and stepped down onto the sidewalk, dragging their trunks behind them. A young black woman dressed in a threadbare coat and a broad-brimmed hat came out of the house next door. She stopped in her tracks and stood, staring. The tribespeople were dressed in their traveling clothes, but these did nothing to disguise the fact the Filipinos didn't belong in these parts.

A group of men in overalls passed on the other side of the street and shouted something at the new arrivals. Julio had become adept at shutting out the racist taunts. The others didn't understand the words the men used, but they knew they had heard them before, in other towns they had visited. One of the men spat on the ground, eyeing them as he did so. Julio looked past them and across the street at an ugly four-story building enclosed by a thick brick wall topped with iron spikes. It was the Shelby County jail. The light from the watchtower lit up the streets for miles around.

North Front Street was in an industrial area, three miles northeast of the Memphis city limits.[1] The district boasted lots of jobs and plenty of local color, though it wouldn't win any beauty contests. It was home to the navy yards, timber mills, breweries, coal yards, the gasworks, and warehouses storing everything from oil to lime and cement. The Illinois Central and the Louisville and Nashville railroad lines ran just yards from where the Igorrotes stood, providing a rattling, whistling soundtrack to the long days and nights. Across the tracks, cargo ships sailed up and down the Wolf River. Drifters, river rats, and passing drunks wandered through the streets looking for a place to get a drink and rest their weary heads.

A straggling group of local children playing in the street watched as Truman herded the Igorrotes inside their new home, away from prying eyes. The showman counted heads as the tribespeople entered. There wasn't room for them all to stand in the narrow hall, so the tribespeople spilled into a neighboring room. Satisfied that everyone was there, Truman swung the door shut and turned the key in the lock. Julio inhaled. The air was musty. There were four small rooms—two overlooked North Front Street and the others looked out onto a vacant lot.[2] You had to pass through a room off the hallway and another room behind it to reach the back door. The walls were covered in a powdery black substance that looked like soot. Truman noticed that the powder had gotten on the sleeve of his suit. He brushed it off. It must be from the coal yard or the railroad out back.

The only toilet was outside. Truman informed the tribespeople they would need permission from him or Callahan to use it. Daipan asked if she could go now. Callahan opened the back door and told her to be quick. He stood at the open door waiting for her to return. There was no back porch, just a few steps leading down to the yard. Not that it could really be called a yard: it wasn't fenced in—it couldn't be, because the L&N Railroad ran through it, within a few feet of the house. While Daipan was in the outhouse, a train thundered past. The house shook and the windows rattled so hard the tribespeople thought the glass might fall in on them.

The place was a hovel, thought Truman, standing in a front room, but the tribespeople slept in much worse at home. It would do fine. He didn't care for the nosy neighbors, but they could deal with them. The windows and doors would remain locked at all times. Except for Julio, no one would be allowed out other than to use the toilet. Truman noticed a group of children peering in through the window. He rapped his knuckles on the glass and shooed them away. They would have to cover the windows.

The tribespeople were tired and hungry after their journey. Julio took out his watch—it was eight o'clock. Truman told the interpreter that they were all to sleep together in one of the rooms at the front. There was a danger they might be seen, thought the showman, but it was preferable to them trying to escape out the back door. Callahan would sleep in the same room with them. Reluctantly, the security man agreed. Then Truman scooped up a pile of the tribe's blankets, a dirty sheet left by the previous tenants, and whatever else he could lay his hands on, and began using them to cover the windows. A couple of the windows had shutters, so Truman pulled them closed.

Julio asked what he was doing. Truman told the interpreter he didn't want people coming round and peering into the house day and night, bothering them. This was true, but he had another reason for keeping the tribe hidden. He didn't want people knowing they were in Memphis in case word got back to McIntyre and the War Department.

Before Truman left to go to his hotel, he told Callahan that he was counting on him to keep them all in line. He didn't want anyone getting out again and causing trouble. If Callahan wanted to keep his job, he must keep the house locked at all times and the windows covered. His security man nodded and Truman handed him the keys. Callahan locked the door behind him and rejoined the tribe in the front room. He lowered himself into a chair and put his feet up on a broken side table. The Igorrotes' guard was not looking forward to the night ahead; he was expected to stay awake all night, and he had no beer to drink and no one to play cards with.

The escape attempt in New Orleans and the letter from the War Department had rattled Truman. He was worried the government would send someone out to check up on him. That was why he had cut short their stay in New Orleans. He also feared the Igorrotes might try to break out again. Truman had purposely kept their bookings short ever since, spending a few days here and there in mostly out-of-the-way places. He had brought them to Memphis on a whim—he had friends in the city and enjoyed it there. He didn't know how long they would be staying.

The Igorrotes' mood was somber on their first night in their new home. Early American visitors to Bontoc had frequently commented on the squalid, primitive, and cramped conditions of the Igorrotes' homes. The tribespeople didn't care for luxuries. But in the Philippines, despite frequently sleeping eight to ten crammed into one small, squat, windowless hut, they had never experienced the claustrophobia they felt now. They were silent as they removed the American clothes, which had become their detested uniform whenever they traveled. There was so much to say but so little point in saying anything. They wondered how long they would be staying in this house, but they hadn't bothered to ask. They no longer trusted a word Truman said.

Maria and Daipan busied themselves at the stove, cooking up the little bit of rice they had left. They had run out of beans. They missed the juicy maize and the sweet camotes they could pick or dig up from the soil whenever they wanted them at home. Julio bought them rice and potatoes every week. He did his best to provide them with fresh fruit and other vegetables, sometimes even a little chicken, but he couldn't always get them. The tribespeople were growing lethargic on their bland, starchy diet, but that was the least of their worries.

When the rice was cooked through, Daipan carried the steaming pot over to where everyone was sitting. Callahan grunted at her to serve him first—he didn't want to eat from the pot after the Filipinos' grubby hands had been in it. Maria rummaged around in a cupboard and found a small bowl. It was chipped and dirty. Using a spoon she scooped some rice into the bowl without bothering to clean it and handed it to the guard. Callahan indicated that he wanted more. Maria and Daipan looked at each other. There would hardly be anything left for the others. Maria gave him more and he ate it greedily. Then the two women told the others to help themselves. Though they hadn't eaten all day, the Igorrotes had lost their appetites.

That night they went to bed early. They were exhausted, but sleep eluded them. Trains rattled through the backyard, just feet from where they lay, but it was not the noise that kept them awake. Feloa lay thinking of his wife and his three young children, wishing he had never left them. The little one was just a baby. He must have grown so big by now. Feloa had made sure his wife had enough to live off for the year that he would be away. But that year was up and he wondered how she was surviving. Their friends and family would help take care of them, but they could only help for so long. No one was rich where they came from. Feloa wasn't the only one with a family at home to support. Dengay thought of his wife and four young children, while Daipan was anxious about her widowed mother. Her mother was a worrier by nature and Daipan knew that she would not rest until she was home.

Julio rose early the next morning. He dressed, putting on a clean white shirt and his favorite beige linen summer suit. There was little point in dressing up, but the interpreter didn't own any informal clothes. Picking up his boater hat, he went through to the next room and asked Callahan if he could go out to use the toilet and to visit the store. The tribe needed food. Callahan nodded. Unlocking the back door, he told him to be quick. There was a store on the corner, two buildings down. Julio went out into the backyard and pulled open the door leading to the outhouse. The wood was rotten. The stench was foul. Holding his breath, he entered. From what he'd overheard Truman and Callahan saying, it didn't sound as though they would be staying long. Though you never knew with Truman. Recently he'd taken to rearranging their schedule at the last minute.

The air in the street was infused with chemicals, but it was preferable to being stuck inside that stuffy box. Julio wondered when they'd see Truman again. He usually reappeared every week or so. Julio guessed he'd gone to Kentucky to see Sallie. Truman had told him she'd had the baby recently. A girl. Maybe seeing them would improve Truman's mood.

The interpreter had noticed that his boss had been drinking more heavily recently. His breath stank of alcohol at all times of the day. The Filipinos had long observed the effect alcohol had on the men in their host country, noting, "the Americans often make themselves mad by things that they [drink]. They [run] about the place shouting or fighting till they [fall] down asleep."[3] Increasingly, Julio tried to stay out of Truman's way. Though the two men were still cordial, the trust between them had never been the same since the incident in the Dallas bar. Julio had become more outspoken. He had been standing up for the tribespeople and challenging his boss, and Truman resented it.

The interpreter wrapped his fingers tightly round the small bundle of notes in his pocket. Over the past six months, he had managed to save over four hundred dollars for the tribe from their souvenir money and tips, which he'd so far kept successfully hidden from Truman.[4] As the only one in the group who wore an American suit at all times, he had more places to hide it. Julio had asked Maria to cut a small hole in the lining of his jacket and waistcoat. He tucked most of the money away in there, then got Maria to sew the lining up again. You could hardly see the joins. He kept a little cash handy inside his pocket, just enough to buy provisions. As far as he knew, Feloa, Dengay, and some of the other men had been keeping some of their own money too.

Julio's fingers were still gripping the money in his pocket as he approached the grocery store and saloon on the corner of North Front and Auction Streets. A weathered sign hanging over the doorway announced that the proprietor was Mrs. Patton. Stepping inside the dark interior, Julio said good morning to the woman behind the counter. The woman, presumably Mrs. Patton, stood silently taking in every inch of him. Julio turned and walked down an aisle. He could feel several sets of eyes boring into his back. Any strangers excited a good deal of interest in this part of town, but Julio's smart clothes, his hat, and his strange accent made him a real oddity. Picking up a bag of rice, Julio turned around to look for potatoes and found that he was being followed by the woman. *Can I help?* she asked abruptly. Lifting a sack of potatoes from a pile on the floor, Julio said no, he could find everything he needed. He picked up a bag of dried beans, watched by two men in oil-stained overalls. Ignoring them, Julio grabbed a box of cookies and some candies as a treat for his friends and put them on the counter.

The woman eyed him suspiciously as she added up the items. There had been a great deal of talk in the store since the previous day about the queer new residents at number 446. Some said they were immigrant laborers, brought in to work on the railroads. According to others, they were prisoners who had recently been released from jail. One of the regulars in the saloon that adjoined the store said he had heard they were a freak show. But, looking at Julio, Mrs. Patton thought he was dressed mighty smart for a circus act. Ignoring all the stares, Julio handed over his money and exited the shop. As he walked back down North Front Street, the young Filipino was trailed by a handful of scruffy-looking children who should have been in school.

Julio couldn't face going back to the house yet. As he approached, he noticed the windows were still covered, so he walked on quickly down the street, his arms laden with groceries. He wouldn't go far, not with Callahan waiting for him, no doubt counting every minute. Julio instinctively followed the noise of the timber yard and stopped outside the gates to watch. The railroad ran alongside it and workers were busy loading freight cars. Julio breathed in the hot, sweet smell of the freshly cut logs. He could have stayed watching the lively scene all morning, but he didn't want to aggravate Callahan. Besides, he felt a little guilty being out, knowing that Maria and the others were cooped up. He turned back toward the house, their own private prison.

Julio knocked on the door. While he waited for it to open, he turned around and gazed up at the towers of the Shelby County jail. This wasn't the first jail he'd seen in America, but he'd never stood so close to one before. He wondered what the inmates were doing inside. Smiling bleakly, he thought their lives might not be all that different from those of their Filipino neighbors. At least the inmates would have work to keep them occupied. Turning back to face the house, Julio noticed someone lifting a corner of the blanket and peering out the window. It was Friday. Julio shook his head at the boy. The last thing they needed was anyone getting caught breaking the rules. Callahan could be easygoing when Truman wasn't around, but he had a quick temper.

Callahan opened the door and began grumbling that Julio had been away too long. Ignoring him, Julio hurried into the front room to show the others what he'd bought. He dug his hand into his packages and began handing out cookies. Maria smiled as he slipped a candy into her open palm. She was pleased to see him in bright spirits. He hadn't been himself lately; he'd been distracted and downhearted. Maria knew he'd been shaken by Truman's lies. Julio had always regarded Truman as a friend. He'd continued to trust him and defend him, even when the others had grown suspicious of the showman's motives. It had taken awhile for Julio to admit it to himself, but there was no hiding from the fact that Julio too had been taken for a ride.

Maria's first responsibility was to her husband, but she also cared for the rest of the group. She was upset by the thought that they were being cheated and taken advantage of. Equally troubling was the knowledge that the tribe's faith in Julio had waned over the past year. Maria dearly hoped that this could be remedied. Julio had never given up arguing their case, even if he hadn't had much evidence of it lately.

Julio offered Feloa a cookie. The tribal chief smiled and helped himself to two. He had developed a very sweet tooth and his growing belly had become a running joke among his countrymen. The roll of fat around his middle helped hide the top of the cloth belt that Feloa wore under the waistband of his G-string. The women had made it for him in New York. The belt was intended to be decorative. But recently he'd begun slitting it open and putting his money inside, then getting the women to sew it back up. It was getting full and he planned to ask Julio if he knew how they could send some of the money back home.[5]

Though Truman demanded that the tribe hand over all their souvenir money, Feloa, Dengay, and Julio were not alone in having hidden some of it from him. The tribespeople no longer dared hide it inside their trunks, for they knew Callahan and Truman had started searching through them. Instead they'd found other, more imaginative places, tucking it under their basket hats, down the fronts of their G-strings, and between their buttocks.

Five hundred miles away, Truman was checking in to the Burnett House hotel in downtown Cincinnati. Though the showman didn't know it, there was a peculiar historical irony to his choice of hotel; not only had the Great Emancipator himself, Abraham Lincoln, stayed in the Burnett House on his journey to Washington, DC, to be sworn in as the sixteenth president of the United States, the hotel's other former guests included Horace Greeley. The antislavery activist would have been horrified by Truman's treatment of the Igorrotes, though the newspaper Greeley founded, the *New York Tribune*, had devoted numerous column inches to the story of the Filipinos at Coney Island.

Truman's brief stay in Cincinnati was packed with business meetings. He had a most enjoyable dinner with the well-connected editor of *Billboard*, the paper of record for carnivals, amusement parks, fairs, and vaudeville. The two men got along famously and spent a long night cementing their new friendship over a bottle of Scotch.

The showman had been traveling a lot that year, arranging bookings, meeting associates, seeing Sallie whenever he could, and keeping tabs on his business partners. Truman visited his Igorrote groups often and always arrived unannounced to collect his share of the takings. The business was full of scam merchants and Truman had learned to trust no one, not even the friends and family he had employed to help in his Igorrote venture. He always studied the gate receipts and admission figures to make sure nothing was amiss. If there was an opportunity to cheat him, he knew someone would take it.

A month had passed since Truman had written to McIntyre at the Bureau of Insular Affairs. At the time Truman had promised to send a monthly report on the Igorrotes. Eager to keep the government at arm's length, Truman decided he would be true to his word and send another report. He was leaving Cincinnati that day and figured he had nothing to lose. His letter wouldn't reveal anything to McIntyre about the current whereabouts of the tribe. He would postdate it and leave it with the bellboy to mail the following week. By the time McIntyre received it, Truman would be long gone.

Truman took out his pen and a piece of the hotel's letterhead stationary, and wrote: "I have the honor to report that there has been no sickness among the people [Igorrotes] with me during the last month. About ten (10) have expressed a desire to return home and will be send [*sic*] with a competent man as soon as Transportation can be arranged also bodies of Dead. Yours Respectfully TK Hunt."[6]

In fact, Truman hadn't seen the tribespeople for days. But there was no harm in letting McIntyre think they'd been in Cincinnati with him. Truman assumed they were all fine. If there was anything to report, Callahan, Fox, or one of his other associates would have been in touch. Most of the Igorrotes were in Memphis with Callahan, where they would soon be joined by the others who had been exhibiting in Hot Springs and Little Rock, Arkansas, with Fox. Truman planned to go and check up on them all very soon.

Back in the house on North Front Street, the Igorrotes thought wistfully of their Coney Island days. If Coney had felt like a prison at times, in hindsight it seemed like liberty itself. Little had they known when they left New York that life was about to get so much worse. At Luna Park they had resented the distortion of their cultural traditions, but now they longed for the days when they were allowed out all day in the fresh air and had work to occupy them. They loathed being idle. With no work to fill their time, they spent their days smoking, chatting, and wondering what might happen to them next. The walls were paper-thin, but the tribespeople were free to speak since Callahan didn't understand them. They rarely spoke about the money Truman owed them anymore. It seemed pointless, especially since they had learned that even Julio hadn't been paid his wages. All he got was a small weekly allowance, taken from their earnings, to buy food and tobacco for the group.

Mealtimes and trips to the privy were the only activities that punctuated the monotony of their wretched existence. As the days passed, they dreamed of the day when the door would be unlocked and they would emerge from the house with its blacked-out windows into the daylight again.

One afternoon there was a loud knock at the door. Callahan ushered the tribespeople into a front room and told them to keep quiet. Feloa peeled back a corner of the blanket covering the window and saw two policemen standing outside on the front porch.[7] Callahan chatted with them for a few minutes. When he came back inside, Julio could see that something was the matter. Callahan called the interpreter aside.

The jailer across the street, a man named Fleetwood, had complained to the police that the Filipinos had been exposing themselves, running around in their skimpy tribal costumes, and upsetting his wife and daughter.[8] From now on, Callahan said irritably, they must all put on their clothes whenever they went outside to use the toilet. Truman had left Callahan in charge and he had no intention of messing up and getting on the wrong side of the boss. Julio thought the jailer was a racist and a fool. His wife and daughter couldn't possibly see around the back of the house unless they'd come looking. Besides, even then, the most they could have seen was an inch of buttock. If the tribe were on show in the city, Julio imagined the jailer's wife and daughter would be rushing to see them. But Julio knew better than to share his opinions with Callahan. He was a racist and a fool himself. What's more, Julio knew that if word of the complaint got back to Truman, the showman would take his anger out on them all. Though it rankled him, it seemed safest to keep quiet and go along with the jailer's request.

That day happened to be Friday, the thirteenth of April, 1906. In five days' time it would be exactly a year since Truman and the Igorrotes had arrived in Vancouver, full of hope and ambition. Julio was the only one who'd been keeping track of the days and he was alone in following the Western calendar, not the ten-month Igorrote version. If Truman had been good to his word, they would all be back in the Philippines by now. Julio wouldn't mention the significance of the date to Maria. There was no point in making anyone else feel worse than they already did.

Most of the tribespeople were already asleep when there was another knock at the door. Julio jumped up and ran over to the window. He lifted an edge of the blanket. He could hardly believe his eyes. Outside were Tainan and the rest of the Igorrotes who'd left New Orleans with Fox. Soon the hallway was filled with familiar voices. *They're back*, Julio shouted in Bontoc, *the others are back!* The sleeping Igorrotes stirred and followed Julio out into the hall. The two groups hadn't seen each other since New Orleans and were overjoyed to be reunited again.

Tainan began to chatter excitedly, telling them they'd just got off the train from Little Rock. That evening Tainan and the others in Fox's group entertained their countrymen and women with stories of their travels. The tribespeople laughed as Tainan told them about the large dog Fox had started traveling with, which he pretended was a fierce guard dog. The Igorrotes had had to pose with the mutt for a photographer from a local paper in Little Rock, pretending they were about to skin it alive for one of their feasts. But instead of looking afraid, the dog had kept rolling over to have its belly tickled.

To celebrate their reunion, the women cooked up a big pot of rice, potatoes, and beans. Afterward they ate what remained of the candies Julio had bought in Mrs. Patton's store. Some of the younger ones began to talk about what they would do when they went home. Though she knew it was foolish, Maria allowed herself to imagine her own reunion with her family. What a feast they would have. The thought made her happy and sad all at once. Over the past year, Maria and Julio had almost always enjoyed the luxury of having their own place to sleep. But in Memphis they had no choice but to bed down with all the others. Maria missed the privacy, but at the same time she was glad that she and Julio had the opportunity to bond with the others again.

The tribespeople were eating a meal together the following day when another visitor came to the house. Hardly anyone had visited in the ten days or so that they had been staying there, just the police officers who'd been once, maybe twice, and Fox and the other Igorrote group.

The tribespeople crowded round the window of the front room and listened. Tainan lifted the edge of the blanket and peered out, but he couldn't see anyone. The person at the door seemed to have come inside. Feloa pulled Tainan away from the window. The Igorrotes heard voices in the hallway. A moment or two later the door swung open. Truman walked in, followed by Callahan.[9]

Julio could see that Truman was holding a letter of some sort. He seemed stirred up, possibly drunk. Usually their boss made small talk. Not today. Standing in the doorway, Truman held up his hand containing the piece of paper. He said it was a telegram from Washington he had just received. The telegram instructed him to take all of the Igorrotes' money from them. He offered no explanation as to why. The tribespeople began to protest. Feloa, Dengay, and Julio pushed to the front. Standing before Truman, Feloa said the showman had already taken all their money. They had just a few dollars left between them and it was theirs. Julio translated, his face solemn.

But the showman persisted. *Give it to me*, he yelled, holding out his hand. Feloa took another step forward. He could smell the liquor on Truman's breath. Drawing himself up to his full height, the tribesman shouted one of the few English words he'd learned during his time in America: *No*. His face flushed. He began to speak in his own tongue, his words tumbling over each other in his anger. *None of us are giving you our money. It is ours. You cannot take it.*

Truman seemed momentarily thrown by their defiance. Suddenly the showman's face was contorted by a rage he couldn't control. At Truman's signal, Callahan grabbed Feloa and pulled off the coat he had draped over his shoulders. Raising his right hand, Truman lunged at the tribal chief. Feloa ducked, thinking Truman was going to hit him again. But instead Truman thrust his hand under his waistband and ripped off the money belt the chief had been hiding there. The others looked on, aghast. They had never seen Feloa look so vulnerable. Taking a knife from his pocket, the showman slit Feloa's belt open. Silver half-dollars rained down on the floor. There were dozens of them. Truman stared angrily at the tribal chief as if in silent rebuke. The men wanted to do something to help, but they felt powerless. They had never seen Truman like this.

Delighted to have made an example of their leader, Truman bent down to scoop up the money. The room fell silent while he counted out twenty-eight dollars in coins which Feloa had earned selling rattan rings at five, ten, and fifteen cents each. The knowledge that someone in the park must have helped change the money into half-dollars made Truman madder still.

The women began to wail. Their high-pitched cries made Truman's head ache. Shoveling the money into his pockets, Truman yelled at them to stop. A few began to moan, "Why does he take our money, it is our own."[10] The women's sobs grew louder. Truman leaped to his feet, his arms flailing. He grabbed the nearest woman by the shoulders and began shoving her, screaming at her to get out. He couldn't stand listening to her for a moment longer. Callahan joined in. Together the two of them pushed the women out and into the next room.

The showman returned to address the men. He opened his mouth to say something, but was interrupted by the sound of the women's cries coming from the next room. Truman stormed through to find them cowering in a corner and yelled at them to shut up. He slammed the door, and stomped back to where the men were waiting, still clutching the telegram in his hand.

Feloa walked up to him and, pointing to his money, which now bulged in Truman's pockets, said clearly, "It is mine."[11] Truman waved the telegram in the air again and repeated that he was merely carrying out government instructions. He looked around at the faces of the twenty-six men and boys in the room, then slowly and calmly told them to hand over their money, all of it. Julio was the first to speak: "No,"[12] he stated firmly in a voice that sounded calmer than he felt. Feloa, Dengay, and Fomoaley looked at Julio with a mixture of surprise and admiration.

What? demanded Truman, incredulous that his assistant was defying him.

The money is ours, Julio said. *We earned it.*

Truman lowered his voice and placed a hand on his assistant's shoulder. In a conspiratorial tone, he said in English that he understood why they were upset and stressed again that he was merely following orders from the government. The money would be returned to them in due course. Julio asked Truman to show him the letter. That was out of the question, said the showman. It was confidential.

Julio spoke again, this time louder than before: he didn't believe Washington had told Truman to take their money; he was stealing it for himself. Truman was furious. He didn't expect such insolence from Julio. How dare he answer back. The showman looked at Julio and said he was asking them one last time to hand over their money. If they handed it over without making a fuss, they could forget the whole matter. If they refused he would have no choice but to use force. *No*, said Julio, *you are lying. We aren't giving you our money.*

Overcome with rage, Truman savagely wrenched at Julio's clothes, ripping his beautiful cream shirt down the front. The mother-of-pearl buttons, which had Maria lovingly sewn, flew across the floor. The room was silent. Truman yanked Julio's jacket off his back and began clawing at the lining. The showman's face was triumphant as he pulled out a wad of notes, more than four hundred dollars, and stuffed them into his own pocket. He had just stolen their only chance of escape.

That's my money, Julio shouted, but Truman kept manically tearing at the jacket. Julio's beloved gold watch he had bought in St. Louis the previous year fell out of an inside pocket and onto the floor. Truman picked it up and stuffed it into his pocket. When he was sure there was nothing of value left inside, Truman contemptuously tossed the ruined jacket onto the floor. But their tussle wasn't over. Truman looked at Julio then lunged for him again.

Callahan grabbed Julio by the wrist. Feloa pushed forward to help his countryman, but Callahan shoved him back. Standing squarely in front of Julio, Truman thrust his hands into his assistant's pants pockets. Julio tried to wrestle free, but it was useless. Truman had the strength of a madman. His nails dug into the interpreter's flesh as he grabbed for every last cent in his pockets.

At last it was finished. Julio looked at Truman, then down at the clothes he had once worn with such pride. His pants pockets were ripped. His shirt was shredded. In that instant Julio saw himself through Truman's eyes; for the first time, it was clear that Truman saw him not as special or different but as just another Igorrote savage. The interpreter stared back at his boss with hatred in his eyes.

Truman barked at the other men in the room to hand over their money. Nobody moved. Friday hid behind Feloa's legs. Holding out his hand, Truman turned to Dengay. When the Filipino shook his head, Truman swung his knife at Dengay's head and with one deft stroke, he slit the tribesman's basket hat open. Coins, tobacco, and a smoking pipe fell to the floor. Truman scooped them up. Then he started tugging at the waistbands of the men's G-strings and rifling through their blankets and traveling clothes. He found money which two of the other men, Filian and Gatonan, had hidden in the belts of their breechcloths. Then, as quickly as he had appeared, Truman turned and left the room without saying another word.

Later that evening, the showman scribbled receipts for Julio, Feloa, Dengay, Filian, and Gatonan and asked Callahan to take the pieces of paper to the men.[13] Truman had taken up residence in a back room of the house on North Front Street and planned to spend the night there. He didn't enjoy slumming it, but he needed to keep an eye on his charges. They would leave town the next day, Sunday, and he didn't want anyone pulling any stunts before then. They had hidden long enough. With their money in his pocket, Truman started to feel his old confidence ebbing back. He would split them up into different groups again and maximize his profits.

The moon rose over the eaves of the house. The only man who slept that night was Truman. His explosion of rage had left him purged and he sank into a deep slumber. Callahan was under orders to stay awake all night in the same room as the Filipinos, and with Truman in the house he didn't dare disobey. He eyed the tribespeople warily as they spoke all night in their native tongue. For the first time Julio joined in their low, fierce talk. Jacketless, his shirt torn, he sat on his haunches alongside the others. He was one of them now.

20

Raising the Alarm

CHICAGO, MAY 1906

Schneidewind's Igorrote Village at Riverview Park, Chicago

RICHARD SCHNEIDEWIND STOOD at the head of the table and raised his glass in a toast to the mighty city of Chicago. The table was groaning under the weight of an incredible feast of succulent, golden roasted poultry, piles of crisp potatoes glistening in fat, and mounds of brightly colored vegetables.

Putting down the carving knife, Schneidewind gestured to his guests to dig in. There was more than enough for everyone. The mood was lighthearted and the convivial sounds of conversation and clinking cutlery filled the air. After struggling with their knives and forks, some of the diners began unabashedly using their hands to pick up the food on their plates and greedily shovel it into their mouths. No one seemed to notice, even less care. Along with English and a smattering of German, there was the sound of another, more exotic tongue.

Schneidewind looked around the table at his Filipino charges. Since their arrival in America the previous year, he had taken to hosting dinners for the Igorrotes in his own home. He had grown fond of them and enjoyed their company. There wasn't room for all thirty-five of them at his table, so he had them over in small groups. Tonight he, his young son, Dick, and a few friends were celebrating the Filipinos' safe arrival in Chicago with Antero, the interpreter, along with some of Schneidewind's other favorite members of the tribe. Their new village was due to open the next day.

Schneidewind was especially fond of Antero. The interpreter was around sixteen years of age and had the easy charm of youth, along with a near perfect command of English. He had acted as one of the recruiters and interpreters when the Igorrotes appeared at the St. Louis Fair. He was bright, good-humored, and always had something to say for himself. In the Philippines Antero was popular with the Americans who settled there and he had worked for Jenks, and as Truman and Else Hunt's houseboy for two years. Else Hunt had treated Antero like a son. She had had white duck suits made for him, given him English lessons at her kitchen table, and had sent him to a local school run by an American woman. She had also taught him American songs, which Antero now used to entertain the crowds who came to the Igorrote Village.

Schneidewind's love for the Philippines stemmed from the time he served in the islands. While there he had fallen for a Filipina named Gabina. They were married in 1900, but Gabina died the following year while giving birth to their son, Dick. Dick moved to America with his father in 1904 and spent most of the year living with his aunts and grandmother in the Schneidewind family home in Detroit. But his father arranged for Dick to visit him regularly while he was touring with the tribe.

When the chicken carcasses had finally been picked clean and there was nothing left in any of the side dishes, Schneidewind and his guests reclined in their seats. Their stomachs groaned from all that they had eaten. The Igorrotes had been popular in Chutes Park, but Schneidewind felt confident they would do even better in the Second

City. Chicagoans had a special appetite for amusement parks and the more outlandish the attractions, the better.

Schneidewind looked at his watch and declared it was time they were all getting to bed. They had a busy day ahead of them. He walked the tribespeople back to their village, promising to take them on a tour of Chicago just as soon as they settled into their new home.

Chicago was growing at an astonishing rate in the early years of the twentieth century. In the three and a half decades since the Great Fire, the city's population had boomed from three hundred thousand to two million. Every day new arrivals from Ireland, Germany, Poland, and Sweden swelled the city still further, word having reached them that Chicago was crying out for immigrant labor. In 1900, three-quarters of the city's residents were either foreign-born or born of foreign parents.

If the Great Fire provided the impetus for the building boom that transformed Chicago, the 1893 World's Fair confirmed the city's position as a major center for architecture and design. The fair drew 27.5 million visitors from all over the country, and when it closed Chicagoans craved something more permanent to take its place.

Six years later, they got their wish, with the opening of Sans Souci amusement park. Named after the summer palace of the Prussian King Frederick the Great and meaning "without worry or care," Sans Souci opened in the summer of 1899. The park sprawled over seventy-four fun-filled acres on Chicago's north side and was billed by its owners with hyperbolic extravagance as "the world's largest amusement park."

Compared to the brash and unrestrained Sans Souci, Riverview Park, which opened five years later, was picturesque and polished. Riverview sat on the banks of Chicago's famous river and was landscaped with shaded groves, rolling lawns, and large picnic areas, making it a popular spot for leisurely days out.[1]

In 1905, as the population continued to grow, Chicago got another park. White City sat on the south side of the city, just a mile from Sans Souci and was inspired by the temporary pavilions at the heart of the Chicago World's Fair. The new park was the brainchild of brothers Morris and Joseph Beifeld, who billed White City as Chicago's answer to Coney Island. Determined not to be outdone by this upstart on their own doorstep, the owners of Sans Souci fought back, spending two million dollars on a host of new rides and attractions.

The competition between the three parks was heating up and the Igorrotes were about to be thrust into the heart of the battle.

Schneidewind had been delighted when the owners of Riverview booked his Igorrote group for the entire summer season. The park was a bucolic idyll that he felt certain the tribespeople would enjoy. The Igorrote's enclosure was a pleasant spot, filled with trees, plants, and freshly mown grass. The tribe had labored hard, building eight native houses, a granary, a civic building, and a system of miniature rice fields. Another hut served as a storeroom, which Schneidewind had stocked with rice, onions, potatoes, bananas, macaroni, cans of corn, tomatoes, beans, dried peas, and coffee. He also provided firewood, bedding, clothing, soap, and cigars.[2]

The weather was cold and miserable when Riverview threw its gates open for the new season on May 26, 1906.[3] Strong northeasterly winds forced many of the thirty-two thousand visitors who turned out for opening day to pull up the collars of their coats against the blasts, which seemed to have come straight from the Arctic. Word had gotten out about the exotic new attraction and Chicagoans hurried to the Igorrote Village to see for themselves whether everything they'd heard was true. Did they really eat dogs and cut off human heads? The line to enter the village grew long. Chicagoans were not famous for their patience, but nobody complained about having to wait to get in, not even when the wind picked up.

Schneidewind had planned an elaborate opening ceremony, but as the gale blew, shaking the walls of the tribe's huts, he was forced to cut it short. From eleven o'clock in the morning until eleven o'clock at night, the crowds roared for more and threw their hard-earned money at the Igorrotes' feet as they sang, danced, and engaged in mock battles.[4] Chilled to the bone by the icy winds, the tribespeople danced with increased vigor. At one point when Antero looked up, it appeared to him as if the whole of Chicago had descended on their village.

Schneidewind rose late the following morning. He was tired but happy after the successful grand opening, and decided to reward himself with a leisurely Sunday breakfast. As he ate, he leafed through the newspapers. He noticed, to his pleasure, that several of the reporters who had visited the village the previous day had given the Igorrote exhibit glowing reviews. He couldn't wait to show the articles to Felder. But as he picked up another paper, he read something that wiped the smile clean off his face.

The article mentioned an Igorrote Village at Sans Souci. That must be a mistake. Surely they meant his village at Riverview. Schneidewind read on and his eyes alighted on the name Truman Hunt. He felt his stomach lurch. How could this be? What was Hunt doing in Chicago? And how had Schneidewind not learned this before now?

The owners of Riverview had been advertising Schneidewind's Igorrote Village for weeks before the start of the new season. Surely Truman knew that they were there. Two Igorrote Villages in the same city would mean lower profits for both of them and that wasn't in anybody's interests.

Truman and Schneidewind's paths had crossed before, in the Philippines, and then again at St. Louis, where Schneidewind had operated a cigar concession. The two men hadn't warmed to each other then and Truman's behavior now was not intended to make friends. By coming to Chicago, was he trying to get back at Felder, his former business partner? From what Schneidewind had heard, the two men had a bitter falling-out. But Truman didn't seem the sort to sacrifice profits, not even in the interest of getting even.

One thing Schneidewind could be sure of was that Truman would stop at nothing to get the upper hand. Schneidewind had gone out of his way to persuade Felder of the merits of putting the Igorrotes in a setting that was realistic and respectful of their culture. But would people come and see their authentic village if, for the same price, Truman was promising them dog feasts, canine thefts, gory tales of headhunting battles, grand weddings, and whatever other crowd-pleasing feats he could dream up? Already fearing the worst, Schneidewind resolved to go and see Hunt's rival village for himself.

A roller coaster thundered overhead, the rattling of the cars' wheels drowning out the riders' screams. The colossal wooden track seemed to groan under the weight of its cargo as the cars loaded with passengers began the slow upward climb before the next clattering descent.

Beneath the loop of the Sans Souci roller coaster sat Truman's Igorrote Village, crammed into a muddy scrap of land, surrounded by the ride's twenty-five-foot-high trestlework. The enclosure wasn't so much a "village" as a pen, thought Schneidewind, aghast. There were no trees or plants. Instead the trestlework had been lined with a thin strip of tin that had been crudely painted to resemble mountain scenery. The living accommodations consisted of one half-finished tribal hut and three small A-frame tents. Against this miserable backdrop, the tribespeople were putting on a halfhearted show for the public. The Igorrotes were filthy, their bronze skin caked in dirt.[5]

Schneidewind shuddered. No one should be living like this in twentieth-century America. Their race was immaterial. He didn't want to see any more. He left the village before word got back to Truman that he was there. Schneidewind wondered where the showman was. When he'd asked at the gate who was in charge, he'd been told it was a man named Hill.

Back at Riverview, Schneidewind telegraphed Felder to tell him about the dreadful condition of their rival's village. Felder told his business partner to leave it with him. He knew exactly what they must do.

Col. Edwards, McIntyre's boss at the Bureau of Insular Affairs, was alarmed to receive Felder's letter describing the appalling conditions of Truman's Igorrote Village. Edwards found McIntyre in his office and read a section of the letter out to him: "Mr. Schneidewind has just returned from a trip to [Truman Hunt's] Village, and from his report, to me, I am afraid that sooner or later the conditions under which the Natives are living will get into public print, and bring this Village into disrepute. It is hard enough on us to have the Igorrote

Village pirated as is the case at Sans Souci, but . . . it would do me personally an irreparable harm if my village was confounded in the public mind with the edition now on view at San [*sic*] Souci Park."[6]

Felder clearly had a vested interest in pointing out any shortcomings in his rival's enterprise. But if what he said was true, and Truman's village could become a public disgrace, a delay could cost the War Department dearly. McIntyre informed Edwards that he had just received a similar complaint from a member of the public who had also visited Truman's village. It was not beyond the realms of possibility that the complainant had been put up to it by Felder. Or maybe they were doing the bidding of the American Anti-Imperialist League. Either way, McIntyre and Edwards agreed, the bureau must act. They must send someone to carry out an inspection of Truman's village straight away.

The inspector would need a translator in order to question the Igorrotes. They couldn't use Truman's interpreter—he might be loyal to his boss and have a vested financial interest in protecting him. But finding an alternative wouldn't be easy. There were Filipinos studying in America under a government program, but it was far from certain that any of them spoke the Igorrotes' language. Of the 7.6 million people living in the Philippines, only 2.8 percent of them were Igorrote, and a smaller proportion still were Bontoc Igorrote like those in Truman's group.[7] The government could waste weeks trying to find an interpreter among the students. There was one other option, which wasn't ideal, but it would have to do. They would use Schneidewind's translator.

Ever since they left the Philippines, Antero had been anxious for news of Truman's group. So when Schneidewind came to find his interpreter one day to tell him they were in Chicago and that he, Antero, was going to see them, the young Filipino whooped with delight. Schneidewind hadn't the heart to tell him about the terrible state of their village.

On June 14, 1906, Antero and Major Franklin O. Johnson got off the streetcar and walked through the gates of Sans Souci. With them were two other Igorrote men and two women from Schneidewind's group who had relatives in Truman's troupe and had begged to go too. Johnson noticed a sign advertising the wedding the following week of Daipan and a young man named Sadoy.[8] Antero spied Truman standing by the entrance to the village.

Truman greeted his former house boy like a long-lost friend. Releasing himself from the showman's embrace, Antero glanced up at the roller coaster overhead and covered his ears. Just yards from where they stood, Antero recognized another familiar face. It was Feloa. He had been given the job of barker, cavorting for the crowds at the entrance to the village to tempt them inside. Of all the demeaning tasks they were asked to perform, this was the Igorrotes' least favorite. Mindful of this, Truman had taken to using it as a way to punish anyone who had annoyed him. Catching sight of Antero, Feloa momentarily stopped dancing and accidentally dropped his spear. Looking up, Truman shouted to him to continue.

Turning to Johnson, Truman introduced himself and his business associate, "Happy" Hill. Johnson shook hands with them both and told Truman that he was there to take a look around on behalf of the US government. If Truman was irritated to see them, he concealed it well.

Johnson reached into his pocket for money to pay the admission fee, but Truman shook his head. No, no, they were his guests; he wouldn't hear of them paying. Showing them into the enclosure, Truman asked his visitors to forgive their appearance. The village was still under construction. From what Schneidewind said, it had been open almost three weeks. That was ample time for the industrious Igorrotes to build a village, thought Antero. Yet as they glanced inside, it looked anything but ready.

The enclosure was muddy and cramped. Back home their livestock lived more comfortably than this, thought Antero. *Do the tribespeople sleep here too?* asked Johnson. Truman nodded. As far as the government inspector could see, there wasn't a single hut for them to sleep in. *Where do they bed down for the night?* Johnson asked. Truman pointed to a half-built hut and said that in time there would be several of these, enough to accommodate everyone. But for now they were sleeping over there, said the showman, pointing to three small tents.

Johnson, who had known the Igorrotes when he served in the Philippines in Benguet Province, asked Truman how many tribespeople were living in the village. Eighteen, came the reply. Without a hint of irony, the showman invited the inspector to take a look around. The Igorrotes were all happy, healthy, and well-fed, as he would soon see for himself. Johnson was about to ask where their food store was when he was interrupted by the cries of Truman's Igorrotes. They had just finished giving a display and, spotting Antero and the others, they began running toward them. Johnson noted that they were in desperate need of a wash.

Truman's Igorrotes were overwhelmed to see friendly faces at last. The inspector left them, and went off to explore the "village." No wonder the poor people were filthy. As far as he could see they had no water closet and the only place to bathe or wash their clothes was using water from a hydrant in a tub in an unsheltered corner of the village, where they could be seen by all and sundry.

Johnson walked over to their sleeping quarters and felt his feet slither and slide in the mud. The A-frame tents were packed so tightly together you could hardly slip a hand between them. He peered inside. Boards had been laid on the ground to stop the tribespeople sinking into the mud as they slept. Could eighteen adults really sleep in these three small tents? Johnson wondered how any of them got any rest under such conditions. Truman had been blasé, but Johnson was appalled at the thought of it.

He walked over to another tent, sitting a little farther away. This one had been set up as a storeroom. The only provisions inside were rice, ground coffee, and sugar. He began jotting down impressions in his notebook. At that moment Hill appeared. Johnson asked him if the tribe had use of a water closet and wash block. Ah, said Hill, shifting his not insignificant weight from one foot to another. The changeable weather had delayed construction of these facilities, so they were currently sharing a water closet outside the village with a neighboring concession. When Johnson suggested that the tribespeople were in desperate need of a wash, Hill replied that the Filipinos did not have the same attitudes to cleanliness as Americans did. What nonsense, thought Johnson.

The government inspector walked over to join Antero and the others just as Truman arrived with Julio.

Johnson had asked to speak to the Igorrotes in private and Truman knew that if he refused, the government would simply send another inspector. Truman instructed Julio to stay with the visitors and make sure the tribespeople didn't say anything that could make trouble for him. He no longer entirely trusted his young assistant after his shocking outburst in Memphis, and would have preferred to leave him out of it, but he had no choice.

Truman disappeared, leaving Johnson and the tribespeople alone. Antero looked at Julio, whose appearance was always immaculate, and noticed his clothes were filthy. His jacket looked as if it had been torn and sewn in several places. The two men shook hands and Antero introduced Johnson. Julio whispered to Antero in Bontoc that they needed help. Truman hadn't paid them a penny of their wages and he was keeping them against their will. One of the men was suffering so badly with rheumatism that he could hardly stand up, but Truman was forcing him to work, and the showman had recently kicked one of the others when he demanded he send them home.

Antero didn't recognize the man Julio was describing as his former boss. He had heard the rumors that Truman had stolen some of the St. Louis group's wages. That was one of the reasons Antero hadn't wanted to come to America with him again. But he was stunned to hear of Truman's cruelty. The showman had changed since they left New York at the end of the previous summer, explained Julio. It was as if he had been taken over by a wicked, greedy version of himself. Julio was about to tell Antero about Truman's heavy drinking, his violent outbursts, and the tribe's escape attempt in New Orleans when he noticed Truman and Hill coming toward them.

Johnson got up and asked Truman if he could have a quick word with him in private. What arrangement had the showman made to pay the tribespeople their wages? Lowering his voice, Truman said he was keeping their earnings safe for them. He had put the money in the bank. If they got hold of it now, they would throw it all away on whiskey and gambling. They would be paid on their return to the Philippines. When did Truman propose taking them back? Truman said that three or four of them wanted to go home now, and added that he planned to send them on the steamship *Dakota* in July. The rest, he said, were happy to stay on. When Johnson asked to see the tickets for their return journey, Truman explained that he had not bought them yet because of the unpredictability of traveling with savages. Satisfied that he had seen all he needed to, Johnson told Truman they would not take up any more of his time.

Antero looked back at his countrymen and women before exiting the village. It pained him to leave them there. The roller coaster roared overhead.

21

A Worthy Opponent

THE WAR DEPARTMENT, WASHINGTON, DC, JUNE 21, 1906

Aerial view of Sans Souci Park, Chicago, looking over the roller coaster under which Truman Hunt's Igorrote group lived

DURING HIS YEARS in government service, McIntyre had learned to keep calm under pressure. Whatever the provocation, he never lost his temper. But now he had really had enough. Johnson's report was damning. Not only was Truman Hunt shamelessly exploiting the Igorrotes, he was treating his own government like fools. McIntyre had to get Truman's village closed down before it blew up into a major scandal.

The Truman-Igorrote business had already taken up too much of McIntyre's time. The bureau needed to put their most dogged agent on the case. McIntyre knew just the man for the job, and asked his secretary to send for him immediately. Frederick Barker was everything a good agent should be. The thirty-six-year-old was diligent, dedicated to serving the government, and would not rest until he got a job done. He always played by the rules and loathed injustice of any sort. There was a standing joke in the department that his expense claims were so low, he must survive on thin air when he was away on assignment. He was also a fluent Spanish speaker, which would help him converse with the Igorrotes.

McIntyre's secretary had been instructed to show Barker in the moment he arrived. As she did so, she couldn't help but note the visitor's handsome features, his strong jawline and piercing blue eyes. McIntyre stood up from behind his desk and shook Barker's hand. Then he got straight down to business. He had an assignment that needed to be handled sensitively. It involved a former Bontoc official who was exhibiting a band of Igorrotes in America. Barker listened with interest.

Barker had served as a law clerk in the Philippine Commission's offices in Manila, and had met the Igorrotes during the three years he lived in the islands. He had read about their appearance at Coney the previous year. Though he was not about to share the opinion with his boss, Barker objected strongly to the exhibition of a native tribe in such a demeaning manner. He was both surprised and disappointed to hear they were still in the country. He also knew all about the Americans who went rogue in the Philippines.

He listened to McIntyre describe the poor living conditions of the group under Truman's care, and knew immediately that this was a case he wanted to solve. Yes, he said enthusiastically, he would leave for Chicago the following day.

Barker must treat the case as confidential. The Anti-Imperialist League was trying to make political hay out of the situation. He should be wary of the Chicago press. The *Daily News* had published a report that week describing the sorry state of Truman's group. Taking his leave, the agent reassured McIntyre that he would have the matter resolved as quickly and painlessly as possible. He couldn't wait to tell his wife, Tudie, about his assignment.

Truman was about to encounter his nemesis.

• • •

Barker arrived at the Great Northern Hotel at nine o'clock on the morning of Saturday, June 23, 1906.[1] Designed by the celebrated architects Burnham and Root, the handsome fourteen-story hotel was built in 1892 and occupied a prime location in downtown Chicago. By 1906 it was no longer the smartest hotel in town, but Barker didn't care for luxuries. He wasn't there to relax. After checking in at reception, he went straight up to his room and saw that it was bigger than he needed. He locked up and, taking his bag with him, went back downstairs. At reception he asked whether there was anything cheaper. Eyeing his smart dress, the desk clerk said there was one room, but it was tiny and had no view from the window. It sounded fine, said Barker putting his hand out for the key.

The first person he went to see was Major Johnson. What impression, he wanted to know, had Johnson formed of Truman during his own inspection. A poor one, Johnson conceded, adding that Truman and his associate Hill had struck him as "Entirely unfit persons to have charge of a band of Igorrotes."[2]

The entrance to Sans Souci Park was on the south side of Chicago, on Cottage Grove Avenue, and had been built to resemble a German beer hall. Two park workers were unlocking the gates when Barker strode up to the entrance, at noon on Sunday, June 24, 1906. A large crowd of day-trippers was already gathered outside. Barker knew Truman was a night owl who didn't usually get to the park until midafternoon, and he hoped he might be able to get a look around before the showman arrived. The government agent walked through the grounds, past the Japanese tea garden, the electric fountains, and the grand ballroom, and inhaled the aromas of hot dogs and freshly popped corn. He hadn't slept much and found the atmosphere strangely invigorating.

Outside the ballroom he asked a young ticket seller if she knew where he would find the Igorrote Village. *Well, of course, they're over there,* she said, pointing to a spot in the distance. *They're quite something,* she continued, trying to engage the handsome visitor in small talk. *Be sure to stick around for the dog feast,* she added. But Barker had already hurried off.

He looked up and noticed a large sign inviting the public to come and see the "dog eaters." Was that all that this fascinating tribe's customs had been reduced to, two sensational words? He put his hand in his pocket and dug out a quarter. Handing it over, he went inside. The village was already filling up. Barker pushed through the crowd to get a better look. What he saw made him gasp.

The scene had none of the gaiety of an authentic tribal village. The Igorrotes were famed in their native land for their good humor and love of life. This group looked as if all the joy and energy had been sucked right out of them. Barker gazed around the "village" in dismay. The Igorrotes were filthy. Their home was a muddy scrap of land with one half-built bamboo shed. Several of the women sat around an open fire cooking. In another corner, a section of ground had been fenced off to make an exhibition space. Inside several men struck tom-toms in a slow, melancholy rhythm. Nearby, an American man sat watching over them. Barker knew from the description he'd been given that it wasn't Truman.

The government agent looked at the faces of the visitors and wondered what they were thinking. Were they disgusted by the squalor? Or did they imagine this was how people really lived in the Philippines?

A voice interrupted Barker's thoughts. *You buy souvenir?* said a native woman, pointing to a woven cloth filled with rattan rings, bracelets, and smoking pipes. He picked up a pipe and asked how much it was. *Twenty-five cents,* came the reply. He handed over two quarters and slipped the pipe in his pocket, telling her to keep the change.

Barker walked over to the tents, his feet slipping underneath him. It was a quagmire. He was horrified to think of the poor Filipinos sleeping there. Truman Hunt should be ashamed of himself. Under other circumstances Barker would have complained to the manager, but he didn't want to draw attention to himself. He walked back over to the exit and left the village.

The man in charge at Sans Souci was a Chicago millionaire by the name of Leonard Woolf. Barker found him in his office and, after explaining why he was there, he asked Woolf to describe his arrangement with the Igorrotes' manager. Woolf had a contract with Hill, not Truman, and it gave him the right to exhibit the Igorrotes at Sans Souci for the entire summer season. Hill had told Woolf that he gave 60 percent of the net profits to Truman and kept the other 40 percent himself. After spending an hour or so in Woolf's company, Barker formed the opinion that he was "entirely straightforward . . . reliable" and eager "to act fairly."[3] Getting up to leave, Barker asked Woolf not to mention his visit to anyone. The government feared that Truman might try to flee with the tribe if he learned they had sent an agent to Chicago.

Barker frequently got so caught up in his work that he forgot to eat. But on this occasion, hunger got the better of him and he stopped for a light lunch at a restaurant near the Igorrote Village. At around two o'clock, just as he was leaving, a disturbance broke out at the tribe's enclosure.[4] The park was packed with visitors, as it was every Sunday. Barker moved closer to get a better look.

A smartly dressed man in a pin-striped cream suit with a straw boater shouted that the village was closed. The tribespeople would not be doing any more shows. All visitors were kindly requested to leave immediately. No more tickets would be sold. The man then disappeared without saying any more. People began lining up at the ticket booth, demanding their money back. The Igorrotes looked on in confusion while their village emptied.

Barker returned to Sans Souci the following day and went straight to the Igorrote Village. There he discovered a thick chain and a heavy padlock on the gates. The government agent peered through the fence and saw the tribespeople inside. He went off to find Woolf. Woolf explained that he'd heard rumors that Truman was planning to break contract and take the tribe to a rival park, so the Sans Souci attorney had served the showman with an injunction on behalf of the park owners, preventing him from taking the tribespeople out of the grounds. In retaliation, the Igorrote boss had ordered the tribe not to sing a note or dance a single step until the injunction was lifted. Woolf told Barker to go and speak to the man guarding the village. He knew Truman. He might be able to tell the government agent something of interest.

With a bit of gentle prodding, the park worker proved surprisingly loose-lipped. From what he said, it was clear that he wasn't a fan of Truman. The park worker told Barker that Truman was in the habit of calling at Sans Souci every few days. He was an odd sort, tightly wound and not the easiest to get along with. Some days he was charm itself while others he wouldn't so much as look at you. He liked to flash his money around. He was a drinker too, though that was hardly unusual in the parks.

Truman traveled out of town a lot for work. His wife was living in Chicago with their baby, and by all accounts she was always nagging him for leaving them alone in a city where they knew no one. Just the other day, Mrs. Hunt had been in the park and caused quite a scene. She'd got into a huge argument with Mrs. Hill, the wife of Truman's business associate. The two women had traded insults and hurled all manner of abuse at each other. When finally they were dragged apart, each had screamed at the other that she would sue for slander.[5] What a charming couple the Hunts were, thought Barker. He hoped he might get chance to meet Mrs. Hunt.

Barker's best bet if he wanted information about the doctor would be Julio, the interpreter, said the man at the gate. He met regularly with Truman whenever the showman was in town and often knew more about his whereabouts than anyone else. Barker needed to find out whether Julio was in cahoots with Truman. If he was, Barker must tread carefully. But if the interpreter was as disgruntled as his countrymen and women, he could be a valuable ally.

Was there any chance he could go inside the village for a few moments, to take a look around? The man unlocked the padlock, and told him to make it quick.

The Igorrotes looked surprised to see a visitor. *We are closed*, said one, standing up. Unlike the others, he was dressed in an American suit. His trousers were filthy round the ankles. Barker guessed that this was Julio. The others stared. Barker introduced himself in Spanish and showed them his government identification. Julio eyed it and, addressing Barker in Spanish, asked him what he wanted. The government had heard that the Igorrotes were being mistreated and held against their will, and he had been sent to investigate. Julio translated his words into Bontoc for the benefit of those who had not understood. The tribespeople began speaking noisily among themselves. Barker told Julio not to mention his visit to anyone. Did they know where Truman was?

22

Dr. Hunt, I Presume

SANS SOUCI PARK, CHICAGO, JUNE 25, 1906

EUROPEAN FIREPROOF

Great Northern Hotel

R. H. SOUTHGATE J. C. ROTH, RESIDENT MANAGER

13

Chicago ______ 190

easy for Hunt to spirit the Igorrotes away, & I do not think, in view of the changed situation, that he will attempt to do so— for the present at least.

Capt. McIntyre's telegram reading: "You are authorized conclude agreements & Schneidewind & Hunt as stated your letters & telegrams" received.

It came a few moments ago & I was extremely glad to get it at this juncture. I was doubtful whether the government would care to treat with Hunt at all. In the light of recent developments he has shown himself to be instinctively untruthful and untrustworthy & irresponsible. I am convinced also that the welfare & interests of the

Letter from Barker to the Bureau of Insular Affairs describing Truman as "instinctively untruthful and untrustworthy & irresponsible"

BARKER WAS SITTING in Woolf's office later that day when a visitor called and announced himself as Mr. Quinn, an associate of Truman's. The showman wanted to meet Woolf "with a view to making an agreement for the exhibition of the Igorrotes,"[1] and was waiting in a nearby saloon. Woolf hesitated for a moment.

This was not how he liked to do business, but he was eager to get his top attraction open again, so he reluctantly agreed to go with the man. Without disclosing his identity, Barker went too.

Truman was sitting at the bar, cradling a drink. It was a bright day outside, but the absence of any windows made it gloomy inside. Barker looked around. Aside from two men in work overalls farther along the bar, they were the only customers. Truman stood up to greet Woolf and Barker, assuming they worked together at Sans Souci. He was delighted to make Woolf's acquaintance at last. He'd heard all about him from Hill. Truman was smoking a cigar and had the loquacious demeanor of someone who had been drinking at the bar for a while.

The showman invited his guests to take a seat, then got down to business. For the right price, Woolf could keep some of the Igorrotes in Sans Souci, but Truman would be taking the rest to another park. The Filipinos were the most in-demand exhibit of the season and he could command a lot of money for them. The amount Woolf was paying for them was frankly insulting. He would need to double it at least before Truman could consider letting him keep some. Barker noted Truman's use of the word *some.* He clearly didn't think of the Igorrotes as human beings anymore. Maybe he never had. When Woolf pointed out that he already had a contract with Mr. Hill, Truman scoffed. The deal with Hill was worthless. The Igorrotes had nothing to do with Hill; he had simply been looking after the day-to-day running of the village for Truman while he was out of town.

This was a lie. Truman had leased the Sans Souci Igorrotes out to Hill, but he had since received a better offer from the owners of White City, a rival Chicago park. The tribespeople were his, said Truman, jabbing his index finger into his own chest for emphasis. He had special permission from the government to exhibit them in America. Did Woolf want to make him an offer? Truman took a slug of his drink and slammed the glass back down on the bar, indicating to the barman to fill it up again. Before giving Woolf time to answer, Truman spoke again. There wasn't a city in America that didn't want the Igorrotes. He had had enough inquiries to keep them employed in the country for a decade. They were box-office gold.

Truman rambled on, leaving few gaps for Woolf or Barker to fill. The Igorrotes would not listen to orders from anyone but him. They regarded Truman as their chief and their trusted friend. Barker had expected the showman to be likable, charming even, but the man propping up the bar before him came across as a liar and a drunk. He spoke loosely and "lied incontinently," even going so far as to "state emphatically that he had 98 Igorrotes" in the country, when he had only forty-nine Filipinos, including Julio and Friday.[2] The way he spoke about the tribespeople, as if they were animals or goods to be sold, disgusted Barker.

When he could no longer stand listening to Truman's bragging and lies, Barker interrupted. He had heard all he needed to hear. Taking out his credentials, Barker identified himself as an agent sent by the US government to investigate Truman's tribal enterprise. The showman fell silent for a moment, but it didn't take long for him to regain his composure, quipping that the government's man should be buying the drinks. Barker sat stone-faced. From then on, Truman "confined his prevarications within more or less safe limits."[3] Truman asked Woolf if he would leave them alone for a moment. Woolf obliged.

Turning to Barker, Truman told him that he was wasting his time. The Igorrotes were working for him of their own free will. They were happy and were cared for as if they were members of his own family. Barker resisted the urge to laugh as the lies kept coming. The tribespeople had each signed contracts agreeing to exhibit for one year with an option of continuance for another year. He had agreed to pay them ten dollars a month each (the actual figure was fifteen dollars), with all salaries payable once they reached the Philippines. He added that the souvenir money belonged to him but that, as a goodwill gesture, he was thinking of giving some of it to the tribespeople. It had been his plan all along to take the Igorrotes at Sans Souci to Milwaukee and from there directly on to Manila the previous weekend, but the Sans Souci attorney had raised an injunction, which prevented him taking the tribespeople away from the park.

In view of Truman's unguarded earlier admissions, Barker was under no illusion that Truman was lying. The showman wasn't planning to take the Igorrotes to Manila. He was going to take them away from Sans Souci in order to throw the government off his scent and to sever all contact between his Igorrotes and those in Schneidewind's group, who he knew might try to help them. Whether he had planned to take them to White City or Milwaukee was anybody's guess. No doubt it depended on which bidder was offering the most money.

Barker asked Truman where the rest of the tribespeople from his original group were. *Fifteen of them are in Milwaukee,* replied Truman, *and the other fifteen are in New Haven.* The government agent asked where the bodies of the two dead men were. *Seattle,* Truman replied. Barker made a mental note to look into whether this was true and to find out if they had been buried.

Truman seemed to relax again. Maybe it was the liquor, thought Barker. The government agent asked him about his business partners. From the way Truman spoke, it was clear that all the interested parties—Truman, Fox, Hopkins, Quinn, Hill, and the rest—were at odds with each other and fighting over control of the Igorrotes and the revenue they were bringing in. What a snake pit. Truman presented himself as a refined, gentlemanly sort, with his elegant suit, his expensive cigars, and his bonhomie, but his behavior was that of a scoundrel and a drunkard. The more he heard of Truman, the less Barker liked the showman.

Truman finished his drink and suggested they go to Sans Souci right away to speak with the tribespeople. They could tell Barker themselves how content they were.

The Filipinos looked up expectantly as Truman turned the key in the padlock. *Is the village opening,* Julio asked hopefully. *Not yet,* said Truman, adding that he had brought someone who wanted to talk to them. He introduced Barker as a government agent. Truman knew how much the Filipinos had grown to mistrust US officials and hoped this might act in his favor. Barker asked Truman if he would leave him alone with the tribespeople for half an hour.

That won't be necessary, insisted the showman. *They can speak openly in my presence.* Truman's tone was goading as he told Barker to ask the Igorrotes anything he wanted. Barker turned to Julio and asked him whether it was his wish to remain on exhibition in America. *No,* said Julio, *I want to go home.* Truman interrupted: *He misunderstood the question; he means he wants to go home at the end of the season. No,* repeated Julio boldly, *I want to go home now.* Julio's bravery spread through the tribe. Standing before their boss, the tribespeople seemed suddenly to forget their fear as each of them said they wanted to return to the Philippines.

Barker had assumed it would take him awhile to gain the tribe's trust and to get them to speak out against the showman. It was clear from Truman's face that he too was shocked by their rebellion. Truman blustered on. Some of them had been feeling homesick recently. They did from time to time, but it would soon pass. Savages are changeable, he said by way of explanation. Barker was in no mood for nonsense. Truman must send all those Igorrotes who wished to return home on the next transport. If any of them wanted to stay and continue exhibiting, they could do so, provided Truman furnished an American Surety Company bond for ten thousand dollars guaranteeing the humane care of the tribespeople and their safe return, at his expense, to the Philippines at the end of the season.

Without so much as a word of argument, Truman agreed. Barker knew he was bluffing. The showman had three days to come up with the bond. If he didn't provide it by Thursday, then he would no longer have any claim to the tribespeople. In the meantime Barker was assuming control of the village on behalf of the government. He would keep all the money generated by the tribe and would hold it in trust for them. The Igorrotes had done without work and wages long enough; the village would reopen that evening. For once, Truman was lost for words. He left vowing to return the next day.

That night Barker sat up late in his small, bare hotel room writing a detailed report for Paul Charlton, law officer at the Bureau of Insular Affairs. It took him several hours to compose and by the time he finished it ran to nineteen pages. He didn't hold back in his assessment of Truman, who had "shown himself to be instinctively untruthful and untrustworthy & irresponsible . . . It is plain, too, that he will wiggle out of any agreement he makes if he can."[4] Barker noted that the showman was "a shrewd man and resourceful"[5] and should not be underestimated. As for the well-being of Truman's other Igorrote groups who were traveling with his associates, Barker concluded that it was highly probable from current rumors that they were no better contented or situated than the troupe in Chicago.[6] Barker hoped the bureau would give him the go-ahead to begin legal proceedings soon and had met with the district attorney in Chicago to brief him on the case against Truman.

If the showman failed to come up with the ten-thousand-dollar bond in the next three days, Barker proposed the government do one of two things. The tribespeople could be returned to the Philippines immediately, discontented, penniless, and at great expense to the government, or they could be entrusted to Schneidewind or some other reputable showman for the remainder of the season, which would allow them to earn some money to take home with them come September. Before signing off his letter, Barker explained that he was sending a handwritten letter and not an official typed report because he was "afraid to use public stenographers"[7] for fear that the contents might be leaked to Truman.

Barker asked Charlton to have his secretary make copies of all his correspondence with the bureau and to mail the copies to him in Chicago so that he might have a record of their exchange. He didn't want to take the risk of having his letters copied locally. Perhaps he was being paranoid, but he thought it better to be paranoid than to risk Truman getting hold of highly sensitive information about the case the government was compiling against him. From what Woolf had said, the showman had a network of spies working for him.

Lying on Barker's bed was a copy of the *Daily News*. Under the headline IGORROTES BALK AT COLD AND CALUMNY,[8] the front-page story described the sorry plight of Truman's Igorrotes, who were quoted saying they had not been paid, had nowhere to bathe, were sleeping in three small tents, and had not been given sufficient clothing to keep out the "lake breezes" and "chilly nights." Barker wondered how the reporter had managed to get his interviews given the police guard and the additional security men who had recently been placed in the village. He would have a word with Julio to see if the tribespeople could be persuaded to refrain from speaking to anyone else.

There was another problem that demanded Barker's attention. A party of visitors had written to the government to complain after visiting Truman's Igorrote Village and witnessing a feast at which a "dog was placed upon his back and two or three of the Igorrotes took hold of its legs while another inserted a knife into the bowels of the dog."[9] The group had been so disgusted they had walked out. Outside they asked the ticket seller what the Igorrotes did after killing the dog. He replied that they turned it into cutlets and stew.

Unless the government intervened and put a stop to the dog feasts, the visitors were threatening to write to the newspapers and the Humane Society to complain. Barker sighed. People never ceased to amaze him. Here were eighteen human beings living in squalor and being forced to put on a degrading show for the public and the only complaint this party had was about the treatment of the dog. He felt like writing back and pointing this out but knew the complaint must be handled carefully. The last thing they needed was the distraction of another scandal.

Barker needed to think for a moment. He lay down on his bed and gazed up at the ceiling. His eyes alighted on a cobweb. He climbed up onto the mattress and began trying to swat it with the *Daily News*. He was no arachnophobic, but he loathed the idea of spiders crawling over his head while he slept. He rolled the newspaper up and, standing on his tiptoes, he waved the paper back and forth. Finally he dislodged one corner of the silken web and pulled the whole thing down. Walking over to the window, Barker hauled it open and dropped the spider's web, complete with its supper of flies, into the air.

Thursday came and went and Truman failed to make the bond. He had not been seen or heard of since his trip to the Igorrote Village with Barker. The War Department instructed Barker to act immediately. If Schneidewind provided a contract agreeing to take care of Truman's Igorrotes, pay them $7.50 each a month plus all their souvenir money, and return them to the Philippines at the end of the season, he would be given control of them that day. It wasn't a perfect solution but in the absence of a simpler—and cheaper—option, it would suffice. The government could hardly enter the Igorrote exhibition business itself.

When Barker told him of the plan, Schneidewind could hardly believe his luck. Not only had his competition been wiped out, he now had an additional eighteen Igorrotes. The season would not be over for another two months. This promised to be a highly lucrative summer. Barker knew the Igorrotes at Sans Souci would be disappointed to learn that they weren't going home yet, though he hoped the news that they would never have to work for Truman again might help soften the blow.

With a satisfactory arrangement in place for the care and management of the Sans Souci Igorrotes, Barker turned his attention to Truman and his other tribal groups. The showman had been missing for a week. From what Barker had gleaned from various sources in the park and from McIntyre's investigations, Truman had tribespeople in Milwaukee, New Haven, and Minneapolis. He could be in any one of those places. Or he could be somewhere else entirely, laying low for a while.

Julio had heard Truman talking to Callahan about Milwaukee. Barker knew there was little point staying in Chicago. Truman was unlikely to show his face in this city for a while. The government agent would go to Milwaukee with Julio, Antero, Feloa, and Schneidewind. He didn't imagine Truman would give up "his" Igorrotes without a fight. The others could help if Truman turned nasty. The chase was on.

23

On the Run

MILWAUKEE, JULY 1, 1906

DOG EATERS MUST LEAVE WINNIPEG

Headline from the Winnipeg Telegram, *July 6, 1906*

ALL THAT REMAINED of the Igorrote Village in Wonderland Park, Milwaukee, was a burned-out campfire, a spear, which lay broken in two on the ground, and a crudely painted sign announcing that the dog eaters had once lived there. In the middle of the deserted plot, a man in a lightweight summer suit stood cursing. The park manager had been making his morning rounds of the attractions, visiting each of the whitewashed terra-cotta-tiled pavilions and the sideshows in turn, and had been aghast to discover that his top attraction had disappeared into thin air overnight. What did he pay those wretched security guards for? How could fifteen Igorrotes wearing nothing but G-strings up and leave like that, without being seen? He stormed off to find the head of security.

The Filipinos had been booked to exhibit for another week at Milwaukee's premier amusement park. But Truman had gotten word from a contact in Chicago that Barker was on his way and had fled in the dead of night, taking the Igorrotes with him.

By the time Barker and the others arrived at Wonderland, Truman and the Igorrotes were already hundreds of miles away. Barker stood looking around the empty village. Truman was as slippery as an eel. If the showman ever tired of being a professional rogue, thought Barker wryly, he could have a wonderful career with the circus as a disappearing act. Barker was eager to get his hands on the Igorrotes before the Fourth of July. It was one of the most lucrative days on the amusement park calendar and he wanted to make sure the tribespeople, and not Truman, profited from the holiday crowds.

Where was the showman now? Had he taken the Igorrotes to hide out with him in some remote location? That would be the obvious way to avoid detection. But if Truman was as hard up as rumor had it, he couldn't afford to be without the tribe's earnings for very long. He would need to exhibit them.

Feloa stooped down and picked up the pieces of the broken spear. He recognized it as Dengay's spear from the chips on both sides of the head. Feloa tucked it into the belt of his loincloth.

Before returning to the station, Barker and Schneidewind made inquiries around the park. One man who'd been employed in the Igorrote Village said he'd overheard Truman talking about going to Iowa. That was a possibility, thought Barker—the showman had family there. But it was equally likely that Truman had paid the man to say it.

At the ticket office, Barker took out his government identification and pushed to the front of the line. Had the agent served an American man, around forty years of age with a midwestern accent, who was traveling with a party of fifteen or so dark-skinned foreigners? The agent called over a colleague. Yes, he knew of the party. He hadn't seen them but he'd received a telegram late the previous night requesting a car be arranged to take a party of eighteen on the 12:35 am northbound train from Lake Shore Junction, just north of Milwaukee, to St. Paul, Minnesota.[1] The man who sent the telegram had given them very short notice, but they'd managed to get a car organized.

Thanking him, Barker fought the temptation to get on the next train to St. Paul. Truman and the Igorrotes could have gotten off the train at St. Paul or any one of the stations en route, and from there traveled on to just about anywhere. Besides, the bureau had made it clear that they wanted to be kept informed every step of the way. There was nothing to do but to return to Chicago and see if anyone there had heard anything more. Maybe Sallie would let something slip. Barker would telegraph McIntyre to let him know what he'd learned and await further instruction. The bureau had requested assistance from the Secret Service. With their help it shouldn't take them too long to find the showman.

Outside, Barker bought a newspaper. Truman's midnight flight was recounted under the headline DR. T. K. HUNT CANCELS DATE: MANAGER OF IGORROTES EVADES GOVERNMENT.[2] Barker read on: "The whole trouble between the former Iowan doctor and governor of Bontoc, Philippine Islands, is said to grow out of the fact that Dr. Hunt is not prepared to kill the goose that lays his golden eggs." At least they'd gotten some of the facts right.

Debate was raging within the US government on the topic of what should be done with Truman once he was arrested. Some senior officials wanted to wrap the matter up quickly and quietly with the minimum of fuss, even if that meant letting Truman go unpunished for his crimes. But McIntyre and Paul Charlton, law officer at the bureau, were both of the view that "[Truman] should have the fear of God put into him through proceedings either criminal or quasi-criminal."[3]

There were a number of charges they could pursue, including breach of contract and larceny. However, Charlton feared it was pointless to pursue the showman for breach of contract because Truman was "probably entirely worthless"[4] and therefore without the means to pay the Filipinos even a fraction of what he owed them. In the fourteen months he had been exhibiting the Igorrotes, Truman and his associates must have made hundreds of thousands of dollars. What on earth had the showman spent his share on? Was he a gambler? Surely even he couldn't have drunk his way through that much liquor.

Back in Chicago a telegram arrived for Barker from McIntyre, telling him to go to Minneapolis. Barker didn't want to waste precious time on another wild goose chase, so first he sent a telegram to the Minneapolis chief of police. At Barker's request the police chief sent his men out to all the city show grounds and amusement parks. But they found no sign of Truman or the tribe. Barker was running out of options. He put a call in to the US Secret Service to see if they had heard anything of Truman. Within hours Barker received word that Truman and the Igorrotes were in Winnipeg, Canada. A third group was believed to be in New Haven, Connecticut,[5] possibly with Hopkins.

Of course, thought Barker, Truman had fled across the border. The showman was a cunning opponent. He knew that by taking the tribe out of the US and into another country he would add a layer of complication to Barker's already difficult job.

In the late afternoon of the Fourth of July, Barker sat on a train to Winnipeg with Schneidewind and Julio. The government agent hoped they might still get control of Truman's Igorrotes and the holiday takings before the night was out. But it was a long shot.

Barker had been on the case for a fortnight, and with each passing day, and each Houdini-like disappearance from Truman, his determination had grown to see justice done. The government had sent him to Chicago for political reasons, of course, but his own motives had grown increasingly personal since he had met the tribespeople and heard firsthand about the abuses and indignities they had suffered. He was determined to see Truman punished and to get the Igorrotes at least some of the money they were due.

Barker, Schneidewind, and Julio sat in silence for most of the train journey. They were tired and had exhausted the conversation about Truman and his exploits for now. As the train inched toward the Canadian border, fireworks flashed in the distance as people gathered at parades, parties, and picnics to celebrate Independence Day.

For his part, Schneidewind was rather enjoying chasing across the country after his rival. He had to admit he was looking forward to seeing Truman get his comeuppance. He wondered what had happened to the former doctor, colonial official, and supporter of the Igorrotes to make him behave in such a cruel manner. He knew Truman had long had a reckless streak and that he enjoyed carousing, but that was true of many Americans who'd found themselves in the

Philippines at the turn of the century. From what his business associates told him, Truman, the great braggart, was now a penniless drunk.

Julio gazed through the window. When he first arrived in America, he'd spent their train journeys looking out of the window trying to memorize every detail of the changing landscape. Now he noticed nothing. He was too busy thinking about the twists and turns his life had taken over the last sixteen months. Julio had been hurt and angered by his experience with Truman, but it wasn't enough to put him off America for good. He still felt instinctively that the country could be the making of him, with the myriad opportunities it offered that he would never have at home.

Julio knew that Maria didn't feel the same way. She missed her family and was eager to get back. But if Barker made good on his promises and Truman was sent to prison, Julio hoped it would persuade his wife to give America another chance. Earlier that day Schneidewind had asked Julio how he'd feel about going into business with him and bringing another Igorrote exhibition group to America the following year. Julio was very tempted.

Sixty-two miles north of the border in Winnipeg, it wasn't a national holiday, but that didn't stop the owners of Happyland Park from throwing a huge Fourth of July party. The thirty-two-acre park was brand-new for the 1906 season and had only been operating six weeks when the manager, W. O. Edmunds, secured the Igorrotes for their first and only Canadian appearance. Edmunds had booked the Filipinos for two weeks and paid far more than he wanted to, but Truman was a convincing salesman who had promised his outlay would be repaid ten times over.

The atmosphere was festive in the park. As a holiday special, Happyland was offering free admission for mothers and their children before eight o'clock and had laid on "everything from peanuts to athletic sports and fireworks."[6] Truman announced the Igorrotes would be holding a special holiday dog feast. In one corner of the village, a group of mongrels stood barking and yapping as the Filipinos lit their fires. Before they got started, Truman told Fox, his brother-in-law, that he was leaving. He'd be back in a few days. With that he snatched a fistful of dollars from the ticket booth and slipped out into the crowd.

The Igorrotes were glad to see Truman leave. His moods had grown increasingly unpredictable and he lied constantly. Here they were in yet another new city, holding yet another dog feast. Truman had said nothing about when they might be reunited with the other groups, let alone when they were going home. Even under Truman's loose definition of their contracts, the year they had agreed to exhibit for him was up. The Igorrotes' own copies of their contracts, however, had long since mysteriously disappeared from their luggage.

Fox wasn't much better than Truman. He didn't speak their dialect or Spanish. Instead he used a mixture of sign language and grunts to communicate with them, and his manner was bullying.

After the dog feast, the holiday crowds threw so many coins into the village that Fox ran out of cloth bags to hold them all. Back in the office, he stuffed some of the money into his pocket, then put the rest in the safe for Truman. What a profitable Fourth of July it had been.

By the time Barker's train reached Winnipeg, Happyland was closed for the night and the holiday profits from the Igorrote Village had been locked away. The following morning Barker went to meet with the US consul and the local chief of police. When the government agent described Truman's mistreatment of the Igorrotes, both men offered him every assistance. The police chief provided three police officers to accompany Barker to Happyland.[7]

Fox was standing beside the entrance to the village when Barker approached with Schneidewind and Julio, as if he'd been expecting them. He looked Barker in the eye and told him not to come a step closer. When Barker said he was there on behalf of the US government and with the full blessing of the local police, Fox seemed to notice the three officers at Barker's side for the first time. In that moment Fox stepped aside, as if suddenly overwhelmed by "moral force and the fear of criminal proceedings."[8] Pushing past him, Barker demanded to know where Truman was. Fox claimed he had no idea. Julio rushed inside to tell the Igorrotes that the government was taking them to Chicago to join the others, before sending them home. The news brought tears of joy and relief.

The US consul had provided an official letter to ease their passage over the border, stating that the Igorrotes were traveling to America at the behest of the US government. Barker had now succeeded in taking charge of thirty-three of the forty-nine tribespeople under Truman's control. But he would not rest until he had rounded up the others. The bureau had learned that a third group had recently moved from New Haven, Connecticut, to Syracuse, New York. The government agent hoped all sixteen of the missing Igorrotes were there. If not, then goodness knew where the others were.

Equally pressing was apprehending Truman. Barker had spoken at length with the Filipinos in Chicago and "Every day discloses further ill-treatment by Dr. Hunt . . . he never fed [the tribespeople] on a journey. They often went a day without food."[9] Truman, who had claimed to be a friend, even a father, to the Igorrotes, had treated them as if they were mongrels brought to him from the pound.

24

Luck Be a Lady

SYRACUSE, JULY 1906

Antoinette Funk as a young law student at Wesleyan University in Illinois

Syracuse was a booming manufacturing center at the turn of the twentieth century, producing everything from automobiles, bricks, beer, and brooms to saddles, steel, and soda ash. Towering industrial chimneys raked the sky. Day and night they belched out black smoke and putrid chemicals, which hung heavy on the air. Much of the industry was located near the banks of the Onondaga Lake, whose waters provided fish for New York's finest restaurants.

In 1906 the city's hardworking residents celebrated the opening of a new amusement park. Named, as so many were, White City—after the buildings at the heart of the 1893 Chicago World's Fair—the new park was built by the Syracuse, Lakeshore, and Northern Trolley Company. For a nickel you could board a trolley downtown for the rattling twelve-minute ride to Syracuse's newest attraction.

Despite its pretensions White City was a poor relative of its famous namesake. Created to drive up traffic on the lakeside trolley line, it consisted of a few buildings hastily thrown up in a Syracuse suburb. The opening weeks had been dogged by poor press reviews and low visitor numbers. The park managers were under pressure to find a thrilling new headline act. They made contact with every promoter in the Northeast, and finally struck gold. A former theater manager and associate of Truman's named F. P. Sargent had fifteen Igorrotes available for bookings. The White City managers snapped them up and gave the Filipinos top billing, ahead of Weedon's pack of performing big cats, "seven in number including a cute baby lion."[1]

Oblivious to the fact that the Igorrotes and Truman were now the subject of an international manhunt, the park managers contacted all the local newspapers to announce the tribe's arrival. The Filipinos needed no introduction. Truman's crimes against them might not have become national news yet, but for more than a year the exhibition of the Igorrotes had been reported in newspapers coast to coast.

The group in Syracuse consisted of seven men and seven women along with Tainan. All were members of Truman's original troupe and had previously been touring with Hopkins.

Shortly after their arrival, Sargent rushed to find Tainan. He had some exciting news. Tainan was going to meet the mayor. The boy began jumping around in excitement. He would wear his finest G-string for the occasion. Maybe the women would let him borrow some precious beads.

A large crowd of politicians, dignitaries, and reporters gathered in the mayor's office for the Filipino's visit. Tainan, who was used to large audiences, rose to the occasion. He gave a short speech in which he said it was an honor to meet the mayor and thanked the people of Syracuse for making his tribe so welcome. Then he launched into a selection of American songs including "My Country, 'Tis of Thee" and "I've Got a Feeling for You."[2] When he finished singing, the audience cheered and crowded round him. Emboldened by the warm reception, Tainan invited the mayor to call on the Igorrote Village. The mayor took the boy up on his offer, and gamely posed for photos with the Filipinos, though he politely declined the plate of boiled dog and rice the tribe's leader proffered.

Tainan was enjoying his celebrity. One afternoon he slipped out of the Igorrote Village unnoticed. Moments later, there was a great commotion beside the Shoot the Chutes attraction. As the boats whizzed down the steep tracks toward the lagoon, a small figure could be seen in the water, waving his arms furiously above his head, apparently in danger of drowning. Assuming the person had fallen in and couldn't swim, a bystander rushed to get help. Sargent wandered over, but instead of throwing off his jacket and jumping in to save the boy, he simply laughed. That was Tainan and he wasn't in danger, he was taking a bath, explained the Igorrotes' manager.[3] A crowd gathered to watch. Tainan waved to them. Then, satisfied that he had given them a good show, the boy climbed out of the water. Sargent slipped him a coin.

While Barker was on his way back to Chicago with the second Igorrote group, McIntyre had been in touch with Dr. William Alexander Sutherland, the head of the Philippine *pensionado* program that placed talented Filipino children in US schools and colleges. Tainan himself had been selected for a place in the program. McIntyre asked Sutherland if he would take the train from New York City to inspect the Igorrote Village in Syracuse.

Sutherland was happy to oblige and when he got to White City he was "favorably" impressed with Sargent, who "treats Igorrotes well . . . they are in perfect health and seem contented."[4] Sargent was a kindly boss who gave the tribe permission to keep their souvenir money along with their tips, and provided them with a plentiful supply of rice, vegetables, and chicken, along with tobacco, soap, and blankets. After Syracuse, he had confirmed bookings for them in Binghamton, Buffalo, and Detroit.[5]

Under the terms of their agreement, each week Sargent remitted half of all net profits to Truman, who had insisted he would pay the tribe their wages out of his share. Predictably, he had not done so.

At McIntyre's request, Sutherland instructed Sargent to stop paying Truman his share of the takings immediately. The bureau would make arrangements to hold the money in trust for the tribespeople. The government would transport the Filipinos to Chicago the following week.[6] When Sargent expressed concern that Truman would come looking for his money in a rage, Sutherland explained that the showman had gone into hiding, fearing that if he showed himself he would be arrested.

Back in Chicago the government had instructed Barker to leave the Igorrotes at Sans Souci for the time being instead of moving them across town to Riverview. This was done on the understanding that Schneidewind was in charge of them and the manager of Sans Souci must make their village sanitary and provide suitable accommodations. Schneidewind came regularly to check on them, and he installed a village manager to look after the tribespeople. Woolf and Barker had beefed up security in the village with the addition of a couple of security guards and a policeman. Barker had also hired two Pinkerton detectives to search for Truman.

On the evening of Monday, July 9, 1906, Barker was leaving Woolf's office in Sans Souci when Julio appeared and asked if he could speak privately to him. The story he told was disturbing: associates of Truman's had started coming to the village with messages for the tribe, intended to persuade or intimidate the Filipinos into going back to Truman. *Why are they not stopped by the security guards or the police officer?* asked Barker. *Because*, replied Julio, looking around to make sure no one was listening, *Callahan lets them in*. Barker looked confused. *What's Callahan got to do with it? He's Truman's friend*, replied Julio. He had assumed the agent knew this. Barker was stunned. Why had nobody mentioned Callahan before? Now it all made sense. He must be the source of the leaks.

Barker went straight to the tribe's village and dismissed Callahan on the spot. He must never show his face in the village again. Callahan grunted something and fled, leaving his few possessions behind.

At ten o'clock that night, Barker left the park grounds. A shadowy figure stirred beside the gates. Once he saw Barker exit, Callahan went back inside. It didn't take him long to find Julio. Furious, he confronted the translator and ordered him to come with him.

Julio guessed where they were going. When they reached a bar near Sans Souci, Callahan told the interpreter to enter. Truman was already there. The showman told Julio he had something for him. He pulled some papers out of his jacket pocket. Turning to the last page, he smoothed out the creases and pushed it in front of Julio. *Sign it,* he said, handing the interpreter a pen. Julio picked the document up and began reading. Angered, Truman snatched it back. Putting the document down in front of Julio again, he told him to sign it. Callahan stood up and leaned over Julio, his face menacing. The barman looked over. *Sign it,* said Truman again. Julio shook his head. He wasn't signing anything he hadn't read.[7]

Julio no longer feared Truman. The young Filipino had once looked up to his boss and aspired to be like him. Now he felt nothing but pity and disgust. Truman was a mess. He had a wife and baby daughter to take care of, but was never home. He'd squandered his fortune and what little he had left ran straight through his fingers. Standing up, Julio looked directly into Truman's bloodshot eyes and announced that he was leaving.

Back in the Igorrote Village, Maria was frantic with worry. She had asked the policeman on duty to get an urgent message to Barker that Julio was missing. Barker had returned to the village shortly before midnight. When Maria described how Callahan had taken Julio out of the park with him, the government agent cursed. Why hadn't the men paid to guard the Igorrotes done their job? Barker would ask for a second policeman to be stationed permanently in the village.

Barker had brought with him Schneidewind and an attorney named Louis J. Blum, whom he had hired on behalf of the government to prosecute Truman.[8] Blum ran the respected Chicago law firm Blum and Blum with his brother; the Blums were both bachelors who still lived at home with their Jewish German mother. Louis Blum was fifty pounds overweight, something he put down to his mother's delicious home cooking.

With Julio absent, Barker asked Schneidewind to translate as best he could. Schneidewind introduced Blum and told the tribe the attorney had come to the village to begin gathering evidence for the case against Truman. Barker indicated to Schneidewind, Blum, and the police officer to sit on the ground. He didn't want the Filipinos to feel intimidated. Blum delicately lowered himself to the ground. As he wedged his considerable bulk into a small space beside Feloa, the chief made a mock-horrified face. Turning to one of the other men, the tribal chief whispered, "Taft," a jokey reference to the famously overweight former governor-general of the Philippines.

The park security guards sat on the fence a short distance away. The night was pitch-dark except for the dancing flames of the fire and the sooty light given off by an oil lamp, which the police officer held aloft. Barker invited Feloa to speak first. As the Filipino began to talk, he was interrupted by a familiar voice shouting from the darkness beyond the campfire. It was Julio. He told them he had just come from a saloon where Truman had tried to force him to sign a document without disclosing its contents.

Blum and Barker looked at each other. Blum would have bet one of his mother's superb strudels that the document Truman had tried to get Julio to sign stated that the tribespeople wanted to remain with him. Blum took out his pen and, indicating to the police officer to hold his lamp nearer so he could see, he hurriedly began writing. When he finished, Blum explained to Julio that the document he had just drafted stated that the Igorrotes at Sans Souci were there of their own free will and that they wished to remain under the charge of the US government until July 21, 1906, when they would be returned to the Philippines.

Blum asked Julio to translate for the rest of the tribe. If they were willing, Blum would like them all to sign the document there and then. The attorney explained that he feared Truman was trying to get legal control of the tribespeople so that he could prevent the government from sending them home. If the tribespeople signed Blum's document, it would prevent the unscrupulous showman from taking control of them again.

Julio translated. The tribespeople grew animated. Feloa seemed to be leading the discussion. He addressed the group one by one, as if getting them to cast a vote. Barker and the other American men watched with interest. Julio picked up the pen. Suddenly Feloa shouted something and more lively discussion ensued. Feloa turned to Barker and, with Julio translating, said they would only sign on one condition: that the government guaranteed they would be paid the back salaries Truman owed them.

At this, the usually mild-mannered Barker lost his temper and began to curse. He had done everything he could to help the tribespeople. He understood they were anxious to be paid, but this was not the time for bargaining. They needed to make the government's custodianship of the tribe official without delay. There would be time afterward to iron out the details. To Barker's relief, only Julio and the other Americans present had understood his strong language. Composing himself, the government agent stated plainly that this was the best offer the Igorrotes were going to get. Julio translated, making clear that he thought they should sign.

Julio took the document from Blum and signed it. Then he passed it to Feloa. The chief paused for a moment, then reluctantly scratched a mark beside his name. One by one the others followed. Julio was reminded of a similar scene back in Bontoc sixteen months earlier, when they had signed their contracts with Truman.

It was after two o'clock in the morning by the time Barker got back to his hotel room. He was glad to have Blum working on the case with him. As well as being a talented attorney, Blum had a "ready wit, an "optimistic view of life," and a "congenial" nature, which Barker had immediately warmed to.[9] He sensed they would get along well and had been impressed by the way the Chicago attorney had interacted with the tribespeople, never once talking to them in a way that was badgering or patronizing.

Instead of going straight to bed, the government agent sat up until four o'clock writing up his report for the bureau. In it he described the scene that had just unfolded: "The Igorrotes picturesquely grouped around the open fire, the native huts contrasting with the 19th century rollercoaster [*sic*] in the background, our police officer holding up the only lamp to read by, and the American audience of some half dozen interested persons somewhat anxiously awaiting results—the whole scene was not without artistic and even sociological interest—to an outsider!"[10]

Barker put his pen down and lay on his bed, fully clothed, his hands folded behind his head. The two Pinkerton detectives he had hired to find Truman had so far failed. They'd visited Sallie and the Elks Lodge, but no one was giving anything away. The Igorrotes didn't understand how it was that Callahan and Truman's other associates were able to find the showman whenever they needed to and "yet the government—the All-Powerful—is unable or indisposed" to find him and "take measures to bring [Truman] to book."[11] Barker could see their point. The fact that the showman had been leading them on a wild goose chase for the past fortnight was shameful indeed. Truman was a resourceful opponent with a vast network of informants and loyal friends and an extraordinary ability to vanish into thin air.

The district attorney's assistant in Chicago had advised Barker to have the Igorrotes make a formal demand for the souvenir money, paving the way for Truman to be indicted in state court for embezzlement. In order to have a realistic chance of prosecuting Truman, they would need to retain a minimum of five or six of the Filipinos to act as witnesses. Given that Truman had stolen the largest sums from Feloa, Dengay, and Julio, and that all three had been present when each of the thefts had occurred, it would make sense for them to be among the witnesses. Barker would need to speak to them to find out if they were agreeable. The district attorney's assistant had advised that they pursue criminal and civil proceedings for embezzlement and breach of contract, with a separate charge for each of the forty-nine Filipinos in the party. While raising multiple actions simultaneously would increase their chances of a conviction, this course of action would be costly. Barker would need to speak to the bureau to see if they were willing to go to the expense.

Barker propped himself up on his pillow. In the sixteen days since he arrived in Chicago, he had managed to see Truman only once. He had arranged a second meeting, but the showman had not turned up. Nonetheless Barker had gotten to know a good deal about Truman who, he'd discovered, had made a large number of enemies. Former employees, friends, and business associates had been happy to dish the dirt on a man who they said was more interested in chasing after a fast buck than in using his considerable talents, and who would do anything to make money, including stabbing his friends and business associates in the back. He had three children with three different wives, and was "utterly worthless" and "almost constantly drunk and lying around the saloons in Chicago."[12]

Blum felt that the legal case against Truman was strong. But Barker feared that, in view of Truman's lack of resources, the bureau might decide it wasn't worth prosecuting the showman. It was one thing to spend public money on a costly court case in the hope of recovering the tribe's earnings, but quite another to spend it knowing there was little hope of ever seeing the thousands of dollars stolen from them again.

Across town, Truman paid Sallie a visit in the apartment he'd rented for her. He was drunk. Through his slurs Sallie made out something about being persecuted by the government and somebody called Barker who wanted to take over the Igorrote business for himself.

Sallie begged Truman to come back home for good. Her eyes filled with tears. She missed him. She was lonely. The baby had hardly seen him. She was tired of being cooped up in a tiny apartment with no money and nowhere to go. Truman said he couldn't come back. They were after him. When Sallie asked if she could go and stay with her family, Truman shook his head. He needed her around.

As he walked out the door, Sallie fell to her knees in the dark hallway and sobbed.

At the suggestion of one of his Elks friends, Truman had arranged to meet with an attorney named Antoinette Funk, a prim-looking woman with a stern demeanor. The showman had been skeptical about hiring a woman at first, but when he met her he was impressed by her fighting spirit, her impressive track record, and her dry humor. Truman immediately engaged her services. No case was too difficult and no client was too dishonorable for Funk. In fact, the slimmer the chances of a not-guilty verdict, and the more egregious the crime, the more appealing the case became for her.

"A little woman who does not weigh more than a hundred pounds,"[13] Funk would go on to become a leading member of the suffragette movement despite her surprising view that women did not belong in the professions. Funk, a single mother of two daughters, expressed this opinion in a 1904 interview in the *Washington Post* shortly after she succeeded in getting a high-profile murderer off with a relatively light fourteen-year sentence, as opposed to the death-by-hanging sentence sought by the prosecution. "Few times . . . has the public seen a woman making the kind of fight waged by Mrs. Funk."[14] Funk was well known among her male colleagues for her exhaustive preparation, her vast legal knowledge, and her rare ability to shape the law to suit her needs.[15]

It was Funk who persuaded Truman, on Thursday, July 12, 1906, that it was time to show his face again. He had no need to hide himself away, she reasoned. That night, Truman, Funk, Callahan, Fox, and two other business associates of Truman's named Quinn and Kavanaugh turned up at Barker's hotel room just after nine thirty.[16] Barker invited them to step inside, though there was barely room for him let alone six visitors.

Barker assumed that the one woman in the group must be Truman's wife, though she was older and uglier than he had imagined she would be. When Truman introduced her as his attorney, the government agent looked up in surprise. Barker offered her his only seat. She declined, insisting she was happier standing.

The room was quiet for a moment. Funk pierced the silence with her booming voice: her client wished to come to an agreement that would allow him to continue exhibiting the tribespeople in America. He was willing to put up a bond. He could not afford the ten thousand dollars the government was asking for, but offered instead to put up four thousand. Truman had been a good boss to the tribespeople, said Funk, adding that he felt "positive" they would wish to stay on in America with him on these terms.[17] Barker said he would put the proposal to the chief of the bureau, but he was bluffing. Under no circumstances would the government allow Truman to get his hands on the Igorrotes again. Still, if Truman was now willing to speak to the government, Barker was intrigued to hear what else he had to say.

Next, Truman's attorney turned briskly to the matter of money. Her client hated to think of the tribespeople being without funds and wished to give them some of the souvenir money he had been keeping for them. He could only afford five hundred dollars just now, but he would pay the balance as soon as he had it. Truman reached into his pocket and pulled out a thick wad of rolled-up bank notes, which he handed to Barker. The government agent took it and began counting. There were indeed five hundred dollars there. Barker was surprised Truman had that much money left. He wondered if there was more stashed away.

Barker knew Truman was not paying the money back because he'd had an epiphany and seen the error of his ways. Rather he was simply doing what he could to avoid criminal prosecution. Barker thanked his visitors for coming and said he would be in touch once he had discussed their proposal with the bureau. Was there anything else they wished to say? No, said Truman, except that the government could reach him at any time through Miss Funk's office. Barker nodded and closed the door behind them, glad to have his room back to himself.

On top of the five hundred dollars Truman had just given him, Barker had collected a further thousand dollars in total from the tribe's gate receipts in Chicago, Winnipeg, and Syracuse. The money was only a fraction of what Truman owed them, but it would go some way to paying their back salaries. Aside from those who were staying on as witnesses, the Igorrotes were due to leave Chicago in nine days' time to begin the long journey home. The government agent hoped they might be able to add to the tribe's pot of earnings before they departed.

Barker rose early the following morning and sent a telegram to the bureau, informing them of Truman's proposal that he should be allowed to keep exhibiting the Igorrotes in America in return for paying a four-thousand-dollar bond. The bureau chief responded quickly and decisively: he dismissed Truman's suggestion out of hand and delivered the good news that the bureau had decided to go along with Barker's suggested course of action and pursue criminal and civil proceedings for embezzlement and breach of contract.

Barker went to straight to the Igorrote Village, where he told the tribe he needed a volunteer who was willing to make a charge against Truman under oath before a justice of the peace. Without hesitation, Julio said he would do it. In fact, he said, it would give him a great deal of satisfaction to put his name to the warrant for Truman's arrest.

For once the police officer didn't have any trouble finding Truman. The showman had become sloppy since he'd hired Funk, assuming that his attorney could get him off with anything. On July 15, 1906, he was arrested on a charge of embezzlement. *Who filed the charge?* Truman wanted to know. On hearing that it was Julio, the showman cursed and muttered something under his breath. He was taken to the police station and put in a cell. Shortly after, Funk arrived and had the showman released on two thousand dollars' bond.[18]

Barker had gone to the police station with Blum to make sure Truman put up a proper bond. When he returned to the Igorrote Village, he found Maria in a state of hysteria. Julio was missing. He had last been seen in the village earlier that day, with some of Truman's friends.[19] Maria was frantic with worry. Truman must have learned that Julio was behind his arrest. He must have instructed his associates to do something terrible to the interpreter by way of revenge.

25

An Ultimatum

ENGLEWOOD, CHICAGO, JULY 17, 1906

15 IGORROTES KIDNAPED;
GOVERNMENT IN TANGLE

Newspaper headline from a file the US government kept on Truman

TAINAN WOKE WITH a start as the train screeched to a halt. It was early in the morning, two days after Truman's arrest, and the Syracuse Igorrotes were on their way to Chicago with Dr. Sutherland of the *pensionado* program. Tainan squinted through the window, trying to work out where they were. The low sprawl of industrial and residential buildings didn't look like Chicago, thought the boy, who had passed through the Second City before and had never forgotten the skyscrapers he had seen there. Shouts coming from outside interrupted his thoughts. A group of men ran past the window. There was a commotion on the platform, then the door to their car burst open. Truman, Callahan, Quinn, and Fox appeared, trailed by some other American men and Julio.[1]

The Igorrotes gawked in astonishment at Truman's unexpected arrival. The showman had come to issue an ultimatum. If they wanted their back salaries, they must get off the train and go with him now, he shouted. If they went with the government, they wouldn't see a penny of their money. Dr. Sutherland jumped to his feet and, in Spanish, he instructed the Filipinos to stay where they were. Truman was lying. Hadn't he promised them their money many times before? This was a trick. For one brief moment, everyone in the car froze in confusion. Tainan looked up at Julio, assuming that he would know what to do. But Julio stood silently.

Outside, doors slammed as passengers clambered out of the train, dragging their trunks after them. The conductor shouted for everyone who was not traveling on to La Salle Street Station in Chicago to get off, the train was about to depart. Truman stood firm. He would not make the offer again. The Igorrotes better make up their minds fast. Did they want their money or not?

Sensing an adventure, Tainan got up and ran for the door. One by one, the others rushed after him. The conductor watched as they began piling off the train. *Stop!* shouted Sutherland impotently. But it was too late. Two short blasts on the whistle indicated that the brakes had been released. Next stop Chicago. Sutherland looked out helplessly as the Igorrotes followed Truman along the platform. Despite the government's best efforts, the last group of Igorrotes was back in the arms of Truman Hunt.

Unnoticed by Sutherland, a man stood at the end of the platform and began to follow Truman at a distance.

Standing in his hotel room, Barker could hardly believe his ears. How on earth could Truman have stolen the tribespeople from right under Sutherland's nose? While Barker cursed and tried to figure out what to do next, a messenger arrived with a note from the Pinkerton agency. Barker tore it open. One of their detectives had been tailing Truman when he stormed the train and kidnapped the Igorrotes, and had pursued the showman into Englewood, the old streetcar suburb that was still infamous for being the site where the serial killer H. H. Holmes had built his "murder castle" fifteen years earlier. The detective had followed Truman and the tribespeople to White City, the other big Chicago amusement park, where they were due to open a new village that very day.

Barker had to hand it to Truman: the showman had chutzpah. Not only had he led the tribespeople off a train in broad daylight, now he was exhibiting them right under the government's nose. Why had he not spirited them away to some obscure and distant town? The man was delusional. He must think he was untouchable.

While Barker grappled with the implications of this latest twist in the story, a US marshal arrived at his hotel room and informed him that he and the Igorrotes in his care must appear in court at ten o'clock the following morning, Wednesday, July 18, to answer a writ of habeas corpus. Not content to have snatched fifteen of the tribespeople from the train, Truman was taking Barker to court in an attempt to win back the rest, claiming that the tribespeople "are now held prisoners [by Barker], that they have communicated to [me, Truman Hunt] their desire to join [me] and fulfill their contract but are prevented and restrained from doing so by said F. F. Barker, government agent." In a statement sworn before a notary public, Truman added that he, Truman, was acting on behalf of Julio, who had told him that "Barker has threatened him with arrest in the event of his, Julio's refusing to do the bidding of said Barker."[2]

The marshal handed over the papers and Barker slammed the door after him. He did not know whether to laugh or cry. Could Julio have turned his back on the Igorrotes and joined forces with Truman? It seemed impossible but who knew what promises the showman had made. Barker was certain about one thing, however: he would not let that rogue make a mockery of him, the government, and the American justice system. If Truman wanted a fight in court, Barker would make sure he got it.

26

Judgment Day

CHICAGO, JULY 18, 1906

The Chicago Daily News *reports on the Igorrotes' debut in a federal court. The racist cartoon is typical of the way the tribespeople were portrayed by the press.*

THE CHICAGO COURTROOM of Federal Judge Solomon Bethea was packed. Several hundred spectators crammed the public gallery and spilled out into the corridors. No one but the most high-profile murderers normally attracted this much attention. Pressmen and photographers sat expectantly. A ripple of excitement ran through the room while everyone waited for the Filipinos to appear.[1] The cartoonist from the *Chicago Daily News* sat sketching. The Igorrotes hadn't even entered court yet, but he drew them as a group of nearly naked savages with wild eyes, unruly hair, thick lips, huge hoop earrings, and skin as black as coal.[2]

In the hallway, the Igorrotes stood waiting to be called. "Tell the men they can't smoke in here," bellowed a man's voice down the corridor.[3] At this, the tribespeople removed the pipes from their mouths and stooped to knock the ashes out on the tiled floor. An attendant rushed after them with a brush and shovel. The door leading to the courtroom opened and the bailiff, Tom Currier, stuck his head out. He was promptly engulfed by a cloud of the tribe's tobacco smoke. Coughing and waving the fumes aside, Currier looked the tribespeople up and down, then shouted, "All right, bring 'em in."[4]

Led by Fomoaley, the Filipinos trooped in. Barker looked over at them. He had sent a messenger to buy the tribe new clothes for their court appearance and now, as he gazed at them for the first time, he wondered where the man had found such a motley array of garments. A rummage sale? The tribespeople were certainly eye-catching, in ill-fitting overcoats, pants that were too long or too short, shirts and overalls that drowned their diminutive frames, and brightly colored horse blankets fashioned as skirts.

The bailiff directed the Filipinos to benches reserved for them at the rear of the courtroom. As ever, the tribespeople inspired the pressmen to new heights of journalistic license. One reporter described how the Igorrotes, in "high pitched voices, like those of children, expressed wonder at the magnificence of Uncle Sam's big building."[5] There was, reflected another member of the press pack, "a curious contrast existing between [the tribespeople's] bare brown legs and the white marble walls of the room."[6]

Only when the Igorrotes were seated did Truman enter the court, accompanied by an uncomfortable-looking Julio, dressed immaculately in a new American suit. Barker studied the translator closely. Behind him, Maria craned to get a look at her husband. Julio shot her a worried smile.

"Take off your hat," commanded the bailiff, a giant of a man who weighed in at a colossal three hundred pounds.[7] He pointed at the offending hat on the head of a small Igorrote male. The man shook his head, no. Irritated, Currier jabbed a finger at the man's headgear, stating firmly "Your hat."[8] When the Igorrote shook his head again, Currier raised his voice, explaining that the law dictated that everyone in the courtroom must remove their hats in front of a sitting judge. Antero, who had been invited by Barker to act as the official interpreter, was sitting at a table at the front of the room beside Blum, Barker, and the assistant district attorney, R. W. Childs. Antero explained that the tribesmen could not remove their hats, not due to a lack of respect for the judge, but owing to the fact that the hats were practically woven into their hair. Frowning, Currier approached the judge and explained the predicament. Waving away the bailiff's concerns, the judge ordered that the Igorrotes could keep their hats on. He had no desire to hold up proceedings over something as trivial as hats.[9]

The bailiff read out the names of each Igorrote man, woman, and child involved in the habeas corpus proceeding.

Then the judge invited Antoinette Funk to speak. Truman's attorney stood up to her full four feet, eleven inches, and strode forward. Tipping her head right back so that she could see over the top of the judge's bench, Funk spoke in a deep voice that boomed across the courtroom. Her client had raised the habeas corpus action that had brought them to court that morning in order to prevent the government from deporting the Filipinos. The Igorrotes had been earning a good living in America and wished to stay in the country exhibiting under Truman. Her client was the only person in the room who spoke the Igorrotes' language. He knew better than anyone present what they wanted. They had never asked him to take them home and, frankly, Funk added, the tribespeople were mystified by the government's desire to gain control of them. Funk continued: the Igorrotes had no desire to go with Mr. Barker, the government agent, who had tried to hoodwink the innocent, trusting mountain people.

Barker studied Julio's face but he betrayed no emotion.

The assistant district attorney rose to address the courtroom next. These claims were simply not true, said Childs. The Filipino tribespeople had signed contracts in March 1905 to come to America with Truman and exhibit for one year in return for a salary of fifteen dollars each a month, insisted Childs. Their contracts had expired more than four months ago and they urgently wished to return home. Truman had refused to take them back to the Philippines despite the fact that he was legally obliged to do so. Because of this, the government, represented in court by Barker and Blum, had stepped in and proposed to put them on a ship back to Manila as soon as possible. Irritated, Funk sat tapping her pencil on a book.

Truman had withheld more than ten thousand dollars from the tribe in wages and he had stolen thousands more, which they had earned selling handmade souvenirs. He had failed to properly care for them and had not provided adequate housing. He had dragged them all over the country exhibiting them and was now trying to hold them in America against their will. He had recently boarded a train and kidnapped a group of Igorrotes who were traveling from Syracuse to Chicago where they were due to be taken in to the safe custody of the government.[10]

Truman sat shaking his head as Childs characterized him as a cruel, greedy man who had shamelessly exploited his fellow human beings and was set on wringing every last cent out of the tribespeople. Truman had kept the Filipinos in actual slavery and could not be trusted to care for a dog, let alone a group of human beings, he added.

Lies, all lies, said Funk, with the "unembarrassed directness" for which she was famed in Chicago's courtrooms.[11] Truman Hunt had known the Igorrotes for many years and had been a devoted friend to them. When he lived among them in the Philippines, Truman, a qualified physician, had risked life and limb to care for the sick tribespeople, even when their bodies were ravaged by cholera. Did this sound like the man Mr. Childs was describing?

Funk continued: Truman Hunt had proved himself to be a kind and compassionate manager. His overwhelming desire in bringing the tribespeople to America had been to give them a once-in-a-lifetime opportunity to earn good American wages, so they could build a better future for themselves. Ever since his very first encounter with the tribe, Dr. Hunt had been true to his word, and had not violated a single condition of his contract with them. The tribespeople had earned a good deal of money and wished to continue working for him. Her client had come to court at the request of his dear friend Julio. The government agent, Barker, had threatened Julio with arrest if he did not do his bidding.

Judge Bethea called Truman to the stand. The showman thanked the judge for giving him the opportunity to defend his reputation. The happiness and well-being of the Igorrotes was more important to him than anything else, Truman insisted. To this end, he would willingly sign a bond guaranteeing their safe return to their homeland and deposit their wages in a bank of the government's choosing. He continued, emphatically, "It is absolutely false that I ever had the least trouble with the people who toured under my management. They were well treated and were perfectly willing to go to the different parks where they appeared."[12]

Julio stared intently at Truman.

There was worse to come. Truman claimed that before they left Bontoc, he had informed Julio that the Igorrotes would not be paid a penny of their wages until they returned to the Philippines at the end of their contracts. The tribe's current frustration was due entirely to an error on the interpreter's part.

Julio turned and looked directly at Barker. His face burned with anger. Slowly he shook his head.

The judge called for an adjournment for lunch. A clerk led the Igorrotes out to an anteroom, where they were served rice and water. When they had cleaned the last grains of rice from their plates, the tribespeople lit their pipes. After a while a clerk called to tell them they were wanted by the judge. The Igorrotes extinguished their pipes and trooped back into the courtroom.

Judge Bethea wanted to hear from the tribespeople next. He instructed Antero to ask each of them whether they wished to remain in America with Truman or return to the Philippines under the care of the government. The interpreter worked his way along the first bench of Igorrotes, asking each man, woman, and child what they wished to do. He moved on to the second bench and the third. Each time the answer was the same: *Go home.* The judge nodded and asked whether there was anything else the tribe wanted.

There was a moment's silence.

In that case . . . the judge began.

Julio stood up and asked if he might be permitted to speak. The judge nodded yes. Truman stared hard at him. In a loud, clear voice Julio stated firmly that he and his countrymen and women wanted nothing more to do with Truman, who had treated them wretchedly and stolen their hard-earned wages. He added, "All I want is [my] money. All my people want is [their] money—then we go home."[13]

Truman was aghast. He had not seen this coming.

Barker sighed with relief and sat back in his seat.

Judge Bethea thought for a moment. It was not his job to punish Truman, or to determine who owed whom what. He was simply required to decide into whose custody the Filipinos should be delivered that day. Looking at the showman, however, the judge was unable to refrain from scolding him for parading the Filipinos around the country like "elephants or monkeys."[14] He continued, "I think that these people should be wards of the government. There is no one better able to take care of them. They should not be rushed about like a lot of animals and [Truman Hunt] should not come into court to get them back from the government for that purpose. Dr. Hunt, you should have turned these people over to the government like a man . . . [This writ] is dismissed."[15]

Truman's attorney jumped to her feet. "But, your honor, the government set the example of exhibiting the people. The government was the first to bring them to this country for show purposes," said Funk. Looking at her, Judge Bethea—a prominent member of the Republican Party and a personal friend of President Roosevelt's—declared, "Well, it should not be done." Undeterred, Funk interrupted again, "My client merely followed the example set by the government."[16]

The judge raised an eyebrow. Turning to face the tribe, he said any Igorrotes in Truman's original group who wished to stay in America could do so and those who wished to return to the Philippines would be sent home as soon as possible under the charge of the government.

Truman cursed under his breath and shook his head with the incredulity of a man who'd grown to believe his own lies.

Julio rushed into Maria's arms.

Outside the court Truman stopped to give a brief interview to the press, dismissing the verdict as nonsense and the claims against him as lies, then excused himself and disappeared into the street. He needed a drink.

Judge Bethea's decision made headlines from coast to coast and over the border in Canada. The newspapers described how Truman had squandered the tribe's wages "leading a fast life in Chicago" while abandoning the tribespeople "to the tender mercies of civilization."[17]

Despite Truman and Funk's best efforts to wrest back control of the Igorrotes over the next two days, all the surviving members of Truman's original group were under Barker's care when the time came for them to leave.

Julio had spilled out his story to Maria and Barker. Truman had kidnapped him, kept him in a hotel room, made him drink liquor, ranted and raved and tried to charm him into staying with him. In a final bizarre gesture he had even bought Julio a beautiful new American suit, with the money he had stolen from Julio and his compatriots. Julio was more determined than ever to do everything he could to ensure that Truman was held responsible for his lies.

Julio, Maria, Feloa, Dengay, and Tainan were staying on to act as witnesses in Truman's prosecution. The others would take the train from Chicago to San Francisco, where they would board a ship to Manila. Judge Bethea had ruled that any of them who wished to stay could, but the tribespeople had had enough of their American adventure.

Maria could hardly bring herself to bid farewell to her countrymen and women. She turned to Daipan. How she would miss her dear friend. The two women held each other tight. Barker shouted that it was time to leave. The parting was one of unspeakable sorrow for the tribespeople. They had endured so much together and knew they would never come together as one group again.

27

Vanishing Act

COOK COUNTY COURT, CHICAGO, SEPTEMBER 4, 1906

William Pinkerton in the Chicago offices of the Pinkerton Detective Agency

FOR SEVEN WEEKS, Blum and Barker worked tirelessly to build a case against Truman while the showman raged, drank, and grumbled his way around Chicago, telling anyone who would listen that he was the victim of a conspiracy that went all the way to the top of the US government. Finally, on September 4, 1906, Truman was arrested for embezzlement and taken before Justice Wolff. Wolff found in favor of the Filipinos and Truman was taken to the county jail. But he was not about to go down without a fight. The showman said that he was unable to pay back the money that he was accused of taking and Funk filed a motion, seeking to have her client released under the insolvent debtor's act, a statute under Illinois law. At 10:20 the following morning, Truman was led into the

Cook County courtroom by a deputy sheriff. As he entered, a hush descended. The showman had become a well-known figure in the city since his arrival with the Igorrotes three months earlier. On this particular morning, he looked tired, agitated, and uncharacteristically shabby.

Judge Houston called on Antoinette Funk to speak. She said she was seeking to have her client freed from jail on the grounds that he was insolvent. The judge turned to Truman and asked him to give an account of his assets. The showman, who had frequently boasted that the Igorrotes had earned him hundreds of thousands of dollars, stood up and stated in a loud, clear voice, "[my] entire worldly wealth consists of $2.50."[1] That one of the most successful showmen in the business had so little money sounded incredible and yet, judging by reports of his extravagant spending, it could just be true. Either that or he had hidden his fortune away someplace where the authorities would never find it.

Standing in court watching proceedings was a heavyset man with a bushy gray mustache. He was William Pinkerton, the eldest son of Allan Pinkerton, founder of the world's most famous detective agency. Together William and his brother, Robert, had taken over the running of the agency following their father's death in 1884. The brothers were arguably even greater detectives than their father and had expanded his sleuthing business into an international operation.

Pinkerton was in court at Barker's request. Truman and his attorney didn't know it, but an officer was currently on his way from Tennessee to collect the showman. Fearing that Funk would keep using delaying tactics and underhanded tricks like this infuriating insolvency plea to keep her client at liberty, Blum had recently filed separate larceny charges against Truman in Memphis, where he now believed they stood a better chance of securing a conviction and a prison sentence. The charges related to the violent incident in the North Front Street house, when Truman had stolen money from a number of the men. Barker had taken the precaution of hiring Pinkerton to shadow Truman from the moment he entered the Chicago courtroom until the Memphis officer snapped the handcuffs on his wrists.

After a few minutes' consideration, Judge Houston announced that he was granting Truman a temporary release on a bond of two hundred dollars. He set the hearing for September 16. Truman signed his bond and the deputy sheriff led him toward a door at the rear of the courtroom. Pinkerton watched the door and waited, assuming they would return shortly, as Truman's lawyer and bondsman remained in the room.[2]

Five minutes passed. There was still no sign of Truman. Alarmed, Pinkerton rushed to the back of the courtroom and wrenched open the door. The showman was nowhere to be seen. His heart pounding, Pinkerton ran out into the hallway and began frantically searching the courthouse. It was useless. Truman was gone.[3]

It was a disaster. Pinkerton could not believe that he had made such a rookie mistake. How could he have allowed Truman to get away?

Pinkerton dashed through the lobby and outside into Adams Street. He ran as fast as his bulk and aging limbs would allow through the corridors of the neighboring Unity Building, sticking his head into every door he passed. He stopped for a moment to get his breath back, then hurried across the street to Kavanagh's Saloon. The man behind the bar said he hadn't seen anyone matching Truman's description. Pinkerton continued on to the Goodrich Transportation Company docks. There he made a thorough search of the cabins and holds of the steamships *Virginia* and *Chicago*, the only two vessels that were due to depart that night. Still there was no sign of him. Next Pinkerton went to the Saratoga Hotel and the Grand Pacific Hotel. He examined the registers and talked to the staff, but no one resembling Truman had checked in. At 10:15 p.m., after almost twelve hours of fruitless searching, Pinkerton called off the hunt. Truman had disappeared into thin air.[4]

Back in his office, Pinkerton sat at his heavy mahogany desk with his head in his hands. The room was dark and cluttered, its walls hung with family photos and mementos of successful cases. A row of handsome spaniels peered down at Pinkerton from dark wooden picture frames. There had been nothing dogged about the detective's pursuit of his man that day. Every so often Pinkerton gave a groan.

Sitting opposite him, his younger brother, Robert, couldn't understand how he had let Truman get away. William Pinkerton speculated that the deputy sheriff who had led Truman from court was in cahoots with the showman and had deliberately taken him by the arm to give the impression he was still in custody, thereby giving him chance to escape.

Just then, the telephone rang. Barker was on the other end of the line and he was in a foul mood. William Pinkerton began apologizing but Barker didn't want to hear it. He ordered the Pinkertons to watch the depots and docks and scour the city until Truman was found.[5]

Barker instructed the Pinkertons to circulate a description of Truman among all their detectives and their many contacts. It read:

> Dr. Truman K. Hunt
> Height: about 5'8"
> Weight: 145 lbs or more
> Age: about 36
> Usually dresses well; good figure and bearing; Dark hair; ~~ruddy complexion~~; clean-shaven; round pleasant face; somewhat receding chin; somewhat pop-eyed; nervous manner. Has had good education. Drinks and smokes.[6]

William Pinkerton mobilized an army of the agency's best men and stayed out all night combing the city, but Truman was nowhere to be found. Early the following morning, the Pinkerton brothers met in their offices to discuss their next move. Truman might be a master of the disappearing act, but he was an opportunistic amateur compared to the villains in the Pinkerton back catalog. This was the firm that had captured the notorious "Napoleon of crime," Adam Worth, whose felonies included safecracking, bank and diamond robbery, and the theft of the celebrated Thomas Gainsborough painting *Duchess of Devonshire* from a London art gallery. After twenty-something years at the helm, the Pinkerton brothers weren't about to let a two-bit thief and fraudster like Truman ruin their track record.

When Barker had first encountered Antoinette Funk, he had assumed that as a woman she would be an easy opponent, but she had proved to be "by nature a fighter" and a dirty one at that.[7] Whenever Barker and Blum succeeded in finding Truman and having him arrested, Funk arrived to argue some obscure point of law or to apply for another writ of habeas corpus to have him released. Having the showman released on the grounds that he was insolvent was typical of the woman's strategy. Blum, who had agreed with the government to prosecute all the cases against Truman for a flat fee of five hundred dollars,[8] had learned that Truman had already paid Funk more than seven hundred dollars.[9] For that money she was presumably prepared to do whatever it took to keep him at liberty.

Barker and Blum had taken a scattershot approach to securing a conviction in Chicago, lodging dozens of separate actions against Truman in the hope that one would stick. A judge in the civil court had found the showman guilty of embezzling the Igorrotes' wages and ordered him to pay back ninety-six hundred dollars to the tribespeople.[10] But it was an empty victory because Truman had no money to give them. From what Barker heard, Truman's wife had taken over the role of his banker. Presumably she had tired of her husband squandering their money and of being pursued by his many creditors.[11]

Truman had failed to turn up in court when one of the criminal cases had been called, for the theft of seventy-six dollars from Feloa, and had thereby forfeited his bondsman's thousand dollars.[12] Blum was given the option of collecting the bond and dropping the charges, but declined. According to Funk, her client had been detained by business in New Orleans.[13] Only weeks later had Barker learned that Truman had indeed been in New Orleans, where he had attempted to earn a quick buck by exhibiting a group of "New Orleans negroes as Igorrotes."[14] According to his source, the public was not fooled and "the show broke up after a few days of unsuccessful endeavor."[15]

Over the many weeks he had spent with the Igorrotes, Barker had gradually gained their trust. From their conversations the government agent compiled a timeline of Truman's crimes, noting the date and location of each theft and assault. Shortly before Truman gave William Pinkerton the slip, Barker had traveled to Memphis to meet with a prosecuting attorney to discuss the possibility of pursuing larceny charges against Truman for the money he stole from Feloa,

Dengay, and Julio in the North Front Street house. The attorney had expressed such confidence that they could secure a conviction that Barker had decided their best course of action would be to drop all the charges in Chicago and move their focus to Memphis. There was one important factor in the case being assembled in Memphis that might make it easier to secure a guilty verdict, and a prison sentence, than in Chicago. Crucially, Truman had used physical force to steal the tribe's money, making it a criminal offense in Tennessee.[16]

The only major difficulty to overcome in the South, reflected Blum, would be "the color of the prosecuting witnesses."[17] Blum had visited Truman's business associate turned adversary Col. Hopkins in St. Louis. Hopkins didn't need to be persuaded to testify against Truman, in fact, he'd volunteered for the job. By adding Hopkins and one or two other white-skinned Americans to the list of witnesses, Blum hoped they might be able to overcome any prejudices in the minds of a Memphis jury.[18]

The cost of securing an indictment in Memphis was around $120.[19] On top of that, there would be the expense involved in taking Truman, under guard, to Memphis. The government had already spent $4,193[20] on deporting the Igorrotes who had sailed for the Philippines in July. Added to that would be the legal and detectives' fees, Barker's time, and the cost of travel, food, and accommodations for the Igorrotes and all other witnesses. Barker knew the bureau chief was eager to keep further costs to a minimum, and had been relieved when McIntyre had agreed to pursue a prosecution in Memphis. Had Pinkerton only done what he was assigned to do and kept Truman in his sights, the showman would be in Memphis by now awaiting trial.

At least the five witnesses were happy. Julio, Maria, Feloa, Dengay, and Tainan had been moved to Riverview after their friends departed for the Philippines, and there they were enjoying the company of Schneidewind's group. Julio and Dengay had been enlisted to work on a scholarly side project with Antero and some of the others, assisting Dr. Carl Seidenadel, a linguist who had taken up residence in the village, where he was busy compiling a major study of the language of the Bontoc Igorrote tribe. While the Pinkertons scoured

Chicago for Truman, the tribespeople, who had grown accustomed to the cruelest treatment, rose each morning to explain the basics of their language to the courteous and studious Seidenadel, who sat all day scribbling feverishly in his notebook. The Igorrotes took comfort in the calm routine of the work, which they found stimulating and rewarding. The witnesses felt content for the first time in months, and stopped nagging Barker about when they were going home.[21]

The first American to undertake a major study of the Bontoc Igorrotes' language had been Albert Jenks, who lived among the tribe in Bontoc pueblo for five months in 1903. In the preface to his book, Jenks had thanked an upstanding public servant named Truman Hunt for his generous help. It was a curious irony that the Igorrotes' eventful journey around America was bookended by these two scholarly studies. Much had changed in the intervening years, not least that Truman had turned from hero to villain.

While the Igorrotes helped Seidenadel in Chicago, newspapers across the US reported that a group of Igorrotes had ambushed a party of American soldiers who were shooting the rapids of the Abulung River in northern Luzon on a bamboo raft. Seven Americans were wounded and the party was unable to return fire because the Igorrotes were hidden on the wooded banks of the river. "This outbreak is inexplicable as hitherto the Igorrotes have been peaceable," wrote the agency reporter in Manila.[22]

On September 14, 1906, nine days after he disappeared from right under William Pinkerton's nose, Truman surprised everyone by showing up in court in Chicago again to answer one of the charges against him. Truman regarded the charge as a relatively minor one and presumed his attorney would have no difficulty in getting him off, or at least having the case postponed. Funk hoped that by dragging the cases out her opponents would tire of trying to prosecute Truman and drop all the charges. Truman was conferring with his attorney at the front of the courtroom when a local sheriff approached them and told the showman he was arresting him under requisition from the governor of Tennessee. Truman reacted angrily. He hated surprises.

As he was led from the courtroom, Funk told him that she would have him released in no time.

On October 10, nearly a month later, Truman was still stuck in his flea-ridden jail cell. The showman's mood was bleak. The loss of his liberty had hit him hard. He felt permanently on edge and for the first time he had begun to fear that he might be convicted. What little patience the showman had had long since run out. He had given Funk what remained of his fortune. He wasn't paying her to leave him languishing in a vile jail cell. Sallie had written to him begging for help, describing how she was being pursued day and night by men claiming Truman owed them money. Baby Patty wasn't sleeping at night and Sallie had no money to pay the rent. Truman needed to get out. He called to one of the guards. The two men had become friendly in the weeks since Truman's arrest. The showman asked the guard to get word to his attorney that he wanted to see her.

Truman lay on his mattress, staring at the flaking paint on the opposite wall. He heard footsteps in the distance and the sound of keys. The guard stopped at his cell and unlocked the door. The showman got to his feet, assuming his attorney had at last succeeded in having him released. But instead of Antoinette Funk, a man stood with the guard. In a languid southern drawl, he introduced himself as a sheriff from Tennessee. Truman was getting out of jail but he was not a free man. Handcuffing himself to the showman, the sheriff told Truman that they were going on a journey. They would catch the next train to Memphis.[23]

28

In the Care of the Government

FORT SHERIDAN, ILLINOIS, OCTOBER 11, 1906

The barracks at Fort Sheridan army base, Illinois

THE FIVE FILIPINO witnesses eyed the high iron gates nervously. Fort Sheridan was located thirty miles north of downtown Chicago and was perched high on the bluffs overlooking the steel-gray waters of Lake Michigan. The army base occupied over six hundred acres, its sixty-four buildings linked by landscaped paths and curving roads. The tribespeople looked at the group of soldiers standing guard outside. Feloa said something to the others in Bontoc. Noticing the rifles in the soldiers' hands, Maria reached forward and tried to loop a protective arm around Tainan, but the boy pushed forward and pressed his face between the bars of the gates. A soldier shouted at him to get back.

Barker handed an envelope to one of the guards. Inside was a letter of introduction from the bureau, listing the names of the tribespeople who would be staying at the barracks. Since arriving in America they had seen the inside of amusement parks, courtrooms, and squalid cold-water apartments. Now the five remaining members of Truman's troupe were to become uneasy residents of an American army base. The accommodations weren't ideal, but Barker needed somewhere cheap and secure to put the Filipino witnesses up in Chicago while they waited for Truman's trial date to be set in Memphis.

Though the Igorrotes didn't know it, they already had a historical connection to the base at Fort Sheridan, which had served as a mobilization, training, and administrative center during the 1898 Spanish-American War. Then it had played a role in delivering the Philippines into American hands. Now it would be the place where five displaced Filipinos would wait it out while the wheels of the American justice system slowly turned.

The thirty-five tribespeople in Schneidewind's group had left Chicago on the 6:30 p.m. train the previous night, bound for San Francisco en route to the Philippines. They'd been joined by a woman from Truman's group, Tanao,[1] who had offered to act as a witness but whom Barker had decided they could manage without.[2]

That morning, Feloa, Dengay, Maria, Julio, and Tainan had woken up feeling utterly alone. When they appeared in court, they would represent the whole tribe. The weight of getting Truman convicted rested heavily on their shoulders.

Two and a half months had passed since the other members of Truman's original group had set sail for Manila. After four hundred and sixty days in the United States, twelve thousand miles by train and sea on the outward journey alone, and thousands of tribal performances before millions of Americans in fifty towns and cities, their financial rewards came to just thirty dollars and eighty-five cents each.[3]

Their departure had been celebrated by anti-imperialists, Democrats, and newspaper editorials alike. Together they called for an end to the Igorrote exhibition trade, arguing that the ignorant tribespeople were ripe for exploitation by unscrupulous showmen, "for they are helpless as children in this strange land. Nor is there any good purpose to be served by parading their dog-eating and like barbarous practices before the American public. There is nothing edifying or educational enough in these exhibitions to atone for their evil effects upon the poor savages who are supposed to be the nation's wards, not its playthings."[4]

The soldier at the gate studied the bureau's letter and glanced over at the tribespeople. Then he looked down the list of visitors who were expected that day. Sensing an opportunity, Tainan reached over to touch the cannon that stood in front of the gates. The soldier barked at them to enter, giving Tainan the fright of his life. Another man stepped forward and said he would escort them to the barracks.

He led the Filipinos past a vast oval-shaped parade ground where soldiers were practicing their drills. The parade ground was lined on the south side by barracks, two stories high, which stretched as far as the eye could see, with bachelor officers' quarters and single-family homes varying in size on the east and north sides. Barker noticed the grim expression on Dengay's face as he took in their new surroundings.

Tainan alone was enthusiastic for their new home. The young boy looked up in awe at the huge water tower across from where they stood. It was as tall as a dozen head-hunting watchtowers stacked one on top of the other. The soldier walked over to one of the barracks and pushed the door open, indicating to the tribespeople to enter. Inside, he pointed to a row of bunks and told the tribespeople to make themselves comfortable. The room was dark and dank, but the Filipinos had grown accustomed to much worse.

They laid their possessions down on the cold stone floor. On top of their blankets, they piled a small gong, a few pieces of native jewelry, a copy of the *Independent* featuring an interview with the tribal chief from back when they were at Coney Island, and a postcard showing four Igorrotes posing beside a man dressed as Uncle Sam. It was a pathetic bundle of mementos to show for everything they had endured in America.

They had their trunks too, though they were in storage and contained little beyond their blankets and extra American traveling clothes. When the rest of Truman's group left in July, the showman had refused to give back their trunks. Laughing, he had claimed "he had a lieu [*sic*] on those effects for a breach of contract!"[5] How typical of the man. After weeks of searching, the bureau had finally discovered the trunks, only to find that all the locks had been broken and the lid of one was smashed.[6] The contents had been rifled through and anything of value stolen.

In the fifteen months he had had charge of them, Truman had taken everything he possibly could from the tribespeople. As the showman had grown more desperate, the Igorrotes had become increasingly inventive. One of the few times they had succeeded in preventing Truman from getting his hands on their money, they had hidden it inside their ears.[7] Barker would not have believed this were possible had Julio not demonstrated how they had done it, rolling the dollar bills tight and packing them into their ear canals. They were lucky they hadn't damaged their hearing. How desperate they must have been.

Looking around the cramped, bare interior of the barracks, Maria experienced a deep longing for home. The damp Chicago air pricked her skin, making her yearn for the day when she would again be able to roam free and toil in the rice fields with the sun beating down on her back. She wanted to feel her muscles ache after a day of hard physical labor. Despite her husband's presence, Maria felt lonely. As the only woman left, she would miss the camaraderie she felt with Daipan and the other women. They had confided in each other and kept each other's spirits up. She desperately missed the children, whose innocence and playfulness had been a source of comfort during the darkest moments. Maria blinked back tears and turned her head so no one would see.

Tainan, who was standing at the window, shouted to the others to come and watch the soldiers practicing their drills. Maria saw something of her husband in the boy. He was smart, good-natured, and eager to learn, though not as serious as Julio. She envied Tainan's resilience. He had known pain in his short life but he had been blessed with a carefree attitude. As an orphan he was concerned not with when he was going home to see his family, but with his new life. Maria knew from chatting to the boy that he was full of excitement about going to an American school. When he had completed his education, he would be expected to take up a civil service job in the Philippines. The post would come with a good wage, but Tainan secretly dreamed of staying on in America.

Barker told Julio that they must stay inside the barracks at all times. They would be provided with three hot meals a day. Did they have everything they needed? The interpreter nodded. There was one other matter Barker wished to discuss with them. For some time now he had been trying to ascertain the whereabouts of the bodies of the two Igorrotes who had died in America. He had appealed to Truman for information, but the showman had callously remained silent on the subject. Barker had recently learned that the Bonney-Watson funeral directors in Seattle were holding Falino's embalmed body in storage and were on the verge of interring it, having not heard a word from Truman since the showman had left the body in their care seventeen months previously. Meanwhile, the undertaker in New Orleans, Thomas Lynch, had buried Pucuan's body at his own expense after failing to hear from Truman. Sadly, thought Barker, it was typical of Truman that a perfect stranger had treated the dead Igorrote with more compassion than him. Barker's face was solemn as he addressed the Filipinos: *What would you like us to do with the bodies?* They could be shipped to the Philippines for burial in Bontoc, or left where they were and, in the case of Falino, buried in Seattle. Feloa, Dengay, and Julio began to speak among themselves. Turning to Barker, Julio said they would like the government to leave the bodies where they were; they should not be disturbed. Falino should be buried. From the way they spoke, it was clear the tribespeople did not like the idea of disinterring the dead.[8] Barker nodded and turned to leave.

When are we going home? Feloa asked. He had asked the same question often and with increasing urgency in recent weeks. Barker felt a good deal of sympathy for Feloa and the others. They had been promised repeatedly that they were on the verge of being sent home and here they were again, in yet another new place, with a trip to Memphis on the horizon.

The trials in Memphis would, he hoped, be called soon and wrapped up quickly, said Barker. If the court cases went to plan, the government hoped to be able to send them home within the month. Feloa, Dengay, and Julio had been unwavering in their determination to see Truman punished. They had also been adamant that they would not leave America without their wages. But with the others gone, Barker sensed that their resolve was beginning to weaken.

Feloa, Dengay, and Julio were vital to the prosecution. If they left America, the cases against Truman would collapse. Barker knew that he could use threats, tell the tribespeople that the government would refuse to pay for their return transport if they did not stay on to see the prosecution through to the end, but he had no desire to be so heavy-handed. These people had suffered enough. It was in everybody's interests to treat them kindly. Feloa and Dengay were worried about their families, who they feared had run out of food by now. Barker told them he would ask the bureau to make arrangements with the lieutenant governor of Bontoc to provide them with sufficient provisions to tide them over until Feloa and Dengay returned.[9]

Julio had his own reason for not wanting to be delayed in America too long. He was considering an offer from Schneidewind to become his assistant. From what Barker understood, Schneidewind had made Antero the same offer. The American wanted the two of them to help him gather another, bigger group of Igorrotes and to bring them to America in time for the next show season. The longer Julio was in America, the more likely it was that Schneidewind would ask someone else to take his place. Barker knew Julio was ambitious, but he was surprised the interpreter wanted to have anything more to do with the showmen.

Back in his hotel, the government agent sat in the dining room. He had just finished eating and now turned his attention to composing a report for the bureau. Reflecting that "the situation of these poor homesick people is one of extreme hardship," Barker suggested that if Truman could not be brought to trial within thirty days, the Filipinos should be put out of their misery and sent home.[10]

In a bleak reference to Schneidewind's plans to bring another exhibition group over the following year, Barker said the five witnesses at Fort Sheridan "will all probably be here again next spring anyway."[11] Other enterprising men would undoubtedly follow in Truman and Schneidewind's footsteps, spurred on by tales of the riches the showmen had earned. And despite the fact that the American dream had turned sour for Truman's group, Barker imagined that many more Igorrotes would be lured across the Pacific. After all, it was human nature to yearn for adventure and opportunity. Unless the government put a stop to it, Barker predicted that the Igorrote trade would run and run.

29

A Gentleman Criminal

SHELBY COUNTY JAIL, MEMPHIS, LATE OCTOBER 1906

The Shelby County Courthouse in Memphis, c. 1906

TRUMAN SAT ON the edge of his bed and eyed the dirty rim of the toilet bowl. A fly emerged from inside and flew over to the tiny slit that passed for a window. The showman got up and went over to look out. He stared at the twelve-foot-high brick wall topped with iron spikes that enclosed the jail. If he craned his neck he could just about see the little frame house on the other side of North Front Street where the Igorrotes had stayed the last time they were in Memphis. The irony that he was sitting in a cell just across the street from where he had kept the Igorrotes as virtual prisoners was wasted on Truman. Instead he was filled with a raging sense of injustice. He had offered the Filipinos an escape from their filthy mountain hovels, and then they had turned on him. Once he had viewed the tribespeople as guileless, playful children. Now he saw them as ungrateful savages.

He had befriended many of the guards, and the police officers, who were frequent visitors. They didn't get too many "gentleman criminals" staying with them and "the doc" was treated well.[1] The guards lapped up his stories of his exploits in the Philippines and roared for more when he described his life as a traveling showman, touring the country with a group of nearly naked savages. The one about the Filipinos nearly being lynched by an angry mob after they went skinny-dipping in Atlantic City always went down well. So too did his description of a woman fainting and almost falling into the cooking pot at one of their dog feasts.

The man running the jail was Mr. Fleetwood, the very one who had complained to the police about the Igorrotes upsetting his wife and daughter by running around with no clothes on when they were staying across the road. Truman and Fleetwood had laughed after they made the connection. With the jailer on his side, Truman had been spared the inconvenience of having to share his cell. That alone made it worth putting up with Fleetwood's long-winded stories.

To Truman's annoyance, Antoinette Funk had been unable or unwilling to travel to Memphis to represent him (his outstanding bills might have been a factor). With his fortune spent, the showman's best hope of securing an attorney lay with the Elks. He had been a regular visitor to the lodge on his two previous visits to Memphis and had gotten to know many of its influential members well.

Truman decided to write to the Memphis Elks Lodge appealing for help. His letter was masterly; Truman Hunt, the medical doctor and Spanish-American War veteran, had fallen on hard times, and through a misunderstanding, he had wound up in jail. Might his brother Elks be able to help clear the matter up? One of the Memphis lodge leaders had come to call on him in jail and had insisted that the Elks would provide him with legal representation. The showman could hardly have wished for more. Not only did the lodge leader make good on his promise, the attorney the Elks provided was one of the best in the city and incredibly well connected to boot. Truman had always liked Memphis and now it was smiling on him.

The showman faced two separate larceny charges in the city, for stealing seventeen dollars (worth around four hundred and fifty dollars today) from Dengay and twenty-eight dollars (worth around seven hundred and forty dollars today) from Feloa. Truman's newly appointed attorney, David Frayser, visited him in his cell to prepare for their day in court. Frayser stood just five feet tall and weighed one hundred and thirty pounds, but despite his diminutive proportions, he was famed among his peers for his combative style and considerable presence. His previous career as a newspaperman had taught Frayser a valuable lesson in the art of storytelling, which he displayed to full effect in his courtroom appearances.

Frayser listened as Truman described his long relationship with the Igorrotes and the accusations he expected them to make against him. When the showman mentioned that the tribespeople were pagans, Frayser closed his eyes and stroked his mustache, imagining the compelling narrative he would weave before the judge and jury. Before he left Truman's cell, Frayser reassured his new client that their case was as good as won.

On Friday, November 2, 1906, Barker and Blum came face-to-face with Frayser for the first time. The setting was Shelby County courthouse, formerly a smart hotel named the Overton that had once played host to the Grand Duke Alexis of Russia. The room was filled with potential jurors who were waiting to find out if they would be selected for the *State of Tennessee v. Truman Hunt*, which would try Truman for the theft of seventeen dollars from Dengay.

Barker eyed Frayser. He was a small, wiry man, balding and with sharp features. But when Truman's attorney got up to speak, Barker observed that everyone in the room listened. He had a deliberate, direct way of speaking and a penetrating gaze that would be enough to make the toughest of witnesses squirm like a bug on a pin. Clutching his lapels, he fixed the first potential juryman with a beady eye and asked, *do you believe in God? Yes, sir*, stammered the man. *Did you attend church on Sunday?* Frayser continued. His manner of questioning would have been enough to send any man of lapsed faith running for the pews.[2] When Frayser quizzed one particularly wretched-looking farmhand about the last time he had attended church, Blum thought he saw a tear of remorse in the young man's eye as he confessed it had been some time. Frayser dismissed the man as unsuitable to be on the jury. Blum raised an eyebrow. It wasn't hard to work out what Frayser's game plan was: no doubt with Truman's encouragement, he was going to play up the Igorrotes' paganism and their nonbelief in the Bible in order to undermine their testimony.

If religion was Frayser's trump card, then Blum knew the prosecution had another potential weakness to overcome. In a city "where the color line is drawn more strictly than perhaps anywhere else in the United States"[3] Blum fully expected that the Igorrotes would encounter a degree of racial prejudice. When it was his turn to speak, Blum got slowly to his feet. He tipped the scales at two hundred and fifty pounds and what he lacked in speed he more than made up for in intellect and determination.

Blum questioned the potential jurors and found three men who expressed a bias so strongly in favor of a white man over anyone else that he felt compelled to dismiss them as unsuitable.[4] This would be a difficult case to win, but, after a lifetime prosecuting crooks and scoundrels in Chicago, Blum wasn't easily intimidated. One of the many lessons he had learned during his long career in the law was that subtlety was often more effective than force.

As Barker and Blum predicted, the jury thus selected was "composed almost entirely of God-fearing men of the farming class."[5] Blum couldn't resist leaning over to Barker and remarking that the trial should open not with swearing on the Bible but with a prayer.[6] The two men exchanged a wry smile. With the jury selected, the trial was set to begin the following Monday, November 5, 1906, before Judge John Moss.

Blum was characteristically relaxed but Barker felt anxious. The day's events did not augur well. How could a collection of Tennessee farmers, rural men of limited education who'd never left their home state, empathize with the plight of a group of Filipino tribespeople? Would an all-white, all-Christian jury ever convict a white, professional, supposedly Christian man based on the testimony of dark-skinned pagan savages?

The people of Memphis knew the Igorrotes well. They had been popular visitors when they had appeared at the city's East End Park a year earlier. On the day of the trial, the street outside the Shelby County court took on a festive atmosphere as spectators began arriving early in the hope of catching a glimpse of the tribespeople. To their disappointment, the tattoos, G-strings, and bare flesh they'd come to see had been covered up by long skirts and sober suits, the result of yet another shopping expedition that Barker had undertaken—himself this time—on their behalf. Despite their dismay over the Igorrotes' clothes, the public were thrilled to see the Filipinos and gathered around to inspect them in their new garb.

It took several minutes for Barker and the five witnesses to get through the crowds. Inside the court building, Barker gathered the Filipinos for a pep talk. He knew that they would be judged not just on what they said, but also on their appearance. It was a fact that, Julio aside, the tribespeople found non-native clothes uncomfortable and, as they stood in the corridor, he pleaded with them not to scratch and fidget in court.

Conscious that Frayser would try to make religion an issue, Blum and Barker had quizzed each of the Filipinos beforehand on their beliefs. After doing so, they concluded that "while not by any means orthodox from a Christian's point of view, [the Igorrotes] have decided religious doctrines. They believe in one God, who is omniscient and omnipotent; in a purgatory or Heaven where the wicked will suffer for their misdeeds on earth and the good will enjoy eternal 'leisure.'"[7] This will suffice, thought Barker, acknowledging that he couldn't hope to change the tribespeople's religious beliefs in a matter of hours. To Barker's surprise, Julio, who described himself as Christian, and his wife, Maria, were less religious than the others. Their Christianity appeared "to be confined to a knowledge of the fact that a man by the name of Jesus Christ once lived."[8]

A voice announced that the *State of Tennessee v. Truman Hunt* was up next. Barker gave the tribespeople one last piece of advice before they entered the courtroom. Truman and his attorney might try to put them off, but they must not be intimidated. They just needed to tell the truth.

• • •

Frayser had sent a barber to Truman's jail cell that morning, along with a new suit, and the showman looked characteristically immaculate, though thinner and lined. Barker reflected that his adversary looked as full of himself as ever. How he hoped the jury would be able to see through his posturing and lies.

Dengay was the first of the tribespeople to be called to the stand. Truman was in court to answer the charge that he had stolen seventeen dollars from him, and what Dengay said that day would be crucial. Barker and Blum had done their best to prepare him, but even they had to concede that the language and cultural barriers would be huge hurdles to overcome. The Igorrotes were simple mountain people who described things exactly as they saw them, without emphasis or embellishment, and their matter-of-fact way of speaking could make it difficult to distinguish between what was trivial and what was important.

Dengay looked solemn as he stood before Judge Moss and placed his hand on the Bible. The Igorrote looked down at the battered leather-bound book under his palm and ran the tips of his fingers over the cover. American customs could be so strange. In Bontoc a man could be trusted to tell the truth. Crime was almost unheard of, but in the rare event that someone in the village was suspected of stealing or of committing an assault, adultery, or even murder, then the suspects would be gathered together and made to chew a mouthful of uncooked rice. When the rice was thoroughly masticated, each person would be told to spit it out onto a dish. Each sample was then inspected. The person whose rice was the driest would be considered guilty, for the tribespeople believed the guilty one would be the most nervous during the "trial," thus interfering with normal saliva flow and giving them a dry mouth.[9] Dengay thought how much simpler it would be if they could perform this trial on Truman. But the showman was so wicked and unrepentant, he would probably pass the test.

With Julio standing next to him, translating, Dengay swore to tell the truth. Before he could finish, Frayser leaped to his feet. How, wondered Truman's attorney aloud, could Dengay's testimony be trusted, given that he didn't believe in the Holy Bible on which he'd just sworn? Frayser's gaze wandered from the judge to his hand-picked, God-fearing jury. *Let the man speak*, said Judge Moss, urging Frayser to sit down and instructing the prosecution to begin.

Sitting next to Blum was the Shelby County assistant attorney general, Alexander Humphreys Kortrecht. An avid churchgoer, a Democrat, and the father of five children, Kortrecht was highly respected even among his courtroom opponents for his "wide research and [the] provident care with which he prepares his cases."[10] Despite the tough exterior the forty-six-year-old's job frequently demanded, Kortrecht was kindly and approachable and immediately succeeded in putting Dengay at ease. He began by asking the Filipino when and why the Igorrotes had come to America. They had come the previous year to earn money, and had exhibited for Truman Hunt in many towns and cities, said Dengay. Kortrecht moved on to their stay in the house on North Front Street. He asked his witness whether he had willingly given Truman Hunt his souvenir money on that April day when Truman had come to the house. *Why would I give him the money? It was mine*, responded Dengay. *He came to the house and stole my money. He tore at our clothes and stole the money we had hidden inside them.*

Objection, shouted Frayser. He accused Julio of failing to give true and accurate translations. As a witness for the prosecution, the translator clearly had a vested interest in the case. Mindful of the fact that no one else in Memphis, and quite possibly the entire country, spoke their language and could therefore act as translator, the judge ruled that Julio could continue in the role. To placate the defense, Judge Moss added that Truman, who had a working knowledge of the language, could interrupt whenever an accurate translation was not given.

Sitting next to Frayser, Truman tried hard not to smile. He scribbled something on a scrap of paper in front of him and passed it along to Frayser.

When it was his turn to question the witness, Frayser stood up and stared hard at Dengay. To the Filipino's confusion, the legal man started by asking him to describe the layout and decor of the house on North Front Street, and the method by which the Igorrotes claimed Truman and Callahan had blacked out the windows. As

Frayser asked him more and more questions about precisely where the windows were, how many of them there were, and the way in which each window was covered, Dengay grew tired. Seven months had passed since they stayed in the house. They'd stayed in many, many places since then, and he could no longer remember exactly what it looked like.

Truman kept interrupting Dengay's testimony to complain that Julio's translation was inaccurate. Dengay grew weary and frustrated. Eventually, because of the many interruptions, Judge Moss adjourned the day's proceedings. Dengay would be recalled the following morning.

That night Dengay was uncharacteristically quiet. He had let the tribe down. The legal man had made his head hurt with his questions about the house. Why hadn't he asked him about Truman and the terrible things he had done to them? If the showman walked free, it would be his fault. Barker and Julio sat for more than an hour talking to Dengay, trying to reassure him that all was not lost. But Barker secretly wondered whether the Igorrote's simple, unaffected truth would be enough to convict a man who dealt in hyperbole, exaggeration, and lies.

The following morning, Frayser continued his questioning in the same vein. *How many rooms were there in the house? Four*, replied Dengay. Was he sure? Dengay's evidence became confused, and at times contradictory. *Isn't it true*, asked Frayser, *that when Mr. Blum and Mr. Barker took you to identify the house on North Front Street recently, you couldn't find it?* Barker wondered how on earth the man knew this. Frayser continued: *If this terrible event that you describe really took place, wouldn't it be fair to assume that every detail of the house would be etched in your mind forever?* Dengay was silent for a moment, unable to think as quickly as the man was speaking. When finally the headhunter found his voice, he said simply, *but what I told you is true.*[11]

Barker felt sorry for the savage. The Igorrotes were good, honest people whose straightforward worldview and complete lack of cunning made them pathetically vulnerable to attack in the rough and tumble of the courtroom. When it was his turn to speak, Barker explained his involvement in the case. He described how he had undertaken a thorough examination of the Igorrotes' complaints and had reached the conclusion that Truman Hunt must be prosecuted for his crimes. There was no doubt in his mind, Barker added, that the tribespeople were telling the truth. Julio, Maria, Feloa, and Tainan were each called on to give their version of events. Their accounts differed little from Dengay's, though when they described a minor detail like the position of the outhouse or a window differently, the defense made much of it.

Truman took the stand next. The contrast between the chief prosecution witness and the accused man was stark; Dengay had been faltering and uncertain, Truman was fluent and assured. He spoke for four hours, eloquently and without a break.[12] His performance was polished and persuasive. The enforced sobriety in jail had been good for him. Gone was the ruddy complexion, the forgetfulness, and the near-permanent slur. He still had the puffy bags under his eyes, but those were there to stay. With Frayser at his side, he looked and felt more like the Truman Hunt of old, the one who'd gone off to medical school full of confidence and swagger. Eyeing the judge and then looking slowly from one juror to another, the showman said the Igorrotes had given him their money to keep safe for them. He was not a thief, he insisted—he despised thieves. Darn him, thought Barker, the showman was so plausible. Would the jury see through his lies?

Truman said he had given the tribespeople a receipt. At this, the clerk passed Judge Moss a piece of paper Frayser had given him earlier. The paper was a receipt for $209 written in Truman's hand, and made out to the Igorrotes as an I.O.U. for some of the souvenir money, which, according to Truman's version of events, the Igorrotes had given him voluntarily.[13] *Why would the defendant have issued a receipt if he had stolen the money?* Frayser asked with a quizzical expression as the receipt was passed to the jurors to inspect. *Doesn't the fact that he issued the receipt indicate that he had no intention of keeping the tribe's money?* Barker noted one of the jurors nodding.

Frayser then showed the receipt to Julio and the Igorrotes and asked them if they had ever seen it before. The Filipinos glanced at each other. How they wished that they could bring themselves to lie, but their consciences would not allow it. On behalf of them all, Julio nodded, *yes, Truman gave us the receipt.* What the translator didn't understand was how Truman had gotten his hands on it. He must have stolen it from their trunks. Julio opened his mouth to say something further, but Frayser cut him off. Blum chewed the inside of his cheek. There was no doubt the receipt would weaken their case. His earlier confidence began to ebb away.

After two long days of testimony, argument, and counterargument, Blum gave an impassioned closing statement. Truman was a liar, a cheat, a spendthrift, and a thief who had earned many thousands of dollars from the Igorrotes. Once he had frittered away his fortune, the greedy showman had used physical force to steal more money from the tribespeople. The Igorrotes were primitive people who deserved to be protected, not betrayed and preyed upon. Truman had treated them abominably and kept them against their will, locked up like slaves, after their contracts had expired.

Frayser stood up to give his closing argument. The Truman he described could have passed for an unfortunate saint. He was a caring manager and friend to the Igorrotes who had fallen on hard times after spending a fortune housing and feeding the tribe, and transporting them around the country. He had kept their wages safe for them and had, on occasion, been forced to borrow souvenir money from them, but, as the I.O.U. demonstrated, he had always planned to pay the money back. The incident described by the Igorrotes as having happened on North Front Street never took place, as evidenced by the Filipinos' failure to find the house or to adequately describe it. Frayser added that his client was stunned and wounded by their claims.

The jury retired to consider their verdict. Barker and Blum stepped outside. Though he did not say so to Blum, Barker feared the case was lost. With objections to the tribespeople swearing on the Bible and numerous questions about the Filipinos' pagan beliefs, opposing counsel had done "everything in their power to arouse religious prejudice against these poor savages in the minds of the jury men. The low intelligence of the Igorrote witnesses and the extreme difficulty of getting the questions to them correctly through an interpreter and of securing responsive replies was constantly raising 'reasonable doubts' in the minds of the jurymen which it required Herculean efforts to ally."[14] The fact that they did not speak English, or understand American ways of doing and saying things, was a major disadvantage, making them easy victims to Frayser and Truman's underhanded tricks.[15]

The next one hour and forty minutes were among the longest and most nerve-racking of Barker's life. In his line of work, Blum had grown accustomed to these tense waits. The attorney, who was a voracious reader and "a veritable treasury of information,"[16] took out his newspaper and began to read, breaking off after awhile to do the crossword puzzle. Tainan began to sing the first verse of the popular 1905 song "Everybody Works but Father,"[17] sung from the point of view of a young boy lamenting that while he works all day, his father lounges around in front of the fire smoking his pipe:[18]

Every morning at six o'clock
I go to my work,
Overcoat buttoned up round my neck
No job would I shirk,
Winter wind blows round my head
Cutting up my face,
I tell you what I'd like to have
My dear old father's place.[19]

Barker looked over at the boy. Next to him, the other Filipinos were chatting calmly. The government agent noticed they seemed able to switch off their minds and relax a little by smoking their pipes. But Barker could do nothing except pace up and down the corridor, making a mental map of every single imperfection on the tiled floor. Would the jury be able to see the truth through the Igorrotes' sometimes halting delivery? Would Truman's fluency and poise be enough to persuade them he was a man of honor?

A voice boomed down the corridor. The jury had reached their decision. Everyone filed back into the courtroom. Barker peered intently at the faces of the jury, searching for a clue to their decision. He noticed one of them smiling at Truman. He felt suddenly nauseous.

Judge Moss looked around the courtroom. He called for the jury's verdict.

As the foreman stood, Barker swallowed. His mouth was dry. He looked over and saw Julio was clenching the side of his seat so tightly his knuckles had turned white. The room was silent, save for the sound of the foreman clearing his throat. All eyes were fixed on him as he opened his mouth and uttered the words the Igorrotes had hardly dared hoped for: "We find the defendant guilty."

Barker and Blum turned to each other, speechless. This was an astounding verdict in favor of the pagan Filipino tribespeople from the southern, all-white, Christian jury. It was a truly historic moment, a fact that was wasted on no one in the room. Julio turned to translate for his countrymen, but he didn't need to. His face told them all they needed to know. The tribespeople were "overjoyed"[20] and asked Barker to send word of the result to their friends in the Philippines immediately. There would be feasting in the Bontoc mountains.

Truman's sentence was set at eleven months and twenty-nine days to be served in the Shelby County workhouse. The showman sat back in his chair, his face deathly white.

The tribe's blunt way of speaking, and their emotion as they described Truman's cruelty, had given their testimony a power the twelve jurors had found hard to ignore. Any religious or racial prejudices the jury might have had against the Igorrotes had been overwhelmed by the disgust they felt as the prosecution described the wealth Truman had accumulated and squandered, and the inhumanity he had shown the savages. The very conservatism of the jury, which Truman's lawyer had assumed would act in his client's favor, had acted against him. His callous behavior had offended their sense of decency.

For the first time since he had begun his pursuit of Truman Hunt, Barker allowed himself to believe that his opponent was going to be properly punished for all that he had done.

30

Trials and Tribulations

SHELBY COUNTY COURT, MEMPHIS, NOVEMBER 22, 1906

Attorney David Frayser *Judge Moss*

A FORTNIGHT AFTER SECURING their surprise victory, the Igorrotes returned to the Shelby County court for the second case against Truman. The showman was accused of using force to steal twenty-eight dollars from Feloa while they were staying in the house on North Front Street. On their first court appearance the tribespeople were nervous, naive, and had fallen easily into Frayser's traps; this time they came prepared and gave "dramatic and persuasive" testimony.[1]

When Kortrecht asked Feloa about the incident in the house on North Front Street, the Igorrote described Truman's ultimate betrayal with a poignancy which would have made any man of conscience weep. The showman's face was impassive.

Frayser's cross-examination followed a by-now familiar path. *Do you believe in God and Jesus Christ?* he asked. *No,* said Feloa, *I believe in a supreme being and in a future reward for good and evil.* As he uttered these words, the Igorrote looked at Truman. But if he hoped to detect a glimmer of remorse, he would find none.[2] *Do you pray?* Frayser continued. *No,* replied the Igorrote. *Do you know what prayer is?* Feloa shook his head. *What, then, do you believe?* Frayser demanded to know. *I believe in a soul. What do you mean by a soul?* Truman's attorney asked. *Will,* explained the Igorrote. *Can you elaborate?* Frayser asked. *Good will or ill will,* added Feloa.[3] It was an unusual exchange for a courtroom, on a topic better suited to the Memphis Theological Seminary, but Truman's attorney continued in this manner for most of the afternoon.

At the first trial, Frayser's emphasis on religion had seemed calculated but now it smacked of desperation.

When, on the second day of the trial, it was Truman's turn to speak, he did not take the stand, complaining of a sore throat.[4]

The jury took four hours to reach their verdict: Truman Hunt was guilty. He was sentenced to another six months in the workhouse.

The pressmen hurried off to file their stories. The verdict would make headlines from Los Angeles to Little Rock and from Paducah to New York City. It was a tribute of sorts to Truman's genius for publicity. He had worked long and hard to make the Igorrotes famous. Now the newspapers were rushing to report the downfall of the tribe's manager.

Truman sat speechless. Frayser had let him down badly. It was a travesty of justice. The jurors were idiots. In short, it was everyone's fault but his.

The sheriff came to lead him away. Truman turned to Frayser and ordered his attorney to get him out fast. The showman glared at the tribespeople. If he could have gotten near them, he would have torn them limb from limb.

Barker and Blum adjourned with the Filipinos to an anteroom. *Why,* Julio asked, *is Truman not being sent to the penitentiary? Will his punishment be sufficiently severe in the workhouse?* Barker had wondered this himself and had been reliably informed by several people with knowledge of such matters that the Shelby County workhouse was a much worse place to stay than the penitentiary. The food and accommodations were so bad, and the work the inmates were required to do on the roads and in the fields was so severe, hardened criminals were said to prefer a sentence of two years in the penitentiary to one year in the workhouse.[5] Julio smiled. He translated for the others. Slapping Dengay hard on the back, Feloa jumped to his feet and exploded into a victory dance.

But their celebrations were short-lived. Following the two guilty verdicts, Frayser lodged customary motions for two new trials, arguing that Truman had been convicted on the basis of false evidence given by the Igorrotes and false interpretation by Julio. On December 20, 1906, Judge Moss, who had presided in the first two cases, granted the new trials. Such a move was rare in the Memphis court system. Explaining his reasoning, Moss said his conscience had been "disturbed" by inconsistencies in the Igorrotes' testimony and by his fear that Julio had not acted as an unprejudiced interpreter.[6] The judge had shown no such doubts or fears at the time. What had happened to change his mind? Barker and Blum were furious. They both knew there were no legal grounds whatsoever for a new trial.

The Igorrotes had a strong sense of justice and could hardly believe it when Barker showed up at their Memphis lodgings to share the news. *How can the judge change his mind? What about what the jury said?* Julio wanted to know. The tribespeople felt cheated, and Barker could understand why. He empathized with their anger and frustration, but it was the pained expression on Maria's face that would stay with him that night. Before he left, they had one final, inevitable question: *When are we going home? The government hopes to have you on a ship within the month,* he replied. Everyone in the room knew he had already made—and broken—this promise before.

Blum had been asking around the legal community to see what he could find out about Judge Moss, and had learned several facts which he shared with Barker. Moss was a prominent Mason who had been the subject of an attack in the newspapers awhile back, which was so fierce it looked as if he wouldn't get reelected. The judge had been befriended by Frayser, and the influential former newspaperman had used his contacts to silence the press. Since then the two men had appeared to be in cahoots in a number of cases. Moss was regarded by many of his peers to be lacking "moral backbone" and his "judicial reputation in the local community was very bad."[7] The judge's decision to grant Truman the new trials was, in Blum's view, a "monstrosity of an opinion rendered by a monstrosity on the bench."[8] To Blum and Barker's dismay, Judge Moss himself would hear the new trials.

Against this backdrop, it seemed certain that the guilty verdicts would be overturned. Assistant Attorney General Kortrecht advised Blum and Barker that their best bet of securing a conviction in Memphis would be to bring a new case for the $444.55 that Truman and his security guard Ed Callahan had stolen from Julio during the same assault in the North Front Street house. Originally Kortrecht had advised them to prosecute the Feloa and Dengay cases on the basis that it should be easier to secure guilty convictions for these lesser monetary amounts. But they were running out of options and Kortrecht now felt the larger amount might carry more weight with the jury.

Barker agreed, though with all the corruption and evident failings in the Memphis legal system, he couldn't help but wonder whether it was worth the effort of taking up another case in the city. He had come to learn that many of the men involved in Truman's case were members of the Masons and the Elks, the latter being the very organization that the showman belonged to and that was paying for his legal representation. Were they sticking together to protect one of their own? The government had already spent eight hundred dollars on the Memphis trials, with nothing to show for their money.[9] Try as he might to be positive, Barker was beginning to see the conviction they had fought so hard for slip away.

By January 1907, the new trials had still not been called. They had been postponed repeatedly and Blum suspected foul play. Almost two years had passed since the Igorrotes had signed their contracts with Truman and everyone, including Frayser, knew they were desperate to return home. Blum believed that Frayser was using his considerable influence over the judge to persuade him to delay the trials in the hope that the tribespeople would tire of waiting and demand to be sent back to the Philippines. As soon as they left America, the cases would be dropped and Truman would be freed from jail.

Barker and Blum decided to change tack. Just because Truman's trial in Tennessee had gotten bogged down in quicksand did not mean that he would evade justice. The showman had taken the Igorrotes across America and into Canada, robbing them as they went. The fact they had traveled so widely meant that Truman could be prosecuted in a number of states. Barker and Blum took a train to New Orleans, where they met with the state's attorney and the district attorney to discuss the possibility of securing an indictment against Truman for the wages he embezzled from the tribe in that city.

Both of the New Orleans officials said they would gladly assist in the prosecution of the case, and gave Barker and Blum the impression that the New Orleans legal system was a good deal less corrupt than its counterpart in Memphis. Barker wrote to the bureau suggesting they make one last attempt to secure a conviction against Truman, this time in New Orleans.[10]

To Barker's immense relief, the head of the bureau granted him permission. On January 18, Truman was indicted by the grand jury in New Orleans, charged with embezzling fifty dollars from Feloa.[11] It was a small fraction of the money the showman had stolen from the tribe while they were on show in the city, but the district attorney thought it would be enough to secure a conviction. Barker didn't want Truman or Frayser to know that he was pursuing fresh charges in another state and swore everyone who knew of it to secrecy. He agreed with the bureau that they would not risk discussing it over the wires, lest any confidential information got back to the showman and his associates. Instead they would communicate by mail.[12]

Truman had been in jail for four months. In that time, he had called Barker, Blum—and especially Frayser—every name under the sun. Every other day he sent messages to Frayser and his friends in the Elks, demanding, begging, and pleading that they get him out. The showman swung between bouts of self-pity and outbursts of rage, in which he railed against the injustice of the world, the ingratitude of the Filipinos, and the faults of the Memphis legal system.

Despite being locked up, Truman still had eyes and ears all over the country. They included friends, former business associates, Elks, and rogues who had started visiting the Igorrotes at their Memphis lodgings. One night Julio left the tribe's rooms to use the outside privy. Just as he reached out to open the toilet door, he felt a hand on his shoulder. He stood rooted to the spot. "When are you going home?"[13] asked a voice, referring to the witnesses' return to the Philippines. Without looking round, Julio said he didn't know. "Do you ever go out at night?"[14] the man asked next. Julio replied, "No," then fled back inside without bothering to answer the call of nature. Barker had since learned that the man was a former undercover detective turned criminal, recently released from the penitentiary.[15]

Fearing that Truman planned to interfere with the legal proceedings by using his contacts to intimidate, bribe, or even kidnap the Filipino witnesses, Barker instructed the man he had hired to guard the tribe not to let any of the Filipinos out of his sight, day or night. They couldn't afford to take any chances.

31

A Surprise Reversal

SHELBY COUNTY COURT, MEMPHIS, FEBRUARY 1, 1907

Q Where did he have this money?

A He had the money in his belt he says. And one day Dr. Hunt came and pulled open his coat, and took the belt from his waist and ripped it with a knife, and then poured it out and took the money.

Feloa's court testimony describing, through an interpreter, how Truman stole his money

THREE MONTHS AFTER the Igorrotes made their debut in a Memphis courtroom, the first of the retrials was called, for the theft of twenty-eight dollars from Feloa. The tribespeople had gained confidence since their first court appearance, but they were badly homesick and Barker feared the long wait had sapped their resolve. Their opponents, meanwhile, proved more willing than ever to play dirty. Truman had beefed up his legal team with the addition of two men named Prescott and Powell. Barker assumed the Elks were footing the bill for such hefty legal representation.

Together Truman's attorneys set out again to portray the Igorrotes as un-Christian savages whose testimony could not be trusted. At the original trials, Frayser had referred to Truman's claim that he kept the Igorrotes' money in order to prevent them from squandering it. According to Truman's version of events, when the Igorrotes got hold of money they threw it away on bull pups at twenty dollars apiece and pint bottles of whiskey at five dollars each, and insulted American women by offering them money. Now, standing in the Shelby County courtroom, Frayser put it to Julio that when they were staying in the house on North Front Street, the interpreter had been going to the store to buy whiskey and cigars. "No sir," said Julio firmly.[1] Barker shook his head in annoyance.

Frayser painted Julio as a liar who had been given all the freedom he wanted by Truman, but who had then inexplicably turned on his boss. Frayser continued, "I will ask you if it wasn't a further fact that you people were out on the front, on the front steps and in the back yard [of the North Front Street house], undressed and making such an exhibition of yourself that the policemen were sent down there to make you stay in the house?" "No sir," Julio replied.[2] At one time these ridiculous allegations would have offended the interpreter, but nothing Truman or his allies said could shock or wound Julio anymore.

Frayser's manner of questioning was aggressive and intimidating. When Dengay took the stand, Frayser did his best to tie the Igorrote up in knots, quizzing him about who was present when the alleged larceny took place, and exactly where in the room each person was standing.

A new interpreter had been found for the retrial, an earnest young Filipino named Asterio Favis, who was studying law at Georgetown University in Washington, DC, and who had no involvement in the case. Speaking to the interpreter, Frayser said, "Ask [Dengay] the names of fifteen of those Igorrotes [who were in the room during the alleged larceny]; ask him to name about twenty five of them?"[3]

INTERPRETER: He asks if you mean those from whom [Truman] took money.

FRAYSER: Ask him to name twenty five of those Igorrotes there in the room.

DENGAY *through* INTERPRETER: Filian, Sardoui, Gotaman, [Dengay], Feloa, Julio, Anguito. He forgets the other names.

FRAYSER: I will ask you if you did not on the former trial name all of them; ask him if he didn't name every one he saw there?

INTERPRETER: He wasn't asked, he says.

FRAYSER: Ask him if he didn't give those names on the former trial.

INTERPRETER: No. Because you didn't ask him, he says. He only gave Feloa, and Julio and his own [name].

FRAYSER: He says I didn't ask him and he didn't give me the names of all those that were there?

INTERPRETER: Yes sir.

In the Philippines, the Igorrotes didn't routinely refer to each other by name, but this subtlety of Igorrote culture was not discussed in the courtroom. Additionally many of the tribespeople had changed their names since coming to America, or had been given new ones by Truman and his associates.

Frayser badgered Feloa about the precise nature of the testimony he had given concerning the alleged thefts at the previous trials three months earlier.

FRAYSER *to* INTERPRETER: Ask him exactly what I ask you: if what he is saying here today is the same that he has said at other trials?

FELOA *through* INTERPRETER: Yes he says, he said that the money was taken from [Dengay] and then from him.

FRAYSER: Ask him is everything he said here today the same as he said on former trials.

General Kortrecht got to his feet to object: "I submit if the court please that that is impossible for a man to take a line of evidence like that and state that every word is the same."[4]

Undeterred, Frayser continued. It was an ugly spectacle, intended to portray Feloa and his fellow Filipinos as liars who were too ignorant to understand their own testimony. The scene was about to get uglier.

The other witnesses secured by Barker and Blum to give evidence on behalf of the Igorrotes were two "negresses," Lizzie Williams and Sallie Peoples, who had lived near the Igorrotes and regularly passed the North Front Street house. The two women testified that the only time they ever saw the Filipinos leave the house was when they went to use the outside toilet. Additionally, they said that the windows of the house were covered at all times and the doors were always closed.

During cross-examination, Frayser accused the two women of colluding with each other over their evidence before the trial. He also made a pointed reference to the color of the women's skin, lest any of the jurymen had failed to notice it.

FRAYSER: What condition did you say the windows were in?
PEOPLES: They had the windows down and had blankets over them. Something looked like blankets; they looked like blankets to me.
FRAYSER: Did Lizzie tell you she saw blankets or something up there?
PEOPLES: No, she didn't tell me nothing about it. I told myself because I seen it . . .
FRAYSER: You say she told you?
PEOPLES: No, I seen them myself, I live right there.
FRAYSER: What color blankets were they?
PEOPLES: They looked like old gray blankets to me.
FRAYSER: All of them?
PEOPLES: I don't know whether they were or not.
FRAYSER: How close did you get to those blankets?
PEOPLES: I would be passing there and I would just see them; I would be going to Mrs. Patton's grocery.
FRAYSER: Were they close enough for you to say they were old gray blankets?
PEOPLES: They looked like old gray blankets to me, them I seen.

Frayser then changed the subject, asking Peoples how she had ended up as a witness in the case. She explained that Barker and Blum had visited her at home in Memphis and asked if she had seen the Igorrotes when the tribespeople were staying on North Front Street.

FRAYSER: You told [Blum and Barker] Lizzie Williams knew something about this?
PEOPLES: No, I never told [them] anything about Lizzie Williams.
FRAYSER: Were you as polite to [Blum and Barker] as you are to me?

PEOPLES: I am with you just like I am with everybody else.
FRAYSER: What did you get mad at [them] about?
PEOPLES: I aint mad at [them]. I aint mad at anybody.
FRAYSER: Do you always treat white people when they cross examine you like you are treating me?
PEOPLES: I treat everybody alike.

While Truman's legal team focused on race and religion again, Kortrecht, Blum, and Barker emphasized the honesty and vulnerability of the Igorrotes, and the dishonesty of their former boss. Barker testified that Truman had admitted to him, in the presence of Funk, that "he took one thousand dollars from various Igorrotes in a criminal manner."[5] Funk dismissed the claim as untrue. Undeterred, Barker continued: Truman had admitted to him that he had stolen "something in the neighborhood of $75.00 or $100.00" from Feloa.

The prosecution played their trump card in the form of Col. Hopkins, who had offered to pay his own traveling expenses from St. Louis for the pleasure of testifying against his old adversary. Hopkins testified that Truman had told him he stole the Igorrotes' souvenir money to ensure the tribespeople were entirely dependent on him and that way "he could handle them better."[6] On the subject of Julio and his honesty, Hopkins said that Truman had told him the interpreter was trustworthy and "a very responsible fellow."[7] Hopkins added that he had found both statements to be true.

Of the nine witnesses called to give testimony on behalf of the Igorrotes, only Hopkins and Barker had white skin, a fact which Barker and Blum feared could prejudice the jury against them. The five witnesses who appeared on behalf of Truman were all white men. They included Fleetwood, the former Shelby County jailer whom Truman had befriended and who was now a deputy sheriff, a newspaper reporter from the *Commercial Appeal*, and Callahan, who said under oath that Julio bought "liquor at the store next door, at Mrs. Patton's."[8] He also stated that when Truman visited the North Front Street house the Igorrotes willingly "deposited" their money with him.

The showman's attorney then produced Mr. Smith, a policeman

whose willingness to lie on behalf of Truman was enough to bring his entire profession in to disrepute. The Memphis police officer, whose job it had been to patrol North Front Street when the tribespeople were there, swore under oath that he and his partner had visited the house where the Igorrotes were staying "fifteen times a day."[9] Despite their frequent visits, officer Smith stated that the tribespeople had never made any complaint to himself or his partner about the way they were being treated. He had seen Truman at the house on one or two occasions and had observed that the tribespeople looked "glad to see him."[10] Julio was stunned by the man's lies. The police had come to the house only once in the whole time they were living there, and had stayed for just five minutes.

The trial in the criminal court lasted three and a half days and was "bitter and personal," culminating in each side addressing the jury for five hours.[11] Blum and Kortrecht were "comprehensive" and "convincing."[12] But Prescott, who spoke on Truman's behalf, was utterly "brilliant."[13]

The jury deliberated for twenty-four hours but could not reach an agreement. Three jurors believed Truman was guilty and the other nine favored acquittal on the basis that Truman had merely "borrowed" the tribespeople's money and not stolen it.

With the jury deadlocked, Judge Moss invited the prosecution and defense to address the jury again. Kortrecht and Blum used the opportunity to emphasize the suffering of the tribespeople, who now faced going home with virtually nothing to show for their two years in America, during which they had worked hard and sacrificed much.

Truman's team pushed the race angle hard and stressed "the unreliability of all colored testimony," describing Truman as an innocent man who was being persecuted by the government, and who was the victim of "personal spite, amusement park feuds, and other 'conspiracies.'"[14]

But still the jury could not reach a verdict. In view of this, Judge Moss said he had no option but to declare a mistrial.

The Filipinos stood silently for a moment, trying to make sense of what had just happened. All around them there was noise and movement. People were screaming at them, asking them questions they didn't understand. The judge was banging on his desk. Barker and Blum were speaking but the tribespeople could not hear over the din. The strange sensation reminded Tainan of the first time he had entered the sea and put his head under the water. Mistrial. What did that mean? What about the other cases? Was Truman staying in jail?

Barker took Tainan and Maria by the arm. He indicated to Blum to lead Julio, Feloa, and Dengay out and into the anteroom first. He would follow with the others. Maria leaned against Barker so heavily that the government agent feared she was about to faint. The last few days had been physically and emotionally draining.

No one spoke for several minutes. Barker and Blum looked at each other over the tops of the Filipinos' heads. They too were sickened by the travesty of justice they had witnessed. Though they had seen it coming, they felt ill prepared for this moment. What could they say? Tainan broke the silence. *Did we lose?* he asked. *Yes,* Feloa said before anyone else had a chance to answer. The tribal chief began gesticulating furiously and shouting in his own tongue. Dengay joined in. Barker didn't know what they were saying, but it wasn't hard to imagine. He looked over and saw a tear rolling down Maria's cheek.

How did this happen? Julio asked. *Why did the jury believe Truman's lies this time?* More than any of the others, the interpreter had trusted Barker and Blum to ensure justice was done. When Feloa and Dengay had demanded to go home, Julio had stuck his neck out and assured them that they would win, that Truman would be punished. Now that he had been proved wrong, the interpreter wanted answers. Barker had never seen Julio angry like this before. He didn't know what to say. The Memphis legal system was corrupt and racist. But that was hardly an answer.

Kortrecht had reassured Blum and Barker that he would not allow verdicts of "not guilty" to be entered. He would insist instead that the cases were "retired." The distinction was an important legal one but it would mean nothing to the Igorrotes.[15]

There's still New Orleans, Barker said to the Filipinos, adding that they stood a better chance of a guilty verdict in Louisiana. But he wondered whether any of them, even Julio, had the stomach for another fight. *We won't give up*, insisted Barker. *We will get a conviction.* He looked around the room. No one was listening.

Three days later, on Saturday, February 9, in the Shelby County courtroom of Judge Moss, all three cases against Truman were formally retired at the request of the assistant attorney general. Together with Barker and Blum, Kortrecht had reached the conclusion that there was little point in pursuing the outstanding cases in Memphis—the second retrial and the theft of $444.55 from Julio. On hearing he was a free man at last, Truman punched the air.

He got up to leave and felt a hand on his shoulder. Spinning round, he came face-to-face with Frank Kenner, who identified himself as an inspector with the New Orleans police department.[16] *What do you want?* Truman demanded angrily. *I'm arresting you*, said Kenner holding up the requisition papers. Frayser was stunned. He had not seen this coming. He reassured Truman that he would sort the matter out. Then Frayser picked up his briefcase and fled the room.

Barker smiled. It was exactly how he and Blum had planned it. What was the point in pursuing another case in Memphis? The courts were so corrupt it was bound to end in disappointment. The government's best hope lay in having Truman extradited to New Orleans to stand trial there.

Frayser hurried down the corridor to apply for a writ of habeas corpus in the hope of having Truman released. Judge Jacob Galloway said he would hear the case on Monday morning in the civil court. Truman would be held in custody until then.

Blum was irritated but not surprised to hear of Frayser's latest move. That night Blum met with some legal friends and acquaintances who gave him some troubling information: Judge Galloway was a member of the same Memphis Elks Lodge that Truman had frequented. This was bad news indeed. Blum sincerely hoped that Galloway was not as easily corrupted as some of his colleagues.

The legal prosecution of Truman had taken many twists and turns. What happened next was extraordinary and unprecedented, even in the murky Memphis court system.

On Monday, February 11, at just before eleven o'clock in the morning, Truman was brought into court. Sitting at the bench, Judge Galloway examined the requisition papers that had been sent by the governor of Louisiana. He then invited Frayser and Blum to speak. While Frayser kept his argument uncharacteristically short, Blum gave "an elaborate argument, setting forth the law"[17] regarding the charges against Truman Hunt and outlining the facts of the case. The judge paused for a moment. Then, in a voice so quiet it was barely audible, Galloway said he was dismissing the writ and remanding the prisoner, who would be handed over to Inspector Kenner. With that Judge Galloway got up from the bench and left the courtroom, declaring the morning session over.

Blum gave an audible sigh of relief.

Truman looked at his attorney. This was not what the showman had been expecting. Frayser signaled to Truman to wait, then hurried after the judge.

The court stenographer got up and left the room. So too did Barker. The officer who had brought Truman in to court left too, taking Truman out through another door, which led to the holding cells. Blum stayed behind to write out the order of the court. As he busied himself, the door swung open and a flustered-looking Judge Galloway reentered, followed by a smug-looking Frayser.

Resuming his seat at the bench, the judge announced that he was reversing his decision. He was doing so on the basis of a legal technicality, namely that the governor of Tennessee had issued his warrant before the cases in Memphis were dismissed.[18]

In his twenty-odd years in the legal profession, Blum had never seen a judge perform a U-turn like this. Truman's trials had gone from tragedy to farce.

Blum stormed to the front of the courtroom to protest. The sheriff, Frank Monteverde (another member of the Memphis Elks), was standing nearby and watched as Blum muttered something and Frayser appeared to lunge for him. Sensing that Blum, the largest man in the room, and Frayser, the smallest, were about to come to blows, Monteverde threw himself between them.[19]

At that moment Truman reentered the room with his guard. The showman looked on at the scene before him with surprise and amusement. He would never be able to repay the generosity of the Memphis Elks.

Blum demanded to know how Judge Galloway could say one thing one minute and then, after conferring with Truman's attorney, return with the opposite decision. Such an immediate reversal didn't make sense. The judge said he was merely following the law. He would not discuss it further. Truman Hunt was a free man.

The deputy sheriff unlocked Truman's handcuffs and the showman shook his wrists free. Without waiting a moment longer, Truman fled the courtroom before the judge could change his mind again.

The cool air of a Memphis winter's day tasted especially sweet after five months in jail. Truman would ordinarily have stopped in at the nearest saloon for a victory drink, but he didn't want to chance his luck. It had been in short supply until that morning. He wanted to get as far away from the court as he could. Besides, he didn't have any money to go drinking. What little he had he must use to tell Sallie his good news. Before he did anything else, Truman decided he would pay a visit to his friends in the Elks to see if they could give him a little money to tide him over. Truman had had enough of Memphis, but he sensed that he should stick around awhile longer. He had a lot of powerful friends there. If he stepped outside the state, or even left the city, who knew what might happen to him?

32

The End of the Line

OUTSKIRTS OF MEMPHIS, MARCH 20, 1907

Steam locomotive, c. 1907

TRUMAN STOOD AT the window, peering through a gap in the filthy drapes. The man was still there. Pulling the drapes closed, Truman sat on the edge of the bed. A spring poked through the mattress into his buttock. Callahan lay dozing on the narrow metal-framed bed on the other side of the room. Truman thought momentarily of some of the fine hotels he had slept in at the height of the Igorrotes' fame. He picked up Callahan's cigarette packet, which was lying on the nightstand between their beds. He would've given anything for one of the expensive cigars he used to smoke. He put the cigarette to his lips and, lighting it, took a long drag. The taste caught in the back of his throat, making him cough.

The two men were holed up in a roadhouse four miles outside Memphis. Truman had grown a mustache and Callahan was sporting a full beard. Both men had adopted aliases when they checked in. Though Callahan was no longer a wanted man himself, he remained intensely loyal to the showman and was happy to do what he could to help his friend.

The rooms were bare and looked as if they hadn't been cleaned in years, but the place was cheap and out-of-the-way. They had been hiding there for a couple of weeks.[1] Though if Truman's suspicion was right that the man across the street was a private detective, it appeared that they'd been found. Truman had to hand it to Barker—he was a determined opponent. The showman wondered how much longer the government would pursue the cases against him.

Truman's plan was to hide out until the government tired of the expense and the trouble of pursuing him and dropped the charges. Knowing the tribespeople as well as he did, Truman imagined that they must be begging Barker to send them home by now. The showman sensed that Julio and Feloa would hold out the longest, but even they would have their limits. Frayser had advised Truman to stay in Memphis and lie low until he got word that the Igorrote witnesses were on a ship to Manila. With the Filipinos out of the country, he would have nothing to fear. Frayser cautioned against venturing across state lines until then. In another state he might not find as many friends in the police and the legal system as he had in Tennessee.

The showman stubbed out his cigarette and began pacing the room. He could do with some air but he didn't want to go out. There was nowhere to go around this dump, and besides he didn't want to give the detective the satisfaction of following him. No, he'd rather stay indoors, even if it meant being cooped up with Callahan. He glanced over at his roommate, lying on his bed with his boots on. For weeks they had had no one for company except each other, spending their days playing cards, smoking, and drinking. Now they were out of liquor.

Callahan was easy enough to get along with, but his conversation was limited. He had recently found out that his mother was sick. He was trying to get the money together to go and visit her in Washington, DC, calling in favors from old friends and relatives, but he hadn't raised enough. Truman could have lent him a little but didn't offer, figuring that his own need was greater than that of the friend who had testified to Truman's good character in court.

The enforced isolation was making Truman yearn for Sallie. When he was in jail, she and the baby had gone to stay with her father in Louisville. She had written to Truman regularly, declaring her love for him and updating him on how the baby was doing. She had named her Patty, after her father Patrick. Truman didn't particularly like the name but he knew how much it meant to her. All Sallie's anger about the terrible circumstances he'd left her in in Chicago had evaporated and she had believed him when he said he was an innocent man being persecuted by the government. She was a most loyal and loving companion. Truman pictured his wife in her favorite pink evening gown. He wondered if she still had it. From her letters it sounded as if she'd been forced to sell off much of what they owned. The rest she had presumably left behind when she fled Chicago. Truman's stomach rumbled. He could do with some decent food. He must have lost twenty, maybe thirty pounds while he was incarcerated. Truman picked up the cigarette packet again and noticed there was only one left. He lit it and threw the packet on the floor.

That evening a messenger came to the roadhouse with a note for Truman. It was from Frayser. The attorney had just learned that an officer was on his way from New Orleans with the intention of taking Truman to Louisiana to stand trial. The detective hanging around outside had presumably tipped Barker off that Truman was there, and Barker had told the New Orleans police where to find him. He had to get out of there. He threw the few possessions he had in a bag and told Callahan he was going out. He didn't know when he'd be back.

Detective Smiddy was lurking in a doorway across the street when Truman exited the roadhouse. Pulling the brim of his hat down, Smiddy followed Truman at a safe distance. Conscious he was being followed, Truman did his best to give the detective the slip. He walked quickly, dodging down side streets and dark alleys. A few minutes later, he jumped aboard a streetcar. Smiddy got on too. At the railroad station, Truman alighted, still tailed by the detective. The showman looked around. Momentarily losing sight of Smiddy,

Truman hurried into the ticket office and bought a one-way ride to Louisville.

The agent told him to hurry, the 8:40 p.m. train was leaving shortly. Truman rushed over to the platform. Smiddy followed and watched Truman board the train. The conductor looked across at Smiddy and asked if he was getting on. No, said Smiddy, taking a step back. Inside, Truman caught sight of the detective and frowned. What was he doing? Wasn't he getting on the train?

The conductor signaled to the driver and the train squealed and lurched forward. Truman could hardly believe his luck. With a grin he lifted his hat and tipped it toward Smiddy, who was still standing on the platform, a confused expression on his face. As if suddenly realizing his mistake, Smiddy turned and rushed toward the telegraph office. The detective hadn't wanted to cross state lines without first getting permission from Barker. But now, with Truman as good as lost again, he knew his split-second decision had been the wrong one.

Barker reread Smiddy's telegram, shaking his head in disbelief. He wired back immediately, ordering the detective to get on the next train to Louisville. But the next train didn't depart until noon the following day, four hours after Truman was due to arrive in Sallie's hometown. The showman had been given a generous head start, which they could ill afford. Barker would need to inform Col. Edwards, chief of the bureau. He dreaded his reply. Edwards had recently been taking an increased interest in the Truman Hunt–Igorrote case and Barker sensed that he was rapidly growing tired of it.

The following morning as Detective Smiddy waited for the train, Truman turned in to South Seventh Street. The showman felt invigorated. Spring was in the air, and despite the rain, it was a nice time to be in Louisville. Over the roofs of the modest shotgun houses where most of the Irish immigrants lived, he could see the copper-domed roof and cross of the St. Louis Bertrand Catholic Church in the next street, the very church in which Sallie's parents had married thirty years earlier. Truman found himself absentmindedly walking toward it.

Taking off his hat, he strode up the half dozen steps and entered. Inside, he made his way down the aisle toward the altar. Light streamed through the stained-glass windows. This was the first time Truman had set foot inside a church since the day he and Sallie were married. He'd never been a believer in the power of prayer and that hadn't changed. But he'd had the feeling that someone or something had been looking out for him recently and being alone in the church felt strangely comforting. He hadn't slept on the journey and his head ached from tiredness. He sat down in a pew and let the silence envelop him.

The sound of footsteps startled him. He must've dozed off. A voice over his shoulder made Truman jump. He turned to see the priest standing behind him in his robes. Did he want him to take confession? The showman stood bolt upright. There was no need, he said, picking up his hat. He was late for an appointment.

Truman turned back on to South Seventh Street. Sallie didn't know he was coming and he hoped she would be at home. He knocked firmly on the door and, after a moment or two, heard a voice asking who was there. Good old Sallie. He'd told her not to speak to anyone she didn't know and he was glad to see she was following his instructions. He replied that it was him, Truman. With that Sallie opened the door and threw her arms around him. Truman stepped inside and, explaining that he couldn't stay long, closed the door.

In Washington, DC, the government had recently come under a series of blistering attacks about its involvement in the Philippines. Senator Alexander Clay of Georgia had introduced a resolution in the US Senate that sought to ascertain the cost to the people of the United States of holding the Philippine Islands. Senator Clay estimated that it cost America between sixty-five and seventy-five million dollars a year to run the Philippines, a pronouncement that had stirred up a hornet's nest. The *Labor World* newspaper was just one of many that had pounced on the figure. Under an article headlined COST TO OUR NATION OF PHILIPPINE ISLANDS, the paper accused the government of intentionally deceiving the public and withholding the accounts.

"These figures naturally raise the question in the mind of the average American voter whether the Philippines are worthwhile? Financially, they are not," concluded the article.[2]

Naturally, Edwards, as chief of the Bureau of Insular Affairs, felt under pressure to clear up the Truman Hunt problem promptly, before it cost the American taxpayer any more money. He sat at his desk in Washington with pages of figures spread out in front of him. At the request of his superior in the War Department, the bureau chief was calculating the amount spent by the government trying to prosecute Truman Hunt. Taking in to account all the expenses, from providing accommodations and travel for the Igorrotes and other witnesses, to legal and detective fees, and the costs of shipping the Igorrotes who had already left back to the Philippines, the total came to $8,499.65 ($212,500 in today's money).[3] This was a large amount of public money spent on cleaning up a mess caused by the Philippine Commission's decision to grant Truman permission to import the tribe. If the figure ever became public, it would be a serious political embarrassment.

There were still five Filipinos in America and more money would have to be found to send them home. Barker had been put on the case nine months ago with a brief to round up the Filipinos quickly, send them home, and get some form of financial settlement from Truman. Now Truman had given them the slip again. The bureau had been eager to make an example of the showman. But as far as Edwards could tell, they were no closer to securing a conviction than they had been nine months ago. The whole thing was getting out of hand. The time had come to call the search off and send the Filipinos home.

Barker's explosion of rage took him by surprise. *Damn him,* he shouted, crushing the telegram into a ball and hurling it across the room. He lunged forward, angrily knocking everything off his desk. Only the lamp was left standing. Barker grabbed it and threw it to the floor. Still shaking from his outburst, he sat down on his bed and buried his head in his hands. Slowly, he looked up and glanced around the room. His face reddened. His meticulously transcribed notes were scattered everywhere. A drop of ink from his pen bled into the rug. He walked over to pick up the desk lamp. There was a dent in the shade and the glass was shattered. Kneeling down, he carefully began picking up the pieces and cursed as a bright bead of blood appeared on the tip of his index finger.

Barker had always feared the bureau would tire of the chase, but he had not been prepared for how the news would make him feel.

The Igorrotes were sitting around their Memphis lodgings when Barker called. They looked up at him expectantly. It was with a heavy heart that he told them the government was closing the investigation and dropping all the charges against Truman. They were going back to the Philippines. *Really? Today?* Feloa looked at Barker, his eyes wide with disbelief. Maria buried her face in Julio's chest and began to sob tears of relief. Barker caught the interpreter's eye and the two men exchanged a look. Barker knew that Julio had been every bit as determined as him to see it through. He couldn't help but feel as if he had led them on with his promises of a conviction. Barker expressed his profound regret that Truman had not faced a longer, more severe punishment. *Truman's crimes will catch up with him one day,* he said, but the words sounded hollow in his ears. He sensed that Julio was the only one who was listening. He looked at the others. The joy on the faces of Dengay, Feloa, Maria, and Tainan should have helped ease his burden, but somehow it didn't.

Leaping in the air, Tainan shouted, "We're going home," over and over in English. Then he began to sing. Loud and clear the words rang out through the room. The reference to the pilgrims aside, the song struck Barker as an oddly fitting choice:

My country, 'tis of thee,
Sweet land of liberty,
Of thee I sing;
Land where my fathers died,
Land of the pilgrims' pride,
From ev'ry mountainside
Let freedom ring![4]

The government agent frowned. He could hardly grudge the tribespeople the freedom they wanted above all else.

The air was chilly and the sky was already growing dark when Barker and the Filipinos reached the station in Memphis. In San Francisco they would catch the army ship to Manila. There they might cross paths with the new Igorrote exhibition groups being assembled by Schneidewind and Col. Hopkins for the 1907 summer season. Both men had invited Julio to work for them, but the translator recently confessed to Barker he was having serious doubts about whether he wanted anything more to do with the trade. Hopkins had even asked Barker to abandon his government career and join him in his enterprise. Barker had politely declined. Chasing around after Truman had provided him with more than enough excitement for a while. Besides, he was looking forward to finally getting home to his wife.

Looking down at the tribespeople, Barker could hardly believe that his own adventure with them was coming to an end. He didn't feel ready to bid them farewell. The government agent was not given to displays of emotion, and, as he stood on the platform, his depth of feeling surprised him. Swallowing hard, he wished Julio, Maria, Feloa, Dengay, and little Tainan well. Feeling a lump rise in his throat, he told them to hurry up and board the train. Julio was the last to climb the steps up to the car. At the top he turned around and looked back at Barker. His dark eyes reflected back the sadness Barker felt. The interpreter reached down and shook the government agent firmly by the hand. Then he disappeared off to join the others.

All aboard, cried a voice in the distance. Inside, Tainan pressed his face up against the window. Barker stood motionless on the platform as the train pulled out. He thought of the train journey that had led the Filipinos to Coney Island two years previously. What a lot had happened to them in that time. He wondered what the tribespeople would tell their families when they reached home. Would they tell tales of adventure and excitement and of the fame they had achieved? Or would theirs be a sorry story of how America had let them down? Had he, Barker, let them down? The thought depressed him. He stood looking down the railroad track into the darkness long after the train disappeared in a puff of gray smoke.

Afterword

An Igorrote village in Northern Luzon, Philippine Islands

THE TRAIN CARRYING the Igorrotes homeward bears the Lost Tribe of Coney Island into the mists of time. After nearly two years in America, during which their every move was scrutinized by the press and the paying public, the spotlight dims and goes out. The tribespeople who had captivated the nation with their spear-throwing demonstrations, their tribal dances and songs, disappear from the American consciousness.

Researching the final chapters of this book, I became consumed by a desire to know what happened to the Filipinos after they left America, particularly those who testified against Truman in court. I longed to discover that Truman had gotten his comeuppance in the years after 1907 and that the tribespeople had gone on to have long and happy lives. As I discovered, Truman's life following his release from jail does offer a karmic revenge of sorts, but the story of what happens next to the Filipinos in Truman Hunt's exhibition group is frustratingly incomplete.

Some of that is due to the ravages suffered by the Philippines during World War II, when Japan and America fought for control of the country and a huge volume of the islands' historical and cultural records was destroyed. Vital records relating to entire years and even decades were wiped out.

From those records that survive I have pieced together some details of what happened to the Filipinos in Truman's 1905 group, together with a few of those who toured with Schneidewind. I hope this book might lead to further discoveries about their later lives.

Julio and Maria: Despite Hopkins's and Schneidewind's pleas, Julio and Maria did not return to America for the 1907 summer season. Indeed, from the records that exist, it seems that Julio and Maria never set foot in America again. The interpreter, who had looked up to Truman and even aspired to be like him, had been badly hurt by the showman's betrayal. When he returned to the Philippines after testifying against his boss in court, Julio received earnings totaling just over thirty dollars. This was exactly the same amount as everyone else in the group, and amounted to a little over a dollar for each month Julio had spent in the country. It was a far cry from the twenty-five dollars a month, plus bonuses, that Truman had promised to pay his trusted assistant. Julio had imagined that a year in America would make him rich and open up the possibility of a new life, perhaps in the Promised Land. Instead he returned home to an existence that differed little from the one he had left behind.

Worse, Julio must have wondered if he had only himself to blame. He had turned a deaf ear to the complaints of the Igorrotes who had exhibited in St Louis in 1904 that Truman had stolen their wages, amounting to just under four-thousand dollars.[1] With the benefit of hindsight, Julio must have realized that Truman ordered him to take a circuitous route to Manila with the 1905 group bound for Coney in order to avoid running into officials in Cervantes or one of the other major towns who might have tried to stop him taking the tribespeople out of the country.

Had Julio been suspicious at the time, but kept quiet because he regarded Truman, his boss, as a friend and ally who could further his own ambitions? If so, he must have been haunted by this memory, and his own silence, during Hunt's 1906 and 1907 trials.

Though Julio ultimately fell out of love with America, his influence on American-Filipino relations and the world's understanding of the Bontoc Igorrote tribe was significant and long lasting due to the work he did, while waiting for Truman's trials to come to court, on the linguist Dr. Carl Seidenadel's guide to the Bontoc Igorrote language.[2] In the introduction to his book, which was published in 1909, Seidenadel described Julio and the other tribespeople who assisted him as the "most sympathetic people, men of astonishing intelligence, inborn independence and frankness, strong principles of honesty, kind disposition, a vivid desire for learning, and blessed with the divine gift of healthy humor." By contrast, Seidenadel had nothing but contempt for Truman, whom he described as "unscrupulous" and as having inflicted "manifold wrongs" on the Filipinos.

That he, Julio, along with Antero, Dengay, Tainan, and others, had contributed to such a significant work would undoubtedly have been a source of great pride for the scholarly Julio.

There is a death certificate in the National Archives of the Philippines for a Julio Balanag (note the different spelling), who died of malaria on April 10, 1922, aged thirty-three. If this is Julio, it was an untimely end to a promising life. It would also have made him sixteen when he arrived in America with Truman in April 1905, not twenty-one as stated in the ship's passenger list. There is no way of knowing for certain whether this is him, though the inexact spellings and imprecise and incomplete records at that time in both the Philippines and America indicate it could be. Judging by the photographs of Julio that survive, it is possible that the interpreter was younger than he claimed. If Julio was indeed sixteen when he accompanied Truman to Coney Island then it gives his story an added poignancy—the man whom the Igorrotes looked to as their bulwark against the mysteries of America was only a boy himself. If this is him, his youth would also make his betrayal at the hands of Truman, a man old enough to have been his father, all the harder to bear.

The Philippines National Archives hold a death certificate for a woman named Maria Balinag, who died on December 10, 1914, aged thirty, in Mabini, Bohol, an island one thousand miles south of Bontoc. When she arrived in America, Maria gave her second name as Alijas, not Balinag. Though it is possible that this document refers to Julio's wife, both the location of her death and the discrepancy in her surname mean this is far from certain.

I could find no record of Julio and Maria having children.

By a strange coincidence, Julio's older brother, Nicasio Balinag, a distinguished civil servant, went on to hold Truman Hunt's old post of deputy governor of Bontoc (and later of Kalinga Province) as the administration of the islands passed out of American control and into the hands of the Philippine people.

The *nikimalika:* America's fascination with the Igorrotes continued long after Truman's trial and exit from the tribal exhibition scene. For a decade after the Filipinos were first exhibited in America, showmen continued to travel to the Philippines to gather their own Igorrote groups. In the mountains of northern Luzon, recruiters found no shortage of volunteers despite what Truman had done. The Igorrotes traveled all over America and beyond, to the UK, Cuba, and mainland Europe. From Magic City, Paris, to London's Earl's Court and the Waverley Market in Edinburgh, the tribespeople delighted crowds wherever they went.

And for many years after their Luna Park debut, the Filipinos continued to be a big draw at Coney Island. In May 1909, four years to the day after Truman and the Igorrotes arrived at Coney, the *New York Sun* described how "[o]ver in Dreamland high above the minarets and spires clinging to a bare pole with his naked toes was a Filipino headhunter who looked out over the crowds, shading his eyes with a brown hand. It was so high where he had climbed like a monkey that the savage looked no bigger than a small boy. Suddenly he threw out a shrill cry, caught up a brass gong from the crow's nest at the very top of the pole and began to sound it with slow steady strokes. The strong resonance rose over the multiple voices of Coney and rolled in waves head long after the brown hand ceased to strike."[3] The village was under the management of Captain J. R. McRae, formerly of the Philippine constabulary.

Even without Truman, the Igorrote stories had become self-perpetuating. FILIPINOS WED BAREFOOT, read the headline in the *New York Times* on June 2 that same season. The accompanying article described the wedding of Tu-Go-Dan and A'Lao, which took place at City Hall, presided over by Alderman Smith, and watched, of course, by the Dreamland press agent, the tribal chief Chemingo, "the medicine man," and many of the couple's Filipino friends. "The marriage took place in the basement before a large and interested crowd. The Filipinos were all barefooted and dressed in native costume. The press agent declared that the bride had fortified herself on the trip up from the Island by smoking two long, black cigars."[4] Despite the change of manager, and tribespeople, the stories stayed the same. After the wedding ceremony, it was reported that the Igorrote Village would celebrate with a four-day-long feast at which "four dozen chickens will be roasted and two dozen dogs will be served as a delicacy. Two barrels of rice will be used in making the native wine that will go with the eatables."[5]

As the years went by, the Igorrotes lost none of their ability to stir the hearts of the American people. At the end of the 1909 season, a Coney Island caretaker described how people sent clothes to the tribespeople from all over the country. "Great bundles of clothes of all sorts, worn and half worn. People coming by and feeling sorry for them because they had so few on. Going home and sending them back by the next train. Those Igorrotes just laughed at them, at the idea of putting anything more on than was absolutely necessary . . . Why, we had to send bundles of clothes to the charity people, to the Salvation Army people and the aid societies. We'd have been overrun with old clothes."[6]

Richard Schneidewind: In comparison with Truman, Schneidewind appeared to be a good and paternalistic manager, but he soon became embroiled in his own scandals. In 1907 when Schneidewind brought a new group of Igorrotes to America, officials in the Bureau of Insular Affairs learned that Schneidewind had been employed as a clerk in the Manila post office in 1901 but had been dismissed after it was discovered that he had taken part in a smuggling scheme, sending many packages of valuable goods to a confederate in San Francisco, who sold them there and in Los Angeles. Despite this, Schneidewind established himself as a major figure in the Igorrote show trade. After three successful tours of America, in 1905, 1907, and 1908, Schneidewind set his sights farther afield. In 1911, despite vociferous opposition from Bontoc elders, the Bontoc lieutenant governor John Early, the local Episcopal bishop, and officials of nearby towns, Schneidewind was permitted to take a group of fifty-five Igorrotes from the Philippines to Europe. They exhibited in France, Scotland, England, the Netherlands, and Belgium. Several babies were born on the tours, in Paris, Pennsylvania, and Madison Square Garden, New York.

Schneidewind and his associates were unfamiliar with the European entertainment business, and, after two years on the road, they ran in to serious financial difficulties. What happened next was alarmingly familiar. According to American newspaper reports, a group of starving Igorrotes was found wandering the streets of Ghent, Belgium, in the winter of 1913. The group's interpreters, Ellis Tongai and James Amok, wrote to US president Woodrow Wilson, begging for his assistance. In their letter they complained that they had not been paid for many months and reported the deaths of nine members of the group, including five children.

Schneidewind tried to persuade the Filipinos that their difficulties were only temporary, and promised them that if they stayed on and continued working for him until the 1915 San Francisco Exposition, they would be rewarded with a very handsome wage. Despite the hardships they had endured, about half of the group agreed to stay on with him in Europe. But, fearing another scandal, the US government intervened, and in December 1913 the US consul in Ghent escorted the tribespeople to Marseilles to catch a boat to Manila. The government spent $2,668.26 sending the group home. Intriguingly, the US consul reported that one of the tribesmen managed to separate himself from the rest of the group in Ghent and, according to several railway-station employees, was last seen "boarding an early train leaving for Brussels."[7]

In May 2011 the Belgian government named a tunnel in the Ghent railroad station the "Timichegtunnel," after Timicheg, one of the nine Igorrotes who died on Schneidewind's European tour.

Schneidewind's disastrous European venture did little to help the image of the Igorrote show trade. In 1914 legislation was passed by the Philippine Assembly to put an end to the exhibition of Filipinos abroad. As a measure of the seriousness with which the Philippine lawmakers regarded the subject, the ban was included as an amendment to a new antislavery act.

Schneidewind, like Truman before him, exited the Igorrote show trade. But before he left the business of exhibiting exotic people altogether, he had one last shot, managing a Samoan Village at the 1915 Panama-Pacific Exposition in San Francisco. After that he packed up and moved back to Detroit with his wife, Selma (whom he had met at Riverview Park, Chicago, when he was exhibiting the Igorrotes there and whom he had married in October 1906). There he worked for a streetcar company and later sold cars. Schneidewind died in January 1949. His son, Dick, whom he had with his first wife, a Filipina named Gabina, was a brilliant man who went on to become a professor of metallurgical engineering at the University of Michigan.

Though the exhibition of large Igorrote groups ended in America after 1914, the word *Igorrote* lived on in the American vocabulary. The *Brooklyn Daily Eagle* reported the appearance of "Marquita, the Igorrote girl violinist" at the Hippodrome, Thompson and Dundy's old theater, in 1924.[8] Almost two decades after her tribe's first appearance at Coney Island, the girl needed no further introduction.

And in Memphis, the scene of Truman's violent criminal assault and robbery, the Igorrotes were still being hailed in the press as "one of the best attractions ever brought to East End [Park]" nearly thirty years after their appearance there.[9] The article in the *Commercial Appeal* continued, "Even in cold December days they astonished the residents of Madison Heights by continuing about their daily routine with even less clothes than Gandhi wears."

Today, more than a century after the Igorrotes first wowed crowds at Coney Island, most Americans probably don't know who the Igorrotes were, but a 2012 op-ed in the *New York Times* paid its own tribute of sorts, informing readers that once upon a time a tribe of "scantily clad Philippine Igorots from the Luzon highlands reenacted a daily 'Bow Wow Feast'"[10] in America.

Friday: Friday was separated from Truman Hunt's troupe in the chaotic summer of 1906. By August, while Barker was in Chicago preparing to send most of Truman's Igorrote group home, Friday was six hundred miles away, in an orphanage in Rochester, New York, run by the American Society for the Prevention of Cruelty to Children (ASPCC). The boy, who stood less than three feet tall, settled in quickly. He made friends and started attending school, where he "was progressing rapidly in his studies."[11] Though his English was limited, the Negrito, whose new friends nicknamed him "Gubbo," regaled his classmates with tales of his life as a performer at Coney Island. According to an article in the local newspaper, he gave the other children Spanish lessons and enjoyed playing with toy cars and trains.

The story of how Friday had ended up at the ASPCC was a sorry one. After becoming separated from the rest of Truman's group, Friday had been locked in an enclosure in the Ontario Beach Park in Charlotte, Rochester, on the banks of Lake Ontario. There he was forced to perform a degrading sideshow for crowds of men, women, and children who gawked at him through the iron bars. After being tipped off by a concerned member of the public, Agent W. A. Killip of the ASPCC led a raid on the park and sprang Friday from his torment. Newspaper reports described how an angry American man (possibly Felder or Friday's guardian, Fuller, or one of their associates) tried to prevent Killip taking Friday away, insisting that the boy had been brought to the US under a five-thousand-dollar bond and could not therefore be taken anywhere without the government's permission. The agent assumed the man was bluffing but wrote to the War Department asking if they knew anything about the boy.

Friday begged Killip to let him stay on in Rochester. He was an orphan; he had no family to go back to. He dreamed of completing his education and staying on in America. But in October Agent Killip received a letter from the War Department, confirming that Friday had been brought to the US under bonds and that he must now return home. Friday was distraught.

The War Department sent a man to collect Friday. He was taken to Chicago to join Schneidewind's group. On October 10, 1906, they left Chicago for Manila. The American dream was over for the Negrito boy who had charmed crowds the length and breadth of the country.

It seems likely that Friday had been taken to Ontario Beach by, or with the knowledge of, George Fuller, the Rochester-born businessman who had bought Friday from his relatives in the Philippines. Fuller presented himself as a caring patron who had adopted Friday in order to give the boy an American education and a good start in life. But if this was true, why had Fuller given the boy to Truman to exhibit in America? The only possible answer is that Fuller did so for his own financial gain, or to assist his friend the showman.

Tainan:[12] His bad experience with Truman didn't put Tainan off America or the Igorrote exhibition business. The boy was enormously popular with the public and with the American showmen who followed in Truman's wake. Tainan's youth arguably made him better able to cope with the demands of life as a human exhibit. Every time the showmen came to the mountains of northern Luzon to look for volunteers, Tainan was there, a willing volunteer ready to embark on another adventure. He was part of Schneidewind's group that traveled to Europe in 1911. By the time he returned to the Philippines in 1914, Tainan spoke good English. Though I could find no records describing what became of him, his tours had given him linguistic skills that would have equipped him well for a professional career with the civil service, as a teacher or businessman.

Daipan: The young woman routinely described in the press as "the belle of the village" returned to America in 1908, appearing, among other places, at the Iowa State Fair, the very one that fired Truman's passion for fairs as a boy. According to an article in the *Des Moines News*, Daipan, still "an Igorrote beauty with much charm of manner and a fascinating smile," was expecting her first child with her husband-to-be, Lai-dis. Two years earlier, Daipan had been married in an elaborate wedding ceremony at Sans Souci in Chicago to fifteen-year-old headhunter Sadoy. This sham marriage was presided over, of course, by Truman Hunt.

The other members of Truman's Igorrote group, including Feloa and Dengay, disappear from the written record after they returned to the Philippines.

Antero:[13] Schneidewind's popular interpreter and Truman's former houseboy returned to America with Schneidewind in 1907. This time Antero brought a wife, Takhay Ulapan, and the couple had their first child, a daughter who, according to legend, they named Sylvia because she was born in Pennsylvania. In 1908, the couple had another daughter at Ontario Beach Park in Charlotte, Rochester, New York (the very place where Friday was rescued by the ASPCC). She weighed six pounds and they named her Charlotte. The couple had a third daughter, Maria, on the boat back to the Philippines in 1909. They went on to have ten children—eight daughters and two sons. In 1911 Antero planned to go with Schneidewind to Europe, but officials in Bontoc, who were reluctant to let the tribespeople go, ordered him to stay and continue the work he had started on the Bontoc census. After participating in the Igorrote tours, Antero worked as an interpreter for the government in the Philippines and became a businessman and farmer.

A firm believer in the importance of education, Antero encouraged all of his children, boys and girls, to concentrate on their studies. According to his descendants, Antero remained interested in the world beyond his doorstep throughout his life. He regularly ventured down to the coast to trade and took a keen interest in the foreigners he met in his domestic travels. Along with Julio, Antero made a major contribution to Carl Seidenadel's book on the Bontoc language. Antero died around 1940 and his wife passed away in the early 1980s.

James Robert Amok: Amok was born in 1894 in Bontoc and first traveled to America with Schneidewind. He arguably became the most Americanized of the *nikimalika* (as the Igorrotes who exhibited in America were known at home), and was willing to endure all manner of hardships and degradations in order to stay on in the US.

How he got the names James and Robert varies according to sources: he was either given them by American missionaries in the Philippines or, perhaps more likely, simply adopted them during his travels. Amok, or Jim, as he was known, worked as a translator for Schneidewind's European tour group. He appeared in a variety show at the Waverley Market Carnival in Edinburgh, Scotland, in December 1915 and exhibited in Cuba two years later, most likely as part of a tour organized by Samuel Gumpertz. In Edinburgh Amok was described by one theater critic as possessing "in a marked degree the characteristics of the authentic 'wild man.' He is remarkably dexterous in throwing his native weapons, and he performs on the platform native dances and semi-religious rites which are of a realistic character, and are carried through with an absorption which surpass in effect any possible acting."[14]

Amok went on to become the longest-serving Igorrote at Coney (the government clampdown on Igorrotes being imported to the US for exhibition purposes after 1914 seems to have been applied to groups and not individuals). A 1917 newspaper article referred to Amok appearing in chains in a cage at a Coney sideshow, where visitors paid a dime to peer through the bars at him.[15] He was a regular fixture at the resort right through the 1920s, by which point Coney's heyday had long passed.

During World War I, Amok was conscripted despite the fact he had never been made an American citizen. The once-ferocious headhunter appealed on the grounds that he had become a "peaceful man who should not be made to fight for the United States, not being a citizen thereof."[16] In the same article, Amok was described by the

Coney sideshow barker as "a ferocious cannibal, with an insatiable appetite for gore" but, he insisted, the tribesman's savage nature deserted him outside of "business hours."

Amok's appeal was overruled. He was deployed in France during WWI, where he was praised for his valor as a soldier and, according to newspaper reports, was awarded the Croix de Guerre for bravery in combat.

After the war, he appeared in a variety show in New York that required him to climb a tree and declare war on his enemies at the top of his voice. In press interviews, he described his work as "silly business, but it paid well."[17] Amok died in New York in 1950 and is buried in the Long Island veterans' graveyard. On his death, newspaper headlines lauded the onetime "sideshow freak" as an American hero.

Frederic Thompson and Elmer "Skip" Dundy: The "Kings of Coney" seemed to be untouchable in the summer of 1905. But by 1906, things were unraveling. Thompson had fallen in love with a pretty, mediocre young actress named Mabel Taliaferro, whom he married after a whirlwind courtship. Thompson devoted his career—and much of his wealth—to making her a star, neglecting Luna Park and the Hippodrome. On June 8, 1906, Thompson and Dundy formally resigned their interest in the Hippodrome amid rumors that four hundred thousand dollars obtained for the theater from the National City Bank "had been spent extravagantly."[18]

Dundy died suddenly the following year of a dilation of the heart and an attack of pneumonia. Without his friend and business partner to keep him focused, Thompson lost his grip. His marriage fell apart and alcoholism took hold. Thompson had always relied on Dundy to take care of their money and, without him, he paid no attention to his financial affairs. He spent profusely, hiring a private train car whenever he traveled, taking a suite of six rooms in the Algonquin Hotel, and hiring a cook and two butlers. Thompson was forced to file for bankruptcy in 1912, giving Luna Park over to his creditors. The following year he married a childhood friend. Despite his troubles the showman remained enormously popular. A benefit held in his honor at Coney in 1916 was attended by hundreds of old friends and colleagues and succeeded in raising thirty thousand dollars.

Thompson's capacity to generate ingenious schemes never died, but deprived of the counterbalance offered by his business partner, his grand plans, from founding a permanent World's Fair atop the new Pennsylvania Station in New York to designing and manufacturing airplanes, never got off the ground. Thompson's days as a genius of the show world were over. He contracted Bright's disease, the same condition that led to Truman's death, and died on June 6, 1919, penniless and physically spent. He left an estate of seven hundred dollars, just enough to cover his medical and funeral expenses.

Col. John Hopkins: Anyone who crossed Col. Hopkins did so at his own peril. The vaudeville legend produced a file weighing five pounds on his dealings with Truman Hunt, which he handed to Barker during Truman's trial in the hope that it contained something incriminating that could be used against his business associate turned enemy. It didn't. Two years after appearing in court to testify against Truman, Hopkins threatened to stage a one-act play exposing his associates' true characters and "concerning whom the world needs a clarification of opinion." *Variety* reported in 1908 that his press agent, Mrs. Emille De Howard, was trying to dissuade him.

Hopkins's health deteriorated in the last years of his life but his wit remained pin sharp. During one hospital stay, he was asked by nurses whether he wanted to see a minister, to which he replied, "What would I do with a minister? If you'll send an undertaker and a gravedigger, they might find it of interest to talk to me."[19] Later, as he lay on his deathbed, the vain impresario, who was then seventy-nine, told staff at the Jewish Hospital in St. Louis that he was sixty-three. He died at five o'clock in the afternoon on October 24, 1909.[20]

Samuel Gumpertz: When Dreamland burned to the ground in 1911, the fast-thinking Gumpertz threw up a tent on Surf Avenue and christened it the Dreamland Circus Sideshow. He supplemented his income by taking a select group of his Coney performers, including the Igorrote James Robert Amok, on tour to Europe and Cuba.

Gumpertz earned a living from his Coney sideshow throughout the 1920s, specializing in freak shows, human oddities, and circus attractions. Among his best known performers were the two-foot-tall Baron Paucci, "the world's smallest perfect man"; "Lionel, the dog-faced boy"; and "the famous pinhead Zip What Is It," who worked for him for many years. A great Coney Island enthusiast and promoter, Gumpertz helped organize the annual Mardi Gras parade and served as president of the Coney Island chamber of commerce. In 1929 Gumpertz finally quit Coney and went back to his circus roots, going to work for Ringling Brothers.

Adele von Groyss: The "baroness" rivaled Truman for self-invention and self-promotion. Though she didn't publicly condemn her old friend, she did not remain in contact with Truman after news of his scandalous behavior hit the headlines. However, her relationship with the Igorrotes endured. In 1910 she tried and failed to set up a school and conservatoire for fifty Igorrotes in Fordham, New York. She wanted to do this, she explained, because the Igorrotes were "remarkable musicians" who "with few exceptions, all have good voices."[21] Her plan was blocked and von Groyss blamed the racial prejudice of Fordham residents, stating: "The general impression among Americans is the Igorrotes are a lower order of beings and therefore must have unspeakable vices, but on the contrary they have wonderful natural intelligence. What is more astonishing than all, they don't steal or lie, virtues you will find in few of the other races."

Von Groyss established herself as the hostess of an avant-garde salon in New York. In that role she promoted Dogmena,[22] a young Igorrote tribeswoman as her protégée, and anointed her an Igorrote princess. Dogmena, scantily dressed in scarlet silks, danced to music composed by von Groyss, and her performances climaxed with the Igorrote plunging a spear into an imaginary head on the floor.[23] Dogmena was in demand at high-society gatherings from Delmonico's and the Hotel Astor in Manhattan to meetings of the International Artistic Social Club and private parties in Washington, DC, garnering attention in newspapers as far afield as London and New Zealand.

Intriguingly, in a 1911 interview, von Groyss referred to a young woman named Dookmena (perhaps another journalistic mangling of an Igorrote name) as one of the original Igorrote group who exhibited at the St. Louis Exposition in 1904, adding that "just before it was time to send her back she met a negro named Jackson, who got her away and gave her American clothes. Then she became his wife, and your [American] Government couldn't send her back."[24]

One of nature's survivors, von Groyss worked tirelessly for charity, was a member of the Ladies Auxiliary, and remained a regular fixture in the New York press, turning her hand to everything from writing a recipe column to playing the piano to accompany silent movies in New York theaters. Interestingly, given Truman's Elks connection, in 1931, music students of von Groyss gave a concert at the Elks Club in Patchogue, Long Island.[25]

Frederick Barker: The release of Truman was a rare low point in Barker's career. Shortly after, Barker left government service and went on to have a successful career working as a lawyer for the Guggenheim brothers in Mexico and South America, where they had mining ventures and other business interests. Barker had a son, Francis, and a daughter, Mabel, with his second wife, Josephine. His work took him to Peru, Chile, Bolivia, and Mexico, where he and his family lived from 1907 to 1918. Barker died in Los Angeles in 1954, aged eighty-three.

Frank McIntyre: The Truman Hunt–Igorrote debacle did nothing to harm McIntyre's professional reputation. In 1912 McIntyre was promoted to chief of the Bureau of Insular Affairs. In 1919 he was awarded a distinguished service medal and praised for his "breadth of view and sound judgment,"[26] the same qualities he had applied to pursuing Truman Hunt more than a decade earlier. McIntyre rose to the rank of major general before retiring in 1929 after forty-three years of service with the army. He died at Miami Beach, Florida, on February 16, 1944.

Col. Clarence Edwards: "There is probably no one American who throughout a long period of years has consistently done more to forward the Philippines than [Edwards],"[27] reported a 1917 article in the *New York Sun*. The first chief of the Bureau of Insular Affairs went on to become commander of the 26th Division in World War I. A controversial figure, he inspired great loyalty among his supporters but had a reputation for being outspoken and argumentative, which made him many foes. During World War I Edwards was openly critical of his army superiors, which led to his being relieved of his command. Following his retirement from the army, Edwards served as president of the grocery business his father had founded. He died in Boston in 1931.

Dean Worcester: Truman's onetime friend and ally held the position of secretary of the interior until 1913, making him one of the most powerful men in the Philippines and the longest-serving administrator in the colonial government. During his career Worcester amassed a collection of thousands of photographs of the Philippines' "non-Christian tribes," including the Igorrotes and the Negritos, which he used in public lectures, and magazine and newspaper articles to promote his view that the people of the Islands were not fit for self-rule. He was a controversial figure throughout his career, loathed by Philippine nationalists and US anti-imperialists alike. After resigning from government service, Worcester remained in the Philippines until his death in 1924. He left behind a vast collection of photographs, letters, and other documents, which tell a controversial but fascinating story of early American colonialism.

Judge Moss: Never one to worry about going against the grain of popular opinion, the judge who let Truman walk free from the Shelby County court in 1907 devoted himself to a series of moral crusades during his long career. These included sentencing anyone found loitering in Memphis to sixty days in the workhouse and clamping down on Sunday opening in the city's theaters in 1908. He died in 1914.

David Frayser: In 1915 Memphis newspapers reported that Truman's former attorney had gone missing after buying a train ticket to Knoxville on March 17. He was still missing in May. Family and friends had made every effort to locate him, and reportedly did not know whether he was living or dead. He later reappeared in Memphis, having apparently suffered a nervous breakdown, and returned to his newspaper roots, taking a job with the *Commercial Appeal.* He died in 1932 of bronchial pneumonia, aged seventy.

Truman Hunt: Truman might have escaped the full force of American justice, but his final years were a kind of long, drawn-out punishment. Such a torrent of misfortune befell him that he must have wondered whether the Igorrotes had put a curse on him. The Filipinos were not vindictive people, nor did they practice voodoo, but in the years after 1907 the showman had good reason to be superstitious.

His post-jail life was marked by personal tragedy, financial hardship, and poor health. After scraping some money together, Truman and Sallie left Kentucky and headed west to make a fresh start. Truman, still chasing a fast buck, invested everything he owned in the Oklahoma oil fields. His dreamed-of fortune failed to materialize and his first child with Sallie, Patty, died in March 1908, aged just two. The couple had another two girls. They named them Bonnie and Mary (after one of Sallie's sisters, who died the same year the child was born). Tragically, Bonnie and Mary also died in infancy.

In 1910, six years after Truman bigamously married Sallie, the itinerant showman and his third wife finally settled at their first permanent address, in Tulsa, Oklahoma. Truman returned to medicine and Sallie had a fourth daughter, Catherine, named after the older sister who had been Sallie's rock during Truman's trials and incarceration.

Truman's appetite for reinventing his own life story had not diminished with age: the Iowa-born showman told the 1910 census taker that he was born in Kentucky, and that he was the son of a Kentucky-born father and a New York–born mother. The census taken in Iowa the same year shows eighteen-year-old Calista, Truman's daughter with his first wife, was still living with her grandmother and aunt Dora in Cedar Rapids.

With a new home and a baby daughter, Truman and Sallie hoped finally to put their misfortunes behind them, but Truman began experiencing periods of intense pain caused by Bright's disease, an inflammation of the kidneys, which was likely exacerbated by his fondness for liquor and rich food. His symptoms included dizziness, backache, and stomach pains.

The former showman moved his family back to Iowa, and began peddling miracle cures via a post office box, with the claim "Diseases of Men Cured . . . We Guarantee What Others Simply Promise. I am a recognized specialist in all diseases of men."[28]

In 1913 little Catherine died of complications following measles. By this point Truman was crippled by pain resulting from Bright's disease that frequently prevented him from working. The former showman had no money to bury his and Sallie's fourth daughter, and was too ill to attend her funeral. Sallie's father, Patrick Gallagher, traveled to Iowa to collect the infant's body and he and Sallie had her buried in the Gallagher family plot alongside Sallie's mother at the St. Louis Catholic Cemetery in Louisville.

The same year that Catherine died, Truman and Sallie had a son, Truman Leo, known as Leo. He was an angelic looking boy with blonde hair and big blue eyes. Sallie was smitten with her first son. But at nineteen months, Leo contracted infant polio, which left him crippled. His right leg was five inches shorter than the left. All the muscles in his affected leg were atrophied, rendering the leg useless and making him dependent on a carer at all times. He was mentally sharp but couldn't dress or bathe himself. He walked with two crutches and had a bodily tremor.

Truman's own health deteriorated rapidly. He self-administered regular injections and frequently felt so weary and sick he was forced to take to his bed. He could do nothing for himself and grew irritable and increasingly difficult to be around. When Truman's mother died toward the end of January 1916, Truman, Sallie, and Leo took over her home. Three weeks later, on February 16, 1916, Truman Hunt died in St. Luke's Hospital, Cedar Rapids, Iowa. His funeral was held two days later at St. Joseph's Catholic Church.

The last mention of Truman in the newspapers he had once filled with farfetched stories of his Filipino charges was a small notice placed by his family in the *Cedar Rapids Gazette.* It read: "Card of Thanks: We wish to express our appreciation for the many acts of kindness and for the assistance given us at the time of the Death of Dr. Hunt."[29] It was signed by Sallie, Truman's sister, Dora, and his daughter Calista.

The showman's body was buried in the Mt. Calvary Cemetery in Cedar Rapids. No headstone marks the grave of the great self-publicist.

Truman was forty-nine. Despite the vast wealth the brilliant showman and physician had accumulated during his lifetime, he left no life insurance policy, no assets, and no means of financial support for his wife and disabled child.

Sallie and Leo Hunt: If Truman thought he had been cursed, his third wife had every reason to believe the spell had been passed on to her and their son, Leo, too. With four daughters dead and buried and a severely disabled son, Sallie faced a future of severe hardship and unspeakable sorrow. All she had left of her marriage were memories and her marriage certificate, which "she prizes very highly."[30] Life must have seemed as if it couldn't get any worse, but the year after Truman's death Sallie's beloved father, Patrick, died.

Sallie couldn't work with Leo to care for, and turned to the Veterans Administration for help, applying for a widow's pension for herself and a dependant's allowance for her son. She became a regular correspondent with the VA over the next twenty-two years as she fought to get every penny she could from the government to put food on the table and a roof over the heads of herself and Leo.

In her correspondence she stated: "[Truman and I] had five children born to our marriage but all but one died in infancy and my living child is in poor health and almost constantly under the care of a physician."[31] In another letter she described Leo as "a victim of that dreadful scourge, Infantile Paralysis . . . He is a great expense to me in the way of shoes and of braces and what limited medical treatment

I can afford . . . He is a bright little fellow at the head of his class in the sixth grade and I think exceptionally advanced."[32] The doctor sent by the VA to examine Leo noted the following about the boy's condition. "General appearance Bad; state of nutrition poor; development impaired; carriage languid; gait limp; posture stooped . . . spits up and vomits food often," due to an impairment in his digestive system. The report concluded, "his disability is total."[33]

Sallie claimed in her application that Truman's death from Bright's disease was caused by his military service. If this was found to be true, Sallie would have been entitled to an augmented pension, paying her an additional twenty-five dollars a month. Sallie's claim for the greater amount was "rejected on the ground that claimant is manifestly unable to show that the officer's death, Feby. 15, 1916 from disease of kidneys, was a result of his military service in line of duty, there being no record in the War Department of said fatal disease and no medical or other evidence on file showing origin thereof in service or its existence at date of claimant's discharge, or continuance thereafter."[34] Whether Truman had told Sallie he contracted Bright's disease as a result of his time in the military, or whether she had invented the story in a desperate bid to get money, is lost to history. Either way, her story has the ring of something her husband might have said for financial gain.

Truman's widow was indefatigable and enterprising in the pursuit of her case. She enlisted the help of Congressman Charles Ogden of the Kentucky Fifth District, who in 1920 wrote to the commissioner of the Bureau of Pensions in Washington, DC, describing Sallie as "a personal friend,"[35] and appealing to the commissioner to increase the allowance paid to Leo to help cover his medical expenses. Congressman Ogden referred to Sallie's difficult personal circumstances and portrayed Truman Hunt as a distinguished public servant who had done sterling service in the cholera hospital in Manila in 1902.

Despite his intervention, money remained tight and Sallie and Leo were reliant on the kindness of family, friends, and strangers. Sallie, who had always dreamed of having a house to call her own, trailed around her home state in search of a place to stay. She spent some time in Parr's Rest, a home for indigent women in Louisville, and she and Leo lived for a while with her sister Margaret and her husband, and their five children.

Then, four years after Truman's death, Sallie got married again, to Jacob Wingfield. The couple settled with Leo in Buechel, Jefferson County, Kentucky. Sallie and Jacob had two children together, John, who was born around 1923, and Sara (the name Sallie's parents had given her) around 1927. Jacob worked variously as a farmer and hotel porter but was frequently unemployed and struggled to provide for his family. Meanwhile, Sallie's time was divided between raising her two young children and providing round-the-clock care for Leo.

Leo took after his father intellectually. He showed great promise at school and went on to study political science at the University of Louisville. His teachers described him as a very able student who could go on to a great career. But during his first year at the university, in 1933, his pension was cut from thirty-six to twelve dollars a month. Leo was living with Sallie and Jacob on a farm in Buechel, Kentucky, but the couple were penniless and heavily in debt to the bank.

Sallie was determined her eldest son should complete his education and took her complaint about the drop in her son's pension straight to the White House. Sallie addressed her letter to the first lady, Eleanor Roosevelt, to "My dear Mrs. Roosevelt" and went on to describe the plight of her son, who, "notwithstanding his affliction . . . is ambitious and anxious to acquire a thoro education. Twelve dollars per month hardly pays transportation expenses between our home and the university of Louisville where he is a sophomore in the College of Liberal Arts."[36] Sallie added, "Please do not think me bold in my appeal to you Mrs. Roosevelt. I think you can understand my anxiety in assuming to address you. Our farm is so heavily encumbered by default of payments on loans we will surely have to lose it if something does not materialize soon . . . I mention this to point out how hopeless [is] the boy's chance of aid from home. I shall be most grateful to you for your least effort in behalf on my son. Very truly yours, Mrs. Sallie G. Wingfield."[37]

By 1934 Sallie had enlisted the help of US senator Alben Barkley of Kentucky (later Harry Truman's vice president). Senator Barkley wrote to the acting director of the Widows' and Dependents' Claims Service, requesting that Leo's allowance be increased. He was informed that the boy was entitled to twenty-seven dollars a month and not a penny more, and the decision was final.

Leo was two years into his university degree when, in 1935, the VA sent a field examiner out to reassess his physical condition. In his report the field examiner wrote, that Leo "is a likable boy, smart and ambitious. He is a bad cripple . . . The ward hopes he can find some way to continue his education, as he realizes that this is his only salvation."[38]

The government turned down Sallie's request for another increase in Leo's allowance. By this point Jacob Wingfield was out of work again, and Truman's only surviving son was forced to drop out of university. He died three years later, on January 25, 1938, at age twenty-four, of a pulmonary abscess empyema, in Louisville, Kentucky. His medical and funeral expenses totaled $609.70, including an itemized bill from his hospital doctor, R. R. Slucher, for "Two House visits $6.00, Thirteen Hospital visits $39.00, Two Blood Transfusions $40.00. Total $85." Sallie applied to the government's War Pension Fund for assistance, which was provided.[39]

Sallie's fighting spirit kept her going through decades of torment. She finally gave up the fight on June 31, 1964, when she died in Kentucky, aged seventy-eight. She had outlived Truman by almost half a century and Leo by twenty-six years.

Sallie left behind her own mystery: in her letter applying for a widow's military pension she wrote, "The certified copy of the public record of my marriage to the soldier gives my name as Sallie A. Gallagher. I was baptized under the name of Sara A. Gallagher, but since my marriage to the soldier I have used the name of Sally G. Hunt, and I respectfully request that my name so appears in my pension certificate, if one be issued to me."[40] The document is signed "Sally G. Hunt." To move from "Sallie" to "Sally" is unimportant. But for Sallie to adopt an entirely new first and middle name on her marriage to Truman seems to suggest that Truman was not the only person in his world who enjoyed reinventing himself, and that he drew people into his orbit who had the same desire. Sara A. Gallagher became

Sallie G. Hunt, wiping out her former identity as she stood in the Portland, Oregon, church where she and Truman married. It was only after Truman's death that she needed to excavate the different layers of that transformation.

Calista Hunt: After the death of her mother, Myrtle, in 1893, and the departure of her father, Truman, Calista was raised by her aunt Dora and her grandmother (Truman's mother), Eunice Melissa Hunt. In 1921 Calista met and married Leo Max Creglow in Iowa. He was a farmer and had served in the Sand Storm Division during the Battle of Mons in WWI. In 1924 Calista and Leo had a son, William. Calista died in Santa Monica, California, in 1969, at the age of seventy-seven.

Else and Philip Hunt: Shortly after Truman's release from jail in February 1907, the Bureau of Insular Affairs received a letter from Mrs. Else Hunt asking whether the bureau knew of the whereabouts of her husband, Truman Hunt, whom she'd been trying to find ever since he left Coney Island in September 1905. McIntyre replied that Truman had been a prisoner in Memphis but that he had recently been released. He continued, "I should state in this connection that during Hunt's incarceration in the Memphis jail he was in correspondence with his wife in Louisville, Kentucky."[41]

Else was finally granted a divorce from Truman on May 9, 1908, after she hired a private detective who provided evidence that Truman had committed adultery and had cohabited with Sallie in New York during the summer of 1905. Truman did not show up in court or send a representative. Else was given full custody of their son, Philip Hunt. It was recorded in the divorce documents that Truman was accused of committing adultery not just with Sallie but with several women. The detective had also visited the Reverend Father James Black in Portland, Oregon, who was shown photographs of Truman and Sallie and confirmed in a sworn statement that he had married them in December 1904, when the groom was still married to Else.

Following her divorce, Else wrote Truman out of her life entirely, and described herself as a widow. She raised Philip, her son with Truman, with the help of relatives. When Philip was eleven, Else got married again, to Wilbur Marsh, a Manhattan stockbroker. Their marriage was a long and stable one and Wilbur raised Philip as if he were his own son. Philip dropped the surname Hunt and became Philip Marsh.

For the first time since meeting Truman, life seemed finally to be going well for Else. But then in October 1920, tragedy struck: at age seventeen, Philip died of pneumonia at the Great Lakes Naval Station in Illinois, where he had enlisted earlier that year.

Else died in 1958 at age eighty-seven, six years after her second husband, and forty-two years after Truman.

AMERICA AND THE PHILIPPINES

The debate over America's involvement in the Philippines and the rights of Filipinos to rule their own country reached a milestone with the passing of the Jones Act of 1916, which formally declared the US government's commitment to Philippine independence. But another three decades passed before the issue was finally resolved: on July 4, 1946, America handed sovereignty of the islands back to the Philippine people with the signing of the Treaty of Manila. In the eyes of many Filipinos, the Americans had done nothing but harm; others celebrated the introduction of public education and widespread political elections.

Despite the controversial role that America played in the Philippines for nearly half a century, the ties between the two countries have endured. According to the US Department of State, there are an estimated four million Americans of Philippine ancestry in the United States today, and more than three hundred thousand US citizens in the Philippines.

As I noted in the introduction to this book, the idea of exhibiting human beings for entertainment is rightly considered grotesque today. Understandably, the subject of the Igorrote exhibition trade is regarded by many modern Filipinos as a shocking example of the subjugation and degradation of their forefathers. I hope that this book, in telling the story of the Igorrotes who were taken to America in 1905 does something to honor their extraordinary lives.

A LAST WORD

Much was said in the corridors of power and written in the press about the manifold ways in which America could "civilize" the Igorrotes, but the tribespeople had their own ideas. Before he left Coney Island, Chief Fomoaley shared his impressions with a journalist.

"I have seen many wonders [in America], but we will not bring any of them home to Bontoc. We do not want them there. We have the great sun and moon to light us; what do we want of your little suns [electric lighting]? The houses that fly like birds [trains and cars] would be no good to us, because we do not want to leave Bontoc. When we go home there, we will stay, for it is the best place in all the world."[42]

Acknowledgments

Truman Hunt led the Igorrotes, and later Barker, on a wild dance across America. Tracing every step of that journey has led me on an equally merry dance, through libraries, museums, court and newspaper archives, along with state, city, county, and federal government archives, and has seen me quizzing experts across the globe. Along the way I have developed a huge admiration for the talents and tenacity of librarians from Manila and Bontoc to Little Rock, Arkansas, and from Chicago and New York to Edinburgh and Aberystwyth.

My special thanks go to all the wonderful staff of the New York Public Library, specifically in the Irma and Paul Milstein Division of United States History, Local History, and Genealogy; the Billy Rose Theater Division; the Manuscripts and Archives Division; the Microforms Reading Room; and to Kate Cordes and her colleagues in the Lionel Pincus and Princess Firyal Map Division. I am especially grateful to Sachiko Clayton and Philip Sutton in the Milstein Division, which became my second home as I researched the book.

I would also like to thank the staff of the following institutions: the Vancouver Public Library; Winnipeg Public Library; Adele Heagney and Amanda Bahr-Evola at the St. Louis Public Library; Chicago Public Library; Onondaga County Public Library in Syracuse; State Library of Iowa; Mason City Public Library; Spokane Public Library; Seattle Public Library; Memphis Public Library; Kansas City Public Library; Fiona Laing at the National Library of Scotland; Central Library in Edinburgh; the Hugh Owen Library at Aberystwyth University; Irene Wainwright at the New Orleans Public Library; Ken Wuetcher at the Louisville Free Public Library; Bentley Historical Library, University of Michigan; the Tampa-Hillsborough Public Library in Florida; Boston Public Library; Atlantic City Free Public Library; Nashville Public Library; Multnomah County Library in Portland, Oregon; Dallas Public Library; Connecticut State Library; Westport Public Library in Connecticut; Tulsa City-County Library in Oklahoma; the Research Center at the Chicago History

Museum; New Haven Free Public Library; Brooklyn Public Library; Chris Child at the New England Historic Genealogical Society; Todd Gilbert at the New York Transit Museum; the wonderful staff at the Brooklyn Historical Society; the New-York Historical Society; the Museum of the City of New York; Barbara Mathé at the American Museum of Natural History; the State Historical Society of Missouri; Charlotte Branch Library; Arkansas State Library; Garland County Library; Ronald A. Lee at Tennessee State Library and Archives; Godfrey Memorial Library; Meg Miner at Illinois Wesleyan University; Diane Disbro, Union Branch, Scenic Regional Library, Union, Missouri; the Missouri History Museum and Library and Research Center; Florence M. Jumonville at the Earl K. Long Library, University of New Orleans; Reme Grefalda and colleagues at the Library of Congress; Charleston County Public Library in South Carolina; the University of Michigan; Kara Tershel at Georgetown University; Charlotte Bare at the Washington Memorial Library; Joshua Ruff, curator at the New York City Police Museum; the National Anthropological Archives at the Smithsonian; Ken Cobb at the New York City Municipal Archives; the University of Tennessee; Pennee Bender at the City University of New York; Westport Historical Society; the Newberry library; the Chicago Bar Association; the John Marshall Law School; and the Spertus Institute.

My research took me to many fascinating places. Chief among these were the wonderful archives of the county clerk's office in downtown Manhattan, where Joseph Van Nostrandt went out of his way to help me locate the records of Truman and Else Hunt's divorce, which had been filed on the wrong shelf. This was a vital piece of my puzzle.

The file contained a copy of the wedding certificate for Truman's bigamous third marriage, and the only photograph I managed to find of Sallie Hunt. This photograph, and another of Truman, had been clearly marked exhibit A and exhibit B with a thick black pen, and entered as evidence when Else took Truman to court more than a century ago.

Holding in my hands the documents that proved beyond doubt that Truman was a bigamist was a heart-pounding moment. Truman had always been able to evade the law. Now, ninety-six years after his death, here was cast-iron proof of his wrongdoing. This was a document even the silver-tongued Truman could not have explained away.

At the National Archives and Records Administration, I wish to thank Ashley Mattingly and Wanda Williams in St. Louis, and Amy Reytar in Maryland, whose heart must have sank every time she saw an e-mail from me in her in-box with yet another query about the Truman Hunt files. And to Glenn V. Longacre and Scott Forsythe at the National Archives at Chicago; Guy Hall and Shane Bell at the National Archives at Atlanta; and the staff at the National Archives at Fort Worth, Texas.

A huge thanks to the following people for their assistance with my research: Ginger Frere, Karen Needles, Mary White, Erin McConnaughhay, Anthony Timek, Richard Raichelson, and Dyan Hooper.

Thanks also to Frank Stewart and Vincent Clark, archivists at the Shelby County register, who answered numerous queries with extraordinary patience and provided me with invaluable court documents relating to Truman Hunt's trials in Memphis; to Dozier Hasty at the *Brooklyn Daily Eagle;* Jenny Lister, curator, textiles and fashion at the Victoria and Albert in London, who shared her extensive knowledge of ladies' and gents' fashions at the turn of the century; Scott Daniels at the Oregon Historical Society; military historian Andrew Birtle at the US Army Center of Military History, who helped me to better understand the US military and political presence in the Philippines in the late nineteenth and early twentieth centuries; the staff and volunteers at the US Army Heritage Center Foundation; to Ron Schweiger, Brooklyn borough historian; Michael Miscione, the Manhattan borough historian; the architectural historian John Kriskiewicz; Melissa Knight Nodhturft, Judicial Staff Attorney at Thirteenth Judicial Circuit Legal Department in Tampa; Professor Alfred Brophy at the University of North Carolina School of Law for answering my legal history questions, no matter how obscure they became—and to my friend Professor Eric Miller of Loyola University in Los Angeles, who put me in touch with him; to Steve Bohlen at Bellevue Hospital Center; the National Personnel Records Center in

St. Louis; Dr. Mark Rice; Gene Gill, who was a fantastic source of information on Memphis in the early 1900s and who provided pictures of the Shelby County courthouse and Shelby County jail; the office of the clerk at Cook County Court in Chicago; New Orleans State Supreme Court; Jackson County records office in Iowa; Memphis Police Department; Rachel Diny at the clerk's office of the Hillsborough County Circuit Court in Tampa; the US District Court Western District of Tennessee in Memphis; the filmmaker Marlon Fuentes; the Philippines embassy in London; communications history experts Professor Gerald Brock, Professor Richard R. John, Diane DeBlois, and Nancy Pope; April Sese and Katie Caljean, who did research at Columbia University into the display of indigenous peoples at the 1904 World's Fair; Nan A. Rothschild, director of Museum Studies, Columbia University; Mary Ann Goldberg, principal at Wydown Middle School in St. Louis, which sits on what was once the site of the Philippine Reservation at the 1904 World's Fair; Victor Mendoza; Benito Vergara; Aaron Beebe, the former director of the Coney Island Museum; meteorologist Scott E. Stephens; Max Storm; Joseph T. Gleason, director of archival services at the New York Society for the Prevention of Cruelty to Children; Cherubim A. Quizon, associate professor of anthropology at Seton Hall University; Stephen Greenberg at the National Library of Medicine; Ernest Hook at the School of Public Health at the University of California; Dr. Tonse Raju at the Eunice Kennedy Shriver National Institute of Child Health and Human Development; and everyone else who kindly replied to my medical history queries on the Caduceus medical discussion board.

Many people assisted me with my research in Truman Hunt's home state. They included the staff of the Cedar Rapids Public Library, Marion Public Library, and Des Moines Public Library; Scott Ketelsen at the University of Iowa and Wendy Stevenson at the University of Iowa library; Dale Gurwell and all the other terrific staff and volunteers at the Iowa Genealogical Society library; and Barbara Mayberry and her colleagues at the Jackson County Genealogical Chapter in Maquoketa.

In the Philippines, I would like to thank Emanuel La Vina; the staff at the National Archives of the Philippines; the National Library of the Philippines; the Bontoc Municipal Library and Kalinga Provincial Library; and the British Embassy in Manila.

I am enormously grateful to Tom Tryniski, the man behind www.fultonhistory.com, an incredible archive of newspaper articles published in New York State, which was invaluable to me. I'd like to thank John Hankey, who acted as my expert guide to American trains, railroad schedules, and services at the turn of the century. Additional thanks go to J. E. Sackey at the Northwest Railway Museum in Snoqualmie, Washington. It was to shipping expert John Hamma, to my father-in-law, Cameron Donaldson, and to Ed Greenberg and the archivists at Canadian Pacific that I turned with queries related to all things maritime. I would also like to express my appreciation to Robert Rydell and Karen Abbott, and to Ian Boyle who provided me with a picture of the RMS *Empress of China*, the ship that brought Truman Hunt and the Igorrotes to North America.

Thanks to Gina Inocencio at the Smithsonian, who put me in touch with Alan Bain at the National Anthropological Archives, who in turn connected me with Patricia Afable, who has done extensive research on the Igorrote exhibition groups, and who was extremely generous with her time and knowledge. My telephone conversations with Patricia fired my enthusiasm for this project in the early stages of my research. Patricia put me in touch with Carlyn Weibel, granddaughter of Richard Schneidewind, and Deana Weibel-Swanson, his great-granddaughter. I spoke to Deana and Carlyn at length over the telephone and thoroughly enjoyed their stories and recollections of Richard Schneidewind.

I owe an enormous debt of gratitude to my agent, William Clark, without whom the story of *The Lost Tribe of Coney Island* might never have been told. He believed in this book from the very beginning and his encouragement and early feedback were invaluable. A massive thanks to my editor, Katie Salisbury, who thrilled to every twist and turn in the story, and whose insightful notes and comments greatly improved this book.

Thanks to Claire Coster, Fiona Leith, Laura Vinha, Shari Kaplan, and Eva Soos for their friendship and support. And to Marie Mutsuki Mockett for her generous advice.

The Lost Tribe of Coney Island is a story about a group of human beings who were betrayed by the man who should have been their protector. Truman was an unfaithful husband, a feckless, inattentive father, and a cruel and destructive guardian to the tribesmen and women who relied on him. As I wrote about the inconstant and duplicitous Truman, I was reminded daily of how lucky I am to have my own fantastic family. My biggest thanks of all go to my mum, dad, David, Bram, Al, and Chip. My dad was diagnosed with cancer in the week I learned I had got a publishing deal for *The Lost Tribe of Coney Island*. It is a great sadness that he is not here to see it published. He was a huge champion of my career, was enthralled by this story, and was enormously proud that I was writing this book. Dad loved to tell stories and if I learned anything about how to spot and tell a good tale I owe much of that to him.

My mum is one of life's rocks. Thanks to her for her love, her unwavering support, and for all she does to make everyone else's life better. And thanks to my sister Al for being the kind of supporter everyone should have on their side. My regular telephone chats with mum and Al helped keep me sane when I was spending long days staring at my laptop. And I am forever grateful for all the babysitting Mum did, which enabled me to finish this book—and take much-needed trips to the cinema.

A massive thanks to my husband, David, who was always there to re-enthuse me whenever I hit a roadblock, for reading the manuscript numerous times without complaining, for buying me a box set of *The Golden Girls* to get me through the editing process, and for his insightful feedback at every stage of this book. He once jokingly asked me if he was "the wind beneath my wings." You know the answer, David. And to Bram, whose boundless energy, zest for life, curiosity, and good humor helped keep things real when my obsession with this story threatened to get out of hand.

Notes

Introduction

1. I use "Igorrote," rather than the alternative "Igorot," as this was the spelling commonly used to refer to the tribe in America. I also refer to them as "Igorrote" rather than "Bontoc Igorrote," as this was how the tribespeople were known in America. I use the plural "Igorrotes," which was widely used in the US press in the early 1900s rather than "Igorrote," which is more strictly accurate.
2. Jenks, Albert Ernest. *The Bontoc Igorot.* Bureau of Public Printing, 1905.
3. *The Macon Telegraph*, September 11, 1904.
4. Ibid.

Chapter 1

1. Translation of Simeon A. Villa diary. Manuscripts and Archives Division. The New York Public Library.
2. Ibid.
3. Jenks, Albert Ernest. "Building a Province." *The Outlook*, May 21, 1904.
4. Ibid.
5. *Third Annual Report of the Philippine Commission 1902 Part 1*, Bureau of Insular Affairs, War Department, Washington, Government Printing Office, 1903.
6. *Brooklyn Daily Eagle*, June 4, 1905.
7. Ibid.
8. Jenks, Albert Ernest. "Building a Province." *The Outlook*, May 21, 1904.
9. *The Los Angeles Times*, April 24, 1904.
10. Rydell, Robert. *All the World's a Fair.* The University of Chicago Press, 1984; 171.
11. *The Macon Telegraph*, September 11, 1904.
12. Ibid.
13. Ibid.
14. Ibid.
15. Rasmussen, R. Kent, ed. *Dear Mark Twain: Letters from His Readers.* University of California Press, 2013.

16. Forbes-Lindsay, C. H. *The Philippines Under Spanish and American Rules.* The J. C. Winston Co., 1906; *The New York Times*, January 23, 1921.
17. *The Seattle Daily Times*, April 20, 1905.
18. *The Seattle Daily Times*, December 11, 1904
19. Afable, Patricia O. "Journeys from Bontoc to the Western Fairs, 1904–1915: The 'Nikimalika' and their Interpreters," *Philippine Studies* vol. 52, no. 4 (2004); 445–473. Ateneo de Manila University, 2004.
20. While Truman was in the Philippines, the exhibits from the St. Louis Philippine Reservation were on the way, all fifteen carloads of them, to New York, where they had been secured for the collection of the American Museum of Natural History. The exhibits included bows and arrows, copper pots, woven baskets, fish traps, looms, a full-sized Igorrote hut, and the obligatory G-string. *The New York Sun*, February 18, 1905.

Chapter 2

1. *The Independent*, October 5, 1905.
2. Jenks, Albert Ernest. *The Bontoc Igorot.* Bureau of Public Printing, 1905.
3. *The Independent*, October 5, 1905.
4. *The Seattle Daily Times*, May 17, 1905.
5. Sallie sometimes signed her name Sallie and other times Sally. The spelling varies in government reports and personal and official correspondence. I have used Sallie, which is the spelling used most often in official and personal documents.
6. Blount, James H. *The American Occupation of the Philippines 1898 to 1912.* G.P. Putnam's and Sons, 1913.

Chapter 3

1. *The Independent*, October 5, 1905.
2. Dengay's name sometimes appears in the official record spelled Dangui and Dengui.
3. Ibid.
4. I have used the spelling of Falino Ygnichen's name that appeared on the passenger list of the ship that carried the Filipinos to North America. His name appears in newspaper coverage of the tribe variously as Falino Ygnichen, Falio Yguichen, and Faliao Ygnichen.
5. *The Independent*, October 5, 1905.
6. Ibid.

Chapter 4

1. *The New York Morning Telegraph*, April 13, 1905.
2. Ibid.
3. Ibid.
4. Ibid.
5. Ibid.
6. Newspaper article, February 3, 1912 source unknown, in Clippings, Thompson, Fred., Billy Rose Theater Division, New York Public Library (referred to hereafter as the BRTD and NYPL).
7. *The Buffalo Express*, date unknown, from Clippings, Thompson, Fred., BRTD, NYPL.
8. *The Cleveland Leader*, date unknown, from Elmer Dundy obituary in the Robinson Locke Collection Envelopes 2342A and 2164, BRTD, NYPL.
9. *The New York Morning Telegraph*, April 13, 1905.
10. Ibid.
11. Ibid.

Chapter 5

1. *The Seattle Daily Times*, April 20, 1905.
2. Ibid.
3. Ibid.
4. Ibid.
5. Ibid.
6. National Archives and Records Administration at College Park, Maryland, Record Group 350, Records of the Bureau of Insular Affairs, File No. 10111.
7. Ibid.
8. *The Morning Oregonian*, April 24, 1905.
9. Ibid.
10. *The Seattle Daily Times*, April 25, 1905.
11. Ibid.
12. Ibid.
13. Ibid.
14. Ibid.
15. *The Seattle Daily Times*, April 24, 1905.
16. *The Seattle Daily Times*, April 26, 1905.
17. Ibid.
18. *The Seattle Daily Times*, April 30, 1905.
19. Ibid.

20. Ibid.
21. Jenks, Albert Ernest. *The Bontoc Igorot.* Bureau of Public Printing, 1905.
22. Ibid.
23. Ibid.
24. Ibid.
25. *The Seattle Daily Times,* May 20, 1905.
26. Ibid.
27. Ibid.
28. Ibid.
29. Ibid. The prospect of the Philippine tribes playing baseball was a subject which captured the imagination of the American press. An article in the *Gettysburg Times* on September 27, 1916, referred to the Moro tribe playing baseball in the Philippines and imagined the day the Moros and the Igorrotes would replace head-hunting with baseball—a sure sign that American civilization had caught on with "baseball, the leader of all sports, binding the east and the west in a brotherhood of sympathy and understanding. When baseball becomes universal throughout the islands of the archipelago we may consider that the Filipinos are apt candidates for independence, for they will have learned one prime essential of freedom—the willingness to lose a game by a close decision without murdering the umpire."
30. *The Seattle Daily Times,* May 20, 1905.
31. Ibid.
32. *The Independent,* October 5, 1905.

Chapter 6

1. *The New York Tribune,* May 16, 1905.
2. MTA.info
3. *Buffalo Morning Express,* May 25, 1905.
4. Ibid.
5. Ibid.
6. *The New York Times,* May 15, 1905.
7. Immerso, Michael. *Coney Island: the People's Playground.* Rutgers University Press, 2002.
8. Porter, Edwin, S., dir. *Rube and Mandy at Coney Island,* BRTD, NYPL, M16 A 389 R. Edison Manufacturing Company, 1903.
9. *The New York Tribune,* May 9, 1905.
10. *The New York Sun,* May 22, 1905.

Chapter 7

1. Trager, James. *New York Chronology.* Collins Reference, 2003.
2. He was no relation to Frederic Thompson.
3. *Coney Island Souvenir Guide.* Megaphone Press Co., 1905.
4. *The Illustrated Buffalo Express,* July 9, 1905.
5. *Brooklyn Daily Eagle,* June 4, 1905.
6. *The New York Tribune,* May 26, 1905.
7. *The New York Morning Telegraph,* May 21, 1905.
8. Ibid.
9. *Brooklyn Daily Eagle,* June 4, 1905.
10. Ibid.
11. Ibid.
12. Ibid.
13. Ibid.
14. It seems likely that Fuller was describing a scene related by Albert Jenks in *The Bontoc Igorot.* Bureau of Public Printing, 1905.
15. *The New York Times,* May 28, 1905.

Chapter 8

1. *The New York Morning Telegraph,* July 19, 1905.
2. Ibid.
3. *The New York Daily Tribune,* July 31, 1905.

Chapter 9

1. *New York Tribune,* July 17, 1905.
2. Intriguingly, the *Washington Post* and the *Atlanta Constitution* reported on a double Igorrote wedding at the St. Louis Exposition in 1904, of Laguima to Domingo and Tugmena to Bocosso, in the May 29, 1904, editions of both newspapers. Bocosso and Tugmena are described as belonging to the Suyoc tribe, not the Bontoc Igorrotes. According to the passenger list for the *Empress of China,* the Igorrotes Laguima and Bocosso who came to Coney with Truman Hunt in 1905 had never been to America before. Was this a mistake, an example of the way names were recycled by the showmen, or were they simply common names? The last two of these seem to offer the most likely explanations. Either way, it shows that weddings were a popular way for the American showmen to bring in the crowds.

3. Jenks, Albert Ernest. *The Bontoc Igorot.* Bureau of Public Printing, 1905.
4. *The New York Tribune,* July 17, 1905.
5. Ibid.
6. Ibid.
7. www.elks.org
8. *The New York Tribune,* July 7, 1905.
9. Ibid.
10. *The New York Morning Telegraph,* July 29, 1905.
11. Ibid.
12. Ibid.
13. *The Brooklyn Standard Union,* July 30, 1905.
14. *The Independent,* October 5, 1905. The reporter who wrote this article is not named.
15. Ibid. The accompanying photograph suggests Fomoaley was younger than forty-eight, perhaps as much as a decade younger.
16. Ibid. All the quotes that follow in this section come from the same article in the *Independent,* October 5, 1905.
17. Ibid.
18. Ibid.
19. *The New York Morning Telegraph,* June 19, 1905.
20. As recounted in the *Oswego Palladium,* October 11, 1905.
21. *Vogue,* August 1905.
22. *The Livingston Democrat,* March 4, 1906.
23. *The Los Angeles Times,* December 12, 1905. Five years later, in 1910, Ivory Soap used a picture of the Igorrotes in an advertising campaign with the caption "some people like Ivory Soap so much they have brought it nearly half way 'round the globe for them."
24. *The Syracuse Post Standard,* September 26, 1906.
25. *The New York Tribune,* July 30, 1905.

Chapter 10

1. *The St. Louis Post Dispatch,* October 24, 1909.
2. Ibid.
3. Ibid.
4. *The Spotlight,* July 1908.
5. Ibid.
6. *The New York Times,* August 10, 1905.
7. Ibid.
8. *Brooklyn Daily Eagle,* August 7, 1905.

9. *The New York Press*, August 7, 1905.
10. *The New York Tribune*, August 7, 1905.
11. *The New York Tribune*, August 16, 1905; *Atlantic City Daily Press*, August 16, 1905; *The New York Daily Star*, August 16, 1905.
12. *Atlantic City Daily Press*, August 16, 1905.
13. *New York Herald*, August 15, 1905; see also *New York Herald*, August 14, 1905.
14. *The New York Tribune*, August 28, 1905.
15. *The Long Islander*, August 27, 1905.
16. *The New York Tribune*, August 28, 1905.
17. His name was sometimes spelled Gattoman or Gotaman.
18. *The New York Tribune*, August 14, 1905; *The New York Morning Telegraph*, September 11, 1905.
19. *The New York Tribune*, August 14, 1905.

Chapter 11

1. *The New York Times*, June 12, 2005, quoting a 1939 *New Yorker* article by A. J. Liebling.
2. Ibid.
3. *The New York Times*, August 31, 1905.
4. *The New York Tribune*, August 31, 1905.
5. Ibid.
6. *Brooklyn Daily Eagle*, September 1, 1905; *Brooklyn Daily Eagle*, September 2, 1905.

Chapter 12

1. *The New York Tribune*, September 1, 1905.
2. *The New York Times*, September 1, 1905.
3. *Brooklyn Daily Eagle*, September 1, 1905.
4. *The New York Sun*, September 1, 1905.
5. *The New York Evening Telegram*, September 2, 1905.
6. *The Nashville American*, September 4, 1905.
7. *St. Louis Globe Democrat*, September 3, 1905.

Chapter 14

1. *The Memphis Commercial Appeal*, September 10, 1905.
2. *The Memphis Commercial Appeal*, September 11, 1905.
3. *The Memphis Commercial Appeal*, September 16, 1905.

4. Ibid.
5. Ibid.
6. *The Dallas Morning News*, October 29, 1905; *The Dallas Morning News*, October 30, 1905.
7. *The Dallas Morning News*, October 28, 1905.
8. Ibid.
9. Ibid.
10. Ibid.
11. *The Macon Telegraph*, October 21, 1905.
12. Barreto, Norberto. *Imperial Thoughts: The US Congress and the Philippine Questions*, 1898–1934. Stony Brook University, 2007.
13. *The Macon Telegraph*, November 2, 1905.
14. Quotes in this scene are from the *Dallas Morning News*, October 5, 1905; and the *San Antonio Sunday Light*, November 19, 1905.
15. In fact the bond was equivalent to around five-thousand dollars.
16. *The Dallas Morning News*, October 5, 1905; *The San Antonio Sunday Light*, November 19, 1905.

Chapter 15

1. *The Tampa Morning Tribune*, November 30, 1905.
2. Ibid.
3. Ibid.
4. Ibid.
5. Ibid.
6. *The Macon Daily Telegraph*, November 30, 1905; *The Tampa Morning Tribune*, November 30, 1905; *The Commercial Appeal*, September 5, 1906.
7. NARA RG 350-13847.

Chapter 16

1. Each Igorrote was to be paid fifteen dollars a month and Julio was to be paid twenty-five dollars as interpreter and assistant.
2. NARA RG 350-13847.
3. Ibid.
4. Jenks, Albert Ernest. *The Bontoc Igorot*. Bureau of Public Printing, 1905; NARA RG 350-13431.
5. *The Fort Wayne News*, January 29, 1906.
6. NARA RG 350-13847.
7. Ibid.

8. *The Daily Picayune*, January 18, 1907; NARA RG 350-13847.
9. *The Dallas Morning News*, January 31, 1906.

Chapter 17

1. *The Washington Times*, August 10, 1904.
2. NARA RG 350-13847.
3. Ibid.
4. NARA RG 350-9640.
5. Ibid.
6. Ibid.
7. NARA RG 350-13431.
8. Ibid.
9. Ibid.
10. NARA RG 350-9640.
11. NARA RG 350-13431.
12. NARA RG 350-13847.
13. Ibid.
14. Ibid.
15. *Fourth Annual Report of the Philippine Commission 1903 Part 1*, Bureau of Insular Affairs, War Department, Washington. Government Printing Office, 1904.
16. Ibid.
17. NARA RG 350-13847.
18. Ibid.
19. Ibid.
20. Ibid.
21. Ibid.
22. Ibid.
23. Ibid.
24. Ibid.
25. Newspaper reports and government correspondence show Pucuan died on January 28, 1906, not January 25, 1906, as Truman states in this letter.
26. NARA RG 350-13847.

Chapter 18

1. NARA RG 350-13431.
2. Ibid.
3. Ibid.

4. Ibid.
5. Ibid.

Chapter 19

1. The factual information and events described in this chapter are taken from a wide variety of sources, including the following: NARA RG 350-13847; Sanborn-Perris Company, New York. Insurance Maps of Memphis, Tennessee, 1897, Vol. 1, Sheet 39; Sanborn Map Company, New York. Insurance Maps of Memphis, Tennessee, 1907, Vol. 1, Sheets 4, 5 & 15; R. L. Polk & Co.'s Memphis City Directory, 1906, Memphis; *The Memphis Daily Appeal*, December 10, 1867; *Daily Picayune*, January 18, 1907; *Daily Picayune*, February 15, 1907; *Daily Picayune*, February 16, 1907; *Daily Picayune*, September 2, 1907; *Commercial Appeal*, September 5, 1906; *Commercial Appeal*, September 6, 1906; *Commercial Appeal*, September 15, 1906; *Commercial Appeal*, September 17, 1906; *Commercial Appeal*, November 3, 1906; *Commercial Appeal*, November 6, 1906; *Commercial Appeal*, November 8, 1906; *Commercial Appeal*, November 9, 1906; *Commercial Appeal*, November 11, 1906; *Commercial Appeal*, November 23, 1906; *Commercial Appeal*, November 24, 1906; *Commercial Appeal*, November 25, 1906; *Commercial Appeal*, December 16, 1906; *Commercial Appeal*, December 21, 1906; *Commercial Appeal*, January 19, 1907; *Commercial Appeal*, February 3, 1907; *Commercial Appeal*, February 6, 1907; *Commercial Appeal*, February 7, 1907; *Commercial Appeal*, February 10, 1907; *Commercial Appeal*, February 12, 1907; *Memphis News Scimitar*, September 5, 1906; *Memphis News Scimitar*, September 17, 1906; *Memphis News Scimitar*, November 4, 1906; *Memphis News Scimitar*, November 5, 1906; *Memphis News Scimitar*, November 6, 1906; *Memphis News Scimitar*, November 9, 1906; *Memphis News Scimitar*, November 11, 1906; *Memphis News Scimitar*, November 18, 1906; *Memphis News Scimitar*, November 22, 1906; *Memphis News Scimitar*, November 25, 1906; *Memphis News Scimitar*, December 20, 1906; *Memphis News Scimitar*, February 6, 1907; *Memphis News Scimitar*, February 10, 1907; *Memphis News Scimitar*, February 11, 1907; *The Paducah Evening Sun*, September 5, 1906; *The Paducah Evening Sun*, November 10, 1906; and the author's personal communication with the Shelby County court archivist.
2. NARA RG 350-13847.
3. *The Independent*, October 5, 1905.
4. NARA RG 350-13847.
5. Ibid.
6. Ibid.
7. Ibid.
8. Ibid.

9. Ibid.
10. Ibid.
11. Ibid.
12. Ibid.
13. Ibid.

Chapter 20

1. *The Chicago Daily Tribune,* June 10, 1906.
2. NARA RG 350-13847; *The Chicago Daily Tribune,* May 26, 1907; *The Chicago Daily Tribune,* May 27, 1906.
3. *The Chicago Daily Tribune,* May 27, 1906.
4. Ibid; *The Chicago Daily Tribune,* June 3, 1906.
5. NARA RG 350-13847.
6. NARA RG 350-13431.
7. Sanger, Gen. J. P., dir. *Census of the Philippine Islands Taken under the Direction of the Philippine Commission in the Year 1903,* Vol. 2. United States Bureau of the Census, 1905; Blount, James, H. *The American Occupation of the Philippines 1898 to 1912,* J. P. Putnam's and Sons, Knickerbocker Press, 1913.
8. NARA RG 350-13847.

Chapter 21

1. NARA RG 350-13847.
2. Ibid.
3. Ibid.
4. Ibid.
5. Ibid.

Chapter 22

1. NARA RG 350-13847.
2. Ibid.
3. Ibid.
4. Ibid.
5. Ibid.
6. Ibid.
7. Ibid.
8. Ibid; *The Chicago Daily News,* June 21, 1906.
9. NARA RG 350-13847.

Chapter 23

1. NARA RG 350-13847.
2. Ibid.
3. Ibid.
4. Ibid.
5. Ibid.
6. *The Manitoba Free Press*, July 4, 1906; *The Winnipeg Telegram*, July 6, 1906.
7. NARA RG 350-13847.
8. Ibid.
9. Ibid.

Chapter 24

1. *The Syracuse Post Standard*, June 30, 1906; *Variety*, July 1906.
2. *The Syracuse Post Standard*, July 4, 1906.
3. *The Syracuse Daily Journal*, July 13, 1906.
4. NARA RG 350-13847.
5. Ibid.
6. Ibid.
7. Ibid. Note that the letter in which this incident is described is erroneously dated June 9, 1906, but the context makes clear it was written on July 9, 1906.
8. Ibid.
9. *The Sentinel*, Vol. XXVIII, Number 11, December 15, 1917.
10. NARA RG 350-13847.
11. Ibid.
12. Ibid.
13. *The Syracuse Herald*, February 21, 1904.
14. *The Washington Post*, February 22, 1904.
15. *The Syracuse Herald*, February 21, 1904; *The Washington Post*, February 22, 1904.
16. NARA RG 350-13847.
17. Ibid.
18. Ibid.
19. Ibid.

Chapter 25

1. NARA RG 350-13847; NARA at Chicago, RG 21-9766, US District Court,

Northern District of Illinois, Eastern Division, Chicago, Civil Case Files, 1871–1911.
2. Ibid.

Chapter 26

1. The events described in this chapter are taken from a wide variety of sources, including the following: *The Chicago Daily News*, July 18, 1906; *The Chicago Daily News*, July 19, 1906; NARA RG 21-9766; NARA RG 350-13847; *The Chicago Daily News*, July 16, 1906; *The Chicago Inter Ocean*, July 16, 1906; *The New York Sun*, July 18, 1906; *The Chicago Tribune*, July 19, 1906; *The Nashville American*, July 19, 1906; *The Syracuse Herald*, July 19, 1906; *The Chillicothe Constitution-Tribune*, July 19, 1906; *The Chicago Daily News*, July 26, 1906; *The Lowville Journal and Republican*, July 26, 1906.
2. *The Chicago Daily News*, July 18, 1906.
3. NARA RG 350-13847.
4. Ibid; *The Chicago Daily News*, July 18, 1906; *The Chicago Daily News*, July 19, 1906.
5. NARA RG 350-13847.
6. Ibid.
7. Ibid.
8. Ibid.
9. *The Chicago American Evening Edition*, July 18, 1906; *The Chicago Evening Post*, July 18, 1906; *The Chicago Daily News*, July 18, 1906; *The Chicago Daily News*, July 19, 1906; *The Chicago Chronicle*, July 19, 1906; NARA RG 350-13847.
10. NARA RG 350-13847.
11. *The Chicago Daily Tribune*, December 9, 1906.
12. NARA RG 350-13847.
13. *The Chicago American Evening Edition*, July 18, 1906; NARA RG 350-13847.
14. *The Chicago Inter Ocean*, July 19, 1906; NARA RG 350-13847.
15. NARA RG 350-13847.
16. Ibid.
17. *The Boston Evening Transcript*, July 19, 1906.

Chapter 27

1. NARA RG 350-13847.
2. Ibid.

3. Ibid.
4. Ibid.
5. *The Commercial Appeal,* September 5, 1906; *The Commercial Appeal,* September 6, 1906.
6. NARA RG 350-13847.
7. Ibid.
8. Ibid.
9. Ibid.
10. Ibid.
11. Ibid.
12. Ibid.
13. Ibid.
14. Ibid.
15. Ibid.
16. Ibid.
17. Ibid.
18. Ibid.
19. Ibid.
20. Ibid.
21. Seidenadel, Carl W. *The First Grammar of the Language Spoken by the Bontoc Igorot, with a Vocabulary and Texts, Mythology, Folklore, Historical Episodes, Songs.* Open Court Publishing Company, 1909.
22. *The Albany Evening Journal,* August 6, 1906.
23. NARA RG 350-13847.

Chapter 28

1. Her name also appears in official correspondence as Tanas.
2. NARA RG 350-13847.
3. Ibid.
4. *The New York Tribune,* July 22, 1906.
5. NARA RG 350-13847.
6. Ibid.
7. Ibid.
8. Ibid.
9. Ibid.
10. Ibid.
11. Ibid.

Chapter 29

1. Letter from Barker to Charlton at Bureau of Insular Affairs, NARA RG 350-13847.
2. NARA RG 350-13847.
3. Ibid.
4. Ibid.
5. Ibid.
6. Ibid.
7. Ibid.
8. Ibid.
9. Jenks, Albert Ernest. *The Bontoc Igorot.* Bureau of Public Printing, 1905.
10. Tennessee the Volunteer State 1769–1923: Volume 4. The S. J. Clarke Publishing Company, 1923.
11. NARA RG 350-13847; *The Memphis News Scimitar*, November 5, 1906; *The Commercial Appeal*, November 6, 1906; *The Memphis News Scimitar*, November 6, 1906.
12. *The Commercial Appeal*, November 6, 1906.
13. *The Commercial Appeal*, November 8, 1906.
14. NARA RG 350-13847.
15. Ibid.
16. *The Sentinel*, Vol. XXVIII, Number 11, December 15, 1917.
17. *The Commercial Appeal*, November 3, 1906.
18. The song, a hit in America and Europe, was recorded by Billy Murray (who also recorded "Meet Me Down at Luna, Lena"), and was later featured in the repertoire of Groucho Marx.
19. Havez, Jean, C. "Everybody Works but Father." 1905.
20. NARA RG 350-13847.

Chapter 30

1. NARA RG 350-13847.
2. *The Memphis News Scimitar*, November 22, 1906.
3. Ibid.
4. *The Commercial Appeal*, November 24, 1906.
5. NARA RG 350-13847.
6. Ibid.
7. Ibid.
8. Ibid.

9. Ibid.
10. Ibid.
11. *The Commercial Appeal*, January 19, 1907; NARA RG 350-13847.
12. NARA RG 350-13847.
13. Ibid.
14. Ibid.
15. Ibid.

Chapter 31

1. All quotations from the trial transcription in this chapter are from NARA RG 350-13847.
2. Ibid.
3. Ibid.
4. Ibid.
5. Ibid.
6. Ibid.
7. Ibid.
8. Ibid.
9. Ibid.
10. Ibid.
11. Ibid.
12. Ibid.
13. Ibid.
14. Ibid.
15. Ibid.
16. *The Memphis News Scimitar*, February 10, 1907.
17. NARA RG 350-13847; *The Memphis News Scimitar*, February 10, 1907; *The Memphis News Scimitar*, February 11, 1907.
18. NARA RG 350-13847.
19. Ibid.

Chapter 32

1. NARA RG 350-13847.
2. *The Labor World*, March 16, 1907.
3. NARA RG 350-13847.
4. Smith, Samuel Francis. "My Country, 'Tis of Thee." 1831.

Afterword

1. NARA RG 350-9640.
2. Seidenadel, Carl W. *The First Grammar of the Language Spoken by the Bontoc Igorot, with a Vocabulary and Texts, Mythology, Folklore, Historical Episodes, Songs.* Open Court Publishing, 1909.
3. *The New York Sun,* May 16, 1909.
4. *The New York Times,* June 2, 1909.
5. *The New York Tribune,* June 2, 1909.
6. *The New York Press,* September 19, 1909.
7. NARA RG 350-13431.
8. *The Brooklyn Daily Eagle,* October 19, 1924.
9. *The Commercial Appeal,* January 1933.
10. *The New York Times,* May 7, 2012.
11. *The Rochester Democrat and Chronicle,* September 9, 1906; *The Oswego Daily Palladium,* October 6, 1906; *The Rochester Democrat and Chronicle,* August 31, 1906; *The Rome Daily Sentinel,* October 6, 1906; NARA RG 350-13847.
12. His name was sometimes spelled Taynan.
13. Antero was known as "Balonglong" in his early years.
14. *The Evening News,* December 21, 1915.
15. *The New York Sun,* September 2, 1907.
16. *The Washington Post,* September 2, 1917.
17. *The New York Tribune,* October 6, 1917.
18. *The New York Times,* June 9, 1906.
19. *The St. Louis Post Dispatch,* October 24, 1909.
20. *The New York Times,* October 25 1909.
21. *The New York Press,* February 12, 1911.
22. Her name was sometimes spelled Dogmeena or Doakmena.
23. *The New York Times,* February 13, 1912.
24. *The New York Press,* February 12, 1911.
25. *The Brooklyn Daily Eagle,* September 17, 1931.
26. http://apps.westpointaog.org/Memorials/Article/3106/ Viewed on February 14, 2014.
27. *The New York Sun,* October 14, 1917.
28. *The National Democrat,* January 25, 1912.
29. *The Cedar Rapids Republican,* February 23, 1916.
30. Truman Hunt Military Pension Application File and Compiled Military Service File, NARA, Washington, DC.
31. Ibid.
32. Ibid.

33. Ibid.
34. Ibid.
35. Ibid.
36. Ibid.
37. Ibid.
38. Ibid.
39. Ibid.
40. Ibid.
41. NARA RG 350-9640.
42. *The Independent*, October 5, 1905.

Bibliography

The source materials I consulted to write this book filled many boxes, bookshelves, and filing cabinets. I read thousands of newspaper articles and trawled through vital records and genealogical databases across America, the Philippines, and Europe. Below is a selection of the materials that were of most value to my research.

Archival Sources

Beals, Jessie Tarbox, Photographs from the Philippine Reservation at the St. Louis Exposition, American Museum of Natural History, New York.

Coney Island Folders. Villages and Sections. Milstein Division, New York Public Library (NYPL).

Dinwiddie, William. Papers, 1898–1905. Two boxes. US Army Heritage and Education Center.

Elsa W. Hunt vs. Truman K. Hunt Divorce Papers, New York County Court Archives, New York Supreme Court, County Court of New York.

Folders: Dundy, Elmer S. Billy Rose Theater Division, NYPL.

Folders: Gumpertz, Samuel. Billy Rose Theater Division, NYPL.

Folders: Thompson & Dundy, Billy Rose Theater Division, NYPL.

Folders: Thompson, Fred, Billy Rose Theater Division, NYPL.

Folders: Thompson, Frederic, Billy Rose Theater Division, NYPL.

King, Naomi. Diary, January 1899. Manuscripts Division, NYPL.

Oceania Collection, The University of Pennsylvania Museum of Archaeology and Anthropology.

Philippines Diary of Simeon A. Villa, sub-inspector of military hospitals, 1899–1901. Translated by American Lieutenant J. C. Hixon. Manuscripts Division, NYPL.

Record Group 350, Records of the Bureau of Insular Affairs, National Archives and Records Administration at College Park, MD.

Schneidewind, Richard. Papers, 1899–1914, Michigan Historical Collections, Bentley Historical Library, University of Michigan.

The Lewis and Clark Exposition Collection, Manuscripts Division, Oregon Historical Society.

The Robinson Locke Collection: Frederic Thompson; Thompson & Dundy. Billy Rose Theater Division, NYPL.

Truman Hunt Military Pension Application File and Compiled Military Service File, the National Archives and Records Administration, Washington, DC.

Welling, Richard. Papers, ca. 1876–1946, Manuscripts Division, NYPL.

Worcester, Dean C. Papers 1834–1915, Museum of Anthropology and Special Collections Library, University of Michigan.

Worcester, Dean C. Photographic Collection 1890–1913, Museum of Anthropology, University of Michigan.

Wotherspoon, George. Papers. Billy Rose Theater Division, NYPL, Boxes 1, 2, 3.

Books

Adams, Judith A. *The American Amusement Park Industry: A History of Technology and Thrills.* Boston: Twayne Publishers, 1991.

Alter, Judy. *Amusement Parks: Roller Coasters, Ferris Wheels, and Cotton Candy.* New York: Franklin Watts, 1997.

Andrews, E. Benjamin. *History of the United States from the Earliest Discovery of America to the Present Time*, vol. 5. New York: Charles Scribner's Sons, 1912.

Barton, R. F. *The Half-way Sun: Life Among the Headhunters of the Philippines.* New York: Brewer and Warren Inc., 1930.

Berman, John S. *Portraits of America: Coney Island.* New York: Barnes & Noble, 2003.

Blount, James H. *The American Occupation of the Philippines, 1898–1912.* New York: G. P. Putnam's Sons, 1912.

Breitbart, Eric. *A World on Display: Photographs from the St. Louis World's Fair, 1904.* Albuquerque: University of New Mexico, 1997.

Byron, Joseph. *New York Interiors at the Turn of the Century.* New York: Dover Publications, Inc. 1976.

Clapp, Walter Clayton. *A Vocabulary of Igorot Language as Spoken by the Bontok Igorots: Igorot-English and English-Igorot.* Manila: Bureau of Printing, 1908.

Cudahy, Brian J. *How We Got to Coney Island: The Development of Mass Transportation in Brooklyn and Kings County.* New York: Fordham University Press, 2002.

Cunningham, Joseph and Leonard De Hart. *A History of the New York City Subway System.* New York: J. Schmidt, R. Giglio, and K. Lang, 1993.

Dauncey, Mrs. Campbell. *An Englishwoman in the Philippines.* New York: E. P. Dutton & Co., 1906.

Denson, Charles. *Coney Island and Astroland.* Mount Pleasant, SC: Arcadia Publishing, 2011.

Denson, Charles. *Coney Island: Lost and Found.* Berkeley, CA: Ten Speed Press, 2004.

Ellis, Edward Robb. *The Epic of New York City: A Narrative History.* New York: Basic Books, 1990.

Fermin, Jose D. *1904 World's Fair: The Filipino Experience.* Quezon City: University of the Philippines Press/Infinity Publishing, 2004.

Freer, William B. *The Philippine Experiences of an American Teacher: A Narrative of Work and Travel in the Philippine Islands.* New York: Charles Scribner's Sons, 1906.

Garland-Thomson, Rosemarie, ed. *Freakery: Cultural Spectacles of the Extraordinary Body.* New York: New York University Press, 1996.

Go, Julian and Anne L. Foster, eds., *The American Colonial State in the Philippines: Global Perspectives.* Durham, NC: Duke University Press, 2003.

Go, Julian. *Empire and the Politics of Meaning: Elite Political Cultures in the Philippines and Puerto Rico during U.S. Colonialism.* Durham, NC: Duke University Press, 2008.

Greller, James Clifford and Edward Watson. *Brooklyn Trolleys.* New Jersey: NJ International, 1985.

Greller, James Clifford. *Brooklyn Trolley Cars from the BRT to the B&QT.* New Jersey: Xplorer Press Inc, 2011.

Holt, Hamilton, ed. *The Life Stories of Undistinguished Americans as Told by Themselves.* New York: Routledge, 2000.

Homberger, Eric. *The Historical Atlas of New York City: A Visual Celebration of 400 Years of New York City's History.* New York: Holt Paperbacks, 2nd edition, 2005.

Ierardi, Eric, J. *Gravesend Brooklyn: Coney Island and Sheepshead Bay.* Mount Pleasant, SC: Arcadia Publishing, 1996.

Immerso, Michael. *Coney Island: The People's Playground.* New Brunswick, NJ: Rutgers University Press, 2002.

Jackson, Kenneth T. *The Encyclopedia of New York City.* New Haven, CT: Yale University Press, 1995.

Jenks, Albert Ernest. *The Bontoc Igorot.* Manila: Bureau of Public Printing, 1905.

Jenks, Maud Huntley. *Death Stalks the Philippine Wilds: Letters of Maud Huntley Jenks.* Minneapolis: The Lund Press Inc., 1951.

Kasson, John F. *Amusing the Million: Coney Island at the Turn of the Century.* New York: Hill and Wang, 1978.

Kramer, Frederick A. *Across New York by Trolley.* New York: Quadrant Press, 1975.

Kramer, Paul A. *The Blood of Government: Race, Empire, the United States & the Philippines.* Chapel Hill: University of North Carolina Press, 2006.

Lowenstein, M. J. *The Official Guide to the Louisiana Purchase Exposition at the City of St. Louis, State of Missouri, April 30 to December 1, 1904.* St. Louis: Louisiana Purchase Exposition Company, 1904.

McCauley, Clay. *A Day in the Very Noble City, Manila: A Lecture (1899).* Whitefish, MT: Kessinger Publishing, 2008.

McCullough, Edo. *Good Old Coney Island.* New York: Fordham University Press, 1999.

Official Catalogue: Philippine Exhibits. St. Louis: Official Catalogue Company, 1904.

Official Handbook of the Philippines and Catalogue of the Philippine Exhibit in Two Volumes. Manila: Bureau of Public Printing, 1903.

Parezo, Nancy J. and Don D. Fowler. *Anthropology Goes to the Fair: The 1904 Louisiana Purchase Exposition.* Lincoln, NE: University of Nebraska Press, 2007.

Peiss, Kathy. *Cheap Amusements: Working Women and Leisure in Turn-of-the-Century New York.* Philadelphia: Temple University Press, 1986.

Pilapil, Virgilio R. *Touring the Legacy of the 1904 St. Louis World's Fair: With Special Attention to the Philippine Exhibit.* Springfield, IL: The House of Isidoro Press, 2004.

Pilat, Oliver and Jo Ranson. *Sodom by the Sea: An Affectionate History of Coney Island.* New York: Doubleday, Doran & Co., 1941.

Register, Woody. *The Kid of Coney Island: Fred Thompson and the Rise of American Amusements.* New York: Oxford University Press USA, 2003.

Reiss, Marcia. *Brooklyn Then and Now.* San Diego: Thunder Bay Press, 2002.

Reports of the U.S. Philippine Commission to the Secretary of War, 1901–1909. Washington, DC: Government Printing Office, 1901–1909.

Rydell, Robert W. *All the World's a Fair: Visions of Empire at American International Expositions, 1876–1916.* Chicago: University of Chicago Press, 1984.

Sally, Lynn Kathleen. *Fighting the Flames: The Spectacular Performance of Fire at Coney Island.* New York: Routledge, 2006.

Sansone, Gene. *New York Subways: An Illustrated History of New York City's Transit Cars.* Baltimore: John Hopkins University Press, 2004.

Schroeder Jr., Joseph J., ed. *Sears, Roebuck and Co. Consumers Guide Fall 1900, Catalogue no. 110.* Chicago: DBI Books, Inc., 1970.

Seidenadel, Dr. Carl Wilhelm. *The First Grammar of the Language Spoken by the Bontoc Igorot, with a Vocabulary and Texts.* Chicago: The Open Court Publishing Company, 1909.

Snow, Richard. *Coney Island: A Postcard Journey to the City of Fire.* New York: Brightwaters Press, 1989.

Solomon, Prof. *Coney Island.* Baltimore: Top Hat Press, 1999.

Sonderman, Joe. *St. Louis: The 1904 World's Fair.* Mount Pleasant, SC: Arcadia Publishing, 2008.

Stein, Harvey. *Coney Island.* New York: W. W. Norton & Company, 1998.

Tompkins, Vincent. *American Decades 1900–1909.* Farmington Hills, MI: Gale Group 1996.

Trager, James. *The New York Chronology: The Ultimate Compendium of Events, People, and Anecdotes From the Dutch to the Present.* New York: Collins Reference, 2003.

U.S. Bureau of the Census. Census of the Philippine Islands, 1903. 4 vols. Washington, DC: U.S. Government Printing Office, 1905.

Vaughn, Christopher A. "Ogling Igorots: The politics and commerce of exhibiting cultural otherness, 1898–1913," in *Freakery: Cultural Spectacles of the Extraordinary Body,* ed. Rosemarie Garland Thomson, 219–33. New York: New York University Press, 1996.

Vergara, Benito M. *Displaying Filipinos: Photography and colonialism in early 20th century Philippines.* Quezon City: University of the Philippines Press, 1995.

Who's Who in Tennessee: A Biographical Reference Book of Notable Tennesseans of Today. Memphis: Paul & Douglass Co., Publishers, 1911.

Worcester, Dean C. *The Philippine Islands and Their People.* New York: Macmillan, 1899.

Worcester, Dean C. *The Philippines, Past and Present.* Ed. R. Hayden. New edition in one volume. New York: Macmillan, 1930. First published in 1914.

Journal Articles and Reports

Afable, Patricia, "The Exhibition of Cordillerans in the United States in the Early 1900s." *Igorot Quarterly* 6, no. 2 (1997): 19–22.

Afable, Patricia. "'Nikimalika,' the 'Igorrotes' of the Early Twentieth Century Fairs: A Chronology and Name Lists." *Igorot Quarterly* 9, no. 4 (2000): 18–31.

Afable, Patricia, "Journeys from Bontoc to the Western Fairs, 1904–1915: The 'Nikimalika' and their Interpreters," *Philippine Studies* 52, no. 4 (2004): 445–473.

Civic Affairs, Souvenir Courthouse Edition, Memphis: March 1910.

Fawcett, Waldon. "Henry W. Goode: The Electrical Engineer Now President of the Lewis and Clark Exposition." *American Illustrated Magazine* 60, no. 6 (Oct 1905): 678–681.

Folkmar, Daniel. "The Administration of a Philippine Province." *The Annals of the American Academy of Political and Social Science* 30 (July 1907): 115–122.

"Hippodrome for London is Next." *New York Telegraph*, February 14, 1906.

"Homage to Thompson." *Billboard*, September 18, 1915.

"The Igorrote Tribe from the Philippines," *Lewis & Clark Journal*, October, 1905, The Oregon Historical Society.

Jenks, Albert Ernest. "Building a Province," *The Outlook* (May 21, 1904): 170–176.

Kauffman, Reginald Wright. "Why Is Coney? A Study of the Wonderful Playground and the Men that Made It." *Hampton's Magazine* 23, no. 2 (August 1, 1909): 215–224.

"Luna Park in Trouble." *Billboard*, October 22, 1910.

Mathé, Barbara. "Jessie Tarbox Beals' Photographs for the 1904 Louisiana Purchase Exposition." *VRA Bulletin* 23, no. 4 (Winter 1996): 53–61.

Mendoza, Victor Roman. "Little Brown Students and the Homoerotics of White Love," *Asian American Subgenres: 1853–1941*. Ed. Hsuan Hsu. Spec. double issue of *Genre: Forms of Discourse and Culture* 39, no. 4 (winter 2006): 65–83.

Newell, Alfred C. "The Philippine Peoples." *World's Work* 8, no. 4 (August 1904): 5128–5145.

"New York Hippodrome Under New Regime." *Billboard*, September 8, 1906.

Paine, Albert Bigelow. "The New Coney Island." *The Century Magazine* (August 1904): 528–538.

Rice, Dr. Mark. "Dean Worcester's Photographs and American Perceptions of the Philippines." *Education About Asia* 16, no. 2 (2011): 29–33.

Rice, Dr. Mark. "His Name Was Don Francisco Muro: Reconstructing an Image of American Imperialism," *American Quarterly* 62, no. 1 (March 2010): 49–76, 193.

"Samuel Gumpertz—Superlative Showman." *Billboard*, April 29, 1933.

"Views of an Igorrote Chief." *The Independent* 59, no. 2 (October 5, 1905): 779–785.

Wiltse, H. M. "Igorrote Marriage Customs." *The Journal of American Folklore* 14 (July 1, 1901): 204–205.

Winter, Frank H. and Randy Liebermann. "A Trip to the Moon." *Air and Space* (October/November, 1994).

Worcester, Dean C. "Head-hunters of Northern Luzon," *National Geographic* 23, no. 9 (September 1912): 833–842.

Worcester, Dean C. *Ninth Annual Report of the Secretary of the Interior to the Philippine Commission for the Fiscal Year Ended June 30, 1910*. Manila: Bureau of Printing, 1910.

Worcester, Dean C. "The Non-Christian Peoples of the Philippine Islands," *National Geographic* 24, no. 11 (November 1913): 1158–1194.

Worcester, Dean C. *Report of the Secretary of the Interior to the Philippine Commission for the Year Ending August 31, 1902.* Manila: Bureau of Public Printing, 1902.

Film on Video/DVD

American Experience: Coney Island, directed by Ric Burns. New York: Steeplechase Films for PBS, 1991, DVD.

Bontoc Eulogy, directed by Marlon Fuentes. New York: Cinema Guild, 1995, DVD.

Cake Walk. New York: American Mutoscope and Biograph Company, 1903. Billy Rose Theater Division, New York Public Library, motion picture.

Fighting the Flames, Dreamland. New York: Museum of Modern Art, 1904. Billy Rose Theater Division, NYPL, motion picture.

New York Subway 1905, directed by G. W. Bitzer. New York: American Mutoscope and Biograph, 1905, motion picture.

Rube and Mandy at Coney Island, directed by Edwin S. Porter. New York: Museum of Modern Art, 1903. Billy Rose Theater Division, NYPL, motion picture.

Maps

Bromley G. W. & Co. Atlas of the Borough of Brooklyn, City of New York: from actual surveys and official plans. Philadelphia: G. W. Bromley, 1907–1908, plate 29.

Kings County Census Maps, Assembly District 7, 1905. New York Municipal Archive.

Map of the Business District of New York, Brooklyn and Jersey City. Chicago: Rand McNally & Co., 1904. As reproduced by H & M Productions, 2000, in *Twelve Historical New York City Street and Transit Maps (Volume II: from 1847–1939).*

Map of Mid to Lower Manhattan Showing the Rapid Transit Line. New York: Wanamaker Stores Maps, 1906. As reproduced by H & M Productions, 2000, in *Twelve Historical New York City Street and Transit Maps (Volume II: from 1847–1939).*

New York South Part of the Borough of Manhattan. Printed for the Convention of the New England Water Works Association September, 1905. Buffalo, NY: Matthews, Northrup & Co., 1904.

Passenger Department of the New York Central & Hudson River Railroad Company. Map of the Underground Railway of New York. G. H. Daniels, general passenger agent, 1905.

Sanborn Map Company, New York. Insurance Maps of Memphis, Tennessee, 1907, vol. 1: 4, 5, 15.

Sanborn-Perris Company, New York. Insurance Maps of Memphis, Tennessee, 1897, vol. 1: 39.

City Directories and Guides

Coney Island. Portland, Maine: L. H. Nelson Company, 1905.

Coney Island Souvenir & Traveler's Guide. New York: Lain & Co. Publisher, 1892.

Ennison, W. J. *Souvenir Guide to Coney Island.* New York: The Megaphone Press, 1905.

Glimpses of the New Coney Island: America's Most Popular Pleasure Resort. New York: Isaac H. Blanchard Company, 1904.

Hall, John D. *Banner Guide, Excursion Book and Directory for New York City and Vicinity.* New York: J. D. Hall, 1905.

History of Coney Island. New York: Burroughs & Co., 1904.

Ingersoll, Ernest. *Handy Guide to New York City.* Chicago: Rand McNally & Company, 1905.

Memphis City Directory 1906. Memphis, Tennessee: R.L. Polk & Co., 1906.

New York Standard Guide. New York: Foster & Reynolds Publishers, 1904.

New York Standard Guide. New York: Foster & Reynolds Publishers, 1906.

Staley, Frank W. *Views of Coney Island.* New York: Charles Francis Press, 1908.

The 5 Cent Guide and Street Directory of New York City. New York: W. H. Smith, 1903.

The Tourist's Handbook of New York. New York: The Historical Press, 1905.

Views of Coney Island. Portland, ME: L. H. Nelson, 1905.

Views of Coney Island. Portland, ME: L. H. Nelson, 1907.

Illustration Credits

vii Brooklyn Historical Society V1986.24.1.29

xi *The American Occupation of the Philippines, 1898–1912* by J. H. Blount. G. P. Putnam's Sons, 1913.

xii–xiii NYPL, Maps Division, Record no. b13995708

xix Library of Congress, Prints and Photographs Division, LC-DIG-ggbain-03959

1 New York County Clerk, Division of Old Records, Elsa W. Hunt v. Truman K. Hunt, Equity Actions, Index Number GA-860/1908

10 Library of Congress, Prints and Photographs Division, LC-USZ62-107899

21 Courtesy of Ian Boyle

40 *The Seattle Sunday Times*

57 Library of Congress, Prints and Photographs Division, LC-DIG-det-4a30339

67 *The New York Daily Tribune*

82 *The Independent*

88 Brooklyn Historical Society, V1974.22.6.6

105 Library of Congress, Prints and Photographs Division, LC-DIG-det-4a11111

119 Friends of Ocean Parkway via https://twitter.com/NYCEMSwebsite

125 *The New York Sun*

138 Library of Congress, Prints and Photographs Division, LC-DIG-det-4a17572

142 Memphis Public Library

159 National Archives at College Park, Maryland, RG 350-13847

165 Library of Congress, Prints and Photographs Division, PAN US GEOG—Louisiana no. 12 (F size)

177 Library of Congress, Prints and Photographs Division, LC-DIG-hec-14151

177 Library of Congress, Prints and Photographs Division, LC-DIG-ggbain-05086

188 Richard Schneidewind Papers 1899–1914, Bentley Historical Library, University of Michigan

192 National Archives at College Park, Maryland, RG 350-13847

226 National Archives at College Park, Maryland, RG 350-13847
234 National Archives at College Park, Maryland, RG 350-13847
241 Tate Archives & Special Collections, The Ames Library, Illinois Wesleyan University, Bloomington, Illinois
253 National Archives at College Park, Maryland, RG 350-13847
256 National Archives at College Park, Maryland, RG 350-13847
263 Library of Congress, Prints and Photographs Division, LC-USZ62-42836
271 Library of Congress, Prints and Photographs Division, HABS ILL, 49-FTSH, 1–21
278 Memphis Public Library
290 Civic Affairs, Souvenir Courthouse Edition, Memphis, March 1910
290 Civic Affairs, Souvenir Courthouse Edition, Memphis, March 1910
296 National Archives at College Park, Maryland, RG 350, File 13847-218
314 Library of Congress, Prints and Photographs Division, LC-USZ62-80521

Index

Page numbers in italics refer to illustrations